The Responsibilities of Rhetoric

The Responsibilities of Rhetoric

Michelle Smith
The Pennsylvania State University

Barbara Warnick
University of Pittsburgh

WAVELAND

PRESS, INC.

Long Grove, Illinois

For information about this book, contact:
Waveland Press, Inc.
4180 IL Route 83, Suite 101
Long Grove, IL 60047-9580
(847) 634-0081
info@waveland.com
www.waveland.com

On the cover: This image of the London suffragettes depicts the enactment of responsibilities by rhetors who sought to rectify oppression and the denial of franchise in their society.

10-digit ISBN 1-57766-623-2
13-digit ISBN 978-1-57766-623-3

Printed in the United States of America

7   6   5   4   3   2   1

This book is dedicated to
Jacqueline DeLaat
and
Elizabeth Basse Parmelee

When I stopped seeing my mother with the eyes of a child,
I saw the woman who helped me give birth to myself.
　　　　　　　　　　　　　　　　　　—*Nancy Friday*

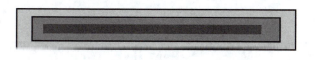

Contents

Editors' Introduction   1

Plenary Address: Reclaiming Rhetoric's Responsibilities   13
David Zarefsky

PART I
Promoting Public Reason   23

1   Rousseau, Rhetoric, and the Promise of Contractual Politics   25
David Tell

2   Rhetoric, Virtue, and the Necessity of Invention   37
William Duffy

3   "Licentia" in the Seventeenth-Century French Pulpit   44
Claudia Carlos

4   The Functions of Polemical Discourse in the Public Sphere   52
Ruth Amossy

5   Form Is a Feminist Issue   62
Eve Wiederhold

6   Knifing Orlan's Mask: Grotesque Aesthetics
as Visceral Resistance to Commodification   70
Jane Munksgaard

7   Audre Lorde's Embodied Invention   80
Lester C. Olson

8   La Frontera y El Chamizal:
Liminality, Territoriality, and Visual Discourse   96
Brian J. McNely

PART II
Forming Publics and Communities 115

9   Public Deliberation and the Rhetorical "Real":
    Balancing Accomplishment and Complication
    in Republican-Democratic Structures   117
    Todd Kelshaw

10 Changing the Public Face of Christian Politics:
    The Rhetoric of Sojourners   129
    Barbara Little Liu

11 The Temporality and Function of
    "Ethical Shifting" in Discursive Interaction   144
    Stephen R. Yarbrough

12 Edit This Page: Wikipedia and
    the Responsibilities of Digital Rhetorics   151
    James J. Brown, Jr.

13 Aesthetics and Rhetoric in *The Oprah Winfrey Show*   159
    Kathleen Dixon

14 Textual and Visual Building Blocks: Agency and Social
    Responsibility in Christine de Pizan's "The City of Ladies" 165
    Julia M. Smith

15 The Constitutive Rhetoric of *Common Sense*   175
    David C. Hoffman

16 Paternalistic Rhetoric and the American People   186
    Jay P. Childers

PART III
Shaping Histories and Envisioning Futures 199

17 Rustic Experience and the Rhetorical Work
    of National Park Architecture   201
    Gregory Clark

18 Eugenics, Nazism, and the Sinister Science
    of the Human Betterment Foundation   214
    Kathleen A. Swift

19 Synecdoche as Figure of the Holocaust   219
    Richard Glejzer & Michael Bernard-Donals

20 The Arabs Did Not "Just" Translate Aristotle:
   Al-Farabi's Logico-Rhetorical Theory   230
   Maha Baddar

21 The Cynic   243
   Charles Johnson

22 Loyalty Oaths and the Letter of the Law:
   Rhetoric, Resistance, and Responsibility   249
   M. Karen Powers

23 Scholarship of Engagement: *Both* a *New Name For*
   and a *Challenge To* the Work of Rhetoric   263
   Richard C. Gebhardt

24 Gender Equity in the Rhetoric Society of America   269
   Cheryl Geisler

PART IV
Preparing Students to Live in
a Rapidly Changing World   279

25 *I* Told *U* So: Classical and Contemporary *Ethos*
   and the Stabilization of *Self*   281
   Nathaniel A. Rivers

26 Coming to Terms with Analogy: Generativity and
   Constraint in the Work of Nagaoka, Gamow, and Freud   289
   Joseph Little & Lisa Jane Kabasin

27 Textual Machinery:
   Authorial Agency and Bot-Written Texts in Wikipedia   303
   Krista Kennedy

28 The Rhetoric of the Graphic Novel   310
   Kathryn E. Dobson

29 The Earth Liberation Front's (ELF)
   Failed Diatribe of Sacramental Arson   326
   Mark Meister & Curt Gilstrap

30 "The Future Is Ours," or Is It?: The Rise and Fall
   of Totalitarian Rhetoric in Poland (and Elsewhere)   340
   Cezar M. Ornatowski

Contributors   355
Name Index   361
Subject Index   365

Editors' Introduction

In his plenary address to the convention, David Zarefsky mused about the conference theme. Noting that one could easily envision the responsibilities of *rhetors* to be responsible and responsive to their publics, or of *rhetoricians* to instruct and empower those who would learn from them and enhance public life, he wondered aloud what might be meant by the responsibilities of *rhetoric*—what might be the responsibilities of this ancient *techne* in our time?

In answering this question, Professor Zarefsky considered four areas of responsibility: (1) the responsibility to promote public reason in society; (2) the responsibility to unite publics and communities; (3) the commitment to provide a vision of what is possible that moves beyond the current moment; and (4) the responsibility to serve as a teaching resource that prepares students to think and deliberate in contemporary society.

In discussing rhetoric's responsibility to promote public reason, Zarefsky reminded his audience of the principles of reasoned discourse that characterize the work of such theorists as Stephen Toulmin, Chaim Perelman, and Lucie Olbrechts-Tyteca. These included a concern for audience and an awareness that reasoned arguments are addressed to and validated by audiences. Rhetoric in this tradition should make use of standards of judgment grounded in community and should be cognizant of people's ability to exercise judgment. Such rhetoric stakes its claim on a faith in the practice of deliberation and the commitment to respectful engagement among people who may hold differing points of view.

In considering rhetoric's second responsibility—to bring people together into publics and communities—Zarefsky emphasized the importance of recognizing common bonds and consubstantiality in a society such as ours, which is often more individualistic than communitarian in nature (Bellah et al.). Further, it is the responsibility of rhetoric to help forge understandings between groups placed in opposition to one another. Zarefsky noted the example of John F. Kennedy, who brought to the mid-twentieth century United States a vision of how the country might revise its attitudes toward the Soviet Union, communism, and peace. Kennedy offered not just a vision of what it meant to be American, but a reminder of what it is to be human.

1

A third significant responsibility of rhetoric discussed by Zarefsky is the commitment to enable a vision of the future that can move a people beyond a current moment and enable them to see how their society can and should change. Here, Zarefsky draws on his previous scholarship on President Lyndon Baines Johnson and the Great Society initiatives. Johnson regarded his utopian vision, first, as unquestionably achievable and second, as not just a *possibility* but a *responsibility* of the great and powerful American nation. Zarefsky calls on us to remember Johnson as a model of a transformative vision of change for a new future, not just for the foreign policy disaster that often dominates his legacy.

The final responsibility considered in the address was that of teaching. Noting that "rhetoric's responsibilities have been enlarged in our time," Zarefsky encouraged his audience to contemplate the need to prepare students to live and thrive in a world that is rapidly changing in ever more dangerous ways—a declining ecology, increasing income disparity, rapidly spreading disease and hunger, terrorism, and genocide. How can rhetoric as a discipline be so shaped as to inspire its audiences and promote public good? As teachers and professors of the art, how best can we enable students to understand and appreciate the benefits and dangers of its practice and its role as a force in its larger social contexts?

The themes that played a role in Professor Zarefsky's plenary address also contributed to many of the presentations and papers submitted for the conference as a whole. A large number of papers were submitted for consideration to be included in our conference volume, and the thirty-one papers that are included represent some very fine work that is directly relevant to these four responsibilities. Our table of contents is designed to reflect the preoccupations of conference presenters who discussed the many facets of rhetoric's responsibilities. In addressing the four above-mentioned themes of Zarefsky's talk, our contributors also expanded on these themes, suggesting related, insightful, and provocative responsibilities for both rhetoric and rhetoricians.

PROMOTING PUBLIC REASON

Each of the authors in this first section discussed the responsibilities of rhetoric by emphasizing Zarefsky's first theme: the need to develop community-based standards of judgment for public discourse, put faith in the processes of public protest and resistance, and follow well-founded standards for public deliberation and debate. Additionally, many of these authors (like other contributors to this year's conference) articulated another related responsibility of rhetoricians: to develop more inclusive models for what counts as public reason and to be willing to acknowledge rhetorics that may not contribute to traditionally lauded goals of consensus and shared values. Thus, the chapters in this section range from essays considering the role of rhetoric in effective, moral public deliberation to those attempting to broaden our sense of what counts as sound public reason so as to include feminist, material, embodied, and spatial perspectives.

The first article in this section considers the fundamental question of the role of rhetoric in the state. Entering the scholarly debate over whether Rousseau's theory of rhetoric and public deliberation is a model for deliberation or a condemnation of it as useless, David Tell's "Rousseau, Rhetoric, and the Promise of Contractual Politics" argues that Rousseau's seemingly ambiguous attitude toward rhetoric becomes clear when viewed in light of the social contract. Suggesting that the political role of rhetoric is limited, though not absent, in Rousseau's formulation, Tell concludes by reconsidering the terms of the social contract in Rousseau's vision, which he views as "unfairly constrict[ing] the role of citizen deliberation." Ultimately, Tell holds on to the promise of a contractual politics in which citizen deliberation is central.

Considering the current state of deliberation and public judgment in society in his essay, "Rhetoric, Virtue, and the Necessity of Invention," William Duffy asks, "How can rhetoricians develop a shared standard for evaluating rhetoric in a public debate?" This question reflects his concern about the extent to which inherited moral discourse is adequate to address the problems of negotiating contemporary moral issues. If interlocutors cannot come to an agreement on what is meant when they employ morally charged language, then controversies will remain unresolved because there are no points of stasis that would allow debate and deliberation to proceed. To engage this problem, Duffy recommends that we turn to forms of truth that are embedded in human experience. Further, intervention in the interactions of people should be committed to the principle that ethically informed communication should be sustained and continued.

The next two essays consider forms of rhetoric that are sometimes maligned but that may yet contribute usefully to public deliberation in certain contexts. In her essay "'Licentia' in the Seventeenth-Century French Pulpit," Claudia Carlos describes a specific situation in the seventeenth-century French court in which "frank speaking," while proscribed generally in French society as a whole, was permitted and even expected when French pulpit speakers spoke to the monarch with moral firmness. She examines the school texts of the period, as well as earlier texts from which they drew material, to describe how the genre of "licentia," or frank speaking, was treated, explained, and taught as a form of rhetoric. She then turns to an analysis of one of Bourdaloue's sermons as delivered to Louis XIV that redressed him and members of his court for impurity, deception, and other improprieties. This essay reminds us of rhetoric's continual responsibilities to articulate the moral ground of principles that ought to regulate public speech.

Ruth Amossy's essay, "The Functions of Polemical Discourse in the Public Sphere," goes against the trend of condemning polemics as failing to meet ethical standards and shape consensus—a trend extending back to antiquity and forward to the present day—to address polemics as a form of argumentation. The essay presents a revised conception of argumentation consisting of a continuum from "a latent form where the opposition of discourses is quite inconspicuous, though by no means absent (an informative newspaper article, for example), to an extreme form where a clash occurs between antagonistic theses (a violent debate on a controversial subject)." At one end of this continuum is polemics, which, Amossy maintains, is vital to a plural public sphere made up of opposing groups with irresolvable differences. Setting the groundwork for future empirical study, this essay offers a clear structure for reconsidering both public argument and the polemical discourse that, like it or not, operates within it.

Eve Wiederhold and Jane Munksgaard both take feminist perspectives on the study of public speech. Wiederhold's essay, "Form is a Feminist Issue," considers how media outlets (FoxNews is her example) blur the acts of informing and advocating on behalf of a specific political agenda, critically analyzing the notions of linguistic authority and accountability. By interrogating the tactics and positioned discourse of those covering the news, Wiederhold draws attention to a sort of journalistic entitlement that enables commentators to position themselves as removed from context and therefore able to assess the overall situation on a systems level. She finds this act of positioning oneself outside of context to be problematic and notes that, often, "The general, the abstract, and the rational garner more cultural regard than the specific, the embodied, and the emotional." To address this problem, Wiederhold encourages a feminist material rhetoric that emerges "from our interactions with complex, historically marked narratives that affect embodied responses to how texts get scrutinized." Jane Munksgaard, in "Knifing Orlan's Mask," studies the work of French multimedia performance artist Orlan, who has used performativity to produce effective resistance by transforming her appearance using current methods of plastic surgery. Orlan has attracted public attention and enacted a mimetic reversal of beautification standards by transforming her own appearance through surgical methods while reading and reciting material during satellite broadcast surgery. In so doing, she has used the process of unmasking to challenge the heterosexual economy and reconsider the question of sexual difference, developing representations of personhood designed to reform social norms.

The two final pieces in this section share the material emphasis of Wiederhold's feminist approach and Munksgaard's work on Orlan. Taking on the role of the body in a different canon of rhetoric, Lester Olson's "Audre Lorde's Embodied Invention" explores bodily experience as a site for rhetorical invention. Through an analysis of Lorde's representations of her struggle with breast cancer, Olson demonstrates the ways in which Lorde's public advocacy drew on this personal physical experience in particular, but also from Black lesbian experience more generally. Olson reconceptualizes inventional practices as occurring on a continuum from abstract impersonal inventional prompts, like the classical *topoi*, to the unabashedly personal and concrete embodied invention displayed by Lorde. Suggesting that embodied invention is likely operative, though unmarked, in rhetorics of the privileged and normative, Olson offers this concept as a new way of exploring and understanding the workings of invention in public discourse.

Addressing the materiality of rhetoric from another angle, Brian McNely's article contributes to the vibrant consideration of rhetoric and spatialization in the field, studying the ways that spaces speak in both dominant and counterhegemonic registers. The article offers the theoretical contribution of "rhetorical stratigraphies," a collage of insights from critical geography, Bakhtinian discourse theory, and Kristie Fleckenstein's work on materiality and semiosis, a model that acknowledges the conflation of spatial and visual rhetoric in practice and the interconnections of the material and discursive. Through an analysis of the space of the Chamizal National Memorial and the graffiti on the actual physical El Paso/Juárez border, McNely demonstrates how rhetorical stratigraphies elucidate "the construction, reception, and circulation of space and visual discourse."

FORMING PUBLICS AND COMMUNITIES

The second section of this collection addresses Zarefsky's emphasis on the responsibility to bring people together. The bulk of the essays in this section consider various roles of deliberation in publics or communities: as a precursor to action, as bridging unfamiliar or opposing positions, as demanding ethical shifts in the perspectives of individuals, and as creating publics out of unexpected assemblages of people. The final two essays raise interesting questions about how we currently conceptualize constitutive rhetoric and suggest, respectively, that some such rhetorics may constitute us not as groups but as individuals and that some powerful constitutive rhetorics can undermine the promise of deliberative democracy.

In his essay, "Public Deliberation and the Rhetorical 'Real': Balancing Accomplishment and Complication in Republican-Democratic Structures," Todd Kelshaw considers the nature of deliberation explicitly. He notes its central role in the formation and growth of publics. The aims of his essay are to revive awareness of the unique contribution of deliberation in society and to distinguish deliberation from dialogue. Kelshaw lauds deliberation's inclusiveness, epistemological openness, and potential to promote understanding of complex public problems. "As such," Kelshaw notes, "public deliberation is . . . an enactment of what is potentially populist, polyphonic, and equivocal about democracy." The idea that rhetoric will only be consequential insofar as its ideas are actionable is threaded through Kelshaw's essay and is also central to Barbara Liu's article, "Changing the Public Face of Christian Politics: The Rhetoric of Sojourners." Liu analyzes the recent growth of a new form of Christian politics—"one that espouses positions usually associated with 'godless' liberals." Investigating Jim Wallis's Sojourners, Liu argues that Wallis's second book, *God's Politics*, extends Wallis's audience to include both progressive evangelicals and liberal Democrat politicians who have helped to confine religion to the private sphere. Most striking, however, is Liu's analysis of Wallis's unique use of the jeremiad as not just a medium but a model of the kind of action he summons this audience to undertake.

An essential dimension of a responsible rhetoric consists of the willingness of all parties to be open to ideas and values that might be quite different from their own. The health of a community is often dependent on its members' readiness to consider and accept perspectives that may be unfamiliar to them. In his essay, "The Temporality and Function of 'Ethical Shifting' in Discursive Interaction," Stephen R. Yarbrough discusses the phenomenon of ethical shifting. Working from George Herbert Mead's view of interactions as events embedded in time and context, Yarbrough notes that social practices are normalized in people's experience. Even in the context of formed communities, participants often must reconsider their ordinary and habitual ways of thinking to adjust to new challenges and changing values. This process can lead them to alter the ethical fields in which their utterances make sense.

In his essay, "Edit This Page: Wikipedia and the Responsibilities of Digital Rhetorics," James J. Brown interrogates the practices of the Wikipedia community, in particular its potential to delegate control to an inner circle of Wikipedians that is balanced and supplemented by a vast array of contributors. Brown observes that such electronic communities allow conflicting interests to be in-community with each other. Their practices also disperse responsibility by allocating the job of monitoring content to users and various contributors. One of the difficulties noted in this study of dispersed community is that its structure offers an example of a site where "identification . . . is always accompanied by disidentification." Brown notes that this tension is due to the recognition that communities formed in the name of shared values are provisional and constantly on shaky ground.

Both Kathleen Dixon and Julia M. Smith take a feminist approach to the study of deliberative communities. In her essay, "Aesthetics and Rhetoric in *The Oprah Winfrey Show*," Dixon considers how various forms of performance, poetics, and artistry bring people together and promote consubstantiality. *The Oprah Winfrey Show* threads together a multimedia mix of the genres of documentary, narrative, entertainment, and journalism to consider significant issues in contemporary culture. Its discourses form a public commons that appeals to Oprah's viewership. The show's repertoire of content and its multimodal formats succeed because they engage the audience's concerns and interests. Julia M. Smith examines a fifteenth-century text—Christine de Pizan's "City of Ladies." She notes that, through rhetorical appeals to her readers, Christine sought to form a like-minded community of literate women within a social culture not conducive to women's intellectual development. Christine's manuscript included illustrations crafted by an artist of the time, and Smith discusses these miniatures in some depth. Her work succeeds in shedding light on how the relationship between image and agency can offer a vision of an alternative lifestyle and a set of priorities. As Smith notes, Christine's work was significant in modeling how women can develop their own rhetorical agency through multiple layers of meaning in a set of manuscripts.

The last two pieces in this section explore some alternative perspectives on constitutive rhetoric, specifically. In "The Constitutive Rhetoric of *Com-*

mon Sense," David Hoffman points out that theories of constitutive rhetoric rely almost entirely on examples of how audiences are constituted as members of some "collective" and "transhistorical" identity. However, Hoffman wonders "must not the subject position of the 'unified and transcendent subject,' the Enlightenment individual . . . also be a product of a constitutive rhetoric?" Hoffman responds in the affirmative and offers Thomas Paine's *Common Sense* as a counterexample to the traditional narrative of constitutive rhetoric, one where the audience is constituted not collectively and transhistorically, but individually and universally. Particularly suggestive is Hoffman's description of Paine's rhetoric as shaping a destiny out of place, not history, in its constitutive function.

Finally, Jay Childers reminds us that not all rhetorics of public formation are responsible or prompt responsible rhetorical actions by others. Jay Childers' "Paternalistic Rhetoric and the American People" traces the construct of the American people, or public, in a recent barrage of "paternalistic rhetoric." Childers argues that the American public is largely constructed by a small group of elites who do not want or need widespread public participation in decision making. The result is a paternalistic rhetoric that formulates the American public as unable to make competent decisions and thus benevolently excludes that public from the public sphere. After situating his concept amongst existing models of constitutive rhetoric, Childers reviews three diverse disseminators of contemporary paternalistic rhetoric: George W. Bush, the Exxon Mobil Corporation, and Bloodsaves, a national nonprofit organization. Childers suggests that it is the responsibility of rhetoricians to watch out for such paternalistic rhetorics that construct individuals as ineffective members of publics and thus curtail democratic self-governance.

SHAPING HISTORIES AND ENVISIONING FUTURES

The third section of this collection stems from Zarefsky's third responsibility of rhetoric: to enable a vision of the future for social change. This section begins with an article demonstrating that rhetorical spaces can supply visions of possible futures. The next two essays address the history of the Holocaust and suggest that responsible rhetorics should learn from the rhetorics that contributed to past atrocities as well as from how those atrocities are constructed and understood in the present. Indeed, in considering our selections, we found that many, if not most, of the discussions of future visions developed from or inferred lessons from the past and/or critiques or analyses of the present. This observation prompted our expansion of Zarefsky's responsibility to include visions of the past as well as the future. The last five essays in this collection address the constructions of pasts and futures of groups familiar to most of our conference participants: academia, rhetorical studies, and the Rhetoric Society of America (RSA) itself. Taken together, these articles show that both responsible histories and projected futures require rigorous analysis of the past and present.

Visions and goals for the future may be promulgated through various means, and Gregory Clark provocatively demonstrates how spaces can promote attitudes that embody hopes for and visions of a different future. Investigating the "sermonic" aspects of the U.S. National Park Service's (NPS) structural and landscape architecture in the first half of the twentieth century, Clark argues that the NPS Rustic design scheme inculcated in visitors attitudes of "reverence" toward nature: "Visitors were directed by design into an alternative way of life that subordinated them and their projects to the sublimity and beauty of nature." These attitudes might lead to associated actions, actions undertaken to preserve the natural environment with a vision of a future where such reverent experiences of nature would remain accessible for future generations.

Visions of the future are often made possible by a knowledge and understanding of past events, and two of these essays address the momentous history of the Holocaust. Kathleen A. Swift, in her essay "Eugenics, Nazism, and the Sinister Science of the Human Betterment Foundation," notes that responsible rhetoric requires understanding rhetorical histories. That is, histories of public controversy and the roles played by rhetoric on a given topic across time should constitute useful genealogies for study by rhetorical critics. To illustrate this point, Swift discusses the history of the "Human Betterment Foundation," an organization formed prior to WWII whose work continued until shortly after the war ended. She traces xenophobic inclinations of the public discourse concerning eugenics during this period. Her archive-based research includes papers produced by the Human Betterment Foundation and a successor organization called EngenderHealth. The significance of her analysis is to reveal standards of community judgment in the early twentieth century that would now be considered shocking.

Richard Glejzer and Michael Bernard-Donals' "Synecdoche as Figure of the Holocaust" argues that Holocaust memoirs are not characterized by metonymy, the construction of a coherent whole, as is commonly assumed, but rather synecdoche, a chain of chaos and disorder that cannot be successfully ordered into a whole. In their analysis of Daniel Mendelsohn's 2006 memoir, *The Lost: A Search for Six of the Six Million*, the authors show that the narrator's attempt to construct a coherent narrative out of various historical fragments is undermined by his synecdochal movement from fragment to fragment; no master piece ever makes the puzzle fall into place. The article raises the question of what other kinds of histories, like Holocaust history, might be driven by the figure of synecdoche, by the displacement that is the essence of all representation.

The next two contributors address, in their own distinct ways, the construction of rhetorical history and historiography. Maha Baddar highlights the absence of Arabs in the medieval rhetorical tradition except as "a military nuisance." "The Arabs Did Not 'Just' Translate Aristotle: Al-Farabi's Logico-Rhetorical Theory" gives an account of the Orientalist view of Arabic philosophy that leads historians to expect only imitative contributions from

Arabic writers and teachers. To counter this trend, her article demonstrates that Abu-Nasr Muhammad al-Farabi did not just translate Aristotle, but theorized rhetoric as a logical art, honed logical and rhetorical terminology in his translations from Greek to Arabic, and adapted Platonic and Aristotelian models for his monotheistic readers. Baddar reminds rhetorical scholars of their responsibility to do the kind of scholarship that not only recovers but also demonstrates the mutations and reformulations of rhetorical theories as they cross national, ethnic, and religious divides.

A unique contributor to the RSA 2008 conference and this collection, the renowned and award-winning public intellectual Charles Johnson presented his short story, "The Cynic," at a plenary session. Depicting the relationships between various schools of thought amongst followers of Socrates, Johnson's story is told from Plato's perspective and illuminates the character of its narrator as well as that of Diogenes, a less-celebrated acolyte of Socrates. Through his ascetic lifestyle and materialist worldview, Diogenes' flamboyance offends but also challenges Plato's sensibilities. Ultimately, "The Dog," as Diogenes is known, confounds an overwhelmed Plato into conceiving an alternative to his idealist view of truth and being and prompts Johnson's readers to consider anew the various streams of rhetorical thought descending from Socrates and their interrelations in the past and present.

The remainder of the essays in this section tackle the construction of the past and future in much closer realms: in academia, in rhetorical scholarship, and in RSA, specifically. Karen Powers' essay "Loyalty Oaths and the Letter of the Law: Rhetoric, Resistance, and Responsibility" expresses concern about the erosion of civil liberties in the post-9/11 era, particularly among members of academia. Noting that nearly two-thirds of the states now require employees such as university professors and those working in public institutions to sign loyalty oaths or complete security questionnaires, Powers sets out to examine this phenomenon. She examines two loyalty oaths—The University of California's loyalty oath requirement in the 1940s and 1950s and an existing loyalty oath and questionnaire in the state of Georgia that emerged at mid-twentieth century. She notes that such structures may be susceptible to "dangerous revisions and reinterpretations," and she therefore presents a vision of the future in which the potential for social change might be impaired.

Recent moves in academia toward what is known as the "scholarship of engagement" have begun to make their mark on the field of rhetoric and composition. Richard Gebhardt's article, "Scholarship of Engagement: *Both* a *New Name For* and a *Challenge To* the Work of Rhetoric," examines what exactly is meant by "engaged scholarship" in these recent initiatives. On the one hand, engaged scholarship might be a new term for what rhetoric and composition faculty generally do—linking rigorous academic inquiry with larger social and public concerns. Yet this optimistic view stems from a broader definition of engaged scholarship than the one presiding in current initiatives, which prescribes not only the subject of the research but also the methodology. Because this definition precludes much of the engaged scholarship of rhetorical scholars, Gebhardt concludes with suggestions of how rhetoric and composition scholars might challenge these narrower understandings of engagement so that future rhetorical scholarship can continue to be valued both institutionally and publicly.

In her essay, "Gender Equity in the Rhetoric Society of America," Cheryl Geisler brings us even closer to home in tracing past and current patterns of professional advancement for women in RSA. She reminds her readers that professional organizations such as the RSA play a vital role in creating opportunities for their members by informing, reviewing, and rewarding scholarly projects. Data she has collected on historic patterns of promotion and tenure among RSA members show a historic discrepancy in the awarding of promotions between men and women—a discrepancy that has declined in recent years. In her conclusion, Geisler offers a vision of the future of RSA in which its women members will be more actively mentored, recognized, supported, and acknowledged. Fortunately, the RSA board is now considering ways in which its Task Force on Gender Equity can work toward these ends.

PREPARING STUDENTS TO LIVE
IN A RAPIDLY CHANGING WORLD

The fourth section of the collection focuses on preparing students to live in a rapidly changing world. As in the previous section, the essays in this section thematize social change, but also emphasize the responsibilities of teachers of rhetoric to provide pedagogical and textual environments in which students can contemplate such topics as resistance, cultural difference, and modes of writing and expression. This section begins with three examples of how teachers might pedagogically employ new models and applications of classic concepts in the field. Another author argues that popular genres can generate student interest and persuade students of the relevance of rhetorical approaches. Finally, the collection closes with two essays that model ways in which the relation of rhetoric and morality might be investigated in classroom settings.

One of the main responsibilities of rhetoricians as instructors is to help students understand rhetorical and discursive concepts in a manner salient to their own times and experiences. The first several articles in this section provide guidance for instructors introducing three such concepts to students: *ethos,* analogy, and agency. In "*I* Told *U* So: Classical and Contemporary *Ethos* and the Stabilization of *Self,*" Nathaniel A. Rivers contrasts the notion of *ethos* as presentation of a stable self with an alternative idea—cultivation of self through interaction with others. In contrast to classical and contemporary notions of *ethos* that view the self as singular, insulated, and authentic, Rivers seeks to put forward a critique of the construct as it is conventionally conceived. In helping students to think about how *ethos* operates in context, Rivers encourages a view of the construct as not fixed or stable but rather drawn from variously authentic cultivations of the self that happen as one engages with the audience. His idea of a malleable self as a resource for cultivation of *ethos* appears to be a promising concept for development in composition studies.

Joseph Little and Lisa Jane Kabasin approach the topic of the rhetorical functions of analogy in scientific discourse. Their article, "Coming to Terms with Analogy: Generativity and Constraint in the Work of Nagaoka, Gamow, and Freud," introduces generativity and constraint as alternatives to former approaches that focus on whether or not a given analogy helped the scientist to "get it right." Generativity and constraint refer to the variety of correspondences aligned with a given analogy and the degree to which the rhetor must address those correspondences in order to keep her arguments in line with the audience's sense of "sound reasoning." Offering three contrasting examples of analogy in operation in science—Nagaoka's Saturnian theory, Gamow's liquid drop theory, and Freud's Clark lecture—the authors demonstrate various rhetorical functions of analogies. They suggest that generativity and constraint, explored via concrete examples, will help students of rhetoric and technical communication to understand the inventional role of analogy in scientific discourse.

In "Writing Machines: Authorial Agency and Bot-Written Texts in Wikipedia," Krista Kennedy leads us to consider another dimension of writing and reading—authorial agency. She asks: What happens when written texts are produced, not by students or other writers, but instead by machines that write? Such questions increase in relevance as mundane textual environments become ever more automated. Authoring in digital environments promotes the distribution of authorship among contributors that coproduce content. Kennedy compares the distributed authorship in Wikipedia with distributed authorship in multiple-authored encyclopedic works. Kennedy then turns to Wikipedia, an environment where texts are written and edited by bots—programs or scripts that can change the text without human intervention. She concludes by noting that in an environment such as Wikipedia, the author has become "the purest sort of textual curator, shaping and showcasing what already exists," rather than the sole source of an original text.

In her essay, "The Rhetoric of the Graphic Novel," Kathryn E. Dobson considers the responsibilities of rhetoric in a genre that is becoming more pervasive—the graphic novel in the form of comics. How do such publications convince reason and move the passions? By combining text and hand-produced visuals, this genre succeeds partly because of its multimodal format. It calls upon teachers and their students to consider how a rethinking of conventional forms of expression may engender new approaches to thought and expression. Dobson urges her readers to take these texts seriously, since they often succeed in engaging student interest in major issues and stimulate a higher level of student attention, contemplation, and response than does sheer text.

This section concludes with two essays exploring questions of morality and rhetoric. Mark Meister and Curt Gilstrap, in "The Earth Liberation Front's (ELF) Failed Diatribe of Sacramental Arson," consider yet another form of expression—use of arson as protest rhetoric. Public articulation of the ELF's views takes the form of diatribe, a historical rhetorical genre that is designed to arouse and shock audiences and alter public perception of social change. Meister and Gilstrap's study focuses on how nondiscursive forms of protest such as arson are conceived, designed, and thrust into public view. They use a form of Burkean analysis to explain ELF's perspective on their actions and their members' view of arson as a means of sanctification and protest against evil. Meister and Gilstrap's essay illustrates how the study of a dramatic resistance movement might encourage readers to consider the moral dimensions of resistance and social protest.

The moral dimensions of Cezar Ornatowski's topic in "'The Future is Ours,' or Is It?: The Rise and Fall of Totalitarian Rhetoric in Poland (and Elsewhere)" are perhaps more apparent. Examining the rhetoric of the "real socialist" regime in Poland, Ornatowski illuminates discursive features that might be considered totalitarian—forced mass identification and the future as already present are two pithy and accessible examples. Besides providing a map for identifying such nondemocratic rhetorics, Ornatowski addresses the relation between rhetoric and regime; ultimately, the article illuminates the link of democracy, as well as totalitarianism, to specific rhetorical characteristics. The question of the relationship of rhetoric to regime and rhetoric to professed ideals is one that all students in a post-9/11 world should consider, and Ornatowski successfully reaffirms the import of rhetorical cues in deciphering the ideals and intentions of both presumed allies and antagonists.

Michelle Smith
Barbara Warnick

Work Cited

Bellah, Robert N., Richard Madsen, William M. Sullivan, Ann Swidler, and Steven M. Tipton. *Habits of the Heart: Individualism and Commitment in American Life*. Berkeley: U of California P, 1985, 1996.

Plenary Address
Reclaiming Rhetoric's Responsibilities

David Zarefsky

For several conferences now, the incoming RSA president has invited the immediate past president to offer remarks in plenary session. Consumed by the responsibility of planning the conference, the new president may be too short-sighted to realize that as you do unto your predecessor, your successor will do unto you. And so here I am. Perhaps you can imagine my rhetorical situation. Should I talk about my own research, on the arrogant assumption that the work I am doing will be of interest to us all? Or should I engage in post-presidential pontification, secure in the delusion that holding this august office imbues one with fresh insight into matters rhetorical? Unable to choose between these appealing prospects, I plan to do both, under the guise of a rumination on this year's conference theme.

Ever since Jack Selzer selected this theme, I have found it puzzling: the responsibilities of rhetoric. Now, I understand that *rhetors* have responsibilities: to be honest and ethical, to respect the audience, to think strategically, to choose wisely. And I understand that we *rhetoricians* have responsibilities: to explain, to assess, and to improve the quality of discourse about topics that matter, and thereby to empower individuals and to enhance our public life. We spend much of our lives trying as best we can to meet these responsibilities. But rhetoric? It is what the ancients regarded as a *techne*, a skill or practice that could be used for good or ill but that was itself neutral. How can we say that rhetoric—our subject matter—has responsibilities?

Yet I believe we can answer that question if we focus our attention on the work that rhetoric does. And here we can take counsel from some of the significant anniversaries we celebrate this year.

Fifty years ago, in 1958, Stephen Toulmin published his second book, *The Uses of Argument*. Largely ignored if not criticized by his fellow philosophers, Toulmin's book would have a significant impact on rhetorical studies. Teachers of composition and public speaking latched on to the Toulmin model because it intuitively seemed a more realistic way to diagram argu-

13

ments than was the traditional syllogism. (I even encountered an intercollegiate debate team during the 1960s that organized its file box according to the parts of the Toulmin model.) But the model was intended to illustrate a larger point: in the world of human affairs, we establish claims not by formal proof but through justification. Proof is concerned with whether statements are true; justification, with whether we should believe them. What determines whether we should believe a claim is whether the inference leading to it is warranted. The warrant is a particularly important part of Toulmin's system (97–102). It is a license authorizing us to move beyond given evidence to infer a claim. It is necessary because, unlike in deductive logic, in ordinary reasoning the claim goes beyond the evidence, telling us something new, and hence does not follow absolutely from it.

The warrant comes not from any formal system or rule, but from people representing the community to which the argument is addressed. Toulmin mentioned that argumentation is often field-specific (36–38) and hence the contents of the warrant may vary from field to field. Meanwhile, the force of the warrant is always the same; namely that the claim is authorized on the basis of the evidence. Although Toulmin does not mention rhetoric, and reportedly was surprised to learn of his book's reception among rhetoricians, he nevertheless invokes rhetorical considerations. His jurisprudential analogy suggests that claims are to be justified; they must be justified *to someone*; hence arguments essentially are addressed and are validated by an audience.

This is no small point, because it gives Toulmin a middle ground between the necessary and the arbitrary. It enables him to posit that arguments in ordinary usage, as well as in many specialized fields, have a logic, though not the logic of formal deduction. And it is an audience-dependent logic. By inference we can hint at Toulmin's view of the responsibility of rhetoric. It is to justify the claims we make upon one another, redeeming the promise of reason through field-based intersubjective standards of judgment that are the expression of a community. To say that the standards of judgment are field-specific also means that they are not universal or hegemonic. Though unintended by Toulmin, this move opened the way for one of the major developments of the past fifty years: recognition of diversity in modes of reasoning and judgment.

The role of rhetoric in reasoning is even more pronounced in Chaim Perelman and Lucie Olbrechts-Tyteca's *The New Rhetoric*, whose publication (in French) also occurred fifty years ago. Traumatized by the ability of the Nazis to capture technical reason and to establish a closed system in which even the Holocaust could be a "valid" conclusion, Perelman sought to rehabilitate the concept of reason rather than to abandon a commitment to reason altogether. For Perelman, arguments depended on their acceptance by an audience for their strength—and not just the particular audience one happened to address but also on the writer or speaker's conception of a universal audience, of reasonable people. Formal rationality was neither a necessary nor a sufficient condition for an argument's being reasonable. Audience judgments determined that. Most of *The New Rhetoric*, on which he collaborated with Olbrechts-Tyteca, is then devoted to an account of argument schemes that increase or decrease the adherence that reasonable people could grant to claims put before them.

It is noteworthy that Perelman and Olbrechts-Tyteca called their book *The New Rhetoric*, even though they were not familiar with the field of rhetoric as most of us know it. But they reached back to the ancient art as the foundation for a humanistic sense of reason grounded in people's ability to exercise judgment. As with Toulmin, a fundamental feature of argumentation is that it is addressed to people, before whom it must pass muster. Rhetoric's responsibility is to enable people to judge whether a claim is reasonable and just.

For both Toulmin and Perelman, then, rhetoric facilitates reason. It is through rhetoric that all the realms of human action outside the boundaries of logical necessity can be rendered reasonable. Although this is a benefit in any area of our lives, it is especially important at moments when we are called together as a public to make decisions under conditions of uncertainty, when the right course is not self-evident but we nevertheless must act. We commemorate this year the anniversary of such a moment.

One hundred years before Toulmin and Perelman and Olbrechts-Tyteca published their books, newspapers reported that the prairies of Illinois were "on fire." The most prominent Senate Democrat, Stephen A. Douglas, was being challenged for his seat by a Springfield lawyer and former congressman, Abraham Lincoln. The heart of their contest would be a series of seven debates held in towns across the state. The centerpiece of the debates, and of the campaign, was the question of whether it was right to permit slavery to extend into new territories—a question that was important to the people of Illinois primarily because it was the issue to which Douglas had hitched his political fortunes. Between two thousand and twenty thousand people attended these epic forensic encounters, enduring the August sun or the October rain for three hours at a stretch, while Lincoln and Douglas declaimed on the issue of the day.

Anyone who has read the debates will recognize that they are not what they are cracked up to be—they are not models of statesmanlike eloquence, cogent reasoning, and powerful evidence. They are consumed instead with allegations of plots and conspiracies, often unencumbered by evidence, by arcane legal disputes about the meaning of constitutional phrases and the finality of court decisions, and by elaborate discussions of what the founders would have thought about the issue had they been on the scene. But to say all this is not to debunk the debates; rather, it is to appreciate them for what they actually do accomplish. First, both debaters make their arguments with a clear sense of their audience: primarily the Old Whigs, whose votes would decide the election, and who in principle were opposed to slavery but also convinced that abolition would be far too drastic a change. Each man appealed to one pole of Whig thought—Lincoln by portraying Douglas as plotting to spread slavery everywhere, Douglas by depicting Lincoln as a closet abolitionist (Zarefsky, *Lincoln, Douglas* 69). Second, however, neither man pandered to his specific audience to the neglect of the larger public. To be sure, they each accused the other of trying—Douglas alleged that Lincoln took different positions in different parts of the state; Lincoln accused his rival of trying to exploit popular prejudices against racial amalgamation. While they both did vary their tone and emphasis for a specific audience, their basic views were consistent throughout. And no wonder—those debates were transcribed and published in the newspapers; neither candidate could hide from an inquisitive public. Third, the debate texts are sufficiently polysemous that they can be read with a universal audience in mind—if, for example, Douglas's role is seen not as an active conspirator in a proslavery plot but as the unintentional instrument of proslavery thought, or if the conspiracy itself is read allegorically to suggest a natural tendency rather than an active design.

Meanwhile, both men offered carefully developed arguments, spelled out the implications of their positions, tried to invite clash, and for the most part engaged what the other had to say. They did not shirk controversy; they did not take refuge in slogans or sound bites; and with only an occasional lapse they did not engage in personal vituperation. Their attacks on each other were more often uses of the circumstantial *ad hominem* than what we today call negative campaigning.

Here was a case where rhetoric met its responsibilities. It facilitated decision making about an important matter, involving claims to the ownership of public memory as well as choices about the future direction of the country. Not everyone made a decision on these grounds, of course, and the rhetorical choices enacted by Lincoln and Douglas ultimately were unable to avoid war. They were in the center of a discourse space that eventually was captured by the extremes, by people who refused to allow themselves to be convinced. But rhetoric cannot do everything. What it did do was to encourage reasoning with an audience in mind, to encourage deliberation, and to engage the citizenry. For all their limitations, the Lincoln–Douglas debates reveal rhetoric in a better light than, say, most contemporary public discussions about the future of Social Security, the fiscal priorities of our government, or the decision to go to war in Iraq.

Important as it is, however, promoting public reason is not rhetoric's only responsibility. I would like to speak more briefly to two others by referring to people who were also writing during the 1950s, even if not precisely in 1958.

As everyone here knows, Kenneth Burke emphasized identification, the perceived consubstantiality of people. It replaced persuasion in his view of the end of rhetoric, and he wrote that it was compensatory to division (20–23). People are naturally divided and fragmented; it is the task of rhetoric to unite them, to lead them to see themselves not as isolated individuals but as a community. Rhetoric brings a public or a community into being. It accomplishes this task by enabling people to recognize common bonds, to see their interests, experiences, and aspirations as consubstantial. Identification is not a natural state but a socially constructed reality. It is not too much to say, then, that rhetoric is the glue that holds a society or culture together, making it something more than a collection of atomized individuals. Providing that glue is a great responsibility indeed.

Communities often are built in response to a perceived external threat. The urgency of the threat causes people to overcome their divisions and stress their solidarity against the enemy. This is a staple in the rhetoric of war and helps to explain why the enemy is simultaneously dehumanized and imbued with great power. The phenomenon is found during metaphorical wars as well as real ones. The enemy might be poverty or drugs, militant Islam or godless communism. During the cold war, widespread fear of communism that was all-powerful yet morally weak, not only united Americans and justified their deferring other goals, but also brought together in common purpose sovereign nations of what we used to call the "free world." More recently, a similar rhetorical map has been used for the war on terror. Because we need to thwart the terrorists, we unite to support even questionable means toward the achievement of this goal. In both cases, interest and power were mobilized by constructing unity in response to threat.

Although creating a community by negating an enemy is a common rhetorical move, occasionally community is created by transcending old categories and heralding a new day—not by warding off danger but by characterizing the moment in a new way. It is too soon to tell, but the current political campaign may be our summons to think anew together on the subject of race. And we saw a rare transcendent moment at the height of the cold war. President Kennedy gave the commencement address at American University in 1963, and he urged his audience to move past the shibboleths of the cold war by rethinking attitudes toward the Soviet Union, toward communism, and toward peace. "Peace" emerged as the central theme of the president's speech for the first time. It was the new transcendent term, overcoming ideological division. Peace, Kennedy said, was the necessary rational end of rational men, because the alternatives would lead to destruction. Then, offering a transcendent vision that overcame divisions, he reminded his listeners, "We all breathe the same air. We all cherish our children's future. And we are all mortal" (Kennedy 460, 462). Specific policy issues may divide us, but these larger values reconstitute us as a community. At moments when that happens, rhetoric fulfills one of its highest responsibilities. It transcends old categories and creates a new sense of who we are.

And when we ask to what end we nurture a sense of community, we are reminded of what *else* rhetoric can do. It can inspire; it can give direction to our thoughts and acts. Richard Weaver had this view of rhetoric in mind when he wrote, also in the 1950s, that rhetoric shows us "better versions of ourselves" (25), motivating us to work and sacrifice so that we move beyond the moment and toward a nobler ideal. I know of no recent public figure who has crafted a utopian vision so forcefully as a person born 100 years ago, President Lyndon Baines Johnson. He sought nothing less than a society free of poverty, illness, ignorance, prejudice, and even ugliness. He believed that it was within our power to shape the civilization we want. "Is a new world coming?" he asked. "We welcome it, and we will bend it to the hopes of man" (Johnson 74). He sought to inspire and motivate Americans to pursue these lofty goals both by appealing to their moral sense and by projecting confidence that the goal could be reached. The richest nation on earth, he often said, had obligations that followed from its wealth: to use its resources to assure opportunity and to better the lives of all. For him this was no idle, visionary dream; it was an achievable utopia. A nation that was able to explore the mysteries of outer space, *a fortiori*, surely should be able to solve its problems here on earth.

With the exception of Medicare, there was no preexisting constituency for most of the Great Society initiatives. Johnson called one into being through his rhetorical appeals. Again and again he conveyed a sense of a possible future, a moral obligation to reach for it, and confidence that it could be done (Zarefsky, "Great Society"). The project of the Great Society foundered, to be sure—partly because Johnson moved too fast, partly because he paid far more attention to securing legislation than to implementing it, partly because he failed to account for the sharp divisions of the country along the lines of race. Mostly, though, Johnson failed because he was diverted. In one of that era's great ironies, the man who could see a better vision of American society and dedicate himself to achieving it, could not do what Kennedy had done at American University—to begin to see beyond the cold war. Imprisoned by cold war assumptions, he risked everything on a war in Vietnam, even as he foresaw that his policy would fail, because he sincerely believed that he had no choice. As a tragic hero, even today Johnson is remembered far more for this foreign policy disaster than for the transformative potential of his domestic vision and his commitment to achieve it.

So far I have drawn on theorists with whom we are familiar, and cases of rhetorical practice on which my research has focused, to suggest three responsibilities of rhetoric. It permits reasoning together about matters that are not certain but about which decisions nevertheless are required. It binds individuals into communities and publics by establishing common bonds among people. And it inspires people to work toward goals by presenting visions of what might be. These are all things that rhetoric is supposed to do, and they are essential to the success of human life and society. Rhetoric has other responsibilities, of course, though I do not discuss them today. It is a means of celebration, commemoration, and consolation. It is the vehicle by which we collectively construct our past. It is a civilized surrogate for violence. In many religious traditions, it is the bridge between the ordinary and the sacred. No doubt many of you can suggest responsibilities of rhetoric to add to this list. The range and significance of rhetoric's responsibilities have both grown over time.

But here's a paradox. Rhetoric cannot will itself into being; it is, after all, a *techne*. Rhetoric cannot meet its own responsibilities; people have to enable it to do that. Individually and together, we must draw on this faculty so that it can do the work it was meant to do. If we were to take stock of how well our culture's rhetorical practice measures up to these responsibilities—if, in the words of our last conference theme, we were to size up rhetoric—we might find the glass half empty or we might find it half full, but we will not find it full enough.

In this country, we have spent the past two decades not just divided into red and blue states, but with a toxic politics that often has seemed to have no objective other than to mobilize a majority for its own sake. Aristotle said that rhetoric was an offshoot of politics, but there is little it can do to ennoble politics that has no objective beyond tactics and strategy. We have seen a flight from rhetoric in the conduct of international affairs, such that deliberation, consultation, negotiation, and persuasion are widely seen as signs of weakness, just as the cold war consensus smothered debate about every foreign policy issue except who could be toughest in standing up to communism. The very real threats posed by terrorism, by asymmetric power, by hostile ideologies, have become not exigencies for collective discussion about how to maintain and adapt our values to a new world, but instead have become trump cards used to threaten, to intimidate, and to silence. We have had no serious discussion lately about how to balance our rights as individuals with our responsibilities to the commons. We have trivialized not only the discourses of our popular and consumer culture but also the discourses of our civic life. And we have not developed a healthy respect for rhetoric itself. Even as we seek inspiration and eloquence, especially in moments of crisis, we think of rhetoric as opposed to reality and we preface the noun with words like "empty" and "mere." We are in a presidential campaign in which the quality of rhetoric has itself become something of an issue. The fact that a candidate is a skilled speaker has been cited as a reason to suspect that the candidate either lacks substance or has something to hide. This is an old but still powerful *topos*.

You may say that I am overstating the case, and you probably would be right. You could point to examples of constructive rhetoric on matters ranging from local zoning to global warming, and I would agree that we should take pride in those. You could even cite some of the same examples of political debate and oratory that have been criticized, and argue instead that they are strong examples of forging collective judgment on difficult issues, and I would agree with that. I myself argued just last week that former Vice President Al Gore's complaint that we have lost the capacity to reason together is oversimplified and naïve (Zarefsky, "Chaim Perelman").

The problem is that as encouraging as the counterevidence may be, it is not enough. Rhetoric's responsibilities have been enlarged in our time. We face such complex predicaments that we need all the rhetorical resources we can get. Our tasks include reconciling unity and diversity, individualism and community, nationalism and global citizenship, liberty and equality, quality and quantity, faith and doubt, the present and the future. None of these pairs consists of opposites in the logical sense; they are not in principle irreconcilable. But they are inherent tensions and often seem to work at cross purposes.

Articulating how they can work together, how we can get the best of both, or how we can transcend the tension, is the task of a responsible rhetoric.

But if rhetoric itself lacks agency, then people must learn how to use it responsibly. Whatever they may have learned so far is not enough. And that is where we come in. It has been observed frequently that the rhetorical tradition is a teaching tradition. What we teach enables men and women to enact rhetoric's social role. And we are not without agency. It is worth reminding ourselves that we as a field probably come closer than anyone else to teaching every student in America. Those of us who teach writing, and some of us who teach speaking, may be presiding over the only required courses remaining in the curriculum. Moreover, many of us work in programs where student demand and enrollments are growing. We flatter ourselves to think that this reflects growing interest in what we do and growing recognition by others of its importance. The work we do is unquestionably important. Yet while it is easy to praise rhetoricians at RSA, I want to ask if we're doing enough to promote the responsibilities of rhetoric.

Fifty years ago, though we were fewer and weaker, we may have had a clearer though narrower sense of what we were about: the study of canonical texts in the history of rhetoric, the pedagogy of writing and public speaking, studies of British and American public discourse by religious and political leaders, argumentation, critical methods. Not every program included all of these topics, but there would be few additions to this list. Moreover, we understood that, by teaching in these areas, we would nurture citizens whose training enabled them to use rhetoric responsibly. That was our product. Both composition studies and what was then called speech were conscious of their ideological heritage in the Progressive movement of the early twentieth century with its commitments to the cultivation of good citizens.

As the program for this conference implies, each of these traditional areas of study remain vibrant today. It is simply not true that the canonical works have been over-studied, with nothing left to say. We still have much to learn from Aristotle and Cicero, and much to learn from nineteenth-century white male orators. We should keep studying them, aided by the conceptual advances of the past fifty years and our ability to see old works in a new light.

But this is not enough. Each of our core subfields encompasses far more than it did then. We have discovered and begun to recover multiple rhetorical traditions. Our canon has been vastly enlarged and the very idea of canonicity has been called into question. Texts and textuality are seen much more broadly than they were then. We have worked to recover voices of those who for far too long were marginalized by their gender, their race, their class, their ethnicity, their sexual orientation. We recognize the many media through which public discourse takes place. We have productively problematized our notions of argumentation, style, effects, and criticism.

And beyond these trends, we have developed entirely new subfields that are, in Justice Douglas's phrase, emanations and penumbras (*Griswold*) of our disciplinary core. These include rhetorics of science and religion, of law and management. They include the rhetorical use of new technologies, vernacular rhetorics, and rhetorics of display—just to name a few.

Today, the scope of our subject is vast—to some, overly so; to some, infinitely so. We speak sometimes of the rhetorical tradition but we know that there are many rhetorics and many traditions. We examine rhetorical practice whether oral, written, visual, or mediated; we study the discourses of science, law, religion, medicine, literature and film, popular culture and violent protest, as well as the discourses traditionally associated with civic life. We bring to our studies theoretical and critical perspectives too numerous to list. Our umbrella is large. What should hold our work together, though, is a focus on what we are about. Our scholarship should deepen and enrich our understanding of rhetoric and its responsibilities. Our teaching should cultivate people who responsibly practice our old and useful art in both their personal and their public lives. Our agency and that of our students will in turn enable rhetoric to reclaim its responsibilities.

Two weeks ago, RSA was admitted into membership of the American Council of Learned Societies. Our application stressed the interdisciplinary nature of our subject and its centrality to public life. The importance of what we do makes it all the more crucial that we meet the challenges posed by this year's conference theme and reclaim rhetoric's responsibilities. At a gathering such as this, we should heed the advice that Adlai Stevenson gave to the seniors at Princeton in a speech he delivered, also during the 1950s: "You will go away with old, good friends. And don't forget, when you leave, why you came" (345).

Works Cited

Burke, Kenneth. *A Rhetoric of Motives.* 1950. Berkeley: U of California P, 1969.

Griswold v. Connecticut. 381 US 479. Supreme Court of the US. 1965.

Johnson, Lyndon B. "The President's Inaugural Address, January 20, 1965." *Public Papers of the Presidents: Lyndon B. Johnson, 1965* 1: 71–74. Washington, DC: U.S. Government Printing Office, 1966.

Kennedy, John F. "Commencement Address at American University in Washington, June 10, 1963." *Public Papers of the Presidents: John F. Kennedy, 1963.* Washington, DC: U.S. Government Printing Office, 1964. 459–64.

Perelman, Chaim, and Lucie Olbrechts-Tyteca. *The New Rhetoric: A Treatise on Argumentation.* Trans. John Wilkinson and Purcell Weaver. Notre Dame, IN: U of Notre Dame P, 1969.

Stevenson, Adlai E. "The Educated Citizen." *The Papers of Adlai E. Stevenson.* Ed. Walter Johnson. 4 vols. Boston: Little, Brown, 1974.

Toulmin, Stephen. *The Uses of Argument.* Cambridge: Cambridge UP, 1958.

Weaver, Richard. *The Ethics of Rhetoric.* Chicago: Regnery, 1953.

Zarefsky, David. "Chaim Perelman, Al Gore, and the Problem of Reason in Our Time." Paper presented at The Promise of Reason Conference, U of Oregon.

———. "The Great Society as a Rhetorical Proposition." *Quarterly Journal of Speech* 65.4 (Dec. 1979): 364–78.

———. *Lincoln, Douglas, and Slavery: In the Crucible of Public Debate.* Chicago: U of Chicago P, 1990.

PART I

Promoting Public Reason

Rousseau, Rhetoric, and the Promise of Contractual Politics

David Tell

Bryan Garsten does not mince words. In unambiguous terms he declares that Rousseau's political thought constitutes "an attack on rhetoric" (58). If, at first glance, Rousseau's praise for ancient eloquence or his republican celebration of political engagement "might lead one to think that Rousseau was friendly to classical rhetoric," Garsten urges us to think again (55–56). Rousseau's political project, he argues, was "an effort to neutralize the power of classical rhetoric" and immunize citizens against "the forms of persuasion recommended by rhetoricians" (70, 80).

Despite the conviction with which Garsten writes, I want to register here his anxiety that someone might mistakenly find Rousseau "friendly" toward rhetoric. This anxiety is well-founded, for some influential scholars have found in Rousseau a political vision in which rhetorical deliberation is the ultimate arbiter of political legitimacy. I am thinking here of Carole Pateman. According to Pateman, "Rousseau might be called the theorist *par excellence* of participation." *The Social Contract* in particular, she claims, "is vital for the theory of participatory democracy" (22).

We have then two contradictory readings of *The Social Contract* and the place of rhetoric therein. And the contradiction is aggravated when we recognize that Garsten and Pateman are hardly the only advocates for their respective positions. While Hannah Arendt argues that *The Social Contract* must "shun the drawn-out wearisome processes of persuasion, negotiation, and compromise" (*On Revolution* 86), Benjamin Barber reaches precisely the opposite conclusion. He argues that Rousseau models a political tradition characterized, in the first instance, by "*common deliberation*: the value of open hearings, public forums, town meetings . . . and other assemblies" (294, 296, emphasis in original).

Is it simply the case that Rousseau was inconsistent regarding the political function of rhetoric? Jean Starobinski thinks so. He writes: "We do [Rousseau] a disservice when we expect him to provide rigorous coherence and systematic thought" (qtd. in de Man 113). Thus, Bonnie Honig accounts for Rousseau's inconsistent evaluations of rhetoric by suggesting that Rousseau could not make up his mind. Sometimes Rousseau had great faith in the capacity of deliberation, Honig explains, and in these moments he character-ized politics "as a process of public deliberation and debate." At other times, however, Honig tells us that Rousseau believed deliberation is hopeless, "that discussion will only fan the flames of factionalism" (20).

Against the backdrop of Starobinski's and Honig's resignation that Rous-seau is simply inconsistent, Derrida's reading of Rousseau in *Of Grammatol-ogy* is all the more impressive. While Derrida does not argue that Rousseau is not contradictory, he does argue that all of the contradictions can be accounted for if we recognize the underlying logic of Rousseau's thought (183, 243).[1] Derrida's findings have important consequences for studying the much-disputed role of rhetoric in Rousseau's thought: they suggest that all the contradictions highlighted above might be accounted for with recourse to an underlying logic.

In this essay I argue that Rousseau's vision of contractual politics *is* that underlying logic. That is, Rousseau's theory of social contracts is fundamen-tal; once we understand this theory, his thoughts on rhetoric no longer seem inconsistent. Seen from this perspective, the contradiction between Garsten and Pateman is illusory, the result of engaging *The Social Contract* on the wrong level. While both Garsten and Pateman have plenty of textual evi-dence to support their claims, neither of them points toward the foundational, contractual logic that regulates the place of rhetoric in *The Social Contract.*

My task, then, is to explain Rousseau's contractual logic and foreground its bearing on the place of rhetoric within his political vision. As I will show, the terms of Rousseau's social contract forced him to declare that citizen delib-eration was of quite limited value; helpful at times, but precisely useless at the most important political moments: moments when basic policy decisions are made. In what follows I focus on Rousseau's theory of social contracts and explain how that theory regulates the political role of rhetoric: sometimes allowing it, most often denying it any role in the formation of the state.

The argument proceeds in three sections. I first consider the rhetorical function of social contracts. Second, I argue that Rousseau's contractual logic delimits the place of rhetoric within his political theory, and third, I conclude by reflecting more generally on the rhetorical promise of contractual politics.

THE RHETORIC OF SOCIAL CONTRACTS

I want to begin by insisting that *The Social Contract* is a book about social contracts. This is not obvious. Indeed, it is striking how much of the second-ary scholarship overlooks this basic fact. Far more common is the approach shared by Jean Starobinski and Jacques Derrida. For all of their differences (recorded in *Of Grammatology*), both scholars read *The Social Contract* as evi-dence of Rousseau's lifelong quest for the perfectly intimate, unmediated communion with others that Starobinski called "transparency" and Derrida "presence." This approach effectively illuminates the philosophical naiveté that characterizes Rousseau's work from the first discourse[2] forward. But here it is important to remember that Rousseau "never pretended" to be a "professional philosopher" (Shklar 1). His thought was provoked by the sight of human suffering, not the sight of human confusion. Accordingly, the deployment of a social contract should be understood as an intervention on the political level—an intervention arranged against suffering itself.

A careful reading of *The Social Contract* reveals that Rousseau introduces the concept of a social contract precisely at the moment when it seems that political foundation requires personal suffering, or personal sacrifice. Listen closely to Rousseau's words and hear the language of sacrifice. The moment of political founding is an "act of total alienation to the whole community of each associate" (*The Social Contract* 18).[3] In reference to this passage, Lester Crocker argues that Rousseau radicalized liberalism by insisting that political foundation requires the ultimate sacrifice. Where liberalism claims that "we sacrifice part of our freedom in order that the remainder of it may be protected," Rousseau "demands a total alienation" (Crocker xvii). "At the moment" of political foundation, Rousseau continues, "every member" of the community "gives himself up to it" along with "all his powers" and his "property" (22). As Garsten notes, political foundation requires the "sacrifice of private judgment" and "the sacrifice of private liberty" (70). Because of these sacrifices, the passage from the state of nature to civilization will always involve loss. Shklar writes: "As long as those Swiss peasants seemed content in their vegetative life, how could Voltaire, or any other champion of civilization, compensate the victims of urban complexity for their lost bliss?" (7). In sum, although Rousseau did not and would not use the word "sacrifice," the concept pervades the opening chapters of *TSC*. Again and again he describes the foundation of politics in sacrificial terms: self-alienation, self-giving, renunciation, and a loss of natural bliss. Crocker rightly concludes that the founding of the body politic "could not be done without sacrifice" (xvi).

What Crocker misses is the fact that *TSC* patently refuses to dwell on this moment of sacrifice. Almost immediately the language of sacrifice gives way, permanently, to the language of exchange. "To say that a man gives himself up for nothing is to say what is absurd and inconceivable" (*TSC* 12). Politics may require self-giving, but this giving is never a sacrifice because "we gain the equivalent of all that we lose" (18). Rousseau puts it this way:

> So untrue is it that in the social contract there is on the part of individuals any real renunciation, that their situation, as a result of this contract, is in reality preferable to what it was before, and that, instead of an alienation, they have only made an advantageous exchange of an uncertain and precarious mode of existence for a better assured one. (35)

The sacrificial character of nation founding has already begun to fade. The reality of self-giving is hidden behind an "advantageous exchange." For the remainder of *TSC,* it is as if the only relevant sacrifice involved is giving up the worthless for the sake of the valuable. Which is, of course, no sacrifice at all.

And this, I want to emphasize, is the rhetorical function of the social contract: it effaces the reality of sacrifice. It transforms the original political move from an act of sacrifice to an act of exchange. In this sense, it is highly significant that Rousseau's seldom-read third discourse, which Peter Gay has described as a "kind of rehearsal for *The Social Contract*," is entitled *Discourse on Political Economy* (111). To Rousseau's mind, a social contract makes the phrase "political economy" a tautology: the political is, by definition, economic, because it is founded on a primordial exchange. "At bottom," Rousseau writes, "all commitments of society are reciprocal in nature" ("Discourse" 117). Thus, in general terms, the rhetorical function of a social contract "consists in our coming to see our society as an 'economy,' an interlocking set of activities of production, exchange, and consumption" (Taylor 181).

It is important to pause here and recognize that Rousseau relied on the language of sacrifice to describe political foundation and then, moments later, introduced a social contract to obscure the fact of sacrifice. It is important because Rousseau's inability to describe the foundations of politics without sacrificial terms indicates that sacrifice is somehow an irremediable aspect of contractual politics. Rousseau's descriptions betray his declarations: while he declares that "we gain the equivalent of all that we lose," his descriptions suggest that sacrifice is basic; it is prior to any exchange or compensation.[4] Without the category of sacrifice, Rousseau's descriptions suggest, private judgment would reign, lawful authority would be reducible to "might makes right," and there would be, by definition, no political realm in which strength is checked by law (*TSC* 10–11).

By insisting on the irremediable character of sacrifice, I am following Danielle Allen, who points us towards sacrifice as "a central and neglected term in the social contract tradition" (37). "The hard truth of democracy," she writes, "is that some citizens are always giving things up for others" (29). Indeed this is a bit of an understatement. Allen's example of sacrifice *par excellence*, the humiliation of Elizabeth Eckford as she attempted to integrate Little Rock's Central High School, suggests just how much is given up for others. She writes: "Beneath the promise and consent that found the social contract is the most extreme loss" (38). In one sense, Allen is here simply repeating, in quieter terms, Foucault's insistence that we recognize the violence that subtends contractual politics. Foucault writes: "The contract may have been regarded as the ideal foundation of law and political power," it may be designed to "fix limits on the exercise of power," but, in fact, Foucault argues, contract theory only hides the fact that the limits of the law are routinely broached and violence is still visited on precisely those whom the contract was designed to protect (222–23). Although neither Allen nor Foucault cite Rousseau, it seems that they both recognize the primary rhetorical function of Rousseau's social contract: it is a response to the loss, the sacrifice, or the violence within political organization.

We have then three responses to a common problem. That is, Foucault, Allen, and Rousseau each recognize the irreducibility of sacrifice, but they respond in different ways. Foucault points to the experience of violence to indict the hypocrisy of liberalism. In Richard Rorty's words, Foucault is simply "unwilling to be a liberal"—he is unwilling to admit that the social contract has any value that is not undermined by the experience of subjection that it is designed to obscure (61). Allen suggests that the loss experienced by Elizabeth Eckford, although extreme to be sure, does not, for that, indicate an essential hypocrisy or limitation. She points to the centrality of sacrifice not to indict contractual politics, but to help us better consider them. She concludes that the challenge to democratic politics is not to eliminate sacrifice, but to recognize it and redistribute it constantly (29, 37). Finally, Rousseau responds to the fact of sacrifice by introducing a primordial agreement in which every party would be compensated for losses accrued.

I will return to Foucault and Allen in the conclusion, but for the moment I want to emphasize that it is precisely Rousseau's recourse to a social contract envisioned as a primordial, compensatory agreement that limits the scope of rhetoric's applicability.

RHETORIC IN *THE SOCIAL CONTRACT*

It is important to remember that a contract is an exchange of goods or services. A social contract is no different. Over and over again, Rousseau describes the social contract in terms of a loss of physical strength and a more-than-compensatory gain in legal protections. "The passage from the state of nature to the civil state," Rousseau writes, occurs when "law succeeds appetite" (*TSC* 22), when the inequalities of physical strength give way to lawful equality (26), when the power to injure another through force gives way to inviolable rights (35), or when the right of physically occupying a piece of land gives way to "lawful possession" (24–25). In sum, the constitution of society requires "substituting a social and moral existence for the independent and physical existence which we have all received from nature. In a word, it is necessary to deprive man of his native powers [strength] in order to endow him with some which are alien to him [the law]" (43).

It is for this reason that Rousseau opens *TSC* with the assertion that "might does not make right" (11). From Rousseau's perspective, right, understood as a uniquely legal form of protection, is available only to the extent that might is sacrificed. But because legal protection is itself stronger than (physical) strength, the political obligation of alienating one's strength is not understood as a loss:

> Instead of alienation, they have only made an advantageous exchange of an uncertain and precarious mode of existence for a better and more assured one . . . of the power to injure others for their own safety, and of their strength, which others might overcome, for a right which the social union renders inviolable. (35)

In sum, the social contract is an exchange of natural, physical strength for legal, or what Rousseau refers to elsewhere as moral or political, protection. This is stated most clearly in his Second Discourse:

> I conceive of two sorts of inequality in the human species: one, which I call natural or physical, because it is established by nature and consists in the difference of ages, health, bodily strengths, and qualities of mind or soul; the other, which may be called moral or political inequality, because it depends on a sort of convention and is established, or at least authorized, by the consent of men. (*The First* 101)

Throughout Rousseau's writings, these two realms—the physical/natural on the one hand and the moral/legal/political on the other—are strictly distinguished.[5] In Rousseau's political writings, the advent of civilization is marked by the passage from the state of nature in which "might makes right" to a civilization in which the inequalities of physical strength are politically irrelevant because each, no matter how strong, submits to the law. When the social contract is violated, Rousseau writes, "it is no longer apparent what right or what interest could maintain the populace in social union, unless it is restrained by force alone, which brings about the dissolution of the civil state" ("Discourse" 122).

It is particularly important to note that this distinction, so basic to *TSC*, is central also in Rousseau's famous account of the origin of languages. In both the Second Discourse and the "Essay on the Origin of Languages," Rousseau argues that the acquisition of language coincides with the advent of society. In the state of nature, he writes, man did not "require a language more refined than that of crows or monkeys" (*The First* 145). As John T. Scott puts it, "The origin of communication is tied to the dawning consciousness of fellow humanity that marks man's emergence as a social and moral being" ("Introduction" xxix).

This logic made it difficult to explain the origin of speech itself. As Rousseau puts it in the Second Discourse, "speech seems to have been highly necessary to talk about speech" (*The First* 123).[6] In *TSC* this same conundrum calls into question the capacity for nation founding:

> In order that a newly formed nation might approve sound maxims of politics and observe the fundamental rules of state-policy, it would be necessary that the effect should become the cause; that the social spirit which should be the work of the institution, should preside over the institution itself, and that men should be, prior to the laws, what they ought to become by the means of them. (45)

In other words, nation founding requires that men understand the superiority of legal rights to physical strength, but their pre-political position in the state of nature precludes this insight. The "social spirit," or willingness to sacrifice physical strength, is both a prerequisite for and a consequence of nation founding.

Compounding this problem is the fact that prior to the founding of the nation there is no language to which a founder could appeal. For, of course, language is a function of society. As Rousseau frames the problem in *TSC*, "There are a thousand kinds of ideas which it is impossible to translate into the language of the people" (44). Reading this passage through the Second Discourse and the "Essay," it becomes clear that the reason why thousands of ideas are untranslatable into the vernacular is that the "language of the people" is, prior to the founding of society, the language of crows and monkeys. It is for this reason, Rousseau famously concludes, that the founder "cannot employ either force or reasoning, he must needs have recourse to an authority of a different order, which can compel without violence and persuade without convincing" (*TSC* 45).

I want to dwell briefly on this last phrase: the founder must "persuade without convincing." Whatever it might mean to "persuade without convincing," it is the capacity to do so that distinguishes the founder. Yet it needs to be emphasized that this nation-founding skill, which sounds so rhetorical because it involves "persuasion," is in fact anti-rhetorical. In the "Essay on the Origin of Languages," Rousseau describes in detail what it means to "persuade without convincing." There the phrase is used to describe the natural voice prior to the conventions of society (296). That is, "persuading without convincing" is defined by precisely the same distinction between nature and convention that, in the Second Discourse, authorized Rousseau to define natural language in terms of crows and monkeys. It is thus not surprising that, in the "Essay," Rousseau tells us that "persuading without convincing" is characterized by unarticulated "cries and groans" (295). Garsten concludes that, like the language of animals, "persuading without convincing" is "primitive" and "nonrational" (57). Like the "voice of nature" in the Second Discourse, "persuading without convincing" is the speech act appropriate prior to the conventions of society.

And here we come to the heart of the matter: nation founding requires a "different order" of reasoning. And the "Essay" teaches us that this "different order" of reasoning must be, if it is to found a nation, unconventional—in the strictest sense of that word. In the Geneva Manuscript, an early draft of *TSC*, Rousseau describes the language of the legislator as "superhuman eloquence" (qtd. in Garsten 61). William Connolly explains that Rousseau's "well-ordered state" requires an order of reasoning that "reaches below custom and expresses the claims of nature" (42). Citizen deliberation, precisely because it relies on social conventions, is insufficient for political foundation. Thus Rousseau introduces as a founder an "extraordinary" legislator, a "genius" whose "sublime reason . . . soars beyond the reach of common men" (*TSC* 45). And here we see the place of rhetoric being regulated by Rousseau's vision of contract politics. Because Rousseau determines the content of the social contract in accordance with the same dichotomy that structures his account of language, he cannot, in the name of consistency, allow rhetoric a role in the founding of the body politic. Because the contract makes possible both deliberation and civilization, Rousseau cannot give practices of deliberation any role in the founding of civilization.

As Bonnie Honig has pointed out, the contractual exchange that inaugurates civilization itself—the exchange of man's "native" powers of strength for those that are "alien to him"—requires an alien, or foreigner. And the decisive characteristic of this foreigner is access to a different order of reasoning that can demonstrate to a strong but stateless people the advantages of alienating their strength and founding a polity. The founding of the state is thus pre-rhetorical: it requires the intervention of a foreigner bearing an uncommon language.

However, if Rousseau's contract theory structurally precludes a role for rhetoric in the founding of a nation, it also provides a designated space for rhetoric following the foundation of the state. And here it is important to note Rousseau's otherwise odd insistence that the foreign-speaking founder must leave the state immediately after its founding. "This office, which constitutes the republic, does not enter into its constitution; it is a special and superior office, having nothing in common with human government" (*TSC* 43). The founding accomplished (without rhetoric), government takes over. In Rousseau's political theory, the government is neither sovereign nor legislative; it has no authority to make laws—only the foreign "legislator" makes laws, and he just skipped town. The government is to be understood simply as the "agent" that "puts into action" the directives of the legislator (60). The government is not instituted by a contract (60), it requires no "different order" of reasoning, and thus its power is always subject to the authority of the people assembled in deliberation.

Rousseau argues that "the assemblies of the people . . . are the shield of the body politic and the curb of government" (*TSC* 97). Even a tyrannical government, which would impose its will violently upon the people, finds itself impotent against a people always able to assemble. In a moving passage, Rousseau suggests that tyranny will be defeated wherever "the multitudes assemble in the squares as quickly as the troops in their quarters" (86). Rousseau concludes that the power of the government is "suspended" as "soon as the people are lawfully assembled" (97). The assembly, the site of deliberation *par excellence*, is at the heart of Rousseau's theory of government—it is the principle against which governments are judged and the power against which tyrannies are found wanting. Those, such as Pateman and Barber, who find in Rousseau's work a model of deliberative democracy focus exclusively on Rousseau's theory of government and its subordinate relationship to the authority of the people assembled.

CONCLUSION: CONTRACT THEORIES AND RHETORICS

These passages about the role of rhetoric within the government are difficult to dislike. In them we see rhetoric given a central and authoritative place in political life. As Garsten has put it, these are the "undeniably democratic" aspects of *TSC* (63). As undeniable as the democratic tenor of these passages might be, it is still difficult to conclude with Pateman that *TSC* "is vital for the theory of participatory democracy" just because the government remains accountable to a deliberative assembly. Those who would find in Rousseau a model for democratic politics need to be reminded that although he does subject the government to the people, the government was never powerful to begin with. It has no capacity to shape the fundamental institutions or principles on which society is founded. And the people's power to "suspend" the power of government does not empower them to shape the basic principles of society.

Participatory democracy, it would seem, should provide for citizen participation at the level of the founding. It is not enough that the assembly be authoritative only after—and these are Rousseau's words—the "institutions" of government have been "frame[d]" (*TSC* 42). Whatever power the assembly might have to "curb" the government, then, it cannot reframe the institutions. Thus what separates Rousseau's vision of a deliberative assembly arranged against the government from even Habermas' relatively conservative vision of a critical public sphere is this: Rousseau has, far more than Habermas, structurally limited the powers of critique; the assembly cannot call into question the basic frameworks of society. Rousseau's contract theory has carefully confined the authority of the assembly and the political function of rhetoric; they are operative only after the basic structures of society have been "framed" without them.

Is contract theory then rhetorically bereft? Must we conclude with Foucault that social contracts merely obscure the actual operations of power to such an extent that we would be better off without them? I don't think so. I think there is one very important point on which Rousseau is precisely correct, Foucault is precisely incorrect, and Danielle Allen is silent. That point is this: social contracts are, in fact, a serviceable means of dealing with the intractability of sacrifice. I agree with Rousseau's basic impulse: faced with human suffering and sacrifice, Rousseau's recourse is to a social contract. This much is good. Because a social contract is, at its best, little more than a set of promises mutually exchanged, Rousseau is reminding us here that rhetoric is a critical tool in our capacity to deal with the human condition. This, we might say, is the rhetorical promise of contractual politics.

It should be clear by this point that I disagree with the terms of the contract as Rousseau envisions it. Envisioned as an exchange of physical inequality for legal equality, the contract, as we have seen, unfairly constricts the role of citizen deliberation. Yet, historically speaking, there are other ways of imagining a social contract that enable us to deal with the facticity of sacrifice without sacrificing the centrality of citizen deliberation.

Arendt reminds us that "the seventeenth century clearly distinguished between two kinds of 'social contract'" (*On Revolution* 169). One was the Rousseauian variety, of which no more needs to be said. Arendt identifies the other type of social contract with the experience of the American colonists. She argues that the colonists did not envision themselves contracting with a government, but rather making promises to each other. Thus while Rousseau's theory is premised on an aboriginal exchange, the "content" of the

American colonists' contract was nothing more than a "promise" to remain committed to the others' welfare (*On Revolution* 170). Thus, by virtue of mutual promises, the American experience was, Arendt tells us, "articulated from top to bottom" in terms of "compacts, combinations, cosociations, and confederations" (*On Revolution* 176, 172).[7]

Most importantly, Arendt argues that the impulse behind all these "cosociations"—"from provinces or states down to cities and districts, townships, villages, and counties"—was the basic experience of loss (*On Revolution* 176). "What prompted the colonists 'solemnly and mutually in the Presence of God and one another, [to] covenant and combine [them]selves into a civil Body Politick' . . . were the 'difficulties and discouragements which in all probabilities must be forecast upon the execution of this business'" (173). She continues: "Nothing but the simple and obvious insight into the elementary structure of joint enterprise as such, the need 'for the better encouragement of ourselves and others that shall joyne with us in this action,' caused these men to become obsessed with the notion of compact" (173). In Arendt's telling, the extremity of the colonists' situation, separated from the comforts of the Old World, allowed them to see, with unequaled clarity, the "simple and obvious insight" that political association involves loss, hardship, and sacrifice. And this insight, Arendt argues, "prompted them again and again to promise and bind themselves to one another" (173). When we recall Allen's argument that it is the capacity to *trust* our fellow citizens that allows us to continually redistribute sacrifice, it becomes clear that a social contract can be a means of redistribution.

In sum, while Rousseau's contract theory attempted to compensate for sacrifice by insisting on a primordial exchange and, in so doing, sharply delimited the political function of rhetoric, the American colonists answered the facticity of loss with the power of a particular rhetorical form: the promise. And thus we might say that the promise of contractual politics, only hinted at in Rousseau's text, is that it posits a promise, a rhetorical form, as a principle of resistance to the inevitability of personal sacrifice. And, at least in Arendt's telling, this rhetorical faculty of promising to take care of one another, of bearing one another's burdens and redistributing sacrifices, is itself capable of founding a nation. "There is an element of the world-building capacity of man in the human faculty of making and keeping promises" (*On Revolution* 175). In this, the colonists' version of the social contract, then, rhetoric is not deferred and its space is not delimited. This version of the social contract is, from the start, "friendly to rhetoric"—the counterfactual "general will" has been replaced by a rhetorical form. Unlike a primordial exchange, the faculty of promising does not attempt to cover over the fact of loss with fictional justifications. Rather, it deals with loss by means of cosociation.

Notes

[1] Derrida defines the underlying logic he sees in Rousseau's work with recourse to what he refers to as the "graphic of the supplement" (183). I am following not that particular emphasis

on the supplement, but more Derrida's sense that, if we focus on what matters most to Rousseau, the contradictions disappear.

² Rousseau wrote three discourses: the first is called *Discourse on the Arts and Sciences,* the second is *Discourse on the Origin and Foundations of Inequity,* and the third is *Discourse on Political Economy.* For the ease of the reader, they will be referred to as First Discourse, Second Discourse, and Third Discourse, respectively.

³ Hereafter *The Social Contract* will be abbreviated *TSC.*

⁴ The distinction between Rousseau's "descriptions" and his "declarations" is Derrida's and is illuminated scores of times in the second half of *Of Grammatology* (217, 218, 229, 238, 243, 268, and 307).

⁵ One of the best sources on Rousseau's physical/moral distinction and its application for rhetoric is John T. Scott's "Rousseau and the Melodious Language of Freedom."

⁶ Rousseau seems to solve this problem in the "Essay on the Origin of Languages." There he argues that although speech is a "social institution," it "owes its form only to natural causes" (289).

⁷ See also Arendt's discussion of contract theories in *The Human Condition.* Although no antagonist is stipulated in the following quotation, it is almost certainly Rousseau: "The sovereignty of a body of people bound and kept together, not by an identical will which somehow magically inspires them all, but by an agreed purpose for which alone the promises are valid and binding . . ." (245).

Works Cited

Allen, Danielle S. *Talking to Strangers: Anxieties of Citizenship since* Brown v. Board of Education. Chicago: U of Chicago P, 2004.

Arendt, Hannah. *The Human Condition.* 2nd ed. Chicago: U of Chicago P, 1998.

———. *On Revolution.* New York: Viking P, 1963.

Barber, Benjamin. "Political Participation and the Creation of Res Publica." *Rousseau's Political Writings: Discourse on Inequality, Discourse on Political Economy, on Social Contract.* Ed. Alan Ritter. New York: W.W. Norton, 1988. 292–306.

Connolly, William E. *Political Theory & Modernity.* Ithaca: Cornell UP, 1993.

Crocker, Lester, ed. "Introduction." *The Social Contract and Discourse on the Origin of Inequality.* New York: Washington Square Books, 1967. vii–xxiv.

de Man, Paul. *Blindness and Insight: Essays in the Rhetoric of Contemporary Criticism.* New York: Oxford UP, 1971.

Derrida, Jacques. *Of Grammatology.* Trans. Gayatri Chakravorty Spivak. Baltimore: Johns Hopkins UP, 1976.

Foucault, Michel. *Discipline and Punish: The Birth of the Prison.* Trans. Alan Sheridan. 2nd ed. New York: Vintage, 1995.

Garsten, Bryan. *Saving Persuasion: A Defense of Rhetoric and Judgment.* Cambridge: Harvard UP, 2006.

Gay, Peter. "Introduction." *Jean-Jacques Rousseau Basic Political Writings: Discourse on the Sciences and Arts, Discourse on the Origin of Inequality, Discourse on Political Economy, on the Social Contract.* Ed. Donald C. Cress. Indianapolis: Hackett, 1987.

Honig, Bonnie. *Democracy and the Foreigner.* Princeton: Princeton UP, 2001.

Pateman, Carole. *Participation and Democratic Theory.* Cambridge: Cambridge UP, 1970.

Rorty, Richard. *Contingency, Irony, and Solidarity.* Cambridge: Cambridge UP, 1989.

Rousseau, Jean-Jacques. "Discourse on Political Economy." *Jean-Jacques Rousseau Basic Political Writings: Discourse on the Sciences and Arts, Discourse on the Origin of Inequality, Discourse on Political Economy, on the Social Contract.* Ed. Donald A. Cress. Indianapolis: Hackett, 1987.

———. "Essay on the Origin of Languages." Trans. John T. Scott. *Jean-Jacques Rousseau: Essay on the Origin of Languages and Writings Related to Music.* Ed. John T.

Scott. Vol. 7. The Collected Writings of Rousseau. Hanover, NH: UP of New England, 1998. 289–332.

———. *The First and Second Discourses*. Ed. Roger D. Masters and Judith R. Masters. New York: St. Martin's P, 1964.

———. *The Social Contract and Discourse on the Origin of Inequality*. 1762. Trans. Lester G. Crocker. New York: Washington Square P, 1967.

Scott, John T., ed. "Introduction." *Jean-Jacques Rousseau: Essay on the Origin of Languages and Writings Related to Music*. Vol. 7. The Collected Writings of Rousseau. Hanover, NH: UP of New England, 1998. xxvii–xxxvii.

———. "Rousseau and the Melodious Language of Freedom." *The Journal of Politics* 59.3 (1997): 803–29.

Shklar, Judith N. *Men and Citizens: A Study of Rousseau's Social Theory*. Cambridge: Cambridge UP, 1969.

Starobinski, Jean. *Jean-Jacques Rousseau: Transparency and Obstruction*. Chicago: U of Chicago P, 1988.

Taylor, Charles. *A Secular Age*. Cambridge: Belknap P of Harvard UP, 2007.

2

Rhetoric, Virtue, and the Necessity of Invention

William Duffy

In 1981, philosopher Alasdair MacIntyre published *After Virtue*, his seminal study in moral theory in which he diagnoses the sterility and antagonism inherent in modern moral debate to be the result of a loss of shared ethical standards and concerns. In the preface to his third edition of the book published in 2007, MacIntyre points to the "characteristically shrill" assertions that often stymie moral debate and says that his explanation

> was and is that the precepts that are thus uttered were once at home in, and intelligible in terms of, a context of practical beliefs and of supporting habits of thought, feeling, and action . . . a context in which moral judgments were understood as governed by impersonal standards justified by a shared conception of the human good. (ix)

MacIntyre locates "this shared conception of the human good" through a neoclassical account of virtue and forwards his thesis that a virtue ethical approach to studying moral debate will provide a better awareness of, and ability to intervene in, the passionate moral impasses that affect us today.

Interestingly, MacIntyre suggests that the language of moral discourse we've inherited from the tradition of Western thought is no longer adequate in its ability to address the problems of negotiating contemporary ethical debates. In short, he asserts that we posses in the present what is essentially a cache of empty moral expressions that function merely as simulacra of a shared moral philosophy—they are empty signifiers continuously used in moral debate as if they carried universal meaning. In what is not a dissimilar critique of language, Sharon Crowley, in *Toward a Civic Discourse*, points to the "deliberate impasse that seems to have locked American public discourse in repetition and vituperation" and argues that if we want rhetoric to be its most useful, "the conceptual vocabulary of rhetoric itself must be rethought" (3, 4). Crowley's call for the rethinking of rhetoric's conceptual vocabulary speaks to the problem of accounting for, in terms of rhetorical theory, the "densely articulated belief systems" that rely on similar modes of expression in matters of passionate debate (4). Whether one approaches this question from the standpoint of moral philosophy, like MacIntyre, or from the position of rhetorical theory, like Crowley, the same problem arises every time. Unless interlocutors can come to a common agreement about what is meant when they employ similar morally charged language, matters of debate are more likely to remain unresolved because there exists no point of stasis from which to engage in debate itself.

More importantly, Crowley's concern for better, more productive public discourse points to the necessity of asking the question about how as rhetoricians we should understand the responsibilities of rhetoric, or rather, "What makes rhetoric ethical?" Here I utilize the terms "ethics" and "ethical" to describe a shared set of values used to measure and evaluate the felicity of human interaction. The problem I wish to address in this essay is how rhetoricians can develop a shared standard for evaluating ethical rhetoric in public debate. Specifically, I argue that applying a classical conception of virtue to the rhetorical canon of invention will provide both a theoretical orientation and a helpful vocabulary for achieving this task.[1]

To begin this inquiry it is important to first consider what one believes about the purpose of rhetoric itself. Crowley summarizes the ancient definitions of rhetoric as simply an "art of invention," but she further qualifies this maxim by saying that for the ancients, "any art or practice entitled to be called 'rhetoric' must intervene in some way in the beliefs and practices of the community it serves" (*Toward* 26, 27). Definitions like those of A. S. Hill in the nineteenth century or I. A. Richards in the twentieth, respectively, state that rhetoric is "the art of efficient communication by language" (881) and "the study of misunderstanding and its remedies" (106). While we can continue to further define rhetoric, what is important, however, is that generally speaking definitions of rhetoric reveal that whatever its make-up and specific purpose, rhetoric *aims* at achieving *something*, whether that something is communication, persuasion, the remedy of misunderstanding, or the invention of argument. From a pragmatic standpoint, this observation is significant because it identifies an important commonality among all beliefs about rhetoric, and that is that rhetoric is made intelligible through its ability to act, through its ability to produce certain effects and achieve certain ends. And herein is where I believe we can locate a new vocabulary for discussing the ethics of rhetoric, because if rhetoric is teleological, if it is made true, so to speak, through the achievement of ends, then the integrity of rhetoric can be understood through a conception of *virtue*, what Aristotle defines as neither a feeling nor capacity, but as a "state" or attitude one assumes in relationship to a particular end (1106a, 1107a).

In Aristotelian terms, virtue represents the "mean" or intermediate condition between states of excess and deficiency. One might feel anger, for example, or pity, or joy, or any particular emotion, and the virtues serve as the barometer that informs the adequacy of such feelings. As Aristotle explains, "We can be afraid, for instance, or be confident, or have appetites. . . . But having these feelings at the right times, about the right things, towards the right people, for the right end, and in the right way, is the intermediate and best condition, and this is proper to virtue" (1106b). The virtues are thus attitudes that help us navigate between the vices of excess and deficiency in our daily activities and interactions. Or, put another way, virtues inform the felicity of our actions and help us assess the achievement of ends.

When Aristotle describes the nature of virtue in the *Nicomachean Ethics*, he first explains that all human actions aim for some kind of good, which can be understood as both the reason for a particular action and the thing that, once achieved, signals the completion of that action. But the ultimate aim for human beings, the thing to which all actions eventually point, is what Aristotle calls *eudaimonia*, which is usually translated into "happiness" or "success." He also makes this same claim in the *Rhetoric* when he writes, "Both to an individual privately and to all people generally there is one goal [*skopos*] at which they aim in what they choose to do and in what they avoid. Summarily stated, this is happiness [*eudaimonia*] and its parts" (Kennedy 1361a1). Aristotle appears to use this term to mean something like felicitous achievement. Just as J. L. Austin refers to the happiness of speech acts as understood by the success of performative utterances, so too does Aristotle seem to conceive of *eudaimonia*. Virtues are therefore those attitudes that are most conducive for achieving whatever particular ends to which an action is directed. As a type of action, something that sets out to achieve certain persuasive ends, rhetoric is therefore open to virtual ethical analysis because it locates as its chief concern the communicative interaction within the purposeful realm of human activity. As such, people can begin to understand the goodness of rhetoric only if they first understand the reasons why people use it.

Those reasons, as already pointed out, range from persuasion to communication to the remedy of misunderstandings, outcomes that all share a common requirement for their achievement, and that is invention. As the first of rhetoric's five canons, invention of course refers to that process of developing, as Crowley summarizes it, "more or less systematic procedures for finding arguments appropriate to the rhetorical situation" ("Evolution" 146). Because in this essay I am not concerned with the subject of invention itself, I will refrain from comparing and contrasting how rhetoricians have defined invention since Aristotle. So for my purposes here rhetorical invention will simply refer to the process of constructing beliefs for and within rhetorical exchanges. When it comes to defining how to apply a virtue ethical critique of rhetoric, then, I want to argue that rhetoric can be virtuous only to the extent that it is inventive. That is to say, rhetorical invention is the thing that signifies the beginning of rhetoric's action, and since the success of rhetoric is located in whether and to what extent it meets the expectations and intentions that are brought to and arise in rhetorical exchange, it can be argued that the inventive process signals, or rather anticipates, the efficacy of rhetoric itself. Thus I believe we can identify invention as a morally neutral but nonetheless fundamental ethical standard from which to debate the virtuousness of particular instances of rhetoric.

Here is a good juncture to step back for a moment and recall that the default location for "the ethical" in rhetorical theory is usually found in discussions of *ethos*, the rhetorical appeal that is most often reserved for the office of a rhetor's character. When placed beside the other two rhetorical appeals, *logos* and *pathos*, it becomes easy to classify *ethos* as simply the term we use to describe the persona a rhetor embodies in any given rhetorical situation. In his book *Inventive Intercourse: From Rhetorical Conflict to the Ethical Creation of Novel Truth*, Stephen Yarbrough, however, argues for an interactionist understanding of *ethos*, one that goes beyond the classical concept of individual character and accounts for the social relationships that govern rhetorical interaction. As Yarbrough writes, *ethos* from an interactionist standpoint can be viewed "as the set of social relations we assume to hold in a situation that determine how we evaluate things and events, what we can do with and to things, and how we expect things to interact with us" (154). More than simply accounting for an individual's character, an interactionist theory of *ethos* considers the ethical stances we occupy and assume in relationship to the world. That is to say, how we interact with objects in the world, including people, determines the social relationships that shape our beliefs about the world itself.

What is important here, I believe, is how Yarbrough points to a connection between how we position ourselves in the world, the ethical stances we assume, and how this positioning affects not only how we *solve* problems but how we *view* problems in the first place. The way we live in and respond to the world, including how we conceive of the world itself, is best understood reciprocally as a process of constant response guided by discourse, what Yarbrough says is the human mode of interaction with the world. "All discursive interactions," he says, "are questions of cause and effect, stimulus and response, action and reaction, anticipation and revision" (27). Our ability to shift ethical stances, those positions that define how we understand certain topical relationships that exist among objects, is what affords us the ability to invent novelty. Those who are able to imagine the perspectives of others, those who can willingly assume new ethical stances, are those who are better situated to respond to the exigencies that stymie our interactions.

A virtue ethical approach to studying the ethical dimension of rhetoric is nicely informed by an interactionist approach to *ethos* because the latter promotes what the sociologist George Hebert Mead called "the continuance of a common world" (342). According to Mead, society is the name we give to account for the social tendency of human beings to engage in cooperative activities. As groups get defined by their common interests and experiences, what arises is a common world, but as Mead says, "This common world is continually breaking down. Problems arise in it and demand solutions" (341). A group's ability to account for and reconstruct this common world represents the test for what Mead called the "truth" of any particular solution, and it is through the virtue of rhetorical invention that we account for and reconstruct the common world.

For Mead, the world is made meaningful through the ongoing progression of conduct, marked by what he calls "gestures." As Donald Bushman explains, "[Mead] describes the uses of language as 'a conversation of gestures,' with the term *gesture* referring to all human social activity, any activity that is sensed by another and that evokes a response in another" (254). In short, Mead believes that we use gestures in anticipation of certain responses, and when our anticipations are not met we must revise our gestures, and it is in this way that communication works. Gestures do not become "communication in the full sense," Mead says, "until the gesture tends to arouse the same response in the individual who makes it that it arouses in the others" (312). From Mead's pragmatist standpoint, communication is the word that signifies when gestures have become meaningful, when human interaction becomes intentional and conduct is deliberative. From this perspective, Mead is able to argue that it is through conduct that truth is created.

As a concept "truth" is significant here because it denotes a kind of end; it is something that gives our actions purpose. In true pragmatist form, however, Mead does not believe truth is something that exists outside of experience, that it is something to which our beliefs must correspond. Instead truth for Mead is a concept that represents the test of belief itself; it is what makes the ability for certain beliefs to provoke actions that sustain the continuance of the common world. As he explains, "The criterion of truth does not then transcend experience, but simply regards the conditions of ongoing experience which has become problematic through the inhibitions of the natural processes of human beings. The solution of the problem lies entirely within experience and is found in the resolution of inhibitions" (342). Or put another way, "Truth expresses a relationship between the judgment and reality . . . the relationship lies between reconstruction, which enables conduct to continue, and the reality within which conduct advances" (338). Embedded in this approach to truth is the idea of mutually conditioning conduct—it is through our mutual actions with others that problems arise and problems are solved. Experience is the realm of this interaction, it is not something that exists separate from the cooperative activities of a group's members. Yarbrough sees a connection here between his use of the word *discourse* and Mead's use of the word *experience*. "According to Mead," Yarbrough says, "human interaction within the world, what I call discourse, must be understood as being always already part of the world and not as a different kind of entity and over against other entities" (14). Truth therefore cannot be located outside the realm of experience, the realm of discourse, because that is where all of our interaction with the world takes place.

At this point one can see an important concept emerging about how the ends of rhetoric can be framed in virtue ethical language. Because we are communicative beings who use discourse to negotiate and make sense of our experiences in the world, and because of our ability to respond to exigencies, we seek resolutions to the problems that upset our beliefs and habits. By virtue of rhetorical invention, existing beliefs can be renewed and novel beliefs created in the face of our everyday experiences. If rhetoric is understood as a tool for creating arguments and effecting persuasion (to continue the common world), it is therefore subject to the virtue ethical claim of invention. Why this is so can be found in the reason that discourse—the communicative interaction we share with the world—doesn't exist prior to interaction itself, which is the claim Mead uses to support his theory of truth. As Yarbrough reminds us, Mead's is the first "non-metaphysical explanation" of how communication works, and he quotes Karen Burke LeFevre when she explains that Mead's approach "takes the invention process out of the mind of the individual and into the interaction of real people" (qtd. in Yarbrough 18).

If we agree with Mead's interactionist approach to communication, then rhetoric cannot exist outside of the rhetorical interactions in which human beings participate; and if we agree with Yarbrough that as a concept *ethos* is best understood as the social relationships a speaker can see in relation to a given situation, then it becomes apparent that in order to continue the common word, in order to maintain the progression of human interaction, rhetoric is valuable to the extent that it is inventive, and it is inventive to the extent that the ethical stances rhetors assume allow them to communicate successfully. If we translate these requirements into virtue ethical standards, then rhetoric is "good" to the extent that it fosters the continuation of interaction, and this is so even if rhetoric is not "effective" at achieving persuasion.

In matters of debate, for example, where parties are engaged in a passionate conflict of arguments that are based on seemingly incommensurable beliefs, most likely a novel argument will be required to achieve resolution and to achieve the continuation of the common world. Rhetoric must therefore be inventive.

Crowley in *Toward a Civic Discourse* hopes that rhetorical theory will help promote "just" arguments, but I believe deciding on what counts as just argument is a bigger problem rhetoricians must first face, especially in the political arena where Crowley focuses most of her concern. To her credit, Crowley does essentially argue for a virtue ethical standard focused on invention to be applied to rhetorical theory, but she doesn't use these terms. "The point of ethical rhetorical exchange is never to shut down argumentative possibilities," Crowley says, "but to generate all the positions that are available and articulable in a given moment and situation." "Good rhetoric," she goes on to say, "looks for all available arguments, just as Aristotle insisted. Bad rhetoric, on the other hand, is static and univocal" (56). Crowley's concern to promote debate that goes beyond "static and univocal" argumentation obviously reflects her belief that there is a standard to which the use of rhetoric can be called responsible, to which it can be called "good." But again, applying the tools of virtue ethical reflection to rhetorical theory opens a further line of inquiry for considering how we measure and adjudicate ethical rhetoric. And furthermore it does what it promotes, which is to say it advances inventive possibilities for articulating further connections between rhetoric and moral philosophy.

When invention is situated not only rhetorically (as the canon we use to develop arguments and formulate ideas), but also ethically (as the virtue that denotes rhetoric's goodness), the relationship between ethics and rhetoric can be discussed with more confidence without acquiescing to modern and postmodern theories of moral relativity. Furthermore, subjecting rhetoric to this virtue ethical standard supports an interactionist theory of *ethos* that accounts for the rhetor according to a set of social relationships and not in terms of individual character. A rhetorical situation will bring with it exigencies that will demand the articulation of specific beliefs and the demonstration of values relevant to that situation, and when studying specific occasions it is well to account for these details. But articulating the basic relationship that rhetoric shares with ethics is made less difficult when one uses the classical notion of virtue to identify the ends of rhetoric, which by default allows one to identify those qualities of rhetoric that best help it attain those ends. Using virtue ethical theory to identify invention as an ethical standard for rhetoric not only speaks to Crowley's desire to rethink the conceptual vocabulary of rhetoric itself, but it also supports Mead's pragmatic claim that truth is found in the continuance of the common world. Rhetoric can be both good and effective, a distinction we should remember the ancient rhetors never made.

Note

[1] My interest in the relationship between rhetoric and ethics departs from previous scholarship that has posited virtue as an ethical quality a speaker possesses prior to rhetorical engagement. For example, see Lois Self. "Rhetoric and *Phronesis*: The Aristotelian Ideal." *Philosophy and Rhetoric* 12.2 (1979): 130–45; and Susan K. Nelson. "Virtue in Aristotle's Rhetoric: A Metaphysical and Ethical Capacity." *Philosophy and Rhetoric* 34.3 (2001).

Works Cited

Aristotle. *Nicomachean Ethics*. Trans. Terence Irwin. 2nd ed. Indianapolis: Hackett, 1999.

Austin, J. L. *How to do Things with Words*. Cambridge: Harvard UP, 1962.

Bushman, Donald. "'A Conversation of Gestures': George Herbert Mead's Pragmatic Theory of Language." *Rhetoric Review* 16.2 (1998): 253–67.

Crowley, Sharon. "The Evolution of Invention in Current-Traditional Rhetoric, 1850–1970." *Rhetoric Review* 3.2 (1985): 146–62.

———. *Toward a Civil Discourse: Rhetoric and Fundamentalism*. Pittsburgh: U of Pittsburgh P, 2006.

Hill, A. S. "From *The Principles of Rhetoric*." *The Rhetorical Tradition*. Ed. Patricia Bizzell and Bruce Herzberg. Boston: Bedford/St. Martins, 2001. 881–84.

Kennedy, George A. *Aristotle On Rhetoric: A Theory of Civic Discourse*. New York: Oxford UP, 1991.

MacIntyre, Alasdair. *After Virtue: A Study in Moral Theory*. 3rd ed. Norte Dame: U of Norte Dame P, 2007.

Mead, George Herbert. *Selected Writings*. Ed. Andrew J. Reck. Indianapolis: Bobbs-Merrill, 1964.

Richards, I. A. *Richards on Rhetoric*. Ed. Anne E. Berthoff. New York: Oxford UP, 1991.

Yarbrough, Stephen R. *Inventive Intercourse: From Rhetorical Conflict to the Ethical Creation of Novel Truth*. Carbondale: Southern Illinois UP, 2006.

"Licentia" in the Seventeenth-Century French Pulpit

Claudia Carlos

One of the subthemes of this year's conference on the "responsibilities of rhetoric" involves the consideration of pedagogies that protect civil liberties. This would certainly seem relevant to the contemporary political climate in this country, where—to take just one recent example—we have a government that has been accused of paying its top military generals to appear on television as "independent observers" to promote an unpopular war. Because we take for granted the right of individuals to speak freely against the policies of the government, any suspicion that those views are not being adequately heard automatically provokes outrage, and it is therefore only natural that, as teachers of rhetoric, we reflect on the connection—one that originates in the Greek *polis*—between what we teach and our rights as citizens of a democracy. But is it possible for such reflection to have any relevance to the teaching of rhetoric in historical periods where "free speech" was not a given? This question will be one that underlies what I would like to discuss today, namely the figure of "licentia," or frank speaking, as it was conceived in rhetoric manuals and put into practice by preachers in the seventeenth-century French court.

With its underlying doctrine of unlimited power for a divinely sanctioned ruler, French "absolutism" would seem, by definition, to deny its citizens any possibility of frank expression. Indeed, writers during the Ancien Régime risked imprisonment, banishment, or forced military service if their works failed to pass the review of the royal censors. Yet, as historians of French preaching have long pointed out, there was one domain in the French court where the opportunity to speak frankly to the monarch *did* exist, and that was in the pulpit. In his 1921 edition of sermons by the neoclassical preacher Louis Bourdaloue, Gonzague Truc describes how preachers dared to say "what no other writer or lay orator would have dared to say before the powerful, against the powerful" (19).[1] The pulpit was, in Truc's words, "the only free voice during this period of silence" (19).[2]

But, as we see from sermons, manuals of rhetoric, and historical accounts of the monarchy, French preachers at court were not only *permitted* to criticize their sovereign, they were actually *expected* to do so. According to Jacques Truchet, Louis XIV, "le plus absolu des rois," fully accepted that his preachers would speak to him with moral firmness; it was the preachers engaging in flattery who drew scorn (22). The numerous preaching manuals of the time confirm Truchet's assessment. For example, in Gabriel Guèret's *Entretiens sur l'éloquence de la chaire et du barreau* (1666), a series of dialogues about pulpit and legal eloquence, the main interlocutor, Ariste, complains of preachers who would preach with severity in front of popular crowds about the importance of a rigorous and disciplined life, but then would be seen at the Louvre as "Courtisans commodes & complaisans" (72). Similarly, Marc-Antoine de la Foix in his *L'art de prêcher la parole de Dieu* (1687), warns his readers that public expressions of praise for the powerful "do great wrong to the majesty and authority of the divine Word"[3] and, as a consequence, the preacher's own authority suffers (164). For the preachers of Louis XIV's court, then, speaking openly to those in power was not merely a right that they could exercise, but it was also a moral duty.

Yet, we must ask what meaning such freedom of expression could have within the context of an otherwise repressive regime. To what degree did this frank speaking from the pulpit correspond to what the Greeks referred to as *parrhesia*, or "the right to say everything"? It is by turning to the figure of "licentia" as it appears in three influential rhetorical treatises of the period—Cypriano Soarez's *De arte rhetorica libri tres* (1569), Nicolas Caussin's *Eloquentiae sacrae et humanae parallela* (1627), and René Bary's *La rhétorique françoise* (1665)—that we can begin to explore an answer to this question.

"LICENTIA" IN THREE EARLY MODERN RHETORICAL TREATISES

The figure of "licentia" was prevalent in early modern treatises on rhetoric. In his study of early modern conceptions of *parrhesia* in England, David Colclough notes how this figure inherited a confused set of definitions from the Greek and Roman traditions. For the Greeks, *parrhesia*, as Colclough points out, was not a figure at all but "a quality of the speech that is consistent with a democratic political system as this was understood in fifth and fourth-century Athens" (184); thus Thucydides could describe Pericles as an ideal Athenian leader because of his "willingness to engage in angry admonition" (184)—that is, his *parrhesia*. In Roman times, with manuals such as the *Rhetorica ad Herennium*, *parrhesia* becomes the figure, "licentia," and is described as a right to speak ("pro iure nostro dicimus") within a particular social situation, namely one in which we have reason to fear or revere our audience ("apud eos quos aut vereri aut metuere debemus") (Cicero IV.XXXVI.48). In addition to the idea of speaking boldly, the anonymous author notes that "there will be many means of palliation" (IV.XXXVII.49) by which the speaker can soften the pungency of his remarks—for example, if he mixes his frank speech with praise. But, according to the author, there is also another possibility for speaking frankly that involves a "craftier device" (IV.XXXVII.49); it is when the speaker reproaches the hearers as they wish him to reproach them, or when he expresses fear about how they will take what he says, all the while knowing they will accept it. This last kind of "licentia," then, is really only a feigned boldness, because the orator risks nothing by what he says. Taking this idea of simulation (or, as Colclough puts it, "dissimulation") even further, Quintilian, who does not view the act of frank speaking as a figure at all, describes "licentia" as a pretense of speaking boldly that functions as a mask for flattery.

The three definitions of "licentia" that I am about to examine reveal the contradictions of this classical tradition. The first, by Soarez, is a Spanish Jesuit text for young pupils that was widely used in French schools of the early seventeenth century. What we find unmistakably is the "crafty" sort of "licentia" described in the *Ad Herennium*:

> Licentia is when, before those whom he should respect or fear, the orator says freely something that in no way offends them. Cicero in his pro Ligario says: See how entirely free from fear I am. See how brilliantly the light of your liberality and wisdom rises upon me while speaking before you! As far as I can, I will lift up my voice so that the Roman people may hear me. When the war began, O Caesar, when it was even very greatly advanced toward its end, I, though compelled by no extraneous force, of my own free judgment and inclination went to join that party which had taken up arms against you.[4, 5] (57b)

The main definition is in the first two lines: "Licentia is when, before those whom he should respect or fear, the orator says freely something that in no way offends them." Then we get the reference to Cicero's "Speech in Defense of Q. Ligarius," an example taken directly from Quintilian and one that seems to be standard in French and Spanish treatises that mention "licentia." The "Pro Ligario" example in fact makes it clear that "licentia" is really flattery under the guise of frankness: while Cicero seems bold to tell Caesar that he once chose to participate in armed resistance against him, what this speech actually does is to imply Caesar's magnanimity, and hence to flatter him.

A fuller treatment of "licentia"—and one even more reminiscent of the one in *Ad Herennium*—occurs in the 1627 edition of Caussin's treatise, another Jesuit school text. Caussin classifies figures by their function, and "licentia" comes under a section about "Figures Relating to Disputes and Contests" ("de figuris a velitatione & certamine"). This is interesting because it suggests that the figure may be used in contests among equals—most probably school exercises in declamation—as opposed to a situation in which the recipient of the frank speaking is in a higher social position:

> Licentia, parrhesia, frankness, and confidence in speaking is a kind of speech in which Demosthenes abounds, as in the following: I am afraid it

is an ominous thing to say, but yet the truth. It is both sharp and biting. Another kind is lofty: What? may I not speak of the other misfortunes of the republic?—At all events it is in my power, and it always will be in my power, to uphold my own dignity and to despise death. A third kind is light, which seems to produce sharp points with a certain bitterness that it soothes and mitigates, as in the following example: For it is you, O conscript fathers (it is a grave charge to make, but it must be uttered), it is you, I say, who have deprived Servius Sulpicius of life. For when you saw him pleading his illness as an excuse more by the truth of the fact than by any labored plea of words, you were not indeed cruel (for what can be more impossible for this order to be guilty of than that), but as you hoped that there was nothing that could not be accomplished by his authority and wisdom, you opposed his excuse with great earnestness, and compelled the man, who had always thought your decisions of the greatest weight, to abandon his own opinion. A fourth kind is flattery which imitates frankness, when nevertheless one says things that he knows will be pleasing to the hearers: such as in "Pro Ligario": See how entirely free from fear I am. See how brilliantly the light of your liberality and wisdom rises upon me while speaking before you.[6, 7] (426)

The first thing to note about this passage is that, unlike the previous one, there is no explicit definition given for "licentia"; instead we have a series of examples illustrating how "licentia" may be used. What Caussin gives his readers is actually a tonal scale of frank speaking, ranging from the most vitriolic attack to outright flattery. Thus, if the orator wants to speak boldly and with extreme bitterness, he should imitate the "Third Philippic" of Demosthenes; if he wishes to adopt a tone that is less bitter and to speak with loftiness, then he should imitate Cicero's "First Philippic against Marcus Antonius"; an orator may strike a milder tone if he softens the bitterness of the "sharp points" (*aculeos*) he launches through his speech, and as the example from Cicero's "Ninth Philippic" shows, this is done though mixing criticism with praise; finally, the orator's intention may be to praise his audience indirectly by feigning frankness and, once again, the example from "Pro Ligario" illustrates how the speaker can do this.

Bary's *Rhétorique françoise*, the source of the third definition, is a text intended for a more general audience than those of Soarez and Caussin. Unlike the two Jesuits, Bary was not a member of the clergy, but a philosopher and a historiographer during the early reign of Louis XIV. Like Soarez, Bary gives the figure of "licence" a definition that seems partly drawn from the *Ad Herennium*: "This figure consists of boldly reproving those to whom we owe some sort of respect" (406).[8] However, there is one significant difference in Bary's appropriation: while Soarez described frank speech that would not offend the audience, Bary offers no such condition, nor does he explicitly state, as the anonymous author of the *Ad Herennium* does, that the frankness will seem to the audience to be justified. He then gives two examples in French, the first of which is a biting attack composed entirely of rhetorical questions and directly addressed to a political leader, and the second, a less acerbic plea to judges in a legal setting that appeals to their concern not to appear to the people as self-interested. After these examples, Bary then does something that neither Soarez nor Caussin does, and that is, to apply the use of "licence" to his contemporary world:

> Licentia was in the past a figure of the bar, it is now a figure of the pulpit; Lawyers in the ancient world only used it when the fault that they were criticizing was shameful to the judge and harmful to the public; Preachers use this figure only when the vices that they are finding fault with convince those who acquire them of a strange blindness, and imply in those who flatter them, a pernicious theology; the former sometimes used to soften through praise that which they had made bitter through invective, the others never mix the sweet with the bitter.[9] (407)

In antiquity, then, it was the lawyers who used "licence"—sometimes with unmitigated bitterness and sometimes softened with compliments—for situations in which a fault was, in the eyes of both the judges and public, something shameful. In France, however, it is the preacher who now has a specific use for "licence," which is never mitigated and is reserved for situations in which a person is unusually "blinded" to his sin, a sin so serious that, if the preacher were not to denounce it, he would be suspected of a dangerous theology ("Théologie pernicieuse"). So, it is with Bary that we see the complete adaptation of the classical tradition of "licentia" to the seventeenth-century French court and a confirmation that, in this setting, it is the preacher who occupies the privileged position of being able to attack the powerful.

A significant difference between Bary's version of "licentia" and those of Soarez and Caussin is that his description does not include the idea of simulated boldness. Interestingly, though, in Bary's treatise, what follows the discussion of "licence" is a section entitled "De la feinte," which treats the figure of "praeteritio"—saying something while pretending not to say it. Moreover, even though Bary says that the preacher never mitigates his attacks against a person to whom he owes respect, when discussing the figure of "prosopopée" (*prosopopoeia*), he notes how preachers can use this device to indirectly criticize a sovereign. So, the idea of dissimulation is certainly still present in the treatise as a whole and even in connection with the preacher, despite the fact that it does not come up in relation to "licence."

"Licentia" in Bourdaloue's "Sur l'impureté"

Before concluding, I would like to take a brief look at one example of "licentia" in practice. It comes from the sermon "Sur l'impureté" ("On Impurity"), which was delivered by Bourdaloue in front of Louis XIV, sometime after 1680. Although we do not know the date of the sermon, the royal scandal to which it alludes—the "affaire des poisons"—occurred in January of 1680 and involved accusations of poisoning against the niece of a key political figure during the early reign of Louis XIV[10] and, more significantly, against the king's mistress, Madame de Montespan. The charges against Montespan, who was a prominent member of the court as well as the mother of several legitimized children of the king, included administering what she believed were "love potions" to the king, poisoning another woman whom she thought was a rival for the king's affections, and engaging in "messes noires" ("black masses") to keep the king in her power. Given that Louis XIV, as with all the kings of France, was a "roi très-chrétien" who was God's representative on earth, this scandal was no doubt something that Bourdaloue believed he had to address in the strongest of terms, which he does in the following passage:

> Let us speak without figures. Let us admit that this sin [impurity] is, in reality, the great trouble of the world, because it attracts to it all the other troubles. I submit that, because of it, human blood is shed; listen to me. Where did the cruelest wars and the wars that were most fatal to nations come from, if not from the passion of love? A woman kidnapped by a madman was the spark that set off the most violent fires, and that consumed entire nations. Because a man was unchaste, thousands of men had to perish by iron and fire. But let us not go back so far in time to find proof of this truth: our century, this unhappy century, has much to convince us [of this truth]; and God allowed it to produce monsters only to force us to admit it. We saw them with fright, and so many tragic events have taught us more than we wanted, what a criminal business can produce, not any more in States, but in families, and in the most honorable families. Poison was for us a crime that was unheard of; Hell, in the interest of this passion, has made it commonplace.[11] (77–78)

Bourdaloue begins by warning the audience that he will speak "sans figure"—that is, without any allegorical terms that would hide his meaning. What he says in the passage is in no way acidic in tone (as with some of the examples given by Caussin and Bary), nor is it as blunt as to call the king an "homme impudique" and Montespan a "monster" directly; nevertheless, the allusion to Helen of Troy and the mythological character of Paris makes this a likely conclusion to draw. And there can be no mistake that this is Bourdaloue's meaning when, at the end of the passage, he explicitly laments the once rare crime of "empoisonnement," which has now disgraced "les familles les plus honorables." Other than using a thinly veiled allusion through the Homeric example, Bourdaloue does nothing to mitigate his outrage and, in this sense, the passage would seem to be a clear illustration of Bary's uncompromising preacher and of Caussin's second kind of "licentia" that adopts a lofty tone.

What I believe emerges from this analysis is definite confirmation that the complicated, classical notion of "licentia"—especially as conceived by Roman handbooks—is alive and well in the rhetorical teaching and practice of the seventeenth-century French court, and that this notion, from its purest form of frank speech to its use as a form of flattery, has its greatest relevance in the pulpit. Yet, in comparison to their Roman counterparts in the law courts, preachers in the French court held a position that was, in one important and obvious way, more politically privileged: they always spoke with the voice of God. It is perhaps for this reason that we do not see in French treatises the phenomenon that Colclough noted among some early modern English writers on rhetoric, namely the idea of *"parrhesia"* as a figure in which the speaker mitigates frankness with an apology for speaking (207). French preachers did not need to apologize because God does not apologize. Even so, if there is a conclusion we can draw from the lingering treatment of "licentia" in rhetorical treatises, many of which were written by members of the clergy who were preachers themselves, it is that the teaching of rhetoric, while not protecting an existing civil liberty, did preserve a domain for an unwritten one.

Notes

[1] "ce que nul écrivain, nul orateur laïque, n'aurait osé devant les puissances, contre les puissances"

[2] "la seule voix libre en ce temps de silence"

[3] "font toujours grand tort à la majesté & à l'autorité de la divine parole"

[4] "Licentia est, cum apud eos, quos aut vereri, aut metuere debet orator tamen aliquid pro iure suo dicit quod eos minime offendat. Cicero pro Ligario: Vide, quam non reformidem: vide, quanta lux liberalitatis & sapientiae tuae mihi apud te dicenti oboriatur: quantum potero voce contendam, ut hoc populus Romanus exaudiat. Suscepto bello Caesar gesto etiam magna ex parte, nulla vi coactus, iudicio meo ac voluntate ad ea arma profectus sum, quae erant sumpta contra te."

[5] For the translation of the lines from the "Pro Ligario," I have borrowed from Cicero, *Select Orations*, 252.

[6] "Licentia, *parrhesia*, libertas, & fiducia loquendi quo genere abundat Demosthenes, ut: *hôste dedoika mê blasphêmon men eipein, alêthes*. Vereor ne quid dicam odiosum, sed omnino verum. Acris est ac amarulenta. Altera excelsa: quid? de reliquis reip. malis dignitatem tueri mortem condemnere. Tertia, lenis est, quae videtur exerere aculeos cum aliqua acrimonia, quam mulcet, & mitigat, ut: Vos enim (Patres conscripti) grave ductu est, sed tamen dicendum, vos, inquam, Servium Sulpitium vita privastis: quem cum videretis se magis morbo quam oratione accusantem, non vos quidem crudeles fuistis (quid enim minus in hunc ordinem conuonit) sed cum speraretis nihil esse quod non illius authoritate & sapientia effici posset, vehementias excusationi obstitustis, atque eum, qui semper vestrum consensum gravissimum iudicavisset, de sententia deiecistis. Quarta, adulatoria, quae simulat liberatem, cum tamen ea dicat quae auditoribus scit esse gratissima: talis sunt illa pro Ligario, vide quam non reformidem, vide quanta lux liberalitatis & sapientiae tuae, mihi apud te dicendi oboriatur."

[7] For the translation of quotations from Demosthenes and Cicero, I have borrowed from the following sources: Demosthenes' "Third Philippic" (225); Cicero's "First Philippic against Marcus Antonius" (*Orations* 8); Cicero's "Ninth Philippic against Marcus Antonius" (*Orations* 150–51); and the "Pro Ligario" (*Select Orations* 252).

[8] "Cette figure consiste à reprendre hardiment ceux a qui l'on doit quelque respect."

[9] "La licence estoit autrefois une des figures du bareau, elle est a present une des figures de la chaire; les anciens Advocats n'en usoient que quand le defaut qu'ils reprenoient estoit honteux au Magistrat & nuisible au public; Les Predicateurs ne s'en servent que quand les vices qu'ils reprennent, convainquent ceux qui les contractent, d'un aveuglement estrange, & supposent en ceux qui les flattent, une Théologie pernicieuse; les premiers adoucissoient quelquefois par la loüange ce qu'ils avoient aigre par l'invective, les autres ne mettent jamais le doux avec l'aigre."

[10] The key political figure was Jules Mazarin (1602–1661).

[11] "Parlons sans figure. Avouons que ce péché est en effet le grand désordre du monde, puisqu'il attire après soi tous les autres désordres. Je dis que c'est pour lui que se répand le sang humain; écoutez-moi. D'où sont venues les guerres les plus cruelles et les plus fatales aux peuples,

sinon d'une passion d'amour? Une femme enlevée par un insensé, fut l'étincelle qui excita les plus violents incendies, et qui consuma des nations entières. Parce qu'un homme était impudique, il fallut que des milliers d'hommes périssent par le fer et par le feu. Mais ne remontons point si haut pour avoir des preuves de cette vérité : notre siècle, ce siècle malheureux, a bien de quoi nous convaincre; et Dieu n'a permis qu'il engendrât des monstres, que pour nous forcer à en convenir. Nous les avons vus avec effroi, et tant d'événements tragiques nous ont appris plus que nous ne voulions, ce qu'un commerce criminel peut produire, non plus dans les États, mais dans les familles, et dans les familles les plus honorables. L'empoisonnement était parmi nous un crime inouï; l'enfer, pour l'intérêt de cette passion l'a rendu commun."

Works Cited

Bary, René. *La rhétorique françoise ou l'on trouve de nouveaux exemples sur les Passions & sur les Figures*. Paris: Pierre le Petit, 1665.

Bourdaloue, Louis. *Sermons*. Ed. Gonzague Truc. Paris: Bossard, 1921.

Caussin, Nicolas, S. J. *Eloquentiae sacrae et humanae parallela*. Paris: S. Chappelet, 1627.

Cicero. *The Orations of Marcus Tullius Cicero*. Trans. Charles Duke Yonge. London: Bell, 1879.

———. *Rhetorica ad Herennium*. Trans. Harry Caplan. Cambridge: Harvard UP, 2004.

———. *Select Orations*. Trans. Charles Duke Yonge. New York: Harper, 1889.

Colclough, David. "*Parrhesia*: The Rhetoric of Free Speech in Early Modern England." *Rhetorica* 17.2 (1999): 177–212.

Demosthenes. *Demosthenes, with an English Translation*. Trans. Norman W. Dewitt and Norman J. Dewitt. London: Heinemann, 1949.

Foix, Marc-Antoine de la. *L'art de prêcher la parole de Dieu, contenant les regles de l'eloquence chrétienne*. Paris: Pralard, 1687.

Guèret, Gabriel. *Entretiens sur l'éloquence de la chaire et du barreau*. Paris: Jean Guignard, 1666.

Soarez, Cypriano. *De arte rhetorica libri tres*. Hispali, Seville: A. Escrivani, 1569.

Truchet, Jacques. *Sermon sur la mort et autres sermons*. Paris: GF-Flammarion, 1996.

The Functions of Polemical Discourse in the Public Sphere

Ruth Amossy

For the purposes of this inquiry, I would like to deal with polemical discourse as a legitimate argumentative mode from both a formal and social perspective. This bias goes against the current trend condemning polemical exchange on a rational and ethical basis, a trend grounded in an ideal of critical discussion and conflict resolution. Even though the question of dissent is recently coming to the fore, as can be seen in the theme of the last Ontario Society for the Study of Argumentation conference, "Dissensus and the Search for Common Ground" (2007), the question of polemics remains quite marginal. My working hypotheses are that polemics is an argumentative mode among others, in a continuum going from inconspicuous opposition to brutal confrontation of theses, and that passionate and even violent exchanges of arguments contribute to the possibility of coexistence in the very heart of social and political dissent. In other words, my contention is that polemical discourse fulfils a social function even if it does not necessarily match ethical models of human interaction and, what is more, even if it often falls short of reaching consensus. Such a claim cannot be sustained without an in-depth analysis of numerous cases, still to be undertaken. This presentation is meant to sketch a first theoretical framework for the study of polemics in a revised conception of argumentation, laying the ground for empirical work.[1]

IS POLEMICS PART OF ARGUMENTATION?

Polemics is generally condemned in everyday language as well as in scientific writing. In her lexicographical analysis of the term, going back to its origins and historical developments, Catherine Kerbrat-Orecchioni points out that it is unanimously denounced, not so much in the dictionary definitions, which are supposed to be neutral, but in the selected examples (21). An inquiry by Roselyne Koren into some 60 articles in the French press (71) shows that polemical discourse is accused of resorting to forms of violence incompatible with the good functioning of social life and of depriving the audience of its freedom of thought. From this perspective, *ad hominem* arguments and the brutalization of verbal exchanges are the most frequent objects of denunciation in the media. Christian Plantin's inquiry (398–401) into Frantext (since 1900) and *Le Monde* (400 titles) points to a shift in the conception of "polemicist" that contributes to its discrediting: it is no more a "person practicing or liking polemics," but rather a speaker who, in his aggressive discourse, displays a state of violent passion, if not of emotional disorder *(polémiqueur).* In all these lexical inquiries, polemical discourse is condemned for its association with violence, aggression, and the attempt to eliminate the opponent by discrediting him, and with extreme vehemence, passion, and transgression of rational standards.

The pejorative meaning of the word and its connotations in ordinary use do not differ from the accusations leveled at polemics by contemporary philosophers. The issue is by no means a technical question of definition: as Michel Foucault pointed out, in polemics, "a whole morality is at stake, the one that concerns the search for truth and the relation to the other" (1). According to him, polemics is "an obstacle to the search for the truth" and "a parasitic figure on discussion" (1) because the polemicist wages war on his adversary, thus abolishing him as an interlocutor. It thwarts the nature of dialogue by the polemicist's unconditional drive to ensure the triumph of a cause he refuses to question.

This critique of polemical discourse underlies argumentation theories and rhetoric from antiquity to the present day. The ancient Greeks denigrated eristic dialogue (from *eris*, strife), which was conceived as an art of disputation in which the partners' only objective is victory over the opponent. Defined as a battle where the other has to be defeated rather than convinced, it was criticized for its contempt for truth and its exclusive focus on winning the argument at any price, be it by using fallacies or inflicting humiliation on the opponent. A quite similar bias is to be found in contemporary research looking for validity criteria in argumentation. Douglas Walton's *New Dialectic* includes eristic in the six main types of dialogue (the others being persuasion, inquiries, negotiation, information seeking, and deliberation) but for him, eristic is a degenerate form mostly emerging when the other types of dialogue go wrong.

From this perspective, it is no wonder that the need for regulating discourse has led to a repression of polemics and a consequent refusal to conceptualize it. Thus Hamblin's dialectic, based on a system of rules intended to prevent any impediment to the sound development of verbal exchange, ignores polemics. In its search for the criteria of valid reasoning, informal logic (a branch developing nonformal standards for the analysis of everyday discourse) globally excludes polemics from the realm of argumentation. A discourse aiming at defeating the adversary by any means is perceived as systematically transgressing the rules of reason upon which reasoning should be based. Interest in polemics is thus limited to the attempt to describe fallacies, namely arguments that appear to be valid but are not. One example would be *ad hominem* arguments, which attack the person of the arguer instead of dealing with a relevant topic (*ad rem*). For the pragma-dialectical school of Amsterdam, which is mainly interested in conflict resolution, polemics transgresses not only the rules of Reason but also the cooperative principles without which agreement cannot be achieved.[2] From this perspective, dialogue has to be framed by a series of norms ensuring the success of a common search for solutions. As the discussants have to obey the rules of reason (namely, of critical discussion) and admit the opponent's stand if it proves to be justified (Eemeren et al.), they cannot engage in polemics without betraying their mission.

The situation does not present any noticeable difference when we turn from normative to nonnormative theories of argumentation. The contemporary emphasis on the search for consensus in argumentation studies eliminates polemics. Chaim Perelman and Lucie Olbrechts-Tyteca's most influential book, *The New Rhetoric* (which defines argumentation as the verbal means used to elicit an audience's adherence to a given thesis), does not address polemics at all. Nor do the numerous treatises and textbooks dealing with argumentation and rhetoric that followed their pioneering work.

There are, however, exceptions to this ostracism. They occur in conceptual frameworks where the main objective is not based on an ideal of communication—be it ethical or practical—but is purely descriptive. One of these descriptive approaches is to be found in French discourse analysis, with its emphasis on case studies and its desire to account for the way discourse actually works. Dominique Maingueneau provided a study of polemical discourse based on seventeenth-century texts of the polemics between Jansenists and Jesuits. However, his analysis lies outside the range of argumentation. It presents polemical discourse as based on antagonist isotopies[3] where each arguer inverts the positions of his opponent: the speakers are blocked in symmetric systems forever incompatible in a structure of mutual misunderstanding preventing any possibility of agreement.

A similar observation is made by Marc Angenot (*Dialogues*), who points out that people insist on engaging in argumentation although they regularly fail to persuade each other and endlessly go on with polemics without reaching any agreement whatsoever. However, Angenot (who in 1982 published a remarkable analysis of a polemical genre, the pamphlet) remains within the scope of argumentation studies in his 2008 book, subtitled "antilogic rhetoric"—an expression inspired by the Sophists' attempt to confront antilogies or opposed reasons that cannot be reconciled although neither of them is true nor false (*Dialogues* 42–43). Angenot explores the ways of irreconcilable polemics, in terms of rhetoric, in a theoretical work based on numerous analyses of actual polemics that look like dialogues of the deaf (the anarchists and socialists in the nineteenth century). Thus polemics seems to have become a subject of inquiry on the ruins of classical rhetoric's ideals.

A quite different approach is developed by drawing on interactional studies, where argumentation is a dialogal form of verbal exchange based on the explicit confrontation of two opposed stands. Leaving ample room for polemics, this definition even threatens to blur all limits and confuse it with argumentation. This is why Plantin chooses to distinguish the *actants* (proponent, opponent, third party) from the *actors* of the argumentative exchange: actants refers to roles that embody a position, and actors refers to people. This distinction prevents any confusion between an opposition of discourses and a conflict built on a confrontation between real people. Plantin considers polemical discourse as a public form of verbal antagonism to be analyzed in its relationship with everyday forms of agonistic speech, namely, exchanges representing a form of struggle. In his eyes, the basic situation becomes polemical when actors fully identify with argumentative roles; in other, nonpolemical cases, the same actor can easily shift from one role to the other, or even—as occurs in cases of deliberation—systematically check the different stances in order to make a judicious choice. It is interesting to notice that in the framework of his specific conception of argumentation, Plantin, far from excluding polemics, has to justify why argumentation is not warlike by definition.

In conclusion of this first, panoramic presentation, it thus appears that studies on polemics are promoted only by descriptive, nonnormative approaches that do not rely on exclusive obedience to Reason or on ethical ideals of communication. Obviously, conceptions of polemics and the very willingness to deal with it are dependent on the specific meaning conferred upon argumentation. As a process of reason leading either to the establishment of Truth or to an agreement on the reasonable, or to conflict resolution, argumentation excludes polemics, which is seen as a mere deterioration, if not degeneration, of argumentative exchange. Moreover, as a verbal exchange based on the recognition of otherness, the acceptance of restraint, the willingness to listen to the opponent's stand, and to question one's own convictions, argumentation cannot tolerate the blunt aggressiveness of polemics. Another conceptual framework is thus needed to examine polemical discourse as an argumentative practice in what Perelman called "the realm of argumentation" (*Realm*).

POLEMICS AS A LEGITIMATE ARGUMENTATIVE MODE

In order for polemical discourse to become a legitimate object of inquiry, one has to broaden the scope of argumentation on the basis of what can be observed on the ground—which is what Maingueneau, Angenot, and Plantin do, although along different lines. People do engage in agonistic argumentation, and they do not necessarily limit themselves to the rules of reason and of ethical dialogue. They try to promote their cause by various means, among which are *pathos* and verbal violence. They go on arguing even when they suspect their persuasion enterprise is doomed to failure. Every democratic society seems to feed on the very type of polemical exchange it condemns. Thus the question is not, primarily, if polemics is good or bad, but how it actually works and what functions it fulfills.

I propose to investigate polemical discourse as an integral part of argumentation understood as a continuum from the weakest to the strongest opposition between a discourse and its counterdiscourse. Aimed at bringing about an agreement on an opinion, a point of view, or a way of seeing or experiencing reality through informal reasoning and adaptation to the audience, argumentation goes from a latent form, where the opposition of discourses is quite inconspicuous, though by no means absent (an informative newspaper article, for example), to an extreme form, where a clash occurs between antagonist theses (a violent debate on a controversial subject). On the one hand, this continuum implies that there is an argumentative dimension in discourses that have no argumentative aim (Amossy, "Argumentative"), and on the other hand, that the often violent confrontation of antagonist theses does not fall outside the realm of argumentation. From this perspective, polemics is an argumentative mode among others, to be described in its specificity and explored in its functions.

The first step in our inquiry is thus to see how a discourse endeavoring to attack another rather than to convince him can be defined as an argumentative mode (Amossy, "Modalités"). Let us first look at the basic structure of polemical exchange. It is characterized by a sharp opposition of theses, as each arguer tries to promote his own point of view through a warlike confrontation. Refutation of the opponent takes an agonistic form: it consists of an attempt to disqualify his stand, if not his very person. Whether quoting the adversary's discourse or simply alluding to it, polemical discourse reacts to the other's words in order to better discredit him.

One can of course wonder whether there is any room left for persuasion in a framework where the speaker's goal is eventually "to eject the adversary from the competition" (Oléron 21), "to subdue him and erase him if necessary" (Declercq 18). We have to remember, however, that polemical discourse does not exclusively address the opponent. Another constitutive feature of polemical exchange is its tripartite nature: it is composed not only of a proponent and an opponent, but also of a third party. Rather than gaining the support of the adversary under attack, the persuasion enterprise is generally directed toward the audience invited to follow or watch the contest. Thus polemical exchanges in a political campaign play a role in the effort to gain the votes of citizens. They also attempt to elicit an adherence of minds in television debates. Moreover, it is unlikely that anybody would engage in polemics over a social problem in the papers if she did not think the reader might be persuaded to abandon the opponent's point of view in favor of her own cause.

This does not imply that an attempt at persuasion is always intended for a third party and never addresses the adversary. True, if (as Plantin would have it) polemics occur only when the actors, the real persons, identify with their argumentative role to such an extent that the thesis becomes constitutive of their own identity, then polemical exchanges can never succeed in persuading the opponent—which is precisely the idea developed in Angenot's *Dia-*

logues de Sourds. It seems, however, that two alternative possibilities can be envisaged. In a polemics where a religious nationalist Jew fights the evacuation of Hebron that is called for by an Israeli leftist struggling for peace, the stance of each person is constitutive of his identity and commands his overall way of life. Here the actor and the argumentative role, the individual and the thesis, are one. Clearly, there can be no shift of opinion without a conversion affecting the identity of the arguer. In this case, the adversaries cannot but go on fighting indefinitely—which they actually do. Moreover, attacks on the political and ideological position of the other will necessarily be attacks— whether explicit or implicit—on his very person.

People engaging in a polemical dialogue do not always have, however, to embody a thesis expressing the essence of their being, which brings us to the second possibility. Imagine a polemical dialogue after the Second Lebanon War between an Israeli citizen who thinks Israeli Prime Minister Ehud Olmert should resign and another citizen who thinks he has to remain as head of the government in order to ensure the stability of the country in a difficult situation. If the two citizens are driven by passion and political enthusiasm, they can easily start a polemical exchange, be it in a private conversation, a public debate, or on the pages of a newspaper. However, violent attacks on the other's opinion will not automatically affect the arguer's person. And if the participants share the same values and interests (the welfare of the country), they can eventually adopt a thesis different from the one held to be true at the beginning.

For the final point in this description of polemical discourse, it should be noted that, as a confrontation, i.e., a strong opposition of theses on a given question, polemics is a structure of exchange. But, at the same time, it involves a tone of voice, a way of speaking and arguing. It can be defined as verbal aggressiveness, not to be confused with the argumentative mode as such. Rather, it is a discursive register, based on all forms of direct attack (like accusing or abusing the opponent), but also on the resources of *pathos* (indignation, anger, compassion toward an opponent's victim) or of humor (irony, sarcasm, and so on). In other words, the verbal exchange uses all permissible techniques to fight the adversary in the argumentative confrontation—and these techniques create a sense of violence without which there can be no polemics. Mere verbal violence does not, however, constitute polemics in itself. An exchange of insults between two drivers, for instance, is not polemical. A quarrel between spouses or friends can be violent without being polemical. It is the use of verbal violence (a discursive register) in a structure of strong opposition and confrontation of theses (an argumentative mode) that creates polemical discourse as such.

The role played by verbal violence calls for a better definition of that phenomenon on the linguistic and stylistic levels. Although everyone seems to be sensible to verbal violence when listening to or participating in a debate, it appears that as an intuitive notion it is very difficult to translate into linguistic terms. In general, then, discourse is felt to be violent when:

- The arguer prevents his partner from expressing her point of view (frequently interrupting her, denying her the possibility to develop her argument, etc.);
- The arguer totally rejects the opposite thesis by discrediting it in harsh terms or by ridiculing it, thus excluding her partner from the debate;
- The arguer assimilates the point of view of the person representing it to absolute Evil, thus demonizing her opponent;
- The arguer is moved by extreme feelings of anger, indignation, or disgust as expressed in her discourse through verbal marks of subjectivity;
- The arguer arouses such feelings in her audience without expressing them in her own name; or
- The arguer abuses her opponent by insulting her and using offensive expressions.

Although this list is by no means exhaustive, we can distinguish in it two major categories: the first three points concern the means used to evacuate the adverse point of view; the last three concern the speaker's emotional implication in her discourse. In all cases, the polemical style is characterized by excess. Refusal of nuances, use of hyperbole, and a tendency to go to extremes give it its peculiar flavor.

The part played by violence in verbal confrontation, and the tolerated type of violence, differs widely according to the cultural and institutional frameworks in which the exchange occurs. However, in argumentation, some limits are always imposed on verbal violence. Polemics has to be regulated in order to be efficient: too brutal a transgression of what can be tolerated would ruin the arguer's chances to be heard. In the social arena, one cannot violate taboos without being sanctioned; an excessively brutal disqualification of an opponent would disqualify the speaker herself. Thus polemical discourse, even in its excess, participates in a ritual that shapes agonistic relationships, imposing on them limits and constraints.

THE SOCIAL FUNCTIONS OF POLEMICAL DISCOURSE, OR ARGUMENTATION REVIEWED

Even when constrained, verbal violence associated with sharp confrontation of opposing theses violates the rules of critical discussion and challenges the rules of politeness underlying verbal exchanges. Why, then, is polemics so common in public debate? Why is this kind of discourse severely judged not only from a philosophical and ethical perspective, but also—as the above research on the ordinary use of the word shows—in social terms? The discrepancy between the condemnation of polemics and the frequency of its use calls for a revision of its evaluation and a re-elaboration of the basis on which this evaluation is established.

Let us go back to our broad definition of argumentation, going from discourses where the antagonism is subtle and blurred to obvious violent clashes of opposing stances. As we have already noticed, the undermining of the latter mode in favor of less agonistic kinds of exchanges derives from the preeminence given to consent over dissent, to agreement over conflict. However, the frequency of polemics clearly testifies to the centrality of conflict in public life. It manifests the importance conferred upon the free expression of antagonist views in a democratic sphere where the formulation of dissent and the competition of divergent points of view are basic rights and sacred principles. This is why any study of argumentation that is eager to describe and understand the nature of actual exchanges in our contemporary world cannot dismiss the violent confrontation of antagonist theses.

These considerations explain Pierre-André Taguieff's demand for a revision of Perelman and Olbrechts-Tyteca's *The New Rhetoric*. Claiming that political discourse and public debate are based on conflict and feed off of it, Taguieff calls for a post-Perelmanian approach focusing on polemics in order to go beyond what he calls "contemporary dialogic angelism," an idealism that prefers reason and dialogue while ignoring the core of political interaction—conflict (273). Such an approach should take into account the inevitability of exchanges based on strong dissent and the role of antagonism in democracy, instead of rejecting them on the basis of ethical concerns or rationalist demands for agreement. Thus Chantal Mouffe, stressing that no consensus can be reached without exclusion, likewise affirms the importance of agonistic confrontation in contemporary democracies, noting:

> An adversary is a legitimate enemy, an enemy with whom we have in common a shared adhesion to the ethico-political principles of democracy. But our disagreement concerning their meaning and implementation is not one that could be resolved through deliberation and rational discussion, hence the antagonistic element in the relation. . . . To be sure, compromises are possible; they are part of the process of politics. But they should be seen as temporary respites in an ongoing confrontation. . . . Far from jeopardizing democracy, agonistic confrontation is in fact its very condition of existence. (5)

In this pluralistic perspective, there is no point in longing for a society from which strong dissent and the ensuing polemics are absent, since they are "the very condition of possibility of a striving democratic life" (5). Moreover, polemics is the only way for adversaries sharing the same (national) space to coexist—to live together while sustaining opposing claims and holding antithetical views. Violence is translated into a communication framework, superseding physical fighting or political repression.

This perspective need not undermine the definitions of argumentation as a search for consensus through verbal means. The ideal of rational dialogue respecting all parties involved remains a fundamental one. The need for a coconstruction of the reasonable (as advocated by Perelman and Olbrechts-Tyteca) in order to make common decisions and take action does not lose its centrality. It should not obscure, however, the necessity of a rhetoric exploring violent confrontations in a democratic space where conflict plays a constitutive role. We cannot ignore that, in a given society, various groups elaborate contradictory views on what is acceptable and reasonable, nor can we disregard the fact that they often never can reach a consensus. The argumentative process leading to a specific conclusion depends on the premises, the shared values, and prevalent norms of reasoning characterizing a social group. The differences might be too deep to allow for a meeting of minds. They may even display what Angenot calls cognitive breaks, separating forever populations that think too differently to ever come to an agreement. They make, however, for a plural society. Plurality entails a positive conception of heterogeneity and, consequently, ensures the legitimacy of contradictory opinions provoking passionate antagonisms. Sharing the same space, the conflicting groups who are divided in their worldview cannot just ignore each other. They have to participate in the public debate and fight for the prevalence of their own perspectives. They do so even when they face an antagonist with whom they can only struggle without any hope of future agreement.

Thus the conflicting views translated into polemics over a specific issue allow for the dynamic of public life in a democratic space where passionate debates on common decisions and future orientations develop freely. True, the same polemics can last for a long time without finding any solution. However, when action has to be taken, the institutional frameworks of a given society provide the desired answer: the latter is the result of a vote, of a referendum, of a law, or of a juridical or governmental decision. Even if they do not put an end to the dissent and the ensuing discussions, they create a fact that cannot be dismissed.

From this perspective, it appears that studying the rhetoric of dissent alongside the search for agreement allows for a fuller and richer view of argumentation, avoiding both the idealism of an approach exclusively based on rational consent and the disillusionment of a theory claiming that any persuasion enterprise is doomed to fail. It is in this conceptual framework that I would like to further the development of studies exploring the functioning and functions of polemical discourse in the contemporary democratic world. The importance of the subject is obvious, as is the broadening of argumentation, in its formal, conceptual, and social implications, brought about by the investigation of polemics.

Notes

[1] This paper is part of a new research project called Polemical Discourse and Argumentation in the Contemporary Democratic Sphere: The French Case and was undertaken with the generous help of the Israel Science Foundation.

[2] Pragma-dialectics is a theory of argumentation developed in Amsterdam by Frans van Eemeren and his research group. Aimed at developing a code of conduct for argumentative discourse, it combines linguistic and logical insights. Based on an ideal of critical rationality, it prioritizes conflict resolution.

[3] "Isotopy" is a concept created by A.-J Greimas *(Sémantique)* in the field of structural semantics. It is based on the repetition of a similar feature in the development of the text, giving the message its coherence and allowing for its deciphering by the reader.

Works Cited

Amossy, Ruth. "The Argumentative *Dimension* of Discourse." *Practices of Argumentation.* Ed. Frans van Eemeren and Peter Houtlosser. Amsterdam: John Benjamins, 2005. 87–98.

———. "Modalités Argumentatives et Registres Discursifs: Le Cas du Polémique." *Les registres. Enjeux Pragmatiques et Visées Stylistiques.* Ed. Lucile Gaudin-Bordes and Geneviève Salvan. Louvain-la-Neuve: Academia-Bruylant, 2008.

Angenot, Marc. *Dialogues de Sourds. Traité de Rhétorique Antilogique.* Paris: Mille et une nuits, 2008.

———. *La Parole Pamphlétaire. Typologie des Discours Modernes.* Paris: Payot, 1982.

Declercq, Gilles. "Rhétorique et Polémique." *La Parole Polémique.* Ed. Gilles Declercq, Michel Murat, and Jacqueline Dangel. Paris: Champion, 2003. 17–21.

Eemeren, Frans H. van, Rob Grootendorst, and Francesca Snoek Hoekemans. *Fundamentals of Argumentation Theory.* New Jersey: Lawrence Erlbaum, 1996.

Foucault, Michel. Interview with Paul Rabinow. "Polemics, Politics and Problematizations." Trans. L. Davis. May 1984. "Essential Works of Foucault." *Ethics.* Vol. 1. New York: New P, 1997. <http://foucault.info/foucault/interview.html>.

Greimas, Algirdas Julien. *Sémantique structurale.* Paris: Larousse, 1966.

Hamblin, C. L. *Fallacies.* London: Methuen, 1970.

Kerbrat-Orecchioni, Catherine. "La Polémique et ses Définitions." *Le Discours Polémique.* Ed. N. Gelas and C. Kerbrat-Orecchioni. Lyon: PU de Lyon, 1980.

Koren, Roselyne. "Stratégies et Enjeux de la Dépolitisation du Langage." *La polémique journalistique.* Ed. Benoit Grevisse and Annick Dubied. *Recherches en Communication* 20 (2003): 65–84.

Maingueneau, Dominique. *Sémantique de la Polémique.* Lausanne: L'Age d'Homme, 1983.

Mouffe, Chantal. "Pluralism, Dissensus and Democratic Citizenship." <http://www.rizoma.ufsc.br/pdfs/chantal.pdf 1>.

Oléron, Pierre. "Sur l'Argumentation Polémique." *Hermès* 16, *Argumentation et rhétorique II* (1995): 15–27

Perelman, Chaim. *The Realm of Rhetoric.* Trans. William Kluback. Notre Dame: U of Notre Dame P, 1982.

Perelman, Chaim, and Lucie Olbrechts-Tyteca. *The New Rhetoric. A Treatise on Argumentation.* Trans. John Wilkinson and Purcell Weaver. Notre Dame, IN: U of Notre Dame P, 1969.

Plantin, Christian. "Des Polémistes aux Polémiqueurs." *La Parole Polémique.* Ed. Gilles Declercq, Michel Murat, and Jacqueline Dangel. Paris: Champion, 2003. 377–408.

Taguieff, Pierre-André. "Analyse du Discours et Nouvelle Rhétorique." *Hermès* 8.9 (1990): 261–87.

Walton, Douglas. *The New Dialectic: Conversational Contexts of Argument.* Toronto: U of Toronto P, 1998.

Form Is a Feminist Issue[1]

Eve Wiederhold

This paper asks: What gets marked as a sign of bad politics? And how should we ask that question?

When FoxNews broadcasts its slogan "We Report. You Decide," it is criticized by media analysts and commentators for breaking its promises. "We Report. You Decide" suggests that "we" will neutrally convey information to allow "you," the vigilant citizenry, to sort through competing claims and render fair judgments about issues facing the nation. "We" will make the democratic ideal real by monitoring the sovereign's actions to allow you to observe, debate, and then evaluate the political scene; to discriminate between legitimate and illegitimate behaviors; and to make informed choices when asked to consider controversial politics and policies.

This, of course, is precisely what FoxNews does not do, according to the media analysts and television personalities (e.g., Keith Olbermann) who track the ways in which FoxNews obstructs the viewer's perspective.[2] Rather than live up to a promise to neutrally convey information, the "we" on Fox instead manipulates and informs via omission by "cherry-picking" (favorite TV buzz word in 2007) information in ways that support a conservative political agenda. Indeed, "we" have gone so far as to provide a platform for the right-wing politics of the George W. Bush administration, acting as a mouthpiece for its policies rather than subjecting those policies to critical scrutiny. "We" masquerade. "We" are the simulacra of news.

The exposure of political bias in FoxNews has been critically important to the political health of the nation because it has indicated how this media outlet has blurred the acts of informing and advocating on behalf of a particular governmental administration. Many would agree that the consequences of this blurring—and of the willingness of other media outlets to follow suit—have been devastating. Yet when media critics identify particular news stations as disseminating "bad" news, they raise a thorny interpretive issue. The logic of their arguments suggests that there is, in fact, "good" news that can be identified, a type of news that would emerge from a zone of neutrality and achieve fairness and balance by offering accurate depictions of public

62

events. Constructing FoxNews as an enemy to "the news" simultaneously implies the existence of "friends" without clarifying who they are or how the friendship is forged. The act of invoking the "good/bad" dichotomy expresses unexamined, naturalized conceptions of how to theorize the nature of linguistic authority, action, and accountability in modern democracy. Such conceptions are built upon a belief, shared by conservative as well as progressive media commentators, that representations can be treated as "real truths" and then critiqued or championed accordingly.

Consider, for example, the columns of Frank Rich, a *New York Times* former theatre critic and current commentator on the political scene whose own politics would conventionally be described as the ideological opposite of those at FoxNews. Rich's ability to synthesize seemingly disparate bits of information floating in public spaces often offers a welcome relief from the reductive, sentimentalized portraits repeated by mainstream journalists at FoxNews and elsewhere. And yet it is possible to find in his delivery an attitude about representation that echoes the organizing logic informing the promises made by his associates at Fox. During the 2008 primary season, for example, Rich let his antipathy for Hillary Clinton's campaign drive his observations about the political scene, and in a column that followed Clinton's defeat in North Carolina in May, joined the chorus of media commentators calling for her to quit the race, and then used that inevitability to prompt a reflection on the unpredictable election season as a whole.

> While we wait out her self-immolating exit, it's a good time to pause the 24/7 roller coaster for a second and get our bearings. The reason that politicians and the press have gotten so much wrong is that we keep forgetting what year it is. Only if we reboot to 2008 will the march to November start making sense. (Rich)

Rich goes on to observe that because we are in a "new" historical moment, the tactics that led to Democratic defeat in the past—especially in 1968 and 1988—won't work. Those old models have been depleted of their linguistic force and voters are ready for "the new," a quality that one can find embodied in the person and candidacy of Barack Obama.

> The year 2008 is far more complex—and exhilarating—than the old templates would have us believe. Of course we're in pain . . . yet . . . there is a heartening undertow: we know the page will turn. . . . The repressed sliver of joy beneath the national gloom can be seen in the record registration numbers of new voters and over-the-top turnout in Democratic primaries. (Rich)

Obama, he adds, has the vision to "understand and emphasize that subterranean, nearly universal anticipation of change rather than settle for the narrower band of partisan, dyspeptic Bush-bashing."

Of course, it is important to point out that Rich is a columnist with an attitude who makes no claims of objectivity. Hence the comparison to the FoxNews slogan may not be entirely fair. What I would draw attention to, however, is the premise embedded within his argument that bespeaks a conception of what constitutes political and ethical judgment. That conception invokes that old metaphor of vision to delineate a method for assessing representations through critical reflection. Rich positions himself as the philosopher able to remove himself from the confusion caused by Hillary's continued campaign, and once removed, assess the overall picture. During the week leading up to the North Carolina primary, some—including Clinton—said she would close the gap with voters in the Tar-Heel State. Some wondered why Barack couldn't clinch the deal. But from Rich's perch, one can see that "the majority" has sorted through competing claims and can tell the difference between the authentic representative of the new era and the one that remains stuck in the old models.

In effect, the logic organizing Rich's column is not so different from that underwriting the slogan of FoxNews in that both invoke commonplace conceptions of deliberatory democracy. That is, both put unquestioned faith in existing evaluative standards to appraise expressions of politics, justice, and democratic life. Such standards recall the Platonically inflected model of *mimesis* wherein a given representation aims to re-present a prior authentic essence that the listener/observer should notice when present, and yearn for when absent. Cultivating a capacity to perceive the difference between the presence/absence of authenticity is believed to be foundational to political judgments. Accordingly, one should judge by determining whether a speaker is genuinely attempting to re-present prior truths or is merely seeking audience satisfaction. One should judge by distinguishing those who sincerely care about the state of the nation from those who are motivated by a desire for political power. In Platonically inflected conceptions of political judgment, citizens participate in civic life by perceiving categorical differences and their power to do so emerges from reading competencies that enable a judicious selection from the multiple arguments made available in a free society. With such observatory powers, the "we" invoked in Rich's column is fully capable of telling who will usher in a refreshing "new." We can distinguish a racist ploy from an honest assessment of a candidate's abilities. And, less explicitly, but vaguely implied, that we should feel morally contented with our capacity to render such judgments. Underwriting this perspective is the idea that shared reading competencies activate a process by which a common will can be realized in the form of mutually recognized public purposes, commitments, and ideals.

Here, we may be surprised to find ourselves not in the domain of philosophy, but in that of rhetoric, and it may give us pause to see how rhetoricians can also borrow Platonically inflected models of judgment when theorizing how people weigh and select which arguments are credible and ethically persuasive. In traditional rhetorical conceptions of democratic inquiry, a kind of linguistic equity appears to be guaranteed by virtue of the ability to participate in discourse, as if the conditions that enable rhetorical engagement neutrally unfold to provide an equitable basis for interpretive exchange. The general ability to participate in democratic processes seems to account for a general ethics that is applicable to any specific negotiation of meaning. When all are given a chance to present their case, all are judged according to the effectiveness of their presentation. Arguably, then, Hillary Clinton had all the opportunities in the world to put forth her ideas and convince voters that she should be the Democratic nominee. The failure of her campaign rests with her, not with any inequities within representational systems.

But when it comes to delineating more precisely how individual literacies lead to choices that inform collective judgments, difficulties arise, especially when attempting to account for the provenance of political thought. Media reports not only deliver information about what happened; they also distribute vocabularies that enable readers to understand the cultural significance of select stories. Political judgments rest not only on the recognition of preestablished signifiers, but also on the question of how the familiar and recognizable has affected what gets seen or overlooked, as well as how "the visible" is positioned within an interpretive context to enable any signifier to make sense.[3] In other words, our methods of assessment are themselves thoroughly rhetorical. To reshape models of representational ethics, we need to explore the rhetorical dimensions of what we say about *how* we deliberate.

This reshaping is already occurring within feminist analyses of discourses of power. Feminist rhetoricians have explored the limits of Western philosophical systems that underwrite narratives of how knowledge is produced and recognized. Their alternative interpretive rubrics reject Platonic and Enlightenment models that envision knowledge as an object made available for review, either empirically or through philosophical insight. When Wendy Hesford observes that students writing autobiographies do not reveal essential selves but "negotiate their identities discursively" ("Writing Identities" 135), she takes exception with the idea that insight, personal or otherwise, can be achieved through a neutral and objective contemplation of pure form. When Joy Ritchie and Kathleen Boardman invoke linguistic excess as a trope for composition pedagogy, they effectively question whether representations are capable of encapsulating the authentic and putting it forth for review. Western epistemologies have endorsed narratives that envision the isolated contemplation of pure form as the height of integrity. Feminists point to the consequences of this vision: The general, the abstract, and the rational garner more cultural regard than the specific, the embodied, and the emotional. Those consequences were evident in Rich's argument, which implied that citizens should indicate an allegiance to the Platonic tradition by rendering judgments that "rise above" the vengeful, the desirous, the personally invested, the politically motivated. And citizens should be expected to find hope in the speaker whose expression of big ideas has the awesome strength to overcome a history of Democratic failures.

In effect, a conception of "freedom from" the rhetorical underwrites these claims, as scholars in rhetoric such as Sharon Crowley have made clear. This reductive portrait of what makes a person credible functions to mask points of hesitation in our conceptions of how people interact with public texts. That hesitation is evident in subsequent responses to Obama's speechifying. On the one hand, he has been heralded as a man of extraordinary eloquence, able to fill a 75,000-seat stadium with ardent fans. On the other, since clinching the Democratic nomination, he has indicated that he understands a need to "tone down" his style and "not aim for a lot of high rhetoric."[4] That doubled message bespeaks a cultural anxiety about how to theorize rhetoric's place in political judgment. The simultaneous construction of Obama as a political ingenue and as too invested in "soaring oratory" (Fouhy 3) attests to a continued cultural investment in an old sentimental dream that imagines the virtuous citizen as rhetorically innocent. We are expected to cherish speakers who have a capacity to move audiences, but whose ability to do so is guileless and natural, devoid of verbal trickery that would obstruct clarity of perception—the very phenomena that constituted the crime of President Bill Clinton, according to many. (And a crime that, for many, implicated the candidacy of his wife.)

The appeal of an "innocent rhetoric" implicates public expectations about how language should be used and how credibility should be judged. It shapes expectations about how citizens should participate with language, namely, that they should continue to avoid "rhetoric" that is too overtly rhetorical, too invested in persuading and satisfying, too calculating and strategic. Language users will continue to be expected to "take the high road" and avoid the mess of linguistic seduction, pleasure, and a will to power. They will be expected to read political campaigns in terms of who best approximates the ideal apolitical candidate, as if the idea of "apolitical authenticity" can be converted into a representational real. When Obama promises to bring in "the new," when media commentators find in him proof of that promise delivered and respond as if a state of newness has in fact been achieved, they effectively offer a reassuring narrative about the capacity of language to reflect a desirable quality that can be distinguished from less than desirable ones.[5]

But when acts of naming give ideas a recognizable form, they craft categories that are positioned within discursive networks that influence how a given category will be read. Because the domains of "the political" and "the rhetorical" continue to be culturally denigrated, promises to get beyond their purview get read as signs of "progress" and "the good."

While the legacy of the Enlightenment's depiction of knowledge as an object available for review has been under scrutiny for some time now, we still have a long way to go when exploring how social context, rather than language's grip on Truth, affects whose speech acts get regarded as credible. Derridean-derived critiques of language point out that signifiers do not present information; they communicate by acting within a linguistic system that establishes meaning through acts of deferral. The presence of meaning is always elusive and relational and involves an endless substitution of signifiers that come to be regarded as a true representation of an event, an *ethos*, a perspective.[6] Feminist rhetoricians push on these insights by asking about the significance of the materiality of the sign.[7] How has any given signifier been positioned within prior cultural narratives and how has that particular positioning affected how the sign will be read? A feminist materialist rhetoric would argue that how we identify signifiers of "good" and "bad" emerges from our interactions with complex, historically marked narratives that affect embodied responses to how texts get scrutinized. "Knowledge" is produced from judgments made about what seems plausible, acceptable, and even thinkable. Before we're "in the know," we encounter multiple transactions that ask us to make choices in response to the institutional norms that precede utterances and make them comprehensible.

Consequently, form—that which gets recognized, assigned meaning, debated, made relevant, or dismissed—is a feminist issue. The material form of the signifier matters to how it is regarded. When looking for transcendence, the materiality of the sign matters. For example, our experience of depictions of a candidate's "experience" will be affected by whether we harbor a desire to "move on," "move up," or "move beyond." Our analyses of the pertinence of entrenched identity categories such as gender, race, and class will influence our assessments of who is believable, who is performing badly, who is subjected to, and who seems to escape the call of languages that precede and influence how bodies are read.

Given the anti-material context from which statements about "turning the page" emerge, one might wonder about what exactly is new. Transcendence—the abstraction of hope, the idea of getting past the old and inspiring the new—was made meaningful during the 2008 election season by simultaneously denigrating the female candidate who was by no means innocent, whose tactics deserve scrutiny and critique, but whose very reach for office was narrated by the mainstream media as a lust for power. And the idea of transcendence has also been made meaningful through the vitriolic denouncement of a charismatic minister who was ridiculed for not seeking transcendence—demanding instead that citizens in the United States pay attention to the politics of race. These methods of translating the meaning of "transcendence" have been comprehensible because we have been trained to see the act of "overcoming" life's paradoxes and complexities as a prized activity. We've also learned to read signifiers of embodiment as impediments in the path of transcendence. Further, the idea of transcendence has been made meaningful through what *isn't* said—what hasn't been made visible in the many public conversations about leadership, democratic processes, and questions of enfranchising and alienating. Had Hillary Clinton delivered a speech to the nation that addressed the subtle but continuing problem of sexism, how would that speech have been received?

Rather than repeat the same logics that look for an interpretive stance that rises above the mess of materiality, rather than retain an evaluative apparatus that promises to differentiate "the good" and "the bad" by accessing a domain of authenticity, we can continue the feminist project of devising alternative evaluative methods that would put a halt to subordinating phenomena associated with the domain of the feminine. More specifically, we can advance feminist rhetorical inquires into the ethics of representation by emphasizing the importance of history and embodiment to interpretive acts. This means countering those discourses that valorize the idea that speech should aim beyond rhetoric. It also means taking a closer look at the presupposed relationships between narrative and lived experience when evaluating participation and credibility. To acknowledge embodiment as a contributor to how we know and judge what we think we know requires a rereading of "the body" and a disentangling of embodied readings from normative narratives that would explain what constitutes the parameters of interpretive interactions. It means reviewing, questioning, affirming, and challenging our allegiance to enculturated interpretive methodologies. Any description of how judgments are rendered might instead be understood as oscillating between the lived and the constructed, the genuine and the artificial, requiring citizens to look at what is "in" the context of interpretation as well as what is left out to enable any signifier to make sense. With this changeable context in view, we might then cultivate interpretive perspectives that acknowledge that because we may not know much of anything, our judgments will always be suspect. Rather than be on the lookout for the judgment that a majority would deem transcendent and virtuous, we might instead be propelled to ask, perpetually: What is our responsibility in any given case? And what can we do in response to this unsettled responsibility?

Notes

1. This paper grew out of a course by the same title that I taught at UNCG in Spring 2007. Conversations with students from that course were challenging and inspiring. I would like to thank Brandy Grabow, Belinda Walzer, John Pell, Tonya Hassel, MaryBeth Pennington, Alan Benson, William Duffy, Stephanie, and Kim Reigle for their thoughtful contributions to class discussions.

2. Olbermann, host of the nightly television show *Countdown* (MSNBC-TV), has a running feud with Fox's incendiary host Bill O'Reilly, and regularly offers a recounting of inaccuracies in O'Reilly's reporting. For another critique of the ways in which news is portrayed on FoxNews, see the documentary *Outfoxed*.

3. See Peggy Phelan for a trenchant exploration about the relationship between vision, language, and judgment.

4. Obama made this comment when describing what he planned to say at the Democratic convention. See Fouhy. While scrutiny of Obama's mode of speech was ongoing during the Democratic primary, media commentators seemed to become more overtly critical once he won. "Where's the passion?" asked Joe Klein in a September 2008 column, while in August, Obama was tagged "Little Rhetoric Riding Hood," by George F. Will. See also Sean Wilentz.

5. Hence, it is not insignificant that the context for reading what "change" means shifted once Obama selected Sen. Joseph Biden (D-DE) as his running mate and John McCain countered with a choice of Alaska governor Sarah Palin. Nor is it insignificant that McCain's ability to wrest the mantle of change from Obama coincided with the shift in media coverage that critiqued Obama's rhetorical style.

6. See Derrida, *Of Grammatology* for an exposition of these ideas. For a helpful translation, see Mary Poovey.

7. See, for example, Teresa de Lauretis, Rosemary Hennessy, and Wendy Hesford ("Reading").

Works Cited

Crowley, Sharon. *Composition in the University: Historical and Polemical Essays.* Pittsburgh: U of Pittsburgh P, 1998.

de Lauretis, Teresa. *Alice Doesn't: Feminism, Semiotics, Cinema.* Bloomington: Indiana UP, 1984.

Derrida, Jacques. *Of Grammatology.* Trans. Gayatri Chakravorty Spivak. Baltimore: Johns Hopkins UP, 1974.

Fouhy, Beth. "Obama Plans to Tone Down Oratory." *Washington Post Express* 26 Aug. 2008: 3.

Hennessy, Rosemary. *Materialist Feminism and the Politics of Discourse.* New York: Routledge, 1992.

Hesford, Wendy. "Reading Rape Stories: Material Rhetoric and the Trauma of Representation." *College English* 62.2 (1999): 192–221.

———. "Writing Identities: The Essence of Difference in Multicultural Classrooms." *Writing in Multicultural Settings.* Ed. Carol Severino, Juan C. Guerra, and Johnnella E. Butler. New York: MLA, 1997. 133–49.

Klein, Joe. "In the Arena." *Newsweek* 1 Sept. 2008: 27.

Olbermann, Keith. *Countdown.* MSNBC-TV, New York. Monday–Friday, 8 PM EST.

Outfoxed: Rupert Murdoch's War on Journalism. Dir. Robert Greenwald. With Roger Ailes, Eric Alterman, Christiane Amanpour. MoveOn.org. 2004.

Phelan, Peggy. *UnMarked: The Politics of Performance.* New York: Routledge, 1993.

Poovey, Mary. "Feminism and Deconstruction." *Feminist Studies* 14.1 (1988): 51–65.

Rich, Frank. "Party Like It's 2008." *New York Times.com* 11 May 2008. <http://www.nytimes.com/2008/05/11/opinion/11rich.html?ei=5070&b29cf53484da1ef3>.

Ritchie, Joy, and Kathleen Boardman. "Feminism in Composition: Inclusion, Metonymy, and Disruption." *College Composition and Communication* 50.4 (1999): 585–606.

Wilentz, Sean. "A Liberal's Lament." *Newsweek.com* 1 Sept. 2008. <http://www.newsweek.com/id/154911>.

Will, George F. "Little Rhetoric Riding Hood." *Washington Post* 24 Aug. 2008: B7.

6

Knifing Orlan's Mask
Grotesque Aesthetics as
Visceral Resistance to Commodification

Jane Munksgaard

French multimedia performance artist Orlan is the first person who used plastic surgery as a medium of artistic expression. Her project, The Reincarnation of Saint Orlan, started in 1990 and involved a series of twelve plastic surgeries during which she started to appropriate aspects of canonically celebrated Western paintings and sculptures. Through recording the transformation process, Orlan makes the surgical act, as well as the results, performative. She performs what Judith Butler (*Gender Trouble*) would identify as a parodic double-inversion by using contemporary surgical methods to achieve a series of standardized conceptions of beauty, which collectively amass her grotesque appearance. This paper proposes that the publicity generated through Orlan's tactical performative over-identification with conservative aesthetic ideals, by using her body as a site of improvisation and resistance, marks her politics as uniquely effective. While cynics view Orlan's media-laden exhibition as simply a marketing trick perpetuated by an attention hungry wannabe artist and her tabloidesque circus, this author finds the marketable component of Orlan's strategy as a necessary evil for truly transgressive politics.

Her deviance and subsequent publicity are the result of doing "what is allowed" in a strange sort of way. Orlan over-identifies with contemporary beautification techniques and splendor's traditional measurements by using the same methods as bourgeois suburbanites everywhere. Instead of simply violating and subverting modernist aesthetic categories, her Fontainebleu School *Diane Chasseresse* eyes, Francoise Gerard's *Psyche* nose, Botticelli's *Venus* chin, Moreau's *Europ* lips, and da Vinci's *Mona Lisa* forehead imitate bodily features of iconic art greatness. Her selection of the most celebrated body parts from Renaissance and Baroque periods of art is deliberate and originates from Greek sculptor Xeuxis, who selected several models and replicated ideal individual features to create the most stunning female forms in an effort to obtain the "ideal woman" (Przybylowicz and Sweet). The act of

70

plastic surgery alone, for most, is an attempt to obey normative beauty stan
dards. Orlan heightens the intensity of that act and reverses its intent by following Xeuxis' practice. She over-identifies with beauty and performs a
double-inversion of vanity's methods and standards. Orlan takes the desire to
perfect both art and the body to its logical extreme.

Her over-the-top acts elicit instinctual horror and shock in viewers
exposed to the gravity of aesthetic ideals. The visceral response Orlan creates
is exactly what Carey Lovelace outlines as ground breaking. Her work is
"like a trip to the dentist, it hurts but we know it's good for us" (13). During
these painful gallery performances, typically a third of the crowd will flee as
soon as the surgeon starts sawing. She undergoes local anesthesia and reads
and recites material during the satellite broadcast surgery, incorporating her
own poetry and philosophy combined with French psychoanalytic theory.
Throughout the performance, cameras zoom in on images of her skin being
cut away from her face, spread open, and turned inside out. Stretching the
skin *away* from the body differs from traditional views of plastic surgery,
where "implants 'lift' the skin and pull it taut" (Friedling 132). This inside-
out image is consistent with the psychoanalytic readings selected from
Jacques Lacan, Julia Kristeva, and Antonin Artaud. Revealing what Parveen
Adams describes as an "unmasking," Orlan "uses her head quite literally to
demonstrate an axiom of at least one strand of feminist thought: *there is nothing behind the mask"* (qtd. in Friedling 138). This move performs a theory of
masquerade and mimicry meant to challenge the matrix of the heterosexual
economy and reconsider the question of sexual difference.

By the end of Orlan's "unmasking" only a few people are left in the galleries in which her performances are showcased. Orlan envisions her shocking bodily performance as productively jarring audiences around the world in
order to unearth multifarious sites for resistance. She states:

> Art that interests me has much in common with—belongs to—resistance.
> It must challenge our preconceptions, disrupt our thoughts; it is outside
> the norms, outside the law, against bourgeois order: it is not there to cra-
> dle us, to reinforce comfort, to serve up against what we already know. It
> must take the risk of not being immediately accepted or acceptable. It is
> deviant, and in itself a social project. Art can, art must change the world,
> and it is its only justification. (qtd. in Zugazagoitia 215)

She destabilizes norms of dominant society and in doing so acts to
"reverse and displace" those norms (Butler, *Bodies That Matter*). Orlan's *serial*
performances are necessary for this reversal. In "Gender as Performance,"
Butler expands on this importance of repeatedly applying peculiarities that do
not simply "presume a subject," but instead "contest the very notion of the
subject." For Butler, performativity is "that aspect of discourse that has the
capacity to produce what it names . . . this production actually always happens
through a certain kind of repetition and recitation" ("Gender as Performance"
111–12). Butler adds to this distinction in the introduction to *Bodies That Mat-*

ter by reinforcing that performativity is not a single act. While some may argue that Orlan's work falls into the "primarily theatrical" camp, Orlan's work is not about the singular surgical event. Instead, her artistic mimicry displays Butler's desire for "reiteration of a norm or set of norms" (12). Parveen Adams contextualizes Orlan's project as mimetic inversion. Her body is more than a tool for a simple surgery; instead Orlan's body functions as both the site and the material, performing a mimetic reversal of concrete beautification standards.

> Orlan acts not just on her body, but upon her body, as an instance of a series. What happens is not just surgery. What happens is abstraction in the sense that cosmetic surgery always moves from the concrete to the abstract, from what exists to an image. . . . She has reversed the relations of portraiture; she has inverted the idea of mimesis. She compels nature to imitate art and the scalpel joins the repertoire of the artist. (Adams 123)

Now one must question why a repeated double-inversion of norms is an effective strategy for a change. Instead of denaturalizing conceptions of feminine it may simply render the performing subject as an unintelligible object. Mimicry also risks signifying identification with dominant powers and masking languages of the other, serving to deny narratives that attempt to speak truth to the pain of hegemonic acts. Orlan addresses these concerns by *using* the paradoxes and contradictions in cultural norms that determine who legitimately has access and "reason" to have elective procedures to alter their physical appearance in the first place. Much like the "amputee wannabes" analyzed in John Jordan's *Quarterly Journal of Speech* piece that seek elective removal of their limbs by making arguments to surgeons that resemble mainstream plastic surgery applicants, Orlan articulates cultural desires for completeness. Jordan's work situates the plastic body as a "rhetorically contested substance, with a variety of social agents engaged in efforts to shape its public meaning and, by extension, its corporeal form" (327). According to Jordan, the discourses rationalizing plastic surgery "frame contemporary debates about the human body, its entelechies, and the means by which individuals seek out and justify their desire for a 'better' body" (328).

Orlan's ironic efforts to attain a "better body" clearly demonstrate the extreme imperfection of creating and obtaining aesthetic standards. Her constantly shifting form attempts to oppose the social order. By being deviant and risking rejection, this performance of spectacle is an example of a site of oppositional struggle, appropriation, agency, and social activism. Asen's study of counterpublics illustrates that while counterpublics operate outside of stations of political power, "participants in the public sphere still engage in potentially emancipatory affirmative practice with the hope that power may be reconfigured" (424). In an effort to reconfigure that power, Orlan's methodological approach has changed to incorporate technology, play, and performance. In other words, her performance can be read as activism by using alternative and unexpected measures and media to convey different theoretical ideas and strategies.

Young-Cheon Cho contextualizes counterpublics as productive rhetori
cal and political acts that challenge traditional modes of communication that
exclude violence, pain, and the physical. For Cho, "there are rhetorical and
political dimensions of the body in pain" (11). By reading the rhetoric of
bodily self-immolation in South Korea, Cho shows how focusing on a body
in pain forces us "to reconsider the current discussion of the public sphere
that is usually limited to the bonds of reason and words" (12). Consistent
with the rhetoric of self-immolation, Orlan's bodily politics of pain certainly
challenge normative bounds of reason and intelligibility.

Orlan's move to highlight the body as a site of confrontation and struggle
echoes contemporary calls from feminist scholars to "return to the body."
Barbara Biesecker highlights the importance of theorizing the body as a site
of feminist voice and historical oppression in order to reinvigorate the space
between rhetoric and feminism. Sharon Crowley outlines how rhetorical
scholars are still preoccupied with the discursive turn and textual analysis
and subsequently neglect investigations attending to bodies and matter.
Crowley points out that the "definition and shaping of the body is the focal
point for struggles over the shape of power" (358).

Christina Foust's piece, "Interrupting Neo-liberal Globalization and
Hegemonic Subjectivity," contextualizes how one should retheorize social
change through the modality of bodily protest. Using women at the WTO
protest, or "radical cheerleaders," as the example, Foust explores how radical
agents conform to common ideas of "protest" while alternatively using their
bodies to make a spectacular protest that she explains "through an interpretive
theory of excess" (3). These "radical cheerleaders" wore mismatched and
homemade uniforms, performed gymnastic stunts, shook garbage bag pom-
poms, and taunted the police while opposing free trade. Their over the top juxtaposition of traditional and contemporary protest tactics challenged authorities who did not know what to do with the protestors' dialectical dance.

Orlan's work also functions as protest that combines traditional imagery
with anarchic radical politics. The juxtaposition of her tortured body with
blood, poetry, philosophy, stripping, and dancing is mind bogglingly unintelligible. Much like the "radical cheerleaders" Orlan stops viewers dead in their
tracks and maintains a truly captive audience. A "lively and distracting performance opens new space for resistance" (Foust 6).

Stanford-based performance and English professor Peggy Phelan would
disagree with claims that Orlan's strategy is transgressive, and argues that
once a performance is captured on tape it no longer constitutes an interrup-
tive act. Unlike a live performance, once an act is recorded it trades in its radical value and opens itself up to surveillance, definition, and containment.
According to Phelan, the temptation to read film and photography "*as* transparent record of performance is much like the temptation to read skin color
as racial identity, and gender categories as the consequence of sexual difference" (94). The repetitive viewing facilitated by recording allows the viewer
to simply fetishize the performer as "the reassuring familiar." Documented

images can assuage audiences' initial anxiety about their relationship to the performer as unknown Other. This knowability eliminates the productive anxiety the initial performance provoked.

Phelan's theory appears problematic for a few reasons. Even if a recording allows a performance to become less shocking over time, because the viewer can repeatedly watch and know the performance, arguably the first viewing still invokes productive anxiety-filled reflexivity. Also, the result of Phelan's politics would limit the scope of performances to a localized stage. Mediums that transmit and record acts expand both the reach and the makeup of available audiences. Phelan even concedes that "the degree to which the spectator is made conscious of what the film cannot and/or will not show is the degree to which the film, unwittingly, succeeds" (94). Orlan specifically and productively addresses Phelan's concerns about visual distancing, fetishization, and surveillance. During her live corporeal surgeries broadcast across the world, she takes phone calls and e-mails, addresses her audience, and embraces that her body is a political act subject to definition and surveillance. She directly addresses the anxiety that performance produces and sarcastically apologizes for disrupting the viewers' neat and tidy vision of aesthetics and gender:

> When Orlan ironically apologizes for causing pain to the spectator (the pain she insists on not feeling) and says, "Sorry, for having to make you suffer," pain still is the medium by which the spectator can be reached best. At the same time, what Orlan induces is not the confrontation with the pain deliberately endured by the artist, but far more the spectator's own reactions to pain's representation. (Zimmermann 38)

When Orlan screams "Long live morphium!" she acknowledges limiting pain for both her own body and the potentially distanced viewer.

Political theorist Paul Passavant points out that subjects who embrace surveillance through publicity-based bodily performances are anything but radical. Instead of being progressive, these strategies are inherently exclusionary, as they are only available to the already privileged. Passavant cites rhetorical scholar Michael Warner's theory of counterpublics and contends promotional hounds misconceptualize theories of the subject that result in alienation when "the bourgeois public sphere derives public value through an inverse relationship with the substantive characteristics of one's body" (117). Passavant's problem with obscene expression centers around a Foucaultian repressive hypothesis that contends only subjects already governed and recognized by laws, rights, and social norms can effectively position themselves as actually parodying civility. Only those within dominant conceptions of power can be seen as radically and purposely *performing* against normative ideals instead of simply *being* the obscene Other:

> Texts attach cultural meanings to bodies and prescribe different forms of government and freedom to those differently engraved bodies. . . . This is not, however, an instance of a passive subject being acted upon or

repressed by power. One gains a subject position that allows conduct. One seeks to invoke this form of discursive power in order to be authorized as a speaker. . . . In the moment of claiming a right, one also hails others as Americans with the aspiration that this call will incorporate a public that will recognize the practice in question as an instance of "free speech" rather than as a social problem that must be contained or eradicated for people's welfare . . . much depends on what sort of identity the law fixes upon the one claiming a right. (117–18)

Passavant's description of an acting subject, in a position of power, using bodily acts to challenge social norms of decency and civility articulates a limit to who has access to a recognized position of power in the first place, as well as how "the public" will receive a speaker who uses his or her subject position to challenge social norms. Passavant describes a public that will simply dismiss the radical actor as calling for a right or identity that exists outside legal norms. So for Passavant, the radical bodily act fails at the initial level of inclusion and the subsequent level of interpretation for those who successfully meet the prerequisite social status.

In a rhetorically interesting move, that is certainly consistent with Passavant's argument about dominant public interpretation, there are many that dismiss Orlan's work as egotistical, devoid of any artistic merit, and label her as mentally ill (Friedling 134). Attempts to disgrace important social questions as simply the products of crazed lunatics are nothing new. Malcolm X was mentally disqualified from Army service due to an alleged psychopathic personality disorder and sexual perversion. Joan of Arc is historically viewed as schizophrenic. Abbie Hoffman's followers were dismissed as pot-smoking hippies for protesting the Vietnam War by gathering around the Pentagon, chanting, and waiting for the building to levitate and turn orange. Michael Moore and others who question the government's role in 9/11 are automatically labeled conspiracy theorists. Those that question Orlan's psychological state may be asking a relevant question about her hunger for publicity, or as this author would contend, they are simply playing the interpretive public game that Passavant describes, by discrediting Orlan as uncivil, indecent, and just plain crazy.

Even if Passavant is correct, that only those who already have political power are recognized as performing a parodic act, he doesn't wholly discredit all the subversive attempts. There must be top-down resistance from those who have access to political power in addition to bottom-up work from marginalized subjects. If an act is discredited because of its accessibility, too many tactics for social change will be dismissed. Limiting tactical options simply allows the few that remain to be more easily recognized, regulated, and discredited. Additionally, we must remember that Orlan's work uses the very tools of bourgeois beauty making to demonstrate the perversity of their methods. She uses a standard of beauty to achieve what, in the end, is actually ugliness. Even though broadcasting plastic surgeries to make a larger point about aesthetics and gender norms is a limited methodological approach, the publicity generated by her work ensures her radical interpretation reaches broad audiences, which exponentially increases the likelihood of a successful message.

Even though some ingredients of Orlan's methodological stew contain mechanisms from mainstream advertising, like the enormous billboards reminiscent of 1950s Hollywood posters, such as featuring the surgeons and operating-room technicians, she uses them to embrace and over conform with consumptive practices. Utilizing billboard style advertising is another attempt for Orlan to blur the distinction between pure art and commodified production. According to her critique of traditional aesthetic standards, the pure art/commodified representation distinction is false. The products are the same. This strategy is clearly a critique, not simply a by-product, of traditional capitalism. Unfortunately, while the avant-garde is intended to challenge traditional consumptive practices, inevitably the museum gift shop commodifies it. Much "deviant" postmodern and avant-garde art inevitably becomes co-opted and consumerized. Trendy art circles only reinforce hierarchal standards of taste and, in the process, deprive the art of its transformative potential. Orlan clearly cannot avoid all capitalist appropriation and co-option, yet her tactics are so different that there is part of her performance that excessively exceeds normal methods easily recognizable by consumer materialism. Even though she still utilizes technology, peddles tickets to her show, and sells digitally modified photography, both her methodological approach and her "products" cannot be explained away and contained by hegemonic discourse. "Orlan's connecting body dramatically performs the grotesque cyborg that we are always becoming. It's a hybrid political/technological/organic body that is 100 percent recycled material; it is the materialization of its context" (Reault). Through disgust and revulsion, Orlan successfully avoids complete aesthetic distancing and indulgent consumption. Her grotesque performance makes it difficult to view her art as detached when she manipulates her body, instead of a separate medium.

Using her body as her canvas and as her *materials* challenges dominant creative and interpretive processes. "One cannot limit the 'body as material' to its respective 'use,' for there remains a part which stubbornly resists being used in the way paint, marble, soil or felt are manipulated in the artistic process" (Zimmermann 37). Orlan uses her lost bodily fluids as raw material and distractingly plays with the blood that appears to be everywhere. During one of her twelve surgeries she finger-painted images of her own disfigured face with the blood gushing from her chin. Using her own blood is "indisputably material evidence that her body is her artistic tool and the operating block her studio" (Cros, Le Bon, and Rehberg 152–53). She plays on her own disfiguration and even momentarily stops the surgery so that the surgeons can display bloodied sheets to the audience.

Bodily fluids can be metaphorically and performatively embraced as an embodiment of the corporeal organic body that produces productive rhetorical and physical excess in spite of their nature to remain culturally relegated to the secret and feminine. Orlan seeks to problematize the private aspects of the body including, but not limited to, artificial manipulation. She wants to "show that which is usually kept secret and to establish a comparison between the self-portrait done by the computer-machine and the self-portrait done by the body machine" (Orlan 9). She juxtaposes the "after" pictures of her bruised and bloody skin with an idealized "before" computer-manipulated image of her apparent outcome to demonstrate that not even the surgeon is in complete control of skin.

This series of twelve plastic surgeries is not the only time Orlan has used her own blood as raw material in order to make a point. In another performance entitled Medusa: A Documentary Study, Orlan held open her own genitals with a set of pincers. She used her menstrual blood to paint the pubic hair and create a spectacle drawing attention to a normally private biological function. Viewers' reactions were taped upon walking into the room where Orlan's vagina was framed by a magnifying glass and a sheet with a hole in it. After viewers left the exhibit designed to "turn men into stone" they were handed a copy of a text by Freud about castration anxiety.

Crowley's essay validates vaginal inquiry as an important mechanism to correct Freud's readings that articulate the defining feature of sex as the feminine lack. For Crowley, "Female genitalia raise further interesting questions about the confidence with which we can distinguish between bodily insides and outsides, as Luce Irigaray has convincingly demonstrated" (360). Both Crowley and Butler (*Gender Trouble*) problematize the historical conceptions of the mind/body split and the female/male split through a theory of excess that lends itself nicely to this author's reading of Orlan's work as articulating a unique and important rhetorical and physical excess. Fluid interpretations of traditional conservative visions of beauty allude to a rhetorical third space; where instead of a fixed binary, linguistic paradigms can produce new and productive counterhegemonic interpretations.

Rhetorical excess can be understood as a tactical strategy that utilizes the political potential of errancy. By focusing on instability, failure, gaps, and deviation, one can purposefully use "the technology of the negative" or find an empty space to twist the ambiguity and contradiction in language and culture for one's own ends. Beyond its political significance in violating or eluding patriarchal oppression, excess has theoretical significance, for it highlights rhetoric's capacity to unhinge the existing social order without the aid of hegemony. "Excess denotes a remainder. Like the numbers left dangling off the bracket in a long division problem, excess renders clean or total calculation difficult, if not impossible" (Foust 14). Not all of Orlan's acts can be explained away, or rendered intelligent by hegemonic forces. Her work simultaneously appropriates and exceeds plastic surgery and aesthetic standards of beauty by repeatedly applying their standards and following their standards to their logical (or illegal) extremes.

In addition to resisting the defining features of hegemonic power structures that empty radical pockets of opposition, Orlan still manages to magnify her argument through widespread publicity. In Henry Krips' article "Couching Politics: Zizek's Rules for Radicals," he cites publicity as an integral mechanism for successful acts of resistance. Without a medium for independent investigation any move that attempts to be radical would simply be ignored. Krips argues that this "publicity provides the engine that multiplies the effects of individual acts to the point that they take on social effects" (126). Through this multiplication, local acts of resistance become global. Overidentification as a strategy involves exposure. Her worldwide broadcasts allow Orlan to reach not only her immediate audience, but art galleries around the world. Both the application of surgery and the end result of her body are so strikingly different that she generates publicity as the subject of dozens of art books, videos, scholastic interpretations, and even an interactive DVD.

Without mass media coverage her work would simply be ignored by those outside of the performance art world. Instead, the hundreds of mainstream and scholarly articles, interviews, videos, and photographs enlarge the scope of her unorthodox spectacle. Her combination of radical and bourgeois methods resists narrow interpretations and conservative containment. While clearly Orlan's work will not bring around a gender revolution on its own, it certainly has a lot to teach activists and scholars about holding the attention of multifarious audiences and metaphorically shaking them silly. Krips reminds us that "ends are determined locally. . . . Which is not to deny the importance let alone the existence of global political struggles. But it is to deny that such struggles are a privileged let alone exclusive site of the political" (134). His vision affirms a localized politics that multiplies through publicity, which articulates referent radical acts as part and parcel of political struggle itself.

Works Cited

Adams, Parveen. *The Violence of Paint, The Emptiness of the Image.* New York: Routledge, 1996.

Asen, Robert. "Seeking the 'Counter' in Counterpublics." *Communication Theory* 10.4 (Nov. 2000): 424–27.

Biesecker, Barbara. "Towards a Transactional View of Rhetorical and Feminist Theory: Rereading Hélène Cixous's The Laugh of the Medusa." *Southern Communication Journal* 57 (Winter 1992): 86–96.

Butler, Judith. *Bodies That Matter: On the Discursive Limits of "Sex."* New York: Routledge, 1993.

———. "Gender as Performance." *A Critical Sense: Interviews with Intellectuals.* Ed. Peter Osborne. London: Routledge, 1993. 108–25.

———. *Gender Trouble: Feminism and the Subversion of Identity.* New York: Routledge, 1999.

Cho, Young-Cheon. "The Body in Pain in the Public Sphere: Embodiment, Self-Suspension, and Subaltern Counterpublics." International Communication Association Conference Papers. New York. 2005. 1–29.

Cros, E., L. Le Bon, and V. Rehberg, eds. "Chronophotology." *Orlan: Carnal Art.* Italy: Canale, 2004. 9–184.

Crowley, Sharon. "Afterword: The Material of Rhetoric." *Rhetorical Bodies.* Ed. J. Selzer and S. Crowley. Madison: U of Wisconsin P, 1999. 357–64.

Foust, Christina. "Interrupting Neo-liberal Globalization and Hegemonic Subjectivity: Exploring the Anarcha-Feminist Resistance of Radical Cheerleaders." Critical-Cultural Studies Division of the National Communication Association Conference, Boston, Massachusetts. Nov. 2005.

Friedling, Melissa. *Recovering Women: Feminisms and the Representation of Addiction.* Boulder, CO: Westview P, 2000.

Jordan, John W. "The Rhetorical Limits of the 'Plastic Body.'" *Quarterly Journal of Speech* 90.3 (2004): 327–58.

Krips, Henry. "Couching Politics: Zizek's Rules for Radicals." *Psychoanalysis, Culture, and Society* 9 (2004): 126–41.

Lovelace, Carey. "Orlan: Offensive Acts." *Performing Arts Journal* 17.49 (1995): 13–25.

Orlan. "'I Do Not Want to Look Like' Orlan On Becoming Orlan." *Women's Art* 9 (2000). <http://www.cicv.fr/creation_artistique/online/orlan/women/women.html>.

Passavant, Paul. "The Governmentality of Discussion." *Cultural Studies and Political Theory.* Ed. Jodi Dean. Ithaca: Cornell UP, 2000. 115–31.

Phelan, Peggy. *Unmarked the Politics of Performance.* New York: Routledge, 1993.

Przybylowicz, P., and E. Sweet. "Handouts for Imaging the Body Curriculum: Orlan Lecture Notes." Course Notes, Evergreen State College. 2006. Sept. 2007 <http://academic.evergreen.edu/curricular/imagingthebody/Handouts/OrlanLecture2006.pdf>.

Reault, Jeneatte. "Orlan and the Limits of Materialization." *J_Spot: Journal of Social and Political Thought* 1.2 (1993). <http://www.yorku.ca/jspot/2/jrault.htm>.

Warner, Michael. "Publics and Counterpublics." *Quarterly Journal of Speech* 88.4 (Nov. 2002): 444–54.

Zimmermann, Anja. "'Sorry for Having to Make You Suffer': Body, Spectator, and the Gaze in the Performances of Yves Klein, Gina Pane, and Orlan." *Discourse* 24.3 (Sept. 2002): 27–46.

Zugazagoitia, Julian. "Orlan: The Embodiment of Totality." *Orlan: Carnal Art.* Ed. E. Cros, L. Le Bon, and V. Rehberg. Italy: Canale, 2004. 215–23.

7

Audre Lorde's Embodied Invention

Lester C. Olson

Our labor has become more important than our silence.
—Audre Lorde, "A Song for Many Movements"

Beginning in late autumn 1977, a fundamental transformation is evident throughout the public life and advocacy of Audre Lorde, the internationally acclaimed poet, visionary activist, and public speaker, who described herself as a Black, lesbian, feminist, socialist, mother of two. At this time, Lorde received medical news concerning the diagnosis of a benign breast tumor followed soon afterward in 1978 by news of yet another tumor that was malignant. As she put it, she became "forcibly and essentially aware" of her "mortality" (*Cancer Journals* 20, *Sister Outsider* 41). So dramatic were the resulting changes in her public address that biographer Alexis De Veaux writes of Lorde as having lived two lives—one before the cancer diagnosis in 1978 and another after it: "The impact of cancer performed a transfiguration not only of Lorde's physicality but of her personality, creativity, and social activism" (xii). During this transformation, Lorde came to voice as a public speaker and regularly addressed diverse audiences between 1977 and 1992. A wounded warrior, she tapped her already finely honed talents as a poet to develop a fifteen-year career as an orator (for an overview, see Olson, "Audre").

Lorde's achievements as a public speaker during those fifteen years have been so overshadowed by her accomplishments as a poet that not until 1997 did any rhetoric scholar contribute a sustained discussion of any one single speech. This first article recounted her December 1977 masterpiece, "The Transformation of Silence into Language and Action," which she delivered to the Modern Language Association in Chicago (Olson, "On the Margins"). It was the first of several speeches that Lorde explicitly identified as a speech in its subsequently published form, though she had delivered public papers on earlier occasions. It is probable, however, that some earlier prose, such as Lorde's 1977 essay "Poetry Is Not a Luxury," was based, at least in part, on earlier orations (*Sister Outsider* 36–39). Before publication of the essay, Lorde had delivered similar remarks for a panel, Poetry Makes Something Happen:

The Poet as Teacher, Writer, and Person, at the Midwest Modern Language Association on October 27, 1977, when she appeared with May Sarton. To judge from a typed manuscript held at the Spelman College Archives in Atlanta, Georgia (which holds the most extensive collection of Lorde's unpublished papers), it appears that these conference remarks informed her subsequent essay, "Poetry Is Not a Luxury."

After the 1978 cancer diagnosis, Lorde continued to produce extraordinary poetry, but now, in addition, she developed an exceptional series of speeches that articulated her understandings of what it meant to her to be both "different" and marginalized, even within diverse minority communities in U.S. culture, as a Black, lesbian, feminist, mother in an interracial relationship (for Lorde's views concerning difference, see *Sister Outsider* 114–23, also Olson, "Liabilities"). She regularly explored how those who embody differences of race, sexuality, age, sex, and class might endeavor to survive, despite overt hostility toward such differences.

Long before Lorde's breast cancer diagnosis, her rhetorical invention in her poetry, including her early collections published by Poet's Press at New York, Broadside Press at Detroit, and Eidelon near San Francisco, had drawn primarily on her personal experiences. In her 1977 essay "Poetry Is Not a Luxury," she began,

> The quality of light by which we scrutinize our lives has direct bearing upon the product which we live, and upon the changes which we hope to bring about through those lives. It is within this light that we form those ideas by which we pursue our magic and make it realized. This is poetry as illumination, for it is through poetry that we give name to those ideas which are—until the poem—nameless and formless, about to be birthed, but already felt. (*Sister Outsider* 36)

After the cancer diagnosis and mastectomy, however, Lorde's public advocacy enacted an urgency, directness, and presence that might best be called embodied invention. In these respects, embodied invention is different in degree rather than kind from meditating on specific personal experiences. As she affirmed in a November 19, 1979, entry in her *Cancer Journals*, "There must be some way to integrate death into living, neither ignoring it nor giving in to it" (13).

This essay examines the ways in which Lorde's body, especially through dealing with breast cancer, became a resource for her embodied rhetorical invention. Her portrayals and representations of her experience of the disease were not merely a disruptive ordeal evident throughout her public address, consisting of speeches, poems, essays, open letters, and political pamphlets. Instead, through language and symbolic action, she actively transformed her fear, vulnerability, and even the surgical amputation of her breast into rhetorical resources as potential strengths and bases for concerted community actions. By embodied invention, I mean the ways in which Lorde's public advocacy drew resourcefully, explicitly, and extensively on her own naming of her bodily experiences in her physical, emotional, spiritual, intellectual, and symbolic relationships to others. Her bodily experiences became a wellspring that suffused her remarkably insightful and influential advocacy for political and social changes in U.S. culture.

At one end of a continuum for characterizing salient qualities of rhetorical invention, Lorde's explicit and extensive use of personal experience in her embodied invention can be contrasted sharply with the other end of this continuum, where rhetorical invention consists of impersonal, abstract, and disembodied systems, such as the universal *topoi* of the ancient Greek writers (e.g., from consequence) and even, to a somewhat lesser extent, the *loci* concerning the person and the act in the classical Roman treatises on rhetoric. For while the latter did concentrate on the specific corporeal person and his or her deeds, the person in Roman treatments of the *loci* transcended the specific sociological and political ramifications of race, sexuality, age, class, and sex as they interacted with each other systemically in an individual's lifetime. Such factors account, in part, for my reluctance to use classical Greek treatments of rhetorical invention, such as the *topoi*, to describe Lorde's processes of rhetorical invention, although the Roman discussions of *loci* may be nonetheless useful as I continue to study Lorde's embodied invention because of their emphasis on the person and the act and their relevance for considerations pertaining to justice. The classical and traditional treatments of rhetorical invention nonetheless have tended to presume a unitary speaking subject rather than a plural or multiple understanding of the individual as a cluster of symbolic selves in contingent, contextual relationship to others.

What follows is a preliminary exploration of an aspect of Lorde's public advocacy that deserves more expansive treatment than is possible here. This essay explores how her public address regularly enacted an activity that Lorde had described variously as a "distillation of experience" (*Sister Outsider* 36) or "metabolizing experience." In an 1986 interview with Marion Kraft, Lorde generalized, "Poetry—for me—is a way of living. It's the way I look at myself, it's the way I move through myselves [*sic*], my world, and it's the way I metabolize what happens and present it out again" (Kraft 146). Similarly, on January 23, 1981, during a recorded interview by Jennifer Abod, apparently in preparation for *A Radio Profile of Audre Lorde*, she observed that "When I write prose, I am a poet writing prose. . . . I am speaking of a whole way of looking at life, of moving into it, of using it, of dealing with myself and my experience. I am not speaking of living itself, I am speaking of a use of my living."

I will argue that Lorde transposed her sensibility as a poet into her oratory. This is not to insinuate that her embodied rhetorical invention was either hermetic or narcissistic, but rather that its richly textured layers of consequential public meanings had extensive personal resonances in the moment of her living. She embedded in public speeches oftentimes deeply personal feelings and convictions about her experiences of bias and hatred—especially during her collaborations and confrontations with others, when she would physically internalize emotions ranging from anger and fear to other, life-enhancing feelings, such as what she termed "the erotic" (*Sister Outsider* 53–59). I will first reflect briefly on bodily experiences in Lorde's rhetorical invention before concentrating on her general use of corporeal experiences as a potential common ground for diverse audiences and, ultimately, will consider how Lorde's experiences as a Black lesbian became a powerful resource in her embodied invention during her struggle with breast cancer.

BODILY EXPERIENCE IN LORDE'S RHETORICAL INVENTION

Bodily metaphors evoking life experiences permeated Lorde's public address, at times constituting a corporeal basis for grasping abstract and intangible ideas. She alluded, for instance, to misunderstandings and distortions of her ideas as them having been "bruised" (e.g., *Cancer Journals* 19, *Sister Outsider* 40), an evocative image probably suggesting violence or the threat of violence, or possibly a symptom of life-endangering diseases such as leukemia, to which she once alluded in *The Cancer Journals* (15), although she did not experience that specific illness. Even so, bruises are, more generally, a symptom of cancer. Lorde depicted hatred and biases impacting her life—heterosexism and homophobia, racism, ageism, and sexism—as "forms of human blindness" (e.g., *Sister Outsider* 45, *Cancer Journals* 12 and 14), a disability that her own severely limited eye sight had given a bodily resonance since her youth. But rather than summoning her physical condition to describe her own limited sight, her language called to mind the active and symbolic character of anyone's willed inability to see or recognize others: "Within this country where racial difference creates a constant, if unspoken, distortion of vision, black women have on one hand always been highly visible, and so, on the other hand, have been rendered invisible through the depersonalization of racism" (*Cancer Journals* 21, *Sister Outsider* 42). A commonplace manifestation of bias is to look through, past, and around despised or devalued others. In her view, Black women, both as individuals and a group, were "deeply scarred" by "virulent hostility" and hatred in U.S. culture (*Sister Outsider* 151). Her emphasis on being "scarred" visualized a bodily trace of previous physical injuries to portray analogous harms from bias offences, which do sometimes extend to physical assault, injury, and their legacies. Even if executed through vivid words or symbolic deeds, discrimination can nonetheless injure a person's symbolic sense of place, belonging, and security.

Lorde's public advocacy featured bodily experiences and senses, activities and desires ranging from dancing, birthing, and working to writing poetry and "moving into sunlight against the body of a woman I love" (*Sister Outsider* 58). She recognized, moreover, that powerful emotions such as anger, fear, affection, and what she termed "the erotic" ordinarily have powerful bodily dimensions, too. To deal effectively with her fear of others' hostility, Lorde claimed, "We can learn to work and speak when we are afraid in the same way we have learned to work and speak when we are tired" (*Cancer*

Journals 23, *Sister Outsider* 44), a line that might have special resonance for people familiar with fatigue, depression, and despair as both emotional and physiological consequences of prolonged ordeals or experiences of terror. In her journal and an essay, she wrote that sometimes she was "metabolizing hatred like a daily bread" (*Sister Outsider* 152), a disquieting bodily metaphor in that it suggested feeding on hatred.[1] Yet, as she recognized in her 1973 poem, "For Each of You," "Everything can be used / except what is wasteful / (you will need / to remember this when you are accused of destruction)" (*Sister Outsider* 127, *Collected* 59). In this regard, her "metabolizing" of others' hatred reversed its potentially devastating bodily and symbolic valences by refusing to internalize them and instead converted them into insights of abiding value. She spoke in public concerning potential uses for both the erotic and anger. Neither of these, she stressed, could be experienced second hand, and both, she argued, could become empowering resources, despite the stigmas associated with being either erotic or angry (see *Sister Outsider* 53–59, 124–33). For Lorde, her embodied invention provided a means to enact the transformation of such powerful feelings and bodily experiences into sources of poetic insight in the form of spoken or written language, symbolic deeds to be communicated to others as potential resources for community activism.

Perhaps because Lorde's own body needed, throughout her entire lifetime, to survive diverse discriminatory, oppressive, and supremacist deeds, she was synthetically able to recognize practices adversely affecting varied groups so similarly, but not identically, that in her rhetorical invention those practices, or symbolic deeds, became a potential common ground among vulnerable communities—regardless of others' tidy distinctions and clear hierarchies among oppressions. On some occasions, she commented on the necessity of resisting certain fragmenting pressures to sort out and give priority to specific components of her identity. In a speech during 1980, for example, Lorde commented:

> As a Black lesbian feminist comfortable with the many different ingredients of my identity, and a woman committed to racial and sexual freedom from oppression, I find I am constantly being encouraged to pluck out some one aspect of myself and present this as the meaningful whole, eclipsing or denying the other parts of self. But this is a destructive and fragmenting way to live. My fullest concentration of energy is available to me only when I integrate all the parts of who I am, openly, allowing power from particular sources of my living to flow back and forth freely through all my different selves, without the restrictions of externally imposed definition. (*Sister Outsider* 120–21)

This idea was thematic in Lorde's public advocacy. And yet, Lorde nonetheless felt tensions between self and other, even within already vulnerable social groups, because diverse minority communities are capable of practicing bias across other social differences. In her *Cancer Journals*, she wrote in an entry on October 23, 1979, "I am defined as other in every group I'm a part of. The outsider, both strength and weakness. Yet without community there is certainly no liberation, no future, only the most vulnerable and temporary armistice between me and my oppression" (12–13).

While, with evident ambivalence, Lorde both recognized and resisted such fracturing pressures, and while she nonetheless acknowledged differences within vulnerable social groups, on other occasions she sometimes transposed explicit parallels from one group's commonplace experiences to shed light on other, overlapping groups' concerns (e.g., see *Sister Outsider* 113, 114–15, and *Burst* 21).[2] For example, to encourage Black men and women to comprehend the terror that lesbians routinely experienced from publicly heterosexual populations, including Black heterosexuals, she wrote about bodily presence in an essay for the *Black Scholar*'s readership: "To the racist, Black people are so powerful that the presence of one can contaminate a whole lineage; to the heterosexist, lesbians are so powerful that the presence of one can contaminate the whole sex" (*Sister Outsider* 51). Her rhetorical technique of foregrounding many Black people's firsthand understanding of racism provided the *Black Scholar*'s audience with an experiential basis for common ground with a similar, but not identical, pattern of exaggerated fear that lesbians and gay men encounter routinely, regardless of race. Sometimes such bias was performed by Black people in ways that consequently rehearsed and perpetuated the oppressive practice, thereby harming both overlapping groups by keeping the practice available for use (which was her point).

In summary, Lorde featured corporeal experiences in her bodily metaphors to make abstract and intangible ideas—such as discrimination and bias—vivid and present to her audiences, whether as "bruises" or "blindness." Her rhetoric portrayed bodily experiences and activities, such as feeding or dancing, to characterize specific moments in her embodied invention. An illustration of this was her active "metabolizing" of others' hatred into her own life-affirming nourishment and, ultimately, into her public advocacy. To Lorde, emotions entailed both psychological and bodily dimensions, especially when they were internalized as responses to others' deeds. She drew on bodily experiences of her activities and emotions (ranging from the "uses of anger" to "the erotic") to suggest common ground across differences, to identify similar practices adversely impacting diverse groups, and to encapsulate her ideas about public and political matters. Examples of the latter included evoking "the erotic" to criticize capitalism or "the uses of anger" to characterize intellectual labor during collaboration with others.

Yet using language and symbolic deeds to portray bodily experiences, whether metaphorically or literally, in public advocacy was complicated for Lorde's embodied invention in that experiences and representations of them are always informed by inherited ideologies. This factor made it necessary for her explicitly to connect the personal and the political with exacting discernment. Fraught with hazards precisely because of their ideological dimensions, the language and symbolic actions that Lorde used to convey her bodily experiences meant situating herself explicitly within different, overlapping groups, whose demographic affiliations contributed to fracturing pressures and double binds (such as "choosing" between the extremes of isolation and imagined community), even as she sought to sort out what it meant to be a Black, lesbian, feminist, socialist, mother of two, including one boy, in an interracial relationship. Yet, Lorde found nonetheless powerful corporeal resources for her embodied invention precisely through her varied and multiple relationships to others. Drawing explicitly on her recognition of her plural selves, she would transpose insights from one sociological group's commonplace experiences onto another's as potential common ground or, at least, the recognition of similar social practices.

CORPOREAL EXPERIENCES AS POTENTIAL COMMON GROUND

To illustrate some further observations concerning Lorde's embodied invention, I have selected three quotations, all taken from her 1980 book, *The Cancer Journals*, which chronicled the poet's experiences of undergoing a mastectomy (for essays on breast cancer in Lorde's *oeuvre*, see Wear and Hartman). The first excerpt is her entry for December 29, 1978: "What is there possibly left for us to be afraid of, after we have dealt face to face with death and not embraced it? Once I accept the existence of dying, as a life process, who can ever have power over me again?" (25). Her poignant, maxim-like reflection fused powerful personal emotions, such as the fear of death, with her public reasoning concerning her entwined bodily and symbolic experiences of vulnerability and power. A post-mastectomy woman, Lorde articulated insights concerning her own prospects for continued living in ways that synthesized idealism and materialism, mind and corporeal body. But note, too, how Lorde shifted among pronouns: "What is there possibly left for *us* to be afraid of, after *we* have dealt face to face with death and not embraced it? Once *I* accept the existence of dying, as a life process, who can ever have power over *me* again?" (emphasis added). Who are the *we* and the *us*? And, just as important, who is the *I* and the *me*?

I want to suggest that all these pronouns were ambiguous and evocative in suggesting a corporeal common ground with her audiences of diverse women. Lorde's pronouns tapped a densely woven combination of rhetorical concepts that here I will only mention: presence (Perelman and Olbrechts-Tyteca 116–120; Gross), experience (Scott), enactment (Campbell and Jamieson), performance (Austin), habitus (Bourdieu), and embodiment (Morris). Her pronouns, moreover, pertained to the activity of speaking for and about others—sometimes inhabiting categories along with her as one of her audience members, other times noting the differences between them (Alcoff). This activity entailed risks of appropriation and false identification on the one hand or exaggerated barricades of difference and division on the other (Spelman). And yet, Lorde was emphatic that limitations of personal experience should not be allowed to become an excuse for disengagement with others, because it was one among varied ways of learning and knowing. She noticed, for example, the absence of literature by "women of Color" in

women's studies courses, because of the "excuse" that "they are too difficult
to understand, or that classes cannot 'get into' them because they come out of
experiences that are 'too different.'" She added with incisive, evident humor,

> I have heard this argument presented by white women of otherwise quite
> clear intelligence, women who seem to have no trouble at all teaching
> and reviewing work that comes out of the vastly different experiences of
> Shakespeare, Molière, Dostoyefsky, and Aristophanes. Surely, there must
> be some other explanation. (*Sister Outsider* 117)

Yet experience, to Lorde, was a touchstone, resource, or fount for generating her poems, essays, open letters, political pamphlets, speeches, and
"biomythography." In a 1983 interview with Karla Jay, Lorde commented on
this last term, "biomythography," which she coined in 1982 to describe *Zami*,
a book-length recollection of being young, Black, and lesbian in New York
City during the 1950s. Lorde objected to Jay's questioning about a "biomythography" being "accurate" by affirming, somewhat defensively, that, while
the experiences in the book were not necessarily only her own, they were
"accurate" representations of her life experiences and the lives of those close
to her:

> But I am giving an accurate account of a time and a place, of a connec-
> tion between black women with African roots, in terms of how we raise
> our children, how we maintain strength, how we find ourselves, the ques-
> tion of the Black Goddess, the creator, in all of us, what happens with
> home life. (Jay 110, see especially 109–10)

Lorde's position might have anticipated certain particulars in Joan W.
Scott's insights about evidence from experience in that the very process of
naming and describing life experiences for any "I" is necessarily ideological
and communal, if only because the language and available narratives are
inherited, cultural resources. As such, they transcend any individual's experiences and become necessary conditions for communicating about them.
Lorde's "I" is consciously composed of plural "selves" and is communal, not
merely individual (e.g., *Cancer Journals* 15). She asserted in *The Cancer Journals*, "I could die of difference, or live—myriad selves" (11). Lorde's "we" is
diverse, particular, and social. Despite the fact that she did sometimes speak
as a woman about "women" in general, her "we" is not necessarily essential-
ist, because she did regularly differentiate within such demographic groups
(e.g., see *Cancer Journals* 10).[3]

Lorde's attention to differences within social groups can be illustrated
with a second excerpt, also taken from *The Cancer Journals*, which consists of
Lorde's first two sentences from the introduction: "Each woman responds to
the crisis that breast cancer brings to her life out of a whole pattern, which is
the design of who she is and how her life has been lived. The weave of her
everyday existence is the training ground for how she handles crisis" (9).
These opening lines focused on gender as a cultural factor in women's socialization as a potential resource for inventing each woman's particular response

to undergoing a mastectomy. In other words, gender socialization and biological sex blur together differently through each woman's experience, depending on the varied particularities of each woman's life situation. As I read Lorde's first few pages, beginning with denial ("nothing much has occurred"), "imposed silence," "anger and pain and fear," "isolation," "shame" and, at the same time, the difficult processes of coming to "voice," becoming visible and being "recognized," naming one's experiences for oneself to be "respected" and to enter into community, reclaiming agency and power, working in community as embattled, if wounded, "warriors," I began to ponder a more focused question: In what specific ways, if any, were Lorde's earlier experiences of becoming a life-affirming Black lesbian a potential resource for her embodied invention in dealing with breast cancer?

Let's turn now to a third excerpt, also from the introduction to *The Cancer Journals*: "imposed silence about any area of our lives is a tool for separation and powerlessness" (9). When Lorde made these comments concerning the "travesty of prosthesis" (9) and, later, when she poignantly refused a Reach for Recovery volunteer's emphatic expectation that she conceal her amputation with a pale, pink, false breast for the sake of "the morale of the office" (59), did Lorde's life experiences as life-affirming Black lesbian shape the contours of her rhetorical invention, her embodied, generative response by words and deeds to the crisis concerning breast cancer? I believe that it did, and the impetus for this essay evolved out of that conviction and, later, by extension, the broader ramifications for reflection on embodied invention throughout Lorde's entire career as a public advocate. The next section considers Lorde's embodied invention as a Black lesbian, an invention that helped generate her insightful, provocative views on breast cancer.

BLACK LESBIAN EXPERIENCES AS A POWERFUL RESOURCE FOR EMBODIED INVENTION

This section explores how Lorde drew on her particular experiences as a Black lesbian as an invaluable resource for her embodied rhetorical invention in dealing with breast cancer. For instance, just as invisibility of lesbians tended (and still does) to make such women vulnerable and isolated from each other, Lorde commented on how breast cancer survivors' use of prosthesis made them invisible to each other and, consequently, vulnerable and isolated from communities of similarly situated women. Just as lesbianism, when kept secret or internalized as shameful, made the prospects of meaningful political or social change minute, so too the secrecy and internalized shame surrounding breast cancer severely circumscribed women's ability to change adverse medical practices and harmful cultural norms. The discrepancies between appearance and authentic selves and the battling for survival against all odds likewise were commonalities suggesting that her earlier experiences with becoming visible as a lesbian informed her later sensibility on becoming visible as a cancer survivor. As an integral part of their liberation struggles, moreover, both groups needed also to confront their own complicity by comporting with externally imposed expectations (on complicity, see Mathison; McPhail; Strine).[4]

And yet, Lorde suffused her experiences as a Black lesbian in particular with those of being a woman generally in U.S. culture to conclude that, for her, prosthesis was both a metaphor and an index of women's predicament within a patriarchal culture. After her confrontation with a Reach for Recovery volunteer, Lorde observed: "As I sat in my doctor's office trying to order my perceptions of what had just occurred, I realized that the attitude towards prosthesis after breast cancer is an index of this society's attitudes towards women in general as decoration and externally defined sex object" (*Cancer Journals* 60). That this external expectation was being imposed on Lorde by another woman dramatized differences between these women, even though each of them had endured a mastectomy. The conflict also illustrated the capacity of one woman to oppress another woman because of internalized, cultural conventions. Indeed, in Lorde's view, the volunteer's expectations became a synecdoche for those of the culture. She explained, "Attitudes toward the necessity for prostheses after breast surgery are merely a reflection of those attitudes within our society towards women in general as objectified and depersonalized sexual conveniences" (*Cancer Journals* 64). The "pale pink breast-shaped pad" was also the "wrong color" for her (*Cancer Journals* 42, 44) because its color presumed whiteness, which added racism to the conflict between women.

Moreover, to Lorde, use of a prosthesis meant sacrificing her own internal needs and desires for embodied presence to accommodate the externally imposed expectations of others: "The real truth is that certain other people feel better with that lump stuck into my bra, because they do not have to deal with me nor themselves in terms of mortality nor in terms of difference" (*Cancer Journals* 64). Beyond Lorde's recognition of others' capacity for denial with its ramifications for complacency, Lorde amplified additional, practical consequences of this difference between internal needs and external expectations:

> In order to keep me available to myself, and able to concentrate my energies upon the challenges of those worlds through which I move, I must consider what my body means to me. I must also separate those external demands about how I look and feel to others, from what I really want for my own body, and how I feel to my selves. (*Cancer Journals* 65)

The use of a prosthesis, for Lorde, colluded with externally imposed expectations for women, generally, and for lesbians, in particular, to be invisible, to conform, and to fit in with received notions of bodily presence, appearance, and public conduct. All of this was imposed on a post-mastectomy woman immediately after a surgery when, in Lorde's opinion, reclaiming agency and embodied presence were paramount.

At length, Lorde commented on certain tensions between presence and absence, visibility and invisibility, by contemplating these stark alternatives in relationship to internalized shame, a term that links a commonplace, internalized response to cancer, regardless of sexuality, with certain taboos concerning lesbianism. Notice the layers of potential meanings in her comment: "A mastectomy is not a guilty act that must be hidden in order for me to regain acceptance or protect the sensibilities of others. Pretense has never brought about lasting change or progress" (*Cancer Journals* 65). Guilt and shame, concealment of certain deeds to secure a false "acceptance" by others, valuing the "sensibilities of others" above one's own needs—these phrases powerfully transposed commonplace experiences among many lesbians at the time onto post-mastectomy women's experiences as potential common ground in Lorde's rhetorical invention. She expanded: "Prosthesis offers the empty comfort of 'Nobody will know the difference.' But it is that very difference which I wish to affirm, because I have lived it, and survived it, and wish to share that strength with other women" (*Cancer Journals* 61). Then, in a shift of pronouns from "I" to "we," Lorde generalized: "If we are to translate the silence surrounding breast cancer into language and action against this scourge, then the first step is that women with mastectomies must become visible to each other" (*Cancer Journals* 61). Such visibility to each other was consequential for entering into communities positioned to deal meaningfully with breast cancer and, just as important, to affirm personal pride and worth in the aftermath of surgery. In contrast, Lorde amplified the deleterious ramifications of complicity:

> By accepting the mask of prosthesis, one-breasted women proclaim ourselves as insufficients dependent upon pretense. We reinforce our own isolation and invisibility from each other, as well as the false complacency of a society which would rather not face the results of its own insanities. In addition, we withhold that visibility and support from one another which is such an aid to perspective and self-acceptance. (*Cancer Journals* 61)

As a post-mastectomy woman, Lorde stressed the life-enhancing value of bodily presence as visibly different—one-breasted or no-breasted—women, while she called attention to another tension between the extremes of difference, on the one hand, and apparent similarity or conformity to tacit norms, on the other. To amplify this tension, she gave it an additional rhetorical edge by turning to the alternatives between the authentic or mere appearance. She observed:

> Women have been programmed to view our bodies only in terms of how they look and feel to others, rather than how they feel to ourselves, and how we wish to use them. We are surrounded by media images portraying women as essentially decorative machines of consumer function, constantly doing battle with rampant decay. (*Cancer Journals* 64)

The stark alternative between authenticity and appearance gave Lorde's readership yet another alternative between reclaiming agency and acquiescing with passivity, as well as between being a self-defining adult or accepting infantilization by others (e.g., *Cancer Journals* 64). Lorde affirmed: "I cannot wear a prosthesis right now because it feels like a lie more than merely a costume, and I have already placed this, my body under threat, seeking new ways of strength and trying to find the courage to tell the truth" (*Cancer Journals* 60–61). Openness and candor, visibility and pride, integrity and self-respect—Lorde apparently transposed all of these life-affirming qualities from her prior experience as a Black lesbian during her subsequent embodied invention concerning breast cancer.

Rejecting the appearance of normalcy, the public "lie" through a concealment made possible by prosthesis, Lorde turned to the value of public engagement and group strength as stark alternatives to living in secrecy, shame, and vulnerable isolation. She averred:

> For as we open ourselves more and more to the genuine conditions of our lives, women become less and less willing to tolerate those conditions unaltered, or to passively accept external and destructive controls over our lives and our identities. Any short-circuiting of this quest for self-definition and power, however well-meaning and under whatever guise, must be seen as damaging, for it keeps the post-mastectomy woman in a position of perpetual and secret insufficiency, infantilized and dependent for her identity upon an external definition by appearance. In this way women are kept from expressing the power of our knowledge and experience, and through that expression, developing strengths that challenge those structures within our lives that support the Cancer Establishment. (*Cancer Journals* 58)

Consistent with this insight, the final section of *The Cancer Journals* moved from Lorde's personal experience of a mastectomy to contemplate economic and other systemic roots of breast cancer and its treatment. Perhaps because it is profitable, the American Cancer Society, Lorde suggested, "has consistently focused upon treatment rather than prevention of cancer" (*Cancer Journals* 71).

Lorde's embodied rhetoric enacted her decision to become an active, wounded warrior, not a passive, suffering victim, by affirming: "When I dare to be powerful, to use my strength in the service of my vision, then it becomes less important whether or not I am unafraid" (*Cancer Journals* 15). She asserted:

> I refuse to have my scars hidden or trivialized behind lambswool [*sic*] or silicone gel. I refuse to be reduced in my own eyes or in the eyes of others from warrior to mere victim, simply because it might render me a fraction more acceptable or less dangerous to the still complacent, those who believe if you cover up a problem it ceases to exist. I refuse to hide my body simply because it might make a woman-phobic world more comfortable. (*Cancer Journals* 60)

By her presence as a one-breasted woman warrior, explicitly inspired by the Amazons of Dahomey (*Cancer Journals* 35, also 28, 45, *Sister Outsider* 49), Lorde enacted her own liberation, overtly rejecting complicity with her oppression by her bodily presence and by offering to her readers a model in public action whose words and deeds depended on her embodied rhetorical invention.

CONCLUSION

Although this necessarily brief essay has concentrated on how Lorde's Black lesbian sensibility became an embodied resource for her particular response to breast cancer, there were other periods of momentous changes in her living that permeated her public advocacy. Throughout Lorde's lifetime, she negotiated difficult conflicts between being both an individual and an underrecognized part of various vulnerable communities as a Black, a woman, a lesbian, a feminist, a socialist, and a mother, whose public virago persona was that of a wounded warrior. At present, it is possible to identify at least four periods of deep and intense transformation in Lorde's embodied invention. The first of these sea changes in her sensibility occurred in 1968, during the six weeks that she was a Poet-in-Residence at Tougaloo College in Jackson, Mississippi, where she taught Black students and first met Frances Clayton (see *Sister Outsider* 88–93). It was then that she actively and dramatically sought to draw upon the diverse aspects of herself in synthesizing, integrated ways, not only because she was working with "young Black poets," but also because it was "a crisis situation" and "a siege situation," with white people acting out of racial hostility overtly nearby.[5] A second sea change in Lorde's bodily basis for her rhetorical invention transpired in the early 1970s, about the time that she published her expressly lesbian, erotic "Love Poem" in *Ms Magazine* (*Collected* 127, see *Sister Outsider* 98–99). Though she believed that she had not been secretive concerning her lesbian sexuality—and certain earlier poems, such as "Martha" and "On a Night of the Full Moon," attest to this (*Collected* 37–44, 172, 198–205)—"Love Poem" was a public statement with profound ramifications for her as a faculty member at John Jay College (*Sister Outsider* 98). This poem also had consequential ramifications for her relationship to her publisher at Broadside Press, which had launched the careers of several accomplished Black poets, mostly men (see Thompson 130–31).[6] The third and most dramatic sea change in Lorde's bodily basis for her rhetorical invention resulted from her confrontation with cancer and its ramifications for her own mortality. A fourth pivotal period is more difficult to pinpoint precisely by year, but its broad outlines extend from the late 1970s until the mid-1980s, when she spoke often as a featured poet or keynote speaker at feminist conferences dominated by white and heterosexual women. The most dramatic, public conflict occurred at *The Second Sex* Conference in 1979 (see *Sister Outsider* 110–13), but its ramifications persisted for a time as she sorted through the magnitude of racism, classism, and heterosexism within women's communities as obstacles and barricades for her work. A more comprehensive exploration of Lorde's embodied invention would need to consider each of these precipitating moments in her living, and possibly others.

In a preliminary way, this essay has proposed and sketched the idea of embodied invention, primarily by characterizing it as a rhetorical process for generating public advocacy. Embodied invention draws extensively and explicitly on personal experiences as a resource during the production of ideas and deeds to be expressed through language and symbolic action to others. Such embodied invention for use in public address explicitly reflects on the sociological and political factors impinging ideologically on the rhetor's experiences and plural identities within a specific history and culture. In other words, embodied invention attends to personal experiences as intrinsically social and political, however personal or individual experiences might seem, if only in a bodily or corporeal way. Embodied invention tends to recognize, moreover, that language and symbolic actions provide the cultural conditions for the expression, representation, or communication of experiences to others. Consequently, while experiences might seem individual or merely personal, they are nonetheless profoundly cultural as they are recognized, understood, and portrayed through communal resources.

Future scholarship on embodied invention, so defined and considered, will need to engage such matters as standpoint epistemology, the idea that people construct what they know from specific locations, histories, and life experiences. In addition, future scholarship might examine the complicated processes of centering on an advocate's affiliations with his or her communities rather than either assimilating uncritically with others or accepting detrimental representations by others as different, marginal, or other—processes that also surface within apparently dominant communities, however unnoticed. Last, but not least, scholarship on embodied invention should scrutinize relationships among such rhetorical concepts as presence, experience, enactment, performance, habitus, embodiment, and identification. This list of germane concepts is meant to be evocative and suggestive, not exhaustive or conclusive.

Embodied invention can be situated on one end of a continuum for varied approaches to rhetorical invention with the other end of this continuum consisting of disembodied, impersonal, and abstract approaches, such as the classical *topoi*. Attention to embodied invention can help critics of public advocacy to better synthesize an author's personal biography in descriptive accounts of her or his public address, especially transformations evident in deeds and words during moments of major change or precipitating events. In the case of a speaker such as Audre Lorde, who was situated politically and socially as different against oftentimes unspoken or unrecognized norms, which tended to presume that power resided within whiteness, maleness, heterosexuality, affluence, and the like, it might be particularly evident that there were systemic, cultural factors impinging on her plural identities. And yet such embodied invention might nonetheless be particularly powerful precisely when it goes unnoticed as presumed or normative, a factor suggesting that future scholarship on embodied invention should concentrate on how presumptions about whiteness, maleness, heterosexuality, affluence, and the like may inform the embodied invention by relatively privileged speakers, writers, and social activists who, at times, might presume to speak or write in a universal voice.

Notes

[1] Lorde's germane journal entries on March 6, 1983, were apparently for "Eye to Eye: Black Women, Hatred, and Anger" (the phrase appears again in *Sister Outsider* 152). Lorde's journal for December 21, 1982–August 7/8, 1983 is held at the Spelman College Archives, Spelman College, Georgia. This specific journal is useful for appreciating her complex views concerning the uses of anger.

[2] Two journal entries made explicit Lorde's conscious transposition across different and/or overlapping social groups. The earliest of the two was in a journal for the period extending from November 1977 until May 30, 1978, in which Lorde endeavored on February 13, 1978, to draw on ideas concerning a "Black Aesthetic" to point to the existence of a "Black female aesthetic." Later, in another journal entry on June 21, 1984, concerning the "Poet as Outsider," Lorde explicitly transposed ideas concerning the "Black Aesthetic" into reflections on "the lesbian aesthetic." She wrote, "In the same way as the De Americanization of Black People lies at the heart of the Black Aesthetic so does the de male ization [*sic:* there are spaces after "de" and "male"] of women lie[s] at the heart of the lesbian aesthetic. Categories cross & merge." These two journals, which are held at the Spelman College Archives, are identified currently with round blue stickers numbered "26" and "62" respectively (which are perhaps a temporary means of identifying them until they are processed at the archives).

[3] For a concise discussion of the plural selves and differences within social groups, see Hammond 26–44, especially 30–31.

[4] Because some might find it hard to recognize Black lesbianism as a resource for dealing with breast cancer, I have endeavored in this section to provide ample quotations as evidence to support the section's central claim. I have also made a conscious decision to keep Lorde's voice in the foreground; her voice is deliberately more predominant than my own.

[5] Lorde made the comments on a video among materials transferred by Gloria Joseph to Audre Lorde's papers held at the Spelman College Archives, Spelman College, Atlanta, Georgia.

[6] Julius E. Thompson calculated that "Broadside published at least 270 men and 140 women writers during its first decade. Men were clearly the dominant group published, and authored 66 percent of all Broadside publications produced in the mid-sixties to the mid-seventies, compared to only 34 percent for women" (126). On the political situation for Lorde, see *Sister Outsider* 98–99 and De Veaux, *Warrior Poet* 130–31 and 141.

Works Cited

Abod, Jennifer. Interview with Audre Lorde. Spelman College Archives, Audre Lorde Collection. Audiotape. Spelman College, Atlanta, GA. 23 Jan. 1981.

Alcoff, Linda. "The Problem of Speaking for Others." *Cultural Critique* 20 (Winter 1991–2): 5–32.

Austin, James. "Lecture I." *How To Do Things With Words*. 2nd ed. Ed. J. O. Urmson and Marina Sbisà. Cambridge: Harvard UP, 1975. 1–11.

Bourdieu, Pierre. "Authorized Language: The Social Conditions for the Effectiveness of Ritual Discourse." *Language and Symbolic Power*. Ed. John Thompson, Gino Raymond, and Matthew Adamson. Cambridge: Harvard UP, 1991. 107–16.

Campbell, Karlyn Kohrs, and Kathleen Hall Jamieson, eds. "Introduction to *Form and Genre*." *Form and Genre: Shaping Rhetorical Action*. Falls Church, VA: Speech Communication Association, 1978. 16–32.

De Veaux, Alexis. *Warrior Poet: A Biography of Audre Lorde*. New York: Norton, 2004.

Gross, Alan G. "Presence as Argument." *Rhetoric Society Quarterly* 35.2 (Spring 2005): 5–21.

Hammond, Karla M. "Audre Lorde Interview" [original interview in October 1978]. *Denver Quarterly* 16.1 (1981): 1–27. Rpt. in *Conversations with Audre Lorde.* Ed. Joan Wylie Hall. Jackson: U of Mississippi P, 2004. 26–44.

Hartman, Stephanie. "Reading the Scar in Breast Cancer Poetry." *Feminist Studies* 30.1 (Spring 2004): 155–77.

Jay, Karla. "Speaking the Unspeakable: Poet Audre Lorde" [original interview on 5 Oct. 1983]. *Gay News* [Philadelphia]. 15 Mar. 1984. Rpt. in *Conversations with Audre Lorde.* Ed. Joan Wylie Hall. Jackson: U of Mississippi P, 2004. 109–14.

Kraft, Marion. "The Creative Use of Difference" [original interview in 1986]. *EAST. Englisch Amerikanische Studien* 3.4 (Dec. 1986): 549–56. Rpt. in *Conversations with Audre Lorde.* Ed. Joan Wylie Hall. Jackson: U of Mississippi P, 2004. 146–53.

Lorde, Audre. *A Burst of Light.* Ithaca, NY: Firebrand, 1988.

———. *The Cancer Journals.* San Francisco: Spinsters Ink/Aunt Lute, 1980.

———. *The Collected Poems of Audre Lorde.* New York: Norton, 1997.

———. *Sister Outsider: Essays & Speeches by Audre Lorde.* Freedom, CA: Crossing, 1984.

———. *Zami: A New Spelling of My Name.* Watertown, MA: Persephone, 1982.

Mathison, Maureen. "Complicity as Epistemology: Reinscribing the Historical Categories of 'Woman' Through Standpoint Feminism." *Communication Theory* 7.2 (1997): 149–61.

McPhail, Mark. "(Re)constructing the Color Line: Complicity and Black Conservativism." *Communication Theory* 7.2 (1997): 162–77.

Morris, Margaret Kissam. "Audre Lorde: Textual Authority and the Embodied Self." *Frontiers* 23.1 (2002): 168–88.

Olson, Lester C. "Audre Geraldine Lorde (1934–1992), Professor of English, Poet, Black Lesbian, and Socialist." *American Voices: An Encyclopedia of Contemporary Orators.* Ed. Bernard K. Duffy and Richard W. Leeman. Westport, CT: Greenwood, 2005. 285–92.

———. "Liabilities of Language: Audre Lorde Reclaiming Difference." *Quarterly Journal of Speech* 84.4 (Nov. 1998): 448–70.

———. "On the Margins of Rhetoric: Audre Lorde Transforming Silence into Language and Action." *Quarterly Journal of Speech* 83.1 (Feb. 1997): 49–70.

Perelman, Chaim, and Lucie Olbrechts-Tyteca. *The New Rhetoric: A Treatise on Argumentation.* Trans. John Wilkinson and Purcell Weaver. Notre Dame: U of Notre Dame P, 1969.

Scott, Joan W. "On Experience." *Feminists Theorize the Political.* Ed. Judith Butler and Joan W. Scott. New York: Routledge, 1992. 22–40.

Spelman, Elizabeth. "Changing the Subject: On Making Your Suffering Mine." *Fruits of Sorrow: Framing Our Attention to Suffering.* Boston: Beacon, 1997. 113–32.

Strine, Mary. "Cultural Diversity and the Politics of Inquiry: Response to Mathison and McPhail." *Communication Theory* 7.2 (1997): 178–85.

Thompson, Julius E. *Dudley Randall, Broadside Press, and the Black Arts Movement in Detroit, 1960–1995.* Jefferson, NC: McFarland, 1999.

Wear, Delese. "'Your breasts/sliced off': Literary Images of Breast Cancer." *Women and Health* 20.4 (1993): 81–100.

8

La Frontera y El Chamizal
Liminality, Territoriality, and Visual Discourse

Brian J. McNely

The Chamizal National Memorial is situated near the bustling downtown area of El Paso, Texas, a few steps away from the Border Highway and the Bridge of the Americas, one of the many commercial and cultural links between El Paso and Ciudad Juárez, Mexico. Historically, the Chamizal area was a quintessentially liminal space, stemming from a border dispute that ranged from 1848 to 1963, when the path of the Rio Grande River shifted on multiple occasions, physically and ideologically flexing the border southward. The Chamizal Convention of 1963 reestablished boundaries, rechanneled the river, and created a static public space on the U.S. side of the border, resettling the area's inhabitants and disrupting individual agency. In the process, the border itself was literally and figuratively concretized, creating a new liminal space just south of the Chamizal.

This study explores the Chamizal Memorial and the border (la frontera) from a rhetorical perspective, not strictly as a historical site of struggle (though that context is essential), but in terms of the ways in which these spaces are made to speak today in both dominant and counterhegemonic terms, through competing visual representations that reflect an oppositional *ethos*. One of the fundamental assumptions of this project is that visual and spatial rhetorics may be coterminous and overlapping, and that the construction of any place, or the analysis thereof, must consider both aspects simultaneously. Therefore, in order to approach both the spatial and visual aspects of this contested region, I draw upon research in critical geography and rhetoric to explore the erasure of local historiographies at the site of the memorial as I work toward a rhetorical understanding of liminal spaces and territoriality that foregrounds the conflation of the spatial and the visual. I examine the Chamizal and the physical border as spatio-discursive locations, considering the ways in which the material reality of the built environment is used as a site of ventriloquism for competing interests in liminal and formerly liminal sites of struggle.

Recent scholarship in the field has productively examined the material and discursive construction of space and place, providing a rich precedent for further studies of spatialization from a rhetorical perspective. For example, Gerard Hauser's *Vernacular Voices: The Rhetoric of Publics and Public Spheres* and Gregory Clark's *Rhetorical Landscapes in America* have been tremendously influential as both critical and methodological forays into the rhetorical construction of space and place. Carole Blair's discussion of national memorial sites foregrounds the materiality of rhetoric, while Elizabethada Wright's exploration of the cemetery explores public memories of the material. Jordynn Jack similarly interrogates collective memories of wartime Los Alamos, arguing that "space and time function ideologically to shape memories" (229) that in turn support

Figure 1. Boundary marker at the Chamizal Memorial. © Brian J. McNely.

privileged historiographies. By employing a rhetorical approach to architecture and the built environment, Nancy Jackson argues that "architecture plays a role in the conditions of communication, which take place around, against, near, or inside the built form" (34); she points out that "architecture is rhetorical; it has a communicative function" (37). Finally, recent work by Jessica Enoch examines how schools in the nineteenth century were feminized by rhetorics of space (292). In short, scholars in our field have uncovered and rearticulated spatialization as a rhetorical practice by both drawing from and enriching our disciplinary theory.

In this exploration of the El Paso/Juárez border, I seek to build upon these (and other) seminal works on the rhetorics of place and space by focusing on three strongly interrelated concepts. First, I discuss the historical construction and erasure of liminal space at the site of the Chamizal National Memorial, drawing upon both local histories and rhetorical approaches to history and historiography. Next, I work to articulate a rhetorical perspective of territoriality that conflates the material and the discursive, merging theories in critical geography with the dialogic discourse theory of Mikhail Bakhtin and the dynamic relationship between materiality and semiosis theorized by Kristie Fleckenstein. I argue that the combination of physical territoriality and discursive spatialization creates rhetorical stratigraphies, layers of material and social strata that must be negotiated by inhabitants in liminal areas such as the El Paso/Juárez border. Finally, I examine both concepts through the visual discourse found at two specific sites in this region: the murals painted on the walls of the Chamizal National Memorial and the graffiti that covers la frontera, the concrete border itself.

Images of struggle are visually striking and readily apparent in both of these locations, where the politics of placement are alternatively articulated by rhetorics of sanitization and resistance. The Chamizal's murals, for example, reflect the multicultural vision of the official historiography, expressing the settlement of the borderlands of the El Paso/Juárez region as the peaceful commingling of disparate cultures. These paintings reinforce the commonplaces of melting-pot ideology, erasing struggle and diminishing difference. The visual and the material combine to produce a place that avoids the liminality of the past, which scrubs the area clean of its tenuous and difficult history. In contrast, the border itself has become an arena of political struggle, especially on the Mexican side of the boundary. Like the Chamizal, this space has also been repurposed, this time by a counterhegemonic discourse of resistance to U.S. imperialism and capitalist domination. The graffiti overlaid on top of the concretized border is almost wholly political, and it is viewed daily by thousands of pedestrians and motorists moving across the border by way of El Paso/Juárez's two downtown bridges. Ultimately, this project examines the impact of these visual and spatial rhetorics from both sides of the divide, with particular attention to how space is used to both reinforce and counteract the dominant discourse.

HISTORY AND HISTORIOGRAPHY ALONG A SHIFTING RIVER

El Paso historian Leon Metz has remarked that it is easier to create a country on paper, particularly in the act of mapping, than it is to actually govern and maintain such boundaries. When international boundaries are drawn along the lines of a river, the complications of governance are intensified, for as Jerry Mueller and several others have noted, rivers shift and become "restless." Metz argued that "from social, engineering, and geographical points of view, rivers are the worst possible boundaries" (294). He claimed that rivers "may separate nations and societies, [but] people who live on opposite sides of a river usually have more in common" with each other than they do with others living farther away (294). Rivers are never permanent, and they change course, flood, and even evaporate. Such characteristics are particularly prevalent within the city of El Paso, where just past the downtown area the terrain opens up into plains and former farmland, and the Rio Grande becomes impossible to contain by natural means, meandering and creating overlapping *bancos* that blur the distinctions between territories (see, for example, figure 2).

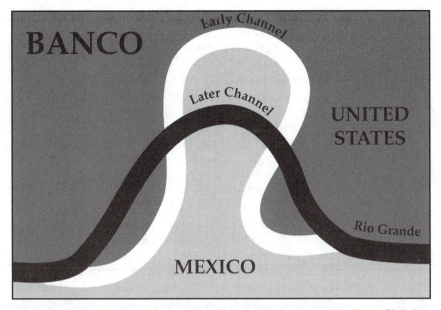

Figure 2. Shifting river boundaries (Metz 316). Permission granted by Texas Christian University Press.

Since the 1848 Treaty of Guadalupe Hidalgo, governance of the border that separates Texas from Mexico along the Rio Grande has been fraught with issues related to the capriciousness of the river. For example, by 1905 another treaty was needed to establish territorial "ownership" of some 58 separate *bancos* (see figure 2) along the lower Rio Grande, where sections of land were awarded alternatively to either the United States or Mexico depending on the movement of the river (Mueller 64). By the 1930s, *banco* disputes in the El Paso/Juárez area had declined, thanks in large part to better flood control and reservoir measures enacted along the river in southern New Mexico (Mueller 64). Interestingly, one of the larger El Paso *bancos* that was perpetually a source of change and conflict continued to be a problem between 1852 and 1963. Mueller explains:

> A hint of the havoc the River would play in disrupting the international boundary occurred as early as 1852 when two surveys . . . showed a southward shift in the channel's position. By 1889 the channel was far south of its 1852 position, in some places as much as a mile. The tract of land between the old and the new channel, some 600 acres, found itself attached to south El Paso at the expense of north Juárez. Named for the brush patch that formerly covered the area, the tract was locally known as *El Chamizal*. (65)

The Chamizal area, gradually shifting and changing shape with the ebb and flow of the river over the 100 years between the treaty of Guadalupe Hidalgo and the 1963 Chamizal Convention (work from which was finally completed

in 1967, as discussed below), became an ambiguous and tertiary space
between two cities and two nations.

At the heart of this ambiguous zone was Cordova Island, a territory "of
Mexico inside the United States, an island irritating local and international
relations" (Metz 307). Cordova Island, one of the larger sections of the
greater Chamizal area, was created by the continual shifts in the channel of
the Rio Grande as described by Mueller and others (see figure 3). Metz has
argued that the area became a haven for smugglers and criminals during pro-
hibition, and that it "blocked El Paso's growth and transportation arteries"
(307). He has also noted that "Mexico retained national jurisdiction as a matter of pride even though it ignored the enclave" (307). Interestingly, the
United States "claimed uninterrupted occupation of Chamizal since 1836"
(Mueller 70), and Cordova Island gradually became another neighborhood of
south El Paso, albeit one that remained marginalized, liminal, and poor.

Lasting solutions to the border dispute surrounding the Chamizal and
Cordova Island were finally negotiated in 1962 and 1963, thus inaugurating
the "official" history of the area. As Metz has shown, the politicization of the
Chamizal had become a moral issue, one that required governmental tact and
acumen on both sides of the dispute. President Kennedy proposed a solution
to the issue that would be "resolved on Mexican terms" (Metz 348), taking
into account the historical territorial claims of the Mexican government. But
the ultimate resolution reflects the power of federal governments and the lack
of power maintained by local inhabitants of the area. U.S. President Kennedy

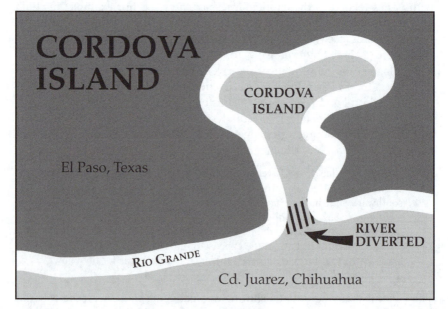

Figure 3. Cordova Island (Metz 308). Permission granted by Texas Christian University Press.

and Mexican President López Mateos were at the forefront of negotiations that led to a six-point plan for the Chamizal, which would include a re-channeled and concretized Rio Grande and the resettlement of all residents occupying the liminal zone. With 5,600 inhabitants and "hundreds of businesses, homes, apartments and tenements" (Metz 348) in the area, providing accommodation for displaced residents became a chief concern. Mexico received a total of 437.18 acres—366 acres to the west of Cordova Island and 264 to the east (for a total of 630), minus the 193 acres of the island ceded to the United States that would become the site of the Chamizal National Memorial (see figure 4). Finally, as a result of the 1963 accord, the rechanneled Rio Grande moved docilely along 4.3 miles of concrete, an edifice of permanent separation and exclusion that was ultimately completed in 1967.

Drawing from the work of Jacqueline Jones Royster, among others, I'd like to make a distinction here between history and historiography, seeing the former as a naturalized artifact imbued with the license of the dominant discourse and the latter as the inherently rhetorical process of history making (which sometimes reinforces the naturalized view of history, but sometimes does not). I do not dispute the general history of the Chamizal area, but I lament the fact that potential border historiographies of dissent have also been plowed under the silt, buried under a permanent concrete boundary that marks the official and natural history of the area. Speaking of the broader problems of the United States' appropriation of land in the Treaty of Guadalupe Hidalgo, Oscar Martinez has argued that Mexicans have remained "deeply distrustful of the United States" due to the potential of losing more territory "to its land-hungry neighbor" (1).

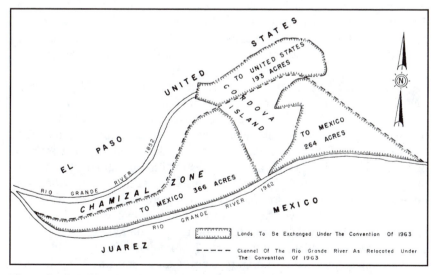

Figure 4. 1963 Chamizal Convention (Bowden 40). Permission granted by Texas Western Press.

A RHETORICAL APPROACH TO TERRITORIALITY

Michel Foucault has argued that "space is fundamental in any exercise of power" ("Space" 252), and nowhere is this more pronounced than in the territorial spaces that accompany international borders. Samuel Truett and Elliot Young point out that "borders are where territorialization becomes real, where physical markers and barriers are erected, and agents of the state regulate the movement of people, goods, and information" (2). In approaching such issues of power, geographer David Delaney has detailed the principle of territorial integrity, which holds so long as borders are not violated or transgressed; this principle plays a key role in social meaning making and official histories along the El Paso/Juárez border. He has noted that "there are innumerable complex territorial configurations and assemblages that shape human social life, relationships, and interactions" (4–5), and I would simply add that what mediates such interactions is discourse. Discourse and territory are interdependent and can be readily witnessed in liminal and formerly liminal zones like the Chamizal and la frontera, where external structures of the built environment dominate culture and become internalized as an overarching spatial component of subjectivity and rhetorical production. Delaney claimed that "territoriality is . . . implicated in the creation, circulation, and interpretation of meaning" (17) and, more specifically, discourse is shaped in no small measure by the territories that delimit and/or enable its circulation. Finally, territory is always relational, and interactions between those inside, outside, or in-between territorial boundaries will continuously affect discursive conventions.

The overriding functions of place and space, therefore, have an inescapable effect on the discourse and culture of those living under such conditions. The conflation of materiality (in the form of places, spaces, and physical boundaries) with semiosis (discursive and extraverbal/imagistic signifying) impacts the ways in which histories are composed and recomposed. A complex interrelation exists between bodies, discourse, and space that undergirds the meaning produced and disseminated in any rhetorical context. Kristie Fleckenstein has termed such interrelations *bodysigns*. Essentially, meaning cannot be separated from the physical context in which it occurs; moreover, in this dynamic, one aspect of meaning cannot be subordinated to the other. She has suggested that our modern Western tradition "increasingly strips us of a sense of our materiality and translates us into pure discursive patterns, into exclusively semiotic beings" (765). This, of course, is problematic, as an understanding of the relationship between materiality and discourse must include the notion that "we cannot escape place, although we can deny it and redefine it" (766). In this sense, meaning is not material, and neither is it semiotic; it is both at the same time—it is mutually constitutive (770).

Delaney argued that territoriality is not wholly comparable to other spatial forms, and I argue here that its effect on discourse and historiography is particularized, as territoriality always already includes significant and conctant issues of power. Borders are often viewed unproblematically—from a distance—as a two-dimensional construct where space on one side of a boundary is distinct from that on the other. However, Delaney argues that verticality is a further component of territories and borders, because these constructs are comprised of layers and layers of social strata and regulatory levels:

> In a modern social order characterized by the comprehensive global regimes of state sovereignty... every physical location... is located within a dense matrix of *multiple, overlapping* territories or territorial configurations. The "meanings" of each of these territories (and the power relations that these meanings imply) are established in relation to other territories across heterogeneous "levels." (31)

Similarly, Sarah Whatmore argues that a complex understanding of territoriality must reject "history as a uni-directional sequence of events" that likewise troubles notions of "geography as a uni-versal plane on which such a history unfolds" (67). In other words, territories are not static, flat constructs; they are complex and shifting assemblages imbued with material, social, historical, and discursive layers.

I want to combine this view of territory with the dialogic discourse theory of Mikhail Bakhtin in a confluence of spatio-discursive meaning making I am calling *rhetorical stratigraphies*. Bakhtin argued that utterances involve the complex imbrication of socio-discursive factors, previous utterances, and vast strata of social meaning and control. He argues that meaning in a given utterance "belongs to an element or *aggregate elements* in their relation to the whole" (1225, emphasis added). More importantly, he stresses that "*the organizing center of any utterance . . . is not within but outside—in the social milieu surrounding the individual*" (1220, emphasis in original). "*Any utterance,*" says Bakhtin, "*is only a moment in the continuous process of verbal communication*" (1221, emphasis in original), a process that is always unique and constantly shifting depending on one's social situatedness, a position that necessarily includes extra-verbal elements such as place and image. In this sense, Bakhtin sees a word as a "*territory* shared by both addresser and addressee" (1215, emphasis added), a central axis where rhetorical and cultural systems collide and meaning is reformulated. When a theory of territorial verticality is combined with Bakhtin's theories of language, we can begin to approximate the rhetorical complexity—the stratigraphy of spatial and discursive meaning—that accompanies both hegemonic and counterhegemonic discursive contexts along the border.

A more fully articulated notion of territory and its relation to discourse must be accompanied by investigations into overriding relationships of power. Power circulates up and down the strata of social and material reality, in relationships between the built environment and people along the border, in the relationships between dominant and subaltern groups, and in the spatial and visual histories that inhabit the landscape, to name but a few. Robert Sack noted that territory has a "place-clearing function" (*Human* 33), that accompanying territorialization is the power to disrupt and remake places and spaces, a characteristic clearly evident in the case of Cordova Island. And Foucault (*Discipline*, "Space") has argued that the built environment is especially reflective of power relations, of the ordering and spatialization of discursive and relational potential between human beings. Sack ("Power") extended Foucauldian arguments about the conflation of space and power, where "territorial rules about what is in or out of place pervade and structure lives" (326), and he also introduced notions of proximity and scale into the exploration of territory. Sack argued that emphasizing the interrelations between distance and power can be articulated in the following manner: "the specific place does not have power but rather . . . it resides in spatial relations, especially the distances, among things" (327). The rechanneled Rio Grande, of course, reinforced spatial and discursive distances, refashioned the actual scale of the border itself, and emphasized the power issues accompanying territoriality.

Spatial practices, De Certeau claimed, structure social life, inclusive of rhetorical meaning making; territorial practices not only structure, but dominate social life in some locations. Such is the case of the history of the Chamizal area, where territorial norms have impacted local discourses for over 100 years. David Sibley has suggested that individuals socialized in a territorial environment would feel anxiety in the presence of liminal zones, and the physical and ideological reconstruction of the Chamizal and the border were no doubt meant to appease some of those cultural anxieties—to reduce the appearance of liminality. The Chamizal Convention reinforced power relations, delimiting inside vs. outside, us vs. them, our space vs. their space. The Chamizal agreement "define[d] the contours of normality and . . . eliminate[d] difference" (Sibley 40), at least in terms of the erasure of liminality. As Sibley explained in his exploration of border crossings, the territorial assertions of both governments in the Chamizal Convention are representative of what he refers to as "the defense of spaces and transgressions" (46). Most importantly, he argued that exclusionary spaces are a key feature of territorial control, that "spatial purification" (77) is integral to the ordering of social space.

El Chamizal and Sanitized Rhetorics

David Sibley's notion of spatial purification is reflected at the Chamizal National Memorial, a 55-acre park situated at the northern end of the former Cordova Island, replete with monuments, a cultural center, and the clean and welcoming ethos of the National Park Service. Delaney echoed Sibley when he noted that territory provides a means of security to those "inside" the boundary from those "outside," and the purification of the formerly liminal zone of Cordova Island through the construction of the memorial is a spatial and architectural practice that reinforces that security. Delaney has suggested that a "quantum of meaning" (29) accompanies territorial/spatial practices, a notion evidenced in the built environment of the Chamizal Memorial, including (but by no means limited to) treaties, international agreements, constitutions, statutes, regulations, ordinances, contracts, deeds, work rules, and innumerable other texts. Any territory can draw upon these texts for a portion of its meanings. More accurately, the meanings of any given modern territory or territorial complex can be derived from a multitude of texts. (29)

Figure 5. Former boundary markers at the memorial. © Brian J. McNely.

This concept reflects some of the rhetorical stratigraphies in place at the Chamizal Memorial, with its conflation of both material and discursive norms. In essence, the memorial is a spatio-discursive representation of the official history of the Chamizal dispute, an argument in architecture and painting for the official representation of a quintessentially liminal area.

De Certeau claimed that spatial practices order social possibilities, and I would argue that the built environment also orders discursive practices at a site like the Chamizal Memorial. The memorial has removed almost any semblance of the daily social practices that once took place on this stretch of land, where people lived, cooked, made love, argued, played, owned business, and raised children. Today, access to the site is available between the hours of 5 AM and 10 PM, and the park is closed on major holidays. A 1.8 mile long walking trail (the "Cordova Island Trail") orders visitors around the edges of the park, most of which is covered with gently rolling hills that are dotted intermittently with large trees. Textual, monumentalized representations of the history of the area are concretized, and the official government history is reified. In short, this is not a place where alternative discourses are welcomed or enacted; an area that was often in flux, existing between territorial boundaries, has been purified, sanitized, and concretized.

Ultimately, the visual representations that merge with the spatial and architectural rhetorics of the memorial further cement the dominant perspective on the history of the area. Murals act as a rhetorical means for the official semiotic history of the Chamizal. When they are overlaid on the monumental, static, and purified spaces of the built environment at the site, they give the space a discursive "voice," a visual history of the Chamizal that is in actuality *not* the Chamizal, but the circumscribed and ordered result of territorial place clearing. W. J. T. Mitchell (*Iconology*) has shown that painting and other visual arts are differentiated from textual works by their reliance upon space; painting—especially of murals and graffiti—is a spatial practice, an action that exemplifies the mutually constitutive nature of materiality and semiosis. The murals at the Chamizal are dependent upon the built environment for their rhetorical meaning, as meaning in this context is dependent upon both factors in the equation, on the spatial and the visual simultaneously.

The Chamizal murals depict an ordered and harmonious hybridity, as seen, for example, in the racial and cultural construction of the idealized Mexican male in figure 6. Native and conquistador merge in the presence of the Mexican man, a design joined visually by the Mexican flag that acts as a background. The striking snake juxtaposed against an aggressive jaguar acknowledges undertones of some cultural animosity; but again, harmony, order, symmetry, and nationalized presence are foregrounded. Not surprisingly, the image of the idealized American citizen (figure 7) is even more blatantly purified and ordered. An indigenous male and an African American (slave?) female recede behind the piercing blue eyes of the dominant white male. Historical conflict is erased, and the three are joined harmoniously by the United States flag in the background, with the presence of the eagle in the fore-

Figure 6. Chamizal mural on west-facing wall of the main memorial building.
© Brian J. McNely.

Figure 7. Chamizal murals on the west- and south-facing walls. © Brian J. McNely.

ground. Finally, the juxtaposition of murals is most striking. Carlos Flores, the artist behind the two main murals that dominate the primary memorial building, titles a second mural "Nuestra Herencia" ("Our Heritage," figures 8 and 9). At the left edge of figure 8, the blue eyes of the idealized white American male peer over the scene, indicative of the ways in which histories and heritage are impacted by the hegemonic gaze of U.S. territorial policy.

La Frontera—Liminality and Counterhegemonic Rhetorics

In stark contrast to the sanitized Chamizal Memorial stands the concrete edifice that controls the rechanneled Rio Grande (see figure 10 on p. 110). After the 1963 erasure of the liminal zone that was Cordova Island, liminality shifted south, to the actual border itself. Delaney has argued that "the life of territory is to be seen in the crossings-over, into and out of . . . meaningful spaces" (27). As we have seen with the memorial, social life has been extinguished, and boundaries and "crossings-over" have shifted to the rechanneled river. The border, once a shifting and natural boundary, has become what Sibley termed a "strongly classified spatial system, consisting of a collection of clearly bounded and homogenous units" (80). More importantly, the rechanneled and concretized border between El Paso and Juárez exemplifies the "abjection" (Sibley 80) that accompanies a strongly classified environ-

Figure 8. "Nuestra Herencia," a south-facing mural with the similarly south-facing American gaze of figure 7 in the background. © Brian J. McNely.

Figure 9. A more detailed view of the south-facing "Nuestra Herencia" mural. © Brian J. McNely.

ment. For the Mexican subaltern especially, this monument to separation and exclusion has clearly become a site where feelings of abjection are reinforced, and such feelings become manifest in the visual discourse found on the border itself.

Mitchell (*Picture Theory*) has pointed out the ways in which violence often accompanies public art, and in the case of the border, histories of violence and struggle are foregrounded within images that take advantage of the architecture of the border itself, that seek to deface and repurpose the monument. As Foucault ("Space") has noted, and as recounted in Fleckenstein above, even in the face of dominant and potentially terrifying spatial and territorial practices, the possibility for resistance remains, especially in liminal areas. For example, Raul Villa, in his discussion of real-life and fictional Chicano resistance, suggested ways in which individuals and counterhegemonic collectives can refigure landscapes of power. In examining graffiti in the new liminal zone of the border, then, spatial and visual rhetorics are again coterminous and interdependent.

In contrast to the harmonious, professional murals that reinforce the static space and official history of the Chamizal Memorial, the liminal zone of la frontera is bold, clear, and above all highly political. The border as canvas becomes a large part of the rhetorical equation, as artists make this space speak in ways that reflect the abjection and violence of this strongly classified environment. Figure 11 is indicative of the kind of spatio-discursive rhetorics found in the new liminal zone, where Che Guevara is an iconic figure of resistance accompanying messages of political struggle such as "PINCHE BUSH" in bold capital (white) letters. These rhetorics indicate the particularized and local historiographies that occur in this liminal environment, the types of voices that were erased and recapitulated by the place-clearing sanitization of Cordova Island. Figure 12 is exemplary of the violence that accompanies the abjection reflected in the public art of the border. An armed figure stands above a message that states "WELCOME TO JUAREZ" in English, while messages in Spanish reflect themes of governmental assassination ("gobiernos asesinos")

Figure 10. Rechanneled and concretized Rio Grande, looking west. © Brian J. McNely.

and punishment ("EL MERECENSER CASTIGADOS"). In short, this is a very different environment than the Chamizal Memorial, one that embodies some of the effects of territorialization in the form of liminal, visual discourse.

Figure 11. Graffiti on the border near the Santa Fe Bridge. © Brian J. McNely.

Figure 12. Graffiti on the border near the Santa Fe Bridge. © Brian J. McNely.

CONCLUSIONS

The history of the Chamizal area is still in flux, despite the attempts of the U.S. government to construct some kind of fixity, both spatially and rhetorically, to the official version of the region. While the liminal characteristics of Cordova Island were erased and sanitized in the form of the national memorial, voices of dissent and counterhegemonic rhetorics persist in the new liminal zone, embodied by the massive concrete border just south of the Chamizal. Today, both places are made to speak, and both hegemonic and counterhegemonic discourses rely on the spaces of territorialization to make meaning. By approaching the territoriality of the U.S.–Mexico border as a vertical construct, one that considers the complex conflation of material and rhetorical stratigraphies, we can examine the ways that inhabitants make meaning by negotiating the social and physical strata that contribute to border life. This investigation of these spatial rhetorics is by no means exhaustive, and I certainly want to be clear that I do not portend to speak for either discourse. Instead, this study provides one window on the ways that spatio-discursive meaning is made in highly politicized territorial locations.

There are several broader implications of this examination of the U.S.–Mexico border that can inform future explorations of space, place, and visual discourse within rhetorical studies. For example, in sites where territorialization is a dominant, ever-present material and discursive reality, the built environment and physical structures like the border dominate cultural

Figure 13. Public mural near the downtown Santa Fe Bridge. © Brian J. McNely.

identification and represent a significant spatial component of subjectivity, positionality, and rhetorical production. Discourse is shaped in large part by the territories that restrict and/or enable its circulation, whether that discourse is written, spoken, or visual. Perhaps more importantly, I have articulated here a rhetorical approach to liminal spaces and territoriality that foregrounds the conflation of the spatial and the visual, the material and the semiotic, and the complex layers and interconnections that comprise rhetorical stratigraphies. While the stratification of spatial and discursive elements may be pronounced in territorial sites like the El Paso/Juárez border, I contend that rhetorical stratigraphies are prevalent in any human construction or organization of space. By approaching space vertically, both in terms of the complex strata of rhetorical production and the multiple, overlapping figurations of territoriality, scholars in rhetoric can enact meaningful interventions into the construction, reception, and circulation of spatial and visual discourse.

Works Cited

Bakhtin, M. M. "From Marxism and the Philosophy of Language." *The Rhetorical Tradition.* Ed. P. Bizzell and B. Herzberg. New York: Bedford/St. Martin's, 1973. 1210–26.

Blair, C. "Contemporary U.S. Memorial Sites as Exemplars of Rhetoric's Materiality." Ed. J. Selzer and S. Crowley. *Rhetorical Bodies.* Madison: U of Wisconsin P, 1999. 16–57.

Bowden, J. J. *The Ponce de Leon Land Grant.* El Paso: Texas Western P, 1969.

Clark, G. *Rhetorical Landscapes in America: Variations on a Theme from Kenneth Burke.* Columbia: U of South Carolina P, 2004.

De Certeau, M. *The Practice of Everyday Life.* Berkeley: U of California P, 1984.

Delaney, D. *Territory: A Short Introduction.* Oxford: Blackwell, 2005.

Enoch, J. "A Woman's Place Is in the School." *College English* 70.3 (2008): 275–95.

Fleckenstein, K. "Bodysigns: A Biorhetoric for Change." *JAC* 21.4 (2001): 761–90.

Foucault, M. *Discipline and Punish: The Birth of the Prison.* New York: Vintage Books, 1979.

———. "Space, Knowledge, and Power." *The Foucault Reader.* Ed. P. Rabinow. New York: Pantheon, 1984. 239–56.

Hauser, G. *Vernacular Voices: The Rhetoric of Publics and Public Spheres.* Columbia: U of South Carolina P, 1999.

Jack, J. "Space, Time, Memory: Gendered Recollections of Wartime Los Alamos." *Rhetoric Society Quarterly* 37.3 (2007): 229–50.

Jackson, N. "The Architectural View: Perspectives on Communication." *Visual Communication Quarterly* 13.1 (2006): 32–45.

Martinez, O. J., ed. *U.S.–Mexico Borderlands: Historical and Contemporary Perspectives.* Wilmington, DE: Scholarly Resources, 1996.

Metz, L. *Border: The U.S.–Mexico Line.* El Paso: Mangan, 1989.

Mitchell, W. J. T. *Iconology: Image, Text, Ideology.* Chicago: U of Chicago P, 1986.

———. *Picture Theory.* Chicago: U of Chicago P, 1994.

Mueller, J. E. *Restless River: International Law and the Behavior of the Rio Grande.* El Paso: Texas Western P, 1975.

Royster, J. J. "Disciplinary Landscaping, or Contemporary Challenges in the History of Rhetoric." *Philosophy and Rhetoric* 36.2 (2003): 148–67.

Sack, R. D. *Human Territoriality: Its Theory and History.* Cambridge: Cambridge UP, 1986.

———. "The Power of Place and Space." *Geographical Review* 83.3 (1993): 326–29.

Sibley, D. *Geographies of Exclusion.* New York: Routledge, 1995.

Truett, S., and E. Young. "Making Transnational History: Nations, Regions, and Borderlands." *Continental Crossroads: Remapping U.S.–Mexico Borderlands History.* Ed. S. Truett and E. Young. Durham, NC: Duke UP, 2004. 1–32.

Villa, R. H. *Barrio-Logos: Space and Place in Urban Chicano Literature and Culture.* Austin: U of Texas P, 2000.

Whatmore, S. *Hybrid Geographies: Natures, Cultures, Spaces.* London: Sage, 2002.

Wright, E. "Rhetorical Spaces in Memorial Places: The Cemetery as a Rhetorical Memory Place/Space." *Rhetoric Society Quarterly* 35.4 (2005): 51–81.

PART II

Forming Publics and Communities

9

Public Deliberation and the Rhetorical "Real"

Balancing Accomplishment and Complication in Republican-Democratic Structures

Todd Kelshaw

In idealizing and describing public deliberation, it is difficult for theorists and practitioners to ignore its inherent messiness. Deliberation is regularly depicted as juxtapositional, complementary, and even antidotal to less dialogic kinds of political talk such as public address, debate, and diatribe. Accordingly we have come to know deliberation as a means for accomplishing various integrative goals in civic discourse. These include the pluralistic inclusion of culturally and epistemologically diverse voices (Bohman 261; Kaveny 313–14), the development of sophisticated understandings about complex public problems (Gastil and Dillard 20–21), and the application of flexible problem solving processes that build cohesive communities (Doble Research Associates 52–53). As such, public deliberation is portrayed as the discursive embodiment of the town hall meeting; an enactment of what is most potentially populist, polyphonic, and equivocal about democracy. In a mass society in which lay citizens rarely participate directly in governance, deliberative public meetings are important opportunities—even if participants usually fulfill mere advisory roles, leaving the real policy decisions to professionals: elected and appointed government officials (Gastil 30–31). Deliberation's inclusive pluralism, complication (rather than simplification) of public problems, potential open-endedness, and questionable efficacy may make it seem inefficient as a civic process. It is, however, clearly attractive to many. Those who are likely to value it above discourses that are comparatively decisive (e.g., debate) and resolute (e.g., majority-rule voting and executive decree) may be thinkers and practitioners who appreciate "muddleheaded anecdotalism" in legal contexts (Simons 22), the "messiness" and "unfinalizability" of relationships (Baxter and Montgomery 232–33), and the "spirit of playfulness" of some approaches to moral conflict (Pearce and Littlejohn 47).

117

But are deliberation's outcomes necessarily so incomplete, indirect in their policy consequences, and abstract? Notwithstanding the United States' alleged dearth of institutional mechanisms for conducting public deliberation and transcribing it into concrete policy (Mathews 14–15), the genre has a telic dimension that is often neglected or minimized in conceptual treatments. If deliberative democrats and other celebrants of public deliberation are to improve the potentials, processes, and outcomes of participatory public governance, it is crucial to forge conceptualizations and practices that appropriately balance decisiveness and materialism on one hand and openness and idealism on the other.

This essay describes public deliberation as a rhetorical modality with great potential for influencing not only individual and public understandings of shared problems but also concrete solutions. It does this by teasing out deliberation and dialogue—two speech genres that are frequently conflated by academics and practitioners (Gastil and Kelshaw 55)—and by stressing deliberation's telic ambition and potential. Specifically, this essay addresses the importance of discursive balance in a republican-democratic society; portrays some prominent forms of republican-democratic talk; and finally speaks to deliberation's rhetorical potential for bridging pluralistic abstraction and the actionable "real." These objectives are motivated by a sense of public deliberation as a crucial civic speech genre that manifests fundamental republican-democratic tensions in a way that no other rhetorical mode does. Public deliberation, this essay asserts, tempers the contradictory needs for complication and accomplishment in public talk, enabling participants to collaboratively realize both unfinalizable abstractions and actionable policy decisions.

REPUBLICAN DEMOCRACY AND ITS RHETORICAL TENSIONS

A large-scale organization that is conceived in ideals of popular self-governance features a broad range of communicative processes. These include information provision, community building, problem solving, and policy making. Since the social structure is too populous to permit full voice and efficacy for all individuals, it is necessary to employ both direct and representational mechanisms. These mechanisms are, respectively, democratic and republican. Simply put, democratic mechanisms enable participants to engage in direct (either face-to-face or mediated) action or interaction whereas republican mechanisms place executive, legislative, and judicial responsibilities in the hands of elected and appointed officials. In the spirit of Gadamer's hermeneutic circle (68), by which understanding is accomplished through the back-and-forth weaving of macro- and micro-contexts (the "whole" and its "parts," respectively), a republican democracy is maintained through the interaction of broad-based representative control and localized democratic engagement.

Communication is subject to various rhetorical tensions across this spectrum of republican-democratic processes. Informed by Bakhtin's dialectical approach, these tensions may be understood as tending, in degrees, centripetally or centrifugally (272–73). Communication processes that tend centripe-tally are relatively decisive, authoritative, stabilizing, and preserving of traditions. They feature speech acts that do things such as convey informa-tion, issue directives, mete out punishments, enact policies, and manifest stratified institutional roles. Conversely, processes that tend centrifugally are relatively open-ended, insurgent, destabilizing, and change-minded. They feature speech acts that problematize information and ask probing questions, resist authority and traditional rules, and empower or give voice to institu-tionally subjugated and marginalized social members.

The array of speech acts and genres that make up any given social struc-ture vary widely in their qualities. Considered in sum, they reveal the struc-ture's general condition. Republican-democratic structures, uniquely, may be recognized by their general temperance of centripetal and centrifugal forces, in which closed-ended (centripetal) and open-ended (centrifugal) rhetorical modes achieve quasi-counterbalance. This is a subtle negotiation in which public policies are both accomplished and complicated in more-or-less equal measure. The "more-or-less"-ness of this imperfect equilibrium reflects the notion that any given social structure is constantly remade in participants' dynamic interaction (Giddens 17), so static balance is impossible.

This definition of republican democracy distinguishes it from other orga-nizational forms. Social structures that experience a preponderance of explicit rules, regulatory controls like censorship and gate keeping, and other centripetally leaning discourses tend toward autocracy or authoritarianism. Their social orders are maintained in unilateral expressions of brute informa-tion and directives that enforce centralized control while stifling insurgence. Designated leadership, established roles, unquestioned traditions, and control mechanisms tend to be formally codified. At the other end of the organiza-tional/rhetorical continuum—the centrifugal one—social structures with few explicit regulations and disciplinary procedures but plenty of equivocal voices lean toward anomie or anarchy. Discursive struggles occur through multilateral decentralization of authority and destabilization of public order. Leadership is emergent and fluid, and implicit social norms are negotiated (and disrupted) among participants rather than imposed from atop or out-side. In contrast to these extremes, republican democracy, as philosophers like Dewey and Bernstein posit, is an ethically grounded ideal, an Aristote-lian golden mean.

Just as some Bakhtin-inspired thinkers apply a dialectical approach to understanding interpersonal relationships (e.g., Baxter and Montgomery 4; Shotter 50), it is fruitful to think similarly about organizational structures. Identifying the *accomplishment/complication* dialectic is the fundamental step in understanding the tensions among a republican democracy's rhetorical genres. Akin to what Kaner (6) describes as a dynamic between "convergent" and "divergent" kinds of thinking during group problem-solving discussion, the accomplishment/complication dialectic encompasses several related con-tinua (see figure 1).

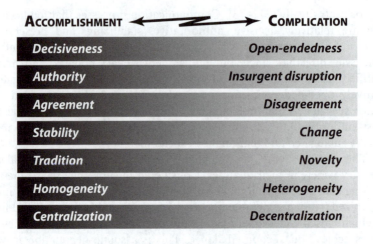

Figure 1.   The accomplishment/complication dialectic.

The more-or-less balancing of these dialectics plays out (or, ideally, *should* play out) in a republican democracy through its enactment of diverse speech genres. Different speech genres such as dialogue, debate, deliberation, public address, and diatribe manifest particular rhetorical modes that fulfill important complementary functions. It is to these genres and their rhetorical functions that the essay now turns.

RHETORICAL MODES OF REPUBLIC DEMOCRACY

The various genres of talk that maintain a republican-democratic body fulfill different rhetorical functions ranging from accomplishment to complication. Considering that a republican democracy strives to temper qualities of speech along this dialectic, it is helpful to briefly describe some prominent forms and the rhetorical functions that they serve.

Along the accomplishment/complication continuum, speech genres manifest different qualities (see figure 2).

Consistent with these qualities, there are particular functions that communication fulfills in a republican democracy. Policy making, law enforcement, budgeting, and information provision are some essential functions that may reflect *accomplishing* qualities. Functions that might reflect *complicating* qualities include civil disobedience, moral conflict enactment, public hearings, and community block parties. The difference between these two sets is, respectively, between resolving and prodding open substantive, procedural, and relational issues.

Among others in republican-democratic discourse, four speech genres are especially prominent: oratory/public address, debate, deliberation, and

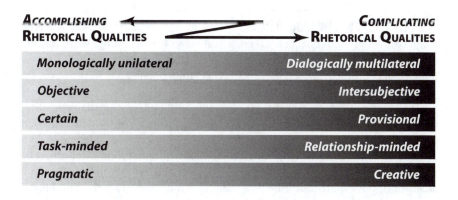

Figure 2. Rhetorical qualities along the accomplishment/complication dialectic.

dialogue. These forms manifest different and, in ways, complementary tendencies along the accomplishing/complicating continuum (see figure 3).

Oratory has predominant centripetal features and thus tends toward the *accomplishing* end of the continuum. The tendency toward monologism that characterizes public address gives this genre what Baxter and Montgomery describe as a penchant to "treat communication as one-sided and univoiced. . . . [T]he focus is on sameness . . . a focus that creates a fiction of consistency and completeness" (46). In oratory, speakers use "heresthetical" and "rhetorical" strategies to affect their audiences. Heresthetic is "the art of setting up situations—composing the alternatives among which political actors must choose" (Riker 9). It is the communicative process of putting an issue or set of issues on the table. Once the table is set, communicators use what Riker calls "rhetorical" strategies to frame those issues in particular ways. This happens through what Aristotle (37–39) describes as conscientious appeals to reason (*logos*), emotions (*pathos*), and the communicator's perceived identity/credibility in relation to the

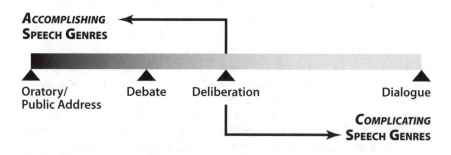

Figure 3. Four prominent republican-democratic speech genres.

topic and the audience (*ethos*). Whereas both heresthetical and rhetorical strategies may be applied in many different speech genres, in address—which is typically conceived and enacted in unilateral ways to do things like inform, persuade, and scold—they may be effective tools of discursive control. Even in the face of centrifugal speech acts such as heckling, public address preserves the primacy of the orator's voice as a controlling force.

Debate, too, leans toward the *accomplishing* end of the dialectic. But, unlike public address, there are two or more distinct voices with different (often mutually exclusive) and potentially equal perspectives. Debate is, in a sense, a confrontation of two or more oratorical addresses, or what might be thought of as "parallel monologues" (Baxter and Montgomery 46), that advance opposing attitudes. Debate can effectively address public problems, but, in cases of entrenched opposition, it can limit productive contact. When that happens, debaters speak as representatives of groups and usually direct their messages to distinct constituents or to an undecided middle. They tend to speak in ways that convey stubborn commitments to points of view (Chasin et al. 326).

On the opposite end of the *accomplishment/complication* dialectic, interactants may engage in dialogue. Dialogue marries the Greek words *dia* and *logos* to signify "meaning through"; that is, joint understandings that emerge through participants during engaged interaction (Bohm 6). Isaacs characterizes dialogue as "a conversation with a center, not sides" that provides a "way of taking the energy of our differences and channeling it toward something that has never been created before" (607). As Anderson, Cissna, and Arnett state, "Dialogue implies more than a simple back-and-forthness of messages in interaction; it points to a particular process and quality of communication in which the participants 'meet,' which allows for changing and being changed" (10). Dialogic communication is useful for building sophisticated understandings of complex cultural and community problems, and for bridging relational, cultural, and moral divides. Whereas these are accomplishments in a particular sense, they cannot be mistaken for firm resolutions of public problems or pronouncements of certainty.

Deliberation, it is important to note, inhabits the middle of the accomplishment/complication scale. This characterization of deliberation as a speech genre that experiences more-or-less balanced measures of centripetal and centrifugal rhetorical forces is this essay's centerpiece. Because public deliberation is typically cast as an antidote to elite control of republic-democratic processes and a means to empower people who have been shut out of politics (Mathews 2–3), it might be easy to think of it as purely dialogic. In fact, one study conducted during 2001 and 2002 found that a significant number of theorists and practitioners used "dialogue" and "deliberation" synonymously (Gastil and Kelshaw 55). But as it enables interactive participants "to weigh carefully both the consequences of various options for action and the views of others" in order to make good, joint decisions (Mathews 110), deliberation has an important goal orientation beyond its dialogic qualities. It is this temperance that establishes public deliberation uniquely as the hallmark of republican-democratic social structures.

PUBLIC DELIBERATION AND THE ENACTMENT OF RHETORICAL BALANCE

As a rhetorical microcosm of republican-democratic processes, public deliberation features both dialogic and monologic rhetorical qualities. Accordingly, it affords opportunities for members of a republican-democratic polity to speak and listen to other diverse voices, forge subtle understandings of complex public problems, and ultimately develop actionable solutions. Public deliberation provides a discursive bridge between abstract understandings of identities, relationships, and common issues on one hand and what may be called "the real" on the other. An appropriate way to explain this is to discuss both the dialogic qualities and the telic (goal-oriented) nature of deliberation.

Dialogic Features of Public Deliberation

As described in detail elsewhere (Kelshaw 4–10), dialogue is defined by several key characteristics—intersubjectivity, openness, relinquishing of control, and destabilization—and participants' attitudes—availability, flexibility, and commitment to the conversation. Dialogue, then, is highly centrifugal; its participants share joint control of potentially contested and unfinalizable meanings through communication behaviors that ensure mutual vulnerability.

Deliberation shares much with dialogue. Cohen (22–23) identifies four aspects of the "ideal deliberative procedure" in civic contexts that reflect dialogic features. The first of these is participants' freedom from authoritative constraints. The emphasis here is on emergent norms and understandings, and on control that is shared among interactants rather than exogenously imposed. This does not mean that public deliberation occurs in a vacuum. Structures and rules (legal, ethical, procedural, etc.) must be in place in order for deliberation to occur at all. As well, deliberation requires *some* discursive rules and limits. In deliberation, though, participants jointly set the terms of their interaction. They collaboratively negotiate their conversation's framework, jointly empowered by what is happening *within* their interaction.

Cohen's second aspect is the provision of reasons to support proposals and criticisms. Whereas this emphasis on rationality does, in a sense, depart from dialogue (which enjoys freedom from exogenous constraints such as formal rules of argument), it is important to observe that "reason" is broader than an authoritative quasi-logical form. Practical reasoning is relationally, culturally, and situationally contingent; the more pluralistic the deliberating group, the more likely that diverse forms of practical reason may affect participants' willingness and abilities to think and talk together flexibly and equally. In forging "ethical collectivism," participants aspire to a "constructed consensus" that is "based upon the collective consideration of the moral opinions of participants in discourse," and that is acceptable if they mutually agree that the discursive process is justified, that all cogent views have been considered, and that "the conclusion agreed upon, judged in the light of the standards of the procedure, is better than any other proposal that has been considered" (Thompson 2).

Cohen's third feature of public deliberation is equality. Equality means that the rules of the deliberative procedure should neither advantage nor disadvantage any individual. Participants should have equal and adequate opportunities to speak and should maintain an egalitarian collective without formal stratification. (Rotating chairship is one good strategy.) Inclusion is part and parcel of equality, as it raises and legitimates diverse perspectives. Diversity aids the challenging of prevailing rules and norms and permits new ways of speaking and thinking about issues.

The fourth aspect in Cohen's list is group effort toward consensus. This is an attitude that precedes any concrete outcomes (to be discussed further along). It privileges not the kinds of tidily resolved decisions of majority-rule voting but rather something much more relationally and substantively complicating. Consensus is not always achievable, but Cohen emphasizes a *spirit* of consensus as a feature of ideal deliberation because it reminds group members that they are bound by common goals.

Telic Features of Public Deliberation

The dialogic features of public deliberation prod things open with regard to inclusively pluralistic participation, relationship building (interpersonally, interculturally, and community-based), and sophisticated understandings of complex problems. These are some of the qualities that are most regularly cited in pro-deliberation literature (e.g., Mathews and McAfee 8–9). Public deliberation potentially does well to complicate the public sphere by bringing diverse people into the civic process and heightening their sophisticated understandings. Of course, these are valuable outcomes of deliberation, but they are *precursors* to the creation and implementation of concrete public policy, and they are prone to inconsequentiality. To conflate dialogue and deliberation is to emphasize these unfinalizable outcomes (which are really ongoing processes) while de-emphasizing deliberation's more actionable products. Doing so would be to paint only half of the picture, so to speak. What must also be addressed is public deliberation's rhetorical penchant for accomplishment.

As described more elaborately elsewhere (Kelshaw 14–16), public deliberation has three characteristics that distinguish it from dialogue and complement its centrifugal features: its concern for task closure, its focus on future courses of action, and its rational weighing of evidence. Simply put, deliberation is "a small-group, discussion-based approach to deciding future courses of action based on careful weighing of evidence" (14). This definition distinguishes deliberation from dialogue, which does not necessarily concern closed-ended decision making, the future tense, and quasi-logical reasoning based in factual evidence.

The first telic-minded characteristic of public deliberation is its concern for task closure. Dialogue cares mostly about the transformation of ideology and relationships through transcendent ways of speaking. Such changes occur through an "ongoing interplay between oppositional features" (Baxter and Montgomery 6) that takes the form of "ongoing messiness" (3). Dialogue's chief product, then, is the process itself: "an open exploration rather than decision making" (Gastil and Kelshaw 55). Public deliberation, further, strives for goals that are concrete, such as policy decisions or, more indirect but still fairly consequential, formal recommendations to institutional officials.

The second important telic aspect of deliberation is its concern for the future tense. In juridical contexts like criminal court cases, for example, deliberation is group decision making that considers facts in the past (guilt or innocence) as well as courses of future action (sentencing). But the language of republican-democratic civic participation focuses on the latter (relying, of course, on participants' understandings of past and enduring facts). This emphasis reflects an understanding of deliberation that dates to ancient Greek democracy. Aristotle (47–78) distinguishes between forensic (*dikanikon*), occasional (*epideiktikon*), and deliberative (*symbouleutikon*) modes of rhetoric. These three types pertain to, respectively, past, present, and future tenses. The rhetorical interactivities of participants in public deliberation deal ultimately with the derivation of policies: future courses of action. However much public deliberation initially builds upon knowledge of past facts and present conditions and, secondly, participants' attitudes and values, it is ultimately an activity of the future tense. This characteristic distinguishes deliberation from dialogue, which focuses largely on the development of participants' beliefs, attitudes, and values—all of which inhabit the present tense.

Public deliberation's third key feature is its concern for analytic consideration of sound evidence. This is a concern that is not prominent in dialogue, a genre that is more permissibly emotional in its preference for empathic over rational communication. Deliberation's requirement of sound argumentation is central as, for example, Habermas' notion of ideal speech (embodied in deliberation) avows. Regardless of the different cultural approaches that diverse participants may bring to the deliberative process, all must be able to articulate individual interests and policy preferences in ways that are understandable and valid (if not agreeable) to others. Participants' reflective and explicit clarifications of their potentially differing standards of reasoning and evidence are crucial to deliberation. Otherwise their communication may fail, creating power imbalances that violate deliberation's dialogic requirements and prohibiting effective decision outcomes.

CONCLUSION: BRIDGING THE ABSTRACT AND THE "REAL"

This essay's purpose is to conceptually tease out public deliberation and dialogue, which are two terms and practices that are at great risk of conflation. The first reason for doing so is that I wish to portray public deliberation as a crucial speech genre of republican democracy—one that actually manifests republican democracy through its tempering application of rhetorical qualities that both accomplish and complicate. Another reason for distinguishing deliberation is that doing so with an emphasis on the genre's oft-neglected telic nature may suggest its capacity for bridging unfinalizable abstractions (such as relationships and ideologies) with "the real."

Communication theorists and practitioners have tremendous responsibility to *do*. This is especially true in the context of republican democracy, in which *doing* (as opposed to having things *done to* one, or simply being *done in* by others) is the basis of social organization. Rhetoric—its study and application—has only minimal consequence if its ideas are not actionable. Along this line, public deliberation, which continues to garner increased attention in academic fields like communication, public administration, political science, and law, must be moved from a philosophical ideal to a relationship and community builder to, ultimately, an institutional force for popular empowerment and ethical policy making.

Today, there are numerous public deliberation projects and programs worldwide, such as the Kettering Foundation's affiliate Study Circles, Citizen Juries, and National Issues Forums. These are laudable efforts that are supported by theoretical and empirical scholarship as well as guidebooks and other resources to be used by facilitators and participants. They help to make public deliberation practicable and practical. But what is largely missing in republican-democratic societies like the United States is an *institutional* component that can function *within* the structure of formal governance to infuse deliberative products into public policy, and not merely policy recommendations or voting behaviors, both of which minimize the democratic dimension of republican democracy.[1]

The definition of republican democracy that was posed early in this essay—a social organizational form in which closed-ended (centripetal) and open-ended (centrifugal) rhetorical modes achieve quasi-counterbalance—is intended to honor the important functions of discourses that both accomplish and complicate. It is a bit too easy sometimes to celebrate dialogue and to demean debate. Both fulfill important functions. The beauty and value of public deliberation is that it is really a *meta*-genre of speech, enabling an array of rhetorical qualities spanning centripetal closure and centrifugal openness. In this sense, it provides a bridge between abstract things like sophisticated understandings of public problems and the messiness of interpersonal, cultural, and community relationships on one hand and, on the other, concrete things like legislation and municipal budgets. This bridge may be thought of, and acted on, as the rhetorical "real."

Note

[1] One example of a potentially deliberative structure that is institutionalized is the Spokane (WA) Community Assembly, which brings representatives of officially recognized Neighborhood Councils together to address public issues. This body, which advises the City Council, is

an actual component of government, as determined by public referendum in 1999. See http://
www.spokaneneighborhoods.org/ and
http://communityassembly.spokaneneighborhoods.org/ for information.

Works Cited

Anderson, Rob, Kenneth N. Cissna, and Ronald C. Arnett, eds. *The Reach of Dialogue: Confirmation, Voice and Community.* Cresskill, NJ: Hampton P, 1994.

Aristotle. *On Rhetoric: A Theory of Civic Discourse.* Trans. George A. Kennedy. New York: Oxford UP, 1991.

Bakhtin, Mikhail M. *The Dialogic Imagination.* Trans. C. Emerson and M. Holquist. Ed. M. Holquist. Austin: U of Texas P, 1981.

Baxter, Leslie A., and Barbara M. Montgomery. *Relating: Dialogues and Dialectics.* New York: Guilford P, 1996.

Bernstein, Richard J. "The Retrieval of the Democratic Ethos." *Cardozo Law Review* 17 (1996): 1127–46.

Bohm, David. *On Dialogue.* Ed. L. Nichol. London: Routledge, 1996.

Bohman, James. "Public Reason and Cultural Pluralism: Political Liberalism and the Problem of Moral Conflict." *Political Theory* 23: 253–79.

Chasin, Richard et al. "From Diatribe to Dialogue on Divisive Public Issues: Approaches Drawn from Family Therapy." *Mediation Quarterly* 13 (1996): 323–44.

Cohen, Joshua. "Deliberation and Democratic Legitimacy." *Deliberative Democracy: Essays on Reason and Politics.* Ed. James Bohman and William Rehg. Cambridge: MIT P, 1997. 17–34.

Dewey, John. "The Ethics of Democracy." *University of Michigan Philosophical Papers.* 2nd series. Ann Arbor, MI: Andrews, 1888.

Doble Research Associates. "Responding to the Critics of Deliberation." Report prepared for the Kettering Foundation. Englewood Cliffs, NJ: Author, 1996.

Gadamer, Hans-Georg. "On the Circle of Understanding." *Hermeneutics Versus Science?* Trans. and Ed. John M. Connolly and Thomas Keutner. Notre Dame, IN: U of Notre Dame P, 1988.

Gastil, John. *By Popular Demand.* Berkeley: U of California P, 2000.

Gastil, John, and James P. Dillard. "Increasing Political Sophistication Through Public Deliberation." *Political Communication* 16 (1999): 3–23.

Gastil, John, and Todd Kelshaw. "What Does it Mean to Deliberate?: A Study of the Meaning of Deliberation in Academic Journals and the On-Line Publications of Membership Associations." Kettering Foundation, Dayton, OH, March 2002.

Giddens, Anthony. *The Constitution of Society.* Berkeley: U of California P, 1984.

Habermas, Jürgen. *Theory of Communicative Action.* Trans. T. A. McCarthy. Vol. 1. Boston: Beacon P, 1984.

Isaacs, William. "A Conversation with a Center, Not Sides." *Bridges Not Walls.* 9th ed. Ed. John Stewart. Boston: McGraw-Hill, 2002. 606–11

Kaner, Sam. *Facilitator's Guide to Participatory Decision-making.* Gabriola Island, BC: New Society, 1996.

Kaveny, M. Cathleen. "Diversity and Deliberation: Bioethics Commissions and Moral Reasoning." *Journal of Religious Ethics* 34 (2006): 311–37.

Kelshaw, Todd. "Understanding Abnormal Public Discourses: Dialogue and Deliberation Defined." *International Journal of Public Participation* 1 (2007).

Mathews, David. *Politics for People: Finding a Responsible Public Voice.* Urbana: U of Illinois P, 1994.

Mathews, David, and Noëlle McAfee. *Making Choices Together: The Power of Public Deliberation.* Dayton, OH: Kettering Foundation, 2001.

Pearce, W. Barnett, and Stephen W. Littlejohn. *Moral Conflict: When Social Worlds Collide.* Thousand Oaks, CA: Sage, 1977.

Riker, William H. *The Strategy of Rhetoric: Campaigning for the American Constitution.* New Haven: Yale UP, 1996.

Shotter, John. *Conversational Realities: Constructing Life through Language.* London: Sage, 1993.

Simons, Herbert W. "In Praise of Muddleheaded Anecdotalism." *Western Journal of Speech Communication* 42 (1978): 21–28.

Thompson, Janna. *Discourse and Knowledge: Defence of a Collectivist Ethics.* London: Routledge, 2002.

10

Changing the Public Face of Christian Politics
The Rhetoric of Sojourners

Barbara Little Liu

At least since the emergence during the 1970s of organizations such as Jerry Falwell's Moral Majority, the political face of Christianity in the U.S. news media has been almost exclusively conservative, Republican, and focused on issues like abortion and school prayer. The generative power of the equation between "Christian" and "conservative" was in impressive evidence when results of a 2004 national election exit poll were reported: when voters were asked to choose the "issue" that mattered most in their vote, the greatest number (22 percent) chose "moral values" and 80 percent of those reported that they voted for Bush ("Election Results"). Based on this flawed poll, many commentators quickly concluded that George W. Bush's conservative stands on such issues as gay marriage and stem cell research had endeared him to Christians, thus garnering him a three million vote margin of victory.

However, since 2004, a different Christian politics has been garnering attention—one that espouses positions usually associated with "godless" liberals. Among others, Jim Wallis, with his best-selling book *God's Politics*, and the organization he heads, Sojourners, are offering the American public and media an alternative view of the relationship between faith and politics, placing more emphasis on eliminating poverty than on closing abortion clinics, on peace than on homosexuality, and on environmental stewardship than stem cells. Perhaps the greatest (but not only) evidence that these voices are being heeded is the Sojourners-sponsored "Forum on Faith, Values, and Poverty," which was broadcast in June 2007 on CNN and featured key Democratic presidential candidates.

As a scholar interested in both political and religious rhetorics and a Christian liberal appalled in the past by the media dominance of the religious Right, I have developed an interest in the rhetoric of Jim Wallis and Sojourners. My focus here is on Wallis's book, *God's Politics: Why the Right Gets It Wrong and the Left Doesn't Get It*. This particular rhetorical artifact draws attention to itself for a number of reasons: it was published early in 2005 and clearly in response to the media's emphasis on the role of "values" in the 2004 election; it was widely promoted by the Sojourners organization through their Web site, their e-mail newsletter (*Sojomail*), their print magazine, and an aggressive e-mail campaign to magazine subscribers. This promotion helped make it a *New York Times* nonfiction best seller for fifteen weeks (Schultz). Additionally, it may have had a significant impact on readers, helping to bring more believers into Sojourners' fold. John Dart, reporting for *Christian Century* magazine, noted that paid subscriptions to *Sojourners* magazine jumped from 24,300 in December 2002 to 45,500 in December 2006, and the percentage of those subscribers identified as "evangelicals" increased from 5 percent to 17 percent. While there may be a number of phenomena influencing this increase (Dart notes excellent writing and sound marketing practices), the appeal of *God's Politics* seems likely to have played a role in drawing attention to the organization Wallis heads.

The wide promotion, popularity, and possible impact of the book may in themselves constitute adequate reasons to examine it further. What is most important in this case, however, is its place at the center of a potentially influential grassroots social movement—one that seeks to correct, or at least complicate, the public face of political Christianity. *God's Politics* occupies this central position in the Sojourners organization and the social movement surrounding it because it is comprehensive in laying out that group's political philosophy and goals, while also including various previously published texts (editorials and ads placed in major media) that constitute manifestos and calls to action for Sojourners. If one wants to understand Sojourners, therefore, one must examine *God's Politics*.

My examination of the book is focused on a few key considerations that can be related to both its substance (its meaning or message) and its form (*how* that meaning/message is communicated). First, by examining the *substance* of Wallis's message, I identify his intended audience or audiences and ascertain his rhetorical goals with regard to those audiences. That is, to whom does his message seem designed to appeal (current members of Sojourners, potential members of Sojourners, or others) and what impact on their action or thought is it designed to bring about? Secondly, I explicate the rhetorical form used to achieve those goals—that is, the way in which delivery of the message is designed to appeal to and influence this audience. I argue that the form of Wallis's message (in this case, the jeremiad) is designed not just to *call his readers to* action, but also to offer a *model for* that action. This approach to substance and form is central to Bonnie J. Dow and Mari Boor Tonn's insightful analysis of the rhetoric of former Texas Governor Ann Richards. They argue that, in her use of feminine style, Richards achieves "a synthesis of form and substance that works to promote an alternative political philosophy reflecting traditional feminine values" (287). In a similar manner,

I will argue that Wallis's rhetoric synthesizes form and substance to "promote an alternative political philosophy" reflecting traditional Christian values in a way not currently associated with Christian political rhetoric.

As I began my examination of the form and substance of *God's Politics*, I expected to discover that Wallis's rhetoric was directed toward religious conservatives with the goal of realigning their religious and moral values with political views that have in recent decades been primarily associated with the secular Left. This hypothesis was validated by the work of other scholars analyzing Wallis's earlier (pre-2004 election) rhetoric. In a 2006 article in the *Journal of Communication and Religion*, rhetorical critics Bohn David Lattin and Steve Underhill analyze Wallis's 1995 book, *The Soul of Politics*. They argue that the primary audience to which Wallis directs his rhetoric is the religious Right (he "directly addresses the 'religious/evangelical Right' thirteen times, while only addressing the 'secular Left' twice") (216). They point to "Wallis's claim of creating a message that transcends the religious Right and Left" (207), but—through an application of Burke's "frames of acceptance"—they argue that "transcendence is not accomplished because Wallis simply invites the Right to become the Left" (216), a move that would be impossible given the Right's deep ideological commitments. Thus, based on Lattin and Underhill's precedent (as well as my own intuition), I expected to find Wallis once again trying to achieve transcendent agreement between the religious Right and the secular Left.

Unexpectedly, sustained analysis suggests a shift in Wallis's primary audiences. I argue that Wallis's message is now geared primarily toward a dual audience of (1) progressive evangelicals who feel left out of the dominant media portrayal of religion and politics and left behind by the Democratic party, as well as (2) liberal Democrat politicians (whether personally religious or secular) who have distanced themselves from religious communities and relegated religion to the private sphere—a group Wallis refers to frequently as "liberal secularists."[1] Rather than arguing, as he may have done in *The Soul of Politics*, that conservative Christians should redefine their politics, in *God's Politics* he contends that (1) moderate and progressive believers— whose views he suggests are more representative of both the greater majority of mainstream Christianity and of the Gospel message—need to become more outspoken and politically active in order to "change the wind" of public sentiment that Washington politicians are always trying to gauge (Wallis 21–22); and (2) the greatest hope for the success of liberal candidates and programs lies in a reclamation of liberalism's ties to religion.

Lattin and Underhill's article also allowed me to hypothesize about the form Wallis's rhetoric might take. They note: "An analysis of Wallis's text reveals that he constructed a *jeremiad*" (211, emphasis added). They briefly and clearly explicate this form and show how *The Soul of Politics* conforms to its expected structure, but the greatest part of their analysis focuses on other elements of rhetorical strategy and the metaphorical clusters within Wallis's rhetoric that might appeal to or conflict with conservative ideological frames of acceptance. Additionally, they fault Wallis for failing "to avail himself of all the available means to persuade his readers," especially suggesting that he "could have cited Biblical texts" but "does not avail himself of this deep resource of invention" (221).

While I am beholden to Lattin and Underhill for their identification of the jeremiad in Wallis's earlier rhetoric, examination of that form takes a much more central role in my analysis of *God's Politics* than it did in their work with *The Soul of Politics*. In *God's Politics*, Wallis makes continuous use of the Bible as a resource of rhetorical invention. He references the Gospel frequently, but his primary biblical references are to the prophets. Key among these prophets is Jeremiah, not only as a source of scriptural evidence, but also as a model for rhetorical action—through the eponymous jeremiad. Wallis looks to Jeremiah's example, then enacts and models the jeremiad as his key rhetorical strategy and form in *God's Politics*. Because it becomes not just the medium for his message but a model for the political and rhetorical action he calls on his readers to take, I argue that Wallis's utilization of the jeremiad is of central importance in *God's Politics* and constitutes a unique use of the form, worthy of scholarly attention.

I will present the analysis that has led to these conclusions by focusing on the first two sections of *God's Politics*, comprised of an introduction and the first six chapters, which lay the philosophical and persuasive groundwork for the more specific issue-by-issue discussion in the rest of the book.

WALLIS'S DUAL AUDIENCE

As noted earlier, Wallis's audience in *God's Politics* is not the religious Right—as I anticipated it would be—but rather a dual group of progressive evangelical Christians and "liberal secularists" (liberal Democrats who have excluded faith-grounded perspectives from the political sphere). I draw this conclusion from an examination of Wallis's descriptions of various groups and his use of inclusive or exclusive language. What are the characteristics of those Wallis describes as "they" and "them" versus the explicitly stated or implied characteristics of the corresponding "we" and "us"? Additionally, whose values and interests are served by the various actions and changes he proposes? I posit that those with whom Wallis works to identify—through either inclusive language or appeals to values and interests—constitute his target audience.

Wallis begins using these various tools of identification from the very first chapter of *God's Politics*, entitled "Take Back the Faith." He addresses his reader as follows:

> Many of us feel that our faith has been stolen, and it's time to take it back. In particular, an enormous public misrepresentation of Christianity has taken place. And because of an almost uniform media misperception, many people around the world now think that Christian faith stands for

political commitments that are almost the opposite of its true meaning. . . .
The problem is in the political arena, where strident voices claim to represent Christians when they clearly don't speak for *most* of us. . . . The religious political Right gets the public meaning of religion mostly wrong—preferring to focus on sexual and cultural issues while ignoring the weightier matters of justice. (3)

Wallis sets up a clear conflict here between conservative and progressive Christianity. And he also clearly takes sides. His tone with regard to the religious Right is accusatory and adversarial. *They* have stolen *our* religion. *Their* commitments are heretical: opposite the faith's "true meaning." *They* get it wrong. *They* don't speak for *us*. At the same time, his consistent use of the word "us" in referring to those he places in opposition to the religious Right makes clear to whom his message is addressed. Any notion that he might be trying in this book to reason with conservative Christians must be quickly dismissed.

The use of adversarial language to portray right-wing Christians continues throughout the first chapters of *God's Politics*, and indeed throughout the entire book. In a section of the first chapter with the heading "The Political Problem of Jesus," Wallis quotes "a nonprofit housing provider for the poor": "I just don't understand how a right-wing economic agenda can be squared with the clear teachings of Jesus on wealth and poverty in Matthew, Mark, Luke, and John" (15). Wallis goes on to ask, "Why are so many conservative evangelicals oblivious to the teaching of Jesus[?]" He concludes: "The politics of Jesus is a problem for the religious Right" (15).

In chapter 5, while discussing fundamentalist Christians' support for a violent response to the violence perpetrated by Islamic fundamentalists on 9/11, Wallis says: "It's always striking to me that when I listen to the Christian fundamentalist justifications for violence I don't hear them asking [the] question, 'What would Jesus do?' From a fundamentalist Christian point of view, shouldn't that be the key question to ask? What is more 'fundamental' to Christianity than Jesus?" (68). Again, Wallis refers to conservative Christians as *they*, and while here the corresponding *us* is not present, it is clearly implied. And again, he points out the heresy of their views as they ignore the teachings that should be at the center of Christianity: the teachings of Christ.

However, the *us* of Wallis's rhetoric, the silenced majority of moderate and progressive Christians, is not his only audience. Wallis also establishes early on a kind of altar call to liberal secularist Democrats. In his introduction, he reminds readers of the divisive 2004 election in which "no matter who won, almost half the population was going to feel absolutely crushed" (xv) and of the exit poll that placed "moral values" at the center of the results. While Wallis notes the flaws in that poll and the more complex view of the relationship between values and a host of related issues offered by later polls, he agrees that "religion was indeed a big factor in this election with moral values talk in the air the entire campaign" (xvii). However, he notes that each party handled religion differently and with different levels of success.

> George W. Bush talked comfortably and frequently about his personal
> faith and ran on what his conservative religious base called the "moral
> issues." . . . Senator John Kerry invoked the New Testament story of the
> Good Samaritan, talked about the importance of loving our neighbors,
> and said that faith without works is dead—but only began talking that
> way at the very end of his campaign. Critics . . . say he got religion too lit-
> tle and too late, while . . . Bush . . . used religion in one of the most parti-
> san ways ever seen. (xvii)

Wallis concludes that "too many Democrats still wanted to restrict religion to the private sphere and were very uncomfortable with the language of
faith and values even when applied to their own agenda" (xvii). He then
points to the kind of success they might achieve if they were to draw from the
well of mainstream Christian values. Quoting a Sojourners petition signed by
over 100,000 people and placed as an ad in more than fifty U.S. newspapers,
he notes that "poverty is a religious issue . . . the environment—protection of
God's creation—is a religious concern . . . war is also a serious religious and
theological matter" and "the number of unborn lives lost to abortion" and
"the one hundred thousand civilian casualties in Iraq . . . are both life issues"
(xviii). He concludes: "If there were ever candidates running with a strong set
of personal moral values *and* a commitment [to] social justice and peace, they
could build many bridges to the other side" (xix). While his portrayal of
Democrats as "secular fundamentalists" is certainly critical, it is not presented in terms as divisive and adversarial as those used in describing the religious Right. This softer tone allows the conclusion that secularist Democrats
function as a secondary audience for Wallis's arguments.

A JEREMIAD FOR PROGRESSIVE CHRISTIANS

Having identified Wallis's likely audiences, I move now to a discussion of
his use of the rhetorical form known as the American jeremiad. In his oft-
cited work, Americanist critic Sacvan Bercovitch traces the development of
the American jeremiad from the political sermons of the first Puritan settlers
in New England to its presence in the civil religion of the twentieth century.
Building on Bercovitch, other scholars continue to identify the form in its various current iterations, from the post-9/11 rhetoric of George Bush (Bostdorff) to Senator Bill Frist's 2001 address to the Society of Thoracic Surgeons
(Bates). Named for the biblical prophet Jeremiah, the form draws parallels
between America as a metaphorical "new Israel" and Americans as "chosen
people" to the rhetorical situation of biblical Israel during the Babylonian
exile (Bates 263). As Bates notes,

> The biblical story of Jeremiah is simple. Yahweh has become dissatisfied
> with the children of Israel because they have failed to fulfill their end of a
> holy covenant. . . . Although Yahweh allows Babylon to seize Israel, He
> has not given up on his chosen people. He allows Jeremiah to give Israel
> one last chance to recommit to the covenant. (262–63)

Bercovitch's work emphasizes the affirmative element unique to the American jeremiad. While the European roots of the form dwelt almost exclusively in a lament over the people's failures, American jeremiads contain an "unshakable optimism" (Bercovitch 7). The New England Puritans believed "God's punishments were corrective, not destructive. . . . His vengeance was a sign of love, a father's rod used to improve the errant child. In short, their punishments confirmed the promise" (8). The resulting characteristics of the American jeremiad, as summarized by Bates, are fourfold:

> First, the speaker must outline a tradition of *obedience to a higher calling* from which the community has deviated. . . . The speaker then identifies *a catastrophe that has befallen the community*, attributing it to deviation. Having made this identification, the speaker *calls on the community to recommit to the sacred covenant*. Last, the speaker *promises* that a recommitment will *return* the community *to prosperity and influence*. (263, emphasis added)

These four characteristics can be seen in Wallis's rhetoric as directed to each of the communities that make up his audience.

Wallis's clearest use of the American jeremiad is directed toward moderate and progressive Christians. In his introduction, Wallis defines "God's politics" by immediately reminding readers of idyllic forerunners who led by principles based in their faith, such as Abraham Lincoln and Martin Luther King, Jr. He notes that these men brought religion into public life not by "claiming God's blessing and endorsement for all our national policies and practices" but by "asking if we are on God's side," behaving in ways that will lead to "penitence and even repentance, humility, reflection, and even accountability" (xiv). The *tradition of obedience to a higher calling* outlined in this jeremiad is prophetic, holding political leadership accountable to its moral ground. As Wallis explains, when one enacts God's politics:

> it *challenges* everything about our politics. God's politics *reminds* us of the people our politics always neglects . . ., *challenges* narrow national, ethnic, economic, or cultural self-interest . . ., *reminds* us of the creation itself, a rich environment in which we are to be good stewards . . ., *pleads* with us to resolve the inevitable conflicts among us, as much as possible, without the terrible cost and consequences of war . . ., [and] *reminds* us of the ancient prophetic prescription to "choose life, so that you and your children may live." (xv, emphasis added)

Wallis's repeated use of active verbs like "challenges," "reminds," and "pleads" highlights the nature of the tradition as he understands it: a prophet does not just suffer silently or grumble to himself, but rather calls attention to the iniquities and inequities by *challenging* the community and its leaders, *reminding* them of their best commitments and values, and *pleading* with them to make a change. Therefore, the *obedience to a higher calling* advocated by Wallis means holding one's leaders to a rigorous and consistent moral standard through continual exhortative participation in the public sphere.

As noted earlier, Wallis begins his first chapter with the lament "our faith has been stolen" (3). This is the *catastrophe* that has befallen the community of mainstream Christians. Their faith is no longer their own; the Christianity recognized in the media bears no resemblance to the Gospels they hold sacred. They have been exiled by their silence.[2] They have not loudly and consistently exhorted their leaders and themselves to do better; in other words, they have not lived up to the prophetic covenant. As a result, "strident voices claim to represent Christians when they clearly don't speak for *most* of us" (3). This silent exile has resulted in the additional catastrophes of the Bush administration for which "other priorities were just more important. . . . Tax cuts that mostly benefited the wealthy were more important, the war in Iraq was more important, and homeland security was more important—all without key recognition of how poverty, despair, family instability, and social disintegration undermine our national security" (12).

At the same time that he describes this catastrophe, Wallis *calls on this community to recommit to the sacred covenant*, by telling them, "It's time to take back our faith in the public square, especially in a time when a more authentic social witness is desperately needed" (3). In his fourth chapter, entitled "Protest Is Good; Alternatives Are Better," Wallis provides an example of the kind of authentic social witness that would return the Christian community to its commitment by telling the story of a six-point plan promoted by Sojourners and a group of U.S. church leaders in the days leading up to the war in Iraq. While he laments the fact that its promotion was too late to gain the necessary momentum needed to stop the war, he argues that, had it come earlier, it could have provided the White House with a serious alternative. He cites support from British Prime Minister Tony Blair and members of his cabinet, interest from UN Secretary General Kofi Annan, and coverage by the *Washington Post* as evidence of the degree to which the plan sensibly addressed the exigencies of the Iraq situation (44–45). The strength of the plan, he argues, is that, unlike protest, it did not just say "no" to war, but offered a credible alternative.

> [The plan] took the threat of Saddam Hussein seriously. It called for his removal from power through an international criminal indictment, the elimination through coercive inspections of any weapons of mass destruction he might have, and the democratic reconstruction of Iraq under international leadership (not U.S. occupation)—all without war. (43)

Building on the potential of the six-point plan, Wallis exhorts his readers to adopt a public rhetoric that doesn't just protest, but offers real alternatives, just as the American jeremiad doesn't just lament the current catastrophe, but suggests the possibility of redemption. He sums up the chapter by tying this approach back to the covenant:

> Offering better visions is in *the best of our traditions* of dissent and protest. Saying "yes" and not just "no" gives political leaders something to consider and debate and not merely something to stop. . . . And, ultimately,

it will be more successful. *It is the tradition of the prophets* who claimed that injustice will not have the last word and that a newer world is not only possible but, indeed, is *the promise of God*. (49, emphasis added)

Wallis's clear call for a return to prophetic traditions, stated here in explicitly biblical terms, suggests that his use of the jeremiad is a conscious and strategic rhetorical choice. He calls on his readers to enact the very form of participation he models in his own rhetoric. As he recalls a higher calling for his readers, he asks them to remind their leaders of that same calling. As he calls for recommitment to the sacred covenant, he asks readers to ask for that same recommitment from their government.

Wallis also promotes prophetic action, by encouraging his evangelical readers to vote "*all* your values" (78, emphasis added). He argues that candidates who profess faith must be called upon to articulate how their faith is expressed in their politics. And they must be held to their own professed standard, the inconsistencies between their talk and their actions pointed out. For example, Wallis asks:

> How does the religious principle of the sacredness of human life challenge all the candidates, for example, on abortion, capital punishment, military spending, missile defense, or gun control? . . . Couldn't both pro-life and pro-choice political leaders agree to common ground actions that would actually reduce the abortion rate, rather than continue to use abortion mostly as a political symbol? Instead of imposing rigid pro-choice and pro-life political litmus tests, why not work together on teen pregnancy, adoption reform and real alternatives for women backed into dangerous and lonely corners? (79)

In other words, a consistent application of Christian values—and hence a return to the sacred covenant—would result neither in reactionary conservatism nor knee-jerk liberalism. But, to be fair, Wallis's applications of "the religious principle of the sacredness of human life" look like liberal politics far more often than they look like the religious Right.

As clearly as he sets out a plan to recommit to covenant, Wallis asserts that recommitment *will return the community to prosperity and influence.* Reminding readers of the current catastrophe, he says: "Perhaps the most mistaken media perception of our time is that religious influence in politics only equates to the politics of the religious Right" (81). He then points to a brighter future: "My prediction is that moderate and progressive religious voices will ultimately shape politics in the coming decades far more significantly than the religious Right will" (81). Wallis predicts that his primary audience will be returned to influence and even come to dominate political discourse; however, the resulting return to prosperity, in Wallis's vision, extends not just to his readers but to all Americans, as it takes the form of an end to partisanship that emphasizes spin and discourages action.

> We would find new agreements across old political boundaries and new common ground among people who agree on values and are ready to chal-

lenge the special interests on all sides who are obstructing the solutions most Americans would support. Ideologies have failed us; values can unite us, especially around our most common democratic visions. (84)

In approaching his primary audience of progressive Christians, then, Wallis's use of the jeremiad takes on a dual role. The form seems perfectly suited to his message and audience as it allows him to chastise them for allowing their current catastrophic situation and emphasize optimistic possibilities for the future—all the while offering them a clear model for the praxis that will bring about that better future.

A Jeremiad for Democrats

While it is clear that Wallis is primarily writing to the "us" of moderate and liberal evangelical Christians, as I demonstrated above, he also hopes to have some impact on the liberal secularists of the Democratic Party. He uses the form of the jeremiad to reach this secondary audience as well by *reminding them of their traditional commitments* and ties to religious communities. Over and over again, Wallis links central tenets of liberal ideology to the progressive evangelical movements of the past. In his introduction, he reminds us of the sermonic rhetoric of both Abraham Lincoln and Martin Luther King, Jr., both icons for civil rights. In chapter 3, he includes the text of an MSNBC column in which he responds to Minnesota governor Jesse Ventura's assertions in a *Playboy* interview that "organized religion is a sham and a crutch for weak-minded people who need strength in numbers" (qtd. in Wallis 38). Wallis tells Ventura:

> I'm sure people have already reminded you about Martin Luther King Jr. and Gandhi, who were pretty tough. Just ask the Southern governors or the British. And I remember watching South African Arch-bishop Desmond Tutu face down armed security police inside his Cathedral in Cape-town, while Nelson Mandela was still in prison. "You have already lost!" he told them, "So why don't you come and join the winning side!" He was smiling when he said it, but not because he was weak-minded. (38)

Similarly, in chapter 6, he reminds readers of the leaders of the anti-apartheid movement, as well as the work of "Archbishop Oscar Romero in El Salvador during the 1980s, church leaders in the Philippines during the revolution that ousted dictator Ferdinand Marcos, [and] the critical opposition to communist rule in Poland" (77).

In all these cases, Wallis pairs cornerstones of American liberal ideology (commitment to human rights, the rule of law, universal suffrage, and representative democracy) to the religious individuals and movements who were their loudest and most successful advocates. He reminds liberal politicians of the times when they have metaphorically and sometimes literally walked arm-in-arm with religious leaders in common political cause, then calls into question the depth of their commitment to liberal ideals when he asks:

> Why do so many liberals seem supportive of religious language when it is
> invoked by black civil rights leaders like Martin Luther King Jr., but
> recoil when such language is employed by white political leaders? Is there
> a subtle kind of racism going on here, where religion is okay for liberals
> as long as it comes from black or poor people? Are black people supposed
> to be culturally religious (love those black choirs), while white believers
> are intellectually suspect? (69–70)

This is certainly pointed criticism, but it does not exclude liberals from his
audience the way his accusations and us-versus-them rhetoric excludes the
religious Right. It is, however, clearly in the tradition of the jeremiad as it
asks liberals to recognize how they have deviated from a higher tradition and
broken a valuable covenant.

Having thoroughly recalled liberalism's religious ties, Wallis *points to the
current catastrophe* of which his readers are all too well aware, not the least element of which is the 2004 presidential election. Looking deeper, Wallis cites
a biblical proverb: "Without a vision, the people perish" (24). The "vision"
for Wallis is a consistent moral standard and set of values rooted in religion,
specifically a correct reading of the Christian gospels. The application of such
a standard could result in a "guiding moral compass that steers our public
life" and engenders thoughtful and consistent policies. Without such a vision,
"powerful interests argue, point fingers at one another, and vie for greater
position and influence, while far less powerful people suffer and are forgotten. . . . We lose all sense of the common good or our shared humanity, . . . a
lack of vision contributes to social unrest, lawlessness, violence, and chaos"
(25). Certainly this is a catastrophic vision.

However, just as he does with his evangelical audience, Wallis calls on
the Democratic Party to *recommit to their sacred covenant, promising a return to
prosperity and influence.* Wallis's rhetoric is always infused with the optimism
of the American jeremiad; God never gives up and His people can always
choose to recommit to the covenant. While Wallis decries the lack of vision
in liberal politics, he quickly offers hope: "The vision is there and merely
awaits us" (28). Laying the groundwork for the more specific issues-based
discussion in the rest of the book, he says,

> This book takes up the most important public questions of our time and
> applies to them the best wisdom of both our prophetic and democratic
> visions. . . . Whenever we deal with social and economic decisions and
> policies, we will always ask what I call the "God question," which is,
> "How are the kids doing?" What happens to the children, our own and
> everybody else's, is always a question that illuminates all the others. (29)

The "God question" becomes the foundation for the vision applied in the rest
of the book and the keystone for recommitment to liberal politics' higher calling. While the latter sections of *God's Politics* apply this vision to a variety of
issues (from terrorism to racism and from peace in the Middle East to domestic and international poverty), a particularly illustrative example can be seen

in his discussion of the hot button issue of abortion. Wallis describes a student forum on social justice at Notre Dame and how one student

> passionately reminded the group that a legal practice that kills four thousand unborn children every day is an urgent moral imperative. But she was then reminded that nine thousand people each day now die of AIDS, thirty thousand children perish every day because of hunger and diseases mostly due to poverty, and as many as half a million are lost each year in international conflicts and wars. All agreed that a more consistent ethic of human life is sorely needed. (301)

The vision of "a more consistent ethic of human life" clearly relates to the question of "what happens to the kids?" and would lead political leaders, Wallis believes, to "really [target] the problems of teen pregnancy and adoption reform, which are so critical to reducing abortion, while offering real support for women, especially low-income women, at greater risk for unwanted pregnancies" (300). In the same chapter, he relates the ethic of human life to the death penalty. In so doing, he shows how its application should lead to a coming together of those currently at opposite ends of the political spectrum. Vehemently pro-choice democrats would need to work more actively to reduce abortions, while conservatives like President Bush would need to repent their support for and use of the death penalty. Thus, in this chapter and others, Wallis works to show how vision is needed in politics and how that vision should combine "what the Old Testament prophets, Jesus, and the New Testament writers had to say" with "our own American traditions [of] democratic ideals" (28). He holds out hope for the community's recommitment to sacred covenant by frequently reminding his audience that "the vision is always there, waiting for us to grasp, embrace, and implement it" (28).

What might the payoff of this return to vision be for Democrats? How will it fulfill the promise of the jeremiad and return them to prosperity and influence? According to Wallis, "Such vision could 'change the wind.' It could change how we think and feel about our public lives, at a deeper level than the shallow spectator sport that our politics has become" (30). Additionally, he states that a change in wind could "significantly alter the framework and spirit of the current debates, which have deadlocked the public discussion and blocked solutions to some of our most serious problems" (30). In other words, a return to vision could lead to a less divisive and more productive American political climate. And, given the positions espoused as the vision is applied throughout *God's Politics*, a polity united under that vision would enact many policies and programs that have long been mainstays of the Democratic Party's platform—from more compassionate safety nets for the working poor to greater protection of human rights. Thus, Wallis's book serves as a jeremiad for both progressive Christians and liberal secularists, promising God-given prosperity and influence to both.

A MORE ACCOMPLISHED MISSIONARY

While Wallis may not have read Lattin and Underhill's critique of *The Soul of Politics*, it seems he does not repeat the rhetorical errors they see in that earlier book. Lattin and Underhill argued that Wallis's rhetoric was not appropriately directed to its primary audience since in order to "accept [his] invitation [to Christian political solidarity], conservatives must abandon their political identity/interests, while accepting liberal identity/interests" (220). Since to do so is to give up core tenets of ideology, such a move is practically impossible, and therefore Wallis's rhetoric is "hostile toward conservatism and fails to address concerns of the religious Right" (220). While Wallis is still largely hostile toward conservatism in *God's Politics*, conservatives are clearly no longer his primary audience. His new audience of progressive Christians and liberal secularist politicians are more ideologically aligned with his positions and are also primed for his message by the catastrophic situations in which they find themselves languishing: silent exile and political failure, respectively. It seems, then, that the potential strength of the rhetoric of *God's Politics* lies in Wallis's capitalizing on the perfect *kairotic* moment. He has found the rhetorical situation most suited to his purpose.

Wallis has also, I would argue, perfected his use of the jeremiad. While Lattin and Underhill noted the presence of the jeremiad in *The Soul of Politics*, their analysis emphasizes the rift between Wallis's predominantly liberal ideology and the conservative ideology of his audience. In *God's Politics*, however, the jeremiad takes on a central role in Wallis's rhetoric. Through his use of the jeremiad Wallis not only effectively communicates a message, but also models the very form of political participation he calls on his progressive Christian readers to adopt. He repeatedly reminds his readers of the role of the biblical prophets (not only Jeremiah but Micah and Amos, among others) who shamed the community for their injustice and reminded them of the promise awaiting them upon their return to the sacred covenant. Wallis calls for a "prophetic politics" that "could offer a way forward beyond our polarized and paralyzed national politics and could be the foundation . . . to provide the new ideas politics always needs" (75). Lattin and Underhill faulted Wallis for failing to "avail himself of [a] deep source of invention" by not citing biblical texts: "No stronger arguments exist for the conservative Christian than the Bible" (221). While, again, his audience may no longer include these conservatives, in *God's Politics* Wallis makes full use of the Bible as a source of rhetorical invention. Not only do biblical citations provide justification for the various political and social positions he espouses, but biblical prophets serve as his rhetorical models. It is difficult to imagine how his argument could be more thoroughly steeped in the Bible.

God's Politics is the work of a rhetor who has identified an apt *kairotic* moment and produced, in response, an artfully structured argument that makes use of the best available means of persuasion. In doing so, he has also used the jeremiad in two ways that might have further relevance for rhetorical critics. First, he uses this form—most often associated with conservatism—to address an audience of progressives. William V. Spanos, in his survey of various literary intersections between the jeremiad and "the fact of the frontier," articulates the conservatism of the form: "the Puritan jeremiad, in its secularized form, became the essential cultural instrument of the dominant Anglo-Protestant core culture in maintaining its hegemony in the face of the astonishing cultural and political transformations America underwent in the long wake of the decline of Puritan theocracy" (38). As noted previously, numerous other critics have articulated the use of the jeremiad by political conservatives. The jeremiad clearly lends itself to conservative ideology as it emphasizes a return to the values and commitments of an idyllic past; however, *progressive* ideology is usually associated with progress and, hence, future change. Wallis is able to couch progressive changes in the usually conservative terms of a return to core values, and while he is not the only rhetor to have done so (Martin Luther King is another example), he is the most contemporary.

Perhaps Wallis is able to make this ideologically oxymoronic use of the jeremiad because he returns the form to its religious roots. This is the second aspect of Wallis's rhetoric that invites further critical interest. Spanos, as quoted above, makes clear that the American jeremiad moved away from its religious roots to become a secular form. Similarly, Mark S. Jendrysik, in his examination of the "declinism" of Bloom, Bennett, and Bork, notes that while the "modern jeremiad shares . . . many goals" with its seventeenth century Puritan precursor, "One of the key differences lies in religious emphasis. In the secularized culture of modern America, explicit religious exhortations run the risk of appearing too sectarian and alienating potential friends. Modern writers therefore rely upon a vague appeal to 'Western tradition'" (362). Certainly, given his Christian audience, it makes sense for Wallis to return to the jeremiad's religious past, but this move is also risky. Contemporary American Christianity is significantly sectarian, and as he appeals to progressives with his message, Wallis alienates the religious Right (as Lattin and Underhill made clear). But his choice of a religious form reveals Wallis's confidence that there is, in fact, a significant audience of progressive Christians who would identify with both the political and religious ideologies he combines in his rhetoric. Wallis himself states: "As I travel the country, I find many people who share this perspective" (75). By returning to the religious roots of the jeremiad form, Wallis is able to put its conservative idealization of the past to a progressive purpose.

Notes

[1] "Secularists" are not necessarily a-religious or anti-religious. Someone with religious beliefs or practices is a "secularist" (in Wallis's use of the term) if he or she keeps their religion almost entirely private and minimizes its influence on their political views and actions.

[2] Interestingly, Jerry Falwell identified a similar catastrophe for religious conservatives in 1980 when he named them a "*silent* majority" (Mitchell and Phipps 56, emphasis added).

Works Cited

Bates, Benjamin R. "Senator Bill Frist and the Medical Jeremiad." *Journal of Medical Humanities* 26.4 (2005): 259–72.

Bercovitch, Sacvan. *The American Jeremiad.* Madison: U of Wisconsin P, 1978.

Bostdorff, Denise M. "George W. Bush's Post-September 11 Rhetoric of Covenant Renewal: Upholding the Faith of the Greatest Generation." *Quarterly Journal of Speech* 89.4 (2003): 293–319.

Dart, John. "The Rise and Fall of Protestant Magazines." 26 Dec. 2006. *The Christian Century.* 28 Mar. 2008. <http://www.christiancentury.org/article.lasso?id=2709>.

Dow, Bonnie J., and Mari Boor Tonn. "'Feminine Style' and Political Judgment in the Rhetoric of Ann Richards." *Quarterly Journal of Speech* 79.3 (1993): 286–302.

"Election Results." 2005. *CNN.com.* 27 Mar. 2008. <http://www.cnn.com/ELECTION/2004/pages/results/states/US/P/00/epolls.0.html>.

Jendrysik, Mark S. "The Modern Jeremiad: Bloom, Bennett, and Bork on American Decline." *Journal of Popular Culture* 36.2 (2002): 361–83.

Lattin, Bohn David, and Steve Underhill. "The Soul of Politics: The Reverend Jim Wallis's Attempt to Transcend the Religious/Secular Left and the Religious Right." *Journal of Communication and Religion* 29 (2006): 205–23.

Mitchell, Nancy E., and Kim S. Phipps. "The Jeremiad in Contemporary Fundamentalism: Jerry Falwell's *Listen America.*" *Religious Communication Today* 8 (Sep. 1985): 54–62.

Schultz, Ray. "Sojourners Uses E-mail to Create a Best-seller." 1 Mar. 2005. *Direct Magazine Online.* 27 Mar. 2008. <http:www.directmag.com/mag/marketing_sojourners_uses_email/index.html>.

Spanos, William V. "American Exceptionalism, the Jeremiad, and the Frontier: From the Puritans to the Neo-Con-Men." *boundary 2* 34.1 (2007): 35–66.

Wallis, Jim. *God's Politics: Why the Right Gets It Wrong and the Left Doesn't Get It.* San Francisco: HarperCollins, 2005.

The Temporality and Function of "Ethical Shifting" in Discursive Interaction

Stephen R. Yarbrough

Donald Davidson reminds us that "we tend to forget that there are no such things [as languages] in the world; there are only speakers and their various written and acoustical products" (*Subjective* 108). Pierre Bourdieu says in *The Logic of Practice* that "to posit, as Saussure does, that the true medium of communication is not speech . . . but language . . ., is to . . . [subordinate] the very substance of communication . . . to a pure construct of which there is no sense experience" (30).

The interactionist perspective these philosophers represent refuses to reify the concept of "language." Kenneth Gergen has expressed the consequence of this refusal succinctly: "Words (or texts) within themselves bear no meaning; they fail to communicate. They only appear to generate meaning by virtue of their place within the realm of human interaction. It is human interchange that gives language its capacity to mean . . ." (263–64).

But *how* does discursive interaction give "language" its apparent capacity to mean? The answer lies in the fact that discourse is a social phenomenon and sociality is itself a temporal phenomenon. In previous work, I have argued that discursive interactions occur through a unitary, inferential process having simultaneously cognitive, ethical, and affective phases.[1] In themselves, cognition and emotion are not actions but *motions*, mechanical causal sequences that machines and insentient organisms can produce. Motion is describable in Newtonian time, what George Herbert Mead called "knife-edge presents" (*Selected* 289). This is structuralist time, what Saussure called "diachronism," a formal relation between timeless synchronic slices. Each synchronic slice is temporally vacuous—that is, the present has no temporal extent and is cut off from the past and future.

When we understand time only diachronically, we can account for social motion, but not for social action. The reason is that cognitive and emotive

144

*motion*s take place habitually within and with respect to a single, already established set of social relations, that is, with respect to a single "ethical field," whereas social *action*s occur between fields. Structural thinkers such as Saussure and Foucault can explain social motion, but not social action. They treat social "moves" as if they were analogous to those we make when we play a board game, such as chess, purely "logically" (cf. Yarbrough, "Force" 353–54). Board games, as such, are played within a single field of objects and relations, and moves in the game make sense only with respect to the already defined roles of the pieces on an already defined field of play with already defined constraints. The consequence is that when we play chess purely "logically"—that is, when we play it *only* with respect to the set of relations that constitutes the game of chess—the game is "timeless" in at least two senses: (1) the "timing" or pace of moves is irrelevant to the game, and (2) the history of the game's moves is equally irrelevant. As far as the game is concerned, it matters not a whit whether the game is played in an hour or a decade, steadily or erratically; and if two people have been playing one another for hours and a third walks up, that third player is just as capable (in theory) of making the next best move as either of the two original players, because the current position of the pieces on the board says it all. Temporality here is no more than a sequence of positional changes whose logic is already formally determined. Time is irrelevant to chess because chess, as such, even when played by human beings, is merely motion. It can just as efficiently—if not more effectively—be played by machines.

Discourse, however, is not analogous to a chess game, as such, and it is necessarily temporal because it is social action. "Sociality," as Mead has defined it, "is the capacity of being several things at once" (*Philosophy* 75). That is to say, it is the capacity to act with respect to more than one set of social relations at once. The moves of an actual chess game *become* meaningful actions and not merely mechanically logical motions to the extent that they enter relations *besides* those that constitute the game. For instance, a player may make a move not in order to win the game, but in order to teach a student the consequences of making such a move; or, although trying to win, a player may make a move not because the game's internal logic demands it, but because having played her opponent many times before, she knows how he will probably respond to it; or, a player may know that he should castle his king, but does not because he knows a friend has bet someone that during that game he would not. The chess player who makes moves "taking into account" other relationships such as these and not merely those of the logic of the game, as such, is acting socially and so necessarily temporally.

Because discursive interactions take place within multiple fields of social relations, the logics of these fields can intersect, and when they do, the conflict interrupts their temporal orders. Such interruptions Mead *(Philosophy)* calls "events." Events are unique; they do not fit the prior patterns of thought and emotion. Events pull the past and the future into the present, reconfiguring both past and future patterns to accommodate that which had been unanticipated. The present, the locus of reality and meaning, therefore, has what Mead calls "a temporal spread"—neither reality nor meaning can "be reduced to instants," and the "earlier stages" of meaningful interaction "must be conditions of later phases" (62).

When we understand temporality in this way, we can see that meaningful cognitive and emotional *actions* necessarily "take place" *between* ethical spaces, in transitions between what Mead (*Philosophy*) calls "consentent sets" of social relationships, relationships that make sense together from a certain perspective or "generalized attitude."

A "consentent set" of relationships unified in a "percipient event" by a "perspective" is similar to what Pierre Bourdieu calls a *field* unified by a *habitus*. A *habitus* is a "system of structured, structuring dispositions . . . which is constituted in practice and is always oriented toward practical functions" (52). Bourdieu emphasizes the individual's passive relation to *habitus*, stressing its function of maintaining the continuity of human interaction. For Bourdieu, the *habitus* creates "a world of already realized ends . . ." (53), and it "ensures the active presence of past experiences, which, . . . in the form of schemes of perception, thought, and action, tend to guarantee the 'correctness' of practices and their constancy over time . . ." (54).

Again, as for Mead, for Bourdieu these sets of relationships among objects that are unified by a *habitus* provide the stable ground against which we experience temporal change. As Bourdieu observes, then, because our practices are "generated by our already established perspective, the *habitus*," they "are adapted in advance to the objective conditions" (62). For example, when I paint my house, the objects and relations I notice, such as the paint flakes on the walls and the mildew on the eaves, and the activities I am disposed to perform and their order, such as scraping, sanding, mixing, and painting, have been adapted to the situation in advance by the *habitus* because it was the *habitus* that created the field in which my house could be seen as needing to be painted in the first place.

Moreover, the practices of those who share a *habitus* will be "immediately intelligible and foreseeable, and hence taken for granted" (58). As a result, Bourdieu insists, "the *habitus* makes questions of intention superfluous, not only in the production but also in the deciphering of practices and works" (58). That's why when my neighbor sees me painting my house, he need not ask me what I'm doing or why I'm doing it. He knows very well why.

Bourdieu's description of the *habitus* may rightly explain those everyday situations in which nothing needs to be said because everything "goes without saying"—those situations in which we do not act *per se* but "go through the motions" and in which the past flows most unaffectedly into the present. But what happens when things do *not* go without saying, when what we or others do or say does not make immediate sense?

What I want to argue here is that, when ordinary habitual discursive practices fail, what interlocutors must alter before they can successfully communicate is, above all, the ethical fields within which their respective utterances make their sense. They must, in other words, make an "ethical shift," and to do that, I suggest, is to reorder time.

We need to reorder time when our interlocutors are moving within a different ethical field from ourselves because, although they may experience the "same" objects and events as we, those objects and events will be in different relationships with one another and therefore have different temporal orders from ours: the same events will have different temporal spreads, and habitual motions will have different rhythms or patterns of emphasis, different urgencies, and so on. Consequently, when we apperceive objects from different ethical perspectives, and so from within different fields, what one person says now may be completely unintelligible to others, not because they are using different "languages," not because they are not familiar with the same concepts, and not because they have different perceptual organs, but because they apperceive the relations among the objects of the discourse differently.

An analogy to this phenomenon is our perception of certain optical illusions, such as Jastrow's famous duck-rabbit sketch. If two people who see only the duck are overheard by a third person who sees only the rabbit, most of what the two say about the duck, however rational and true their words may be to them, to the third person they will seem either utter gibberish or something entirely different from what they intend.

This difference occurs not because the parties speak different languages or see different lines, shades, and so forth, but simply because they relate the same lines and shades to one another in different ways, so that what they are talking about is different. Of course, those who see the duck can learn to see the rabbit, and the one who sees the rabbit can learn to see the duck. Ordinarily, this will not produce a third perspective from which they combine the relationships of both sets so that all see the same thing, a "dabbit" or a "ruck," but each will be able to shift back and forth as need arises, correlate their differences, and recognize that what one sees as ears the other sees as a bill.[2]

We necessarily perform ethical shifts similar to such gestalt shifts all day, every day, because we share the world with others having different purposes from ourselves who therefore apperceive different significant relationships among the world's objects at different times. We accommodate these different fields primarily by altering the timing[3] of our actions within our own current field of conduct. We speed up, slow down, and stop in traffic because of it; we rush our lunch and hurry to a meeting because of it; we adjust our syllabi because of it; we postpone washing our clothes because of it; we wait in line at the theater because of it; and on and on—but, most of all, because of it we adjust what we say (or write) and when we say it.

This ability to shift from one ethical field or consentient set to another, adjusting our sense of temporal order accordingly, is absolutely essential to our sociality and therefore to our discursive competence. Knowing what words typically "mean" is not enough, because "meaning," in that sense, is stuck in the past. In fact, most of the discursive work we traditionally attribute to "language" is actually a function of ethical shifting.

Consider, for instance, a metaphor. When in the *Iliad* we read "Achilleus is a lion," we understand the utterance immediately. Structural theories claim that somehow the meanings of the words have changed.[4] Donald Davidson, in sharp contrast, argues that metaphors do not create special meanings; rather, "metaphors mean what the words, in their most literal interpretation, mean, and nothing more" (*Inquiries* 245). From this point of view, "Achilleus is a lion" is a false statement. However, Davidson says that what metaphors *do* (as opposed to *mean*) is nudge us to notice relationships we've never noticed before. Noticing new relationships, I would argue, initiates an ethical shift, not a linguistic change.

Mead again is helpful here. Joas summarizes Mead's analysis not just of metaphor but of meaningful social events in general: "In every referential system any event can only be of a single kind which is identical with itself." Thus, in our example, Achilleus is Achilleus and a lion is a lion. But, Joas continues, "To be of two different kinds at the same time means, therefore, belonging simultaneously to two referential systems." To say that Achilleus *is* a lion, then, is to ask your interpreter to apperceive Achilleus in relation to two different ethical fields at once, to relate simultaneously to Achilleus the human warrior *and* to Achilleus the ravenous beast. Yet, Joas goes on to say, "Now, an event is in two referential systems only when it is in passing from the one to the other" (182). This passage is the ethical shift—the change of attitude toward Achilleus, and so the change in our expectation of how he will act—that marks time and makes meaning.

The ethical shift toward Achilleus induces, at the same time, a reinterpretation of Achilleus' past acts and a reconception of his probable future acts. Even as we shift from ethically regarding Achilleus as we do human warriors to regarding him as we do irrational ravenous beasts, in order for us to anticipate Achilleus' future actions we reinterpret his past actions from the new perspective. Unlike our response to our opponent's moves in a chess game, where motivations and intentions—causal historical forces—are irrelevant, in meaningful interaction those forces and our ability to follow the arc of their historical trajectory are everything. Reading the *Iliad*, the audience does follow this arc and can anticipate Achilleus' future actions, but being ignorant of Achilleus' previous actions and of the narrator's metaphoric descriptions of them, Hector, during his final confrontation with Achilleus, still regards his enemy from within their presumed shared *habitus* of the warrior society. Before they fight, Hector proposes they swear to uphold their warriors' code and the winner allow the loser a proper funeral. But Achilleus responds, "Hector, talk not to me, thou madman, of covenants. As between lions and men there are no oaths of faith, ... even so it is not possible for thee and me to be friends . . ." (*Iliad* 22: 260). And, even as Hector lies dying, when he asks Achilleus again to be allowed a proper funeral, Achilleus the lion responds with a threat to eat Hector raw.

Literature provides us with numerous examples of such moments when characters succeed or, like Hector, fail to radically reinterpret past and future events, redefine objects, and reevaluate relationships—all in an instant—by performing an ethical shift. Of course, most of the ethical shifts we make continually all day, every day are habitual, commonplace events that require no such radical revision of the past. We notice the food in our refrigerator has spoiled, then we throw it in the trash; we finish a book, then we set it on a shelf: in these cases, what was once food instantly becomes (and will have been) trash to dispose; what was once something to read instantly becomes (and will have been) something to store. The tempo of our daily lives is set by such events. In such quotidian moments the cycle of cognitive expectation, unexpected event, emotional reaction, apperceptual adjustment, reinterpretation, and revised cognitive expectation is familiar, automatic, and unnoticed. However, when an event is unfamiliar—including those times when an interlocutor's use of words is unfamiliar, we must shift our ethical stance more radically.

Through ethical shifting we continually adapt our attitudes, our dispositions to act, and our sense of time to a social world whose objects have their own dispositions that may resist our own and whose temporal orders conflict with our own. Through this interaction our world and our discursive meanings continually evolve.

Notes

[1] See Yarbrough, "On the Very Idea."

[2] Under certain circumstances, such a blending can occur, thus inventing a novel concept. I discuss those circumstances at length in *Inventive Intercourse*.

[3] Timing is usually discussed under the heading of the classical concept of *kairos*. Sipiora and Baumlin offer a representative selection of ancient and contemporary theories of *kairos*; however, each of these reduces timing to a "subjective" matter governed by the perception of mental states or an "objective" matter governed by the conception of physical, causal forces; or they attempt to reconcile the two. Both of these senses of "timing" neglect sociality altogether.

[4] Entire books and innumerable articles have attempted, unsuccessfully, to explain how metaphors can mean. Of course, they usually assume that language is an abstract entity that its function is representational, that in order to represent metaphor must function under a special rule for breaking linguistic rules, that metaphor creates new meanings for old words, and so forth. For a good collection of many of the most influential attempts to explain metaphor, see Johnson.

Works Cited

Bourdieu, Pierre. *The Logic of Practice*. Trans. Richard Nice. Stanford, CA: Stanford UP, 1990.

Davidson, Donald. *Inquiries into Truth and Interpretation*. Oxford, UK: Clarendon P, 1984.

———. *Subjective, Intersubjective, Objective*. Oxford: Oxford UP, 2001.

Foucault, Michel. *The Subject and Power: Afterword*. Ed. Hubert L. Dreyfus and Paul Rabinow. Chicago: U of Chicago P, 1982.

Gergen, Kenneth J. *Realities and Relationships: Soundings in Social Construction*. Cambridge: Harvard UP, 1994.

Homer. *The Iliad*. Trans. A. T. Murray. Vol. 2. Cambridge: Harvard UP, 1925.

Joas, Hans. *G. H. Mead: A Contemporary Re-examination of His Thought*. Trans. Raymond Meyer. Cambridge: MIT P, 1985.

Johnson, Mark, ed. *Philosophical Perspectives on Metaphor.* Minneapolis: U of Minnesota P, 1985.

Mead, George Herbert. *The Philosophy of the Present.* Amherst, NY: Prometheus, 2002.

———. *Selected Writings.* Ed. Andrew J. Reck. Chicago: U of Chicago P, 1964.

Saussure, Ferdinand de. *Course in General Linguistics.* Trans. Wade Baskin. London: Fontana/Collins, 1974.

Sipiora, Phillip, and James S. Baumlin, eds. *Rhetoric and Kairos: Essays in History, Theory, and Praxis.* Albany: State U of New York P, 2002.

Yarbrough, Stephen R. "Force, Power, and Motive." *Philosophy and Rhetoric* 29 (1996): 344–58.

———. *Inventive Intercourse: From Rhetorical Conflict to the Ethical Creation of Novel Truth.* Carbondale: Southern Illinois UP, 2006.

———. "On the Very Idea of Composition: Modes of Persuasion or Phases of Discourse?" *JAC* 25 (2005): 491–512.

Edit This Page
Wikipedia and the
Responsibilities of Digital Rhetorics

James J. Brown, Jr.

On May 26, 2005, the following text was added to Wikipedia's article for John Seigenthaler, Sr.:

> John Seigenthaler Sr. was the assistant to Attorney General Robert Kennedy in the early 1960s. For a short time, he was thought to have been directly involved in the Kennedy assassinations of both John, and his brother, Bobby. Nothing was ever proven. John Seigenthaler moved to the Soviet Union in 1972, and returned to the United States in 1984. He started one of the country's largest public relations firms shortly thereafter. ("Seigenthaler Incident")

Of these five sentences, only the first was accurate. Seigenthaler had indeed worked for Robert Kennedy in the 1960s. However, he was never implicated in the assassination of Robert or John Kennedy, had never moved to the Soviet Union, and was not the founder of a public relations firm (his older brother Thomas founded Seigenthaler Public Relations). In late September 2005, Seigenthaler learned of the faulty Wikipedia article from his friend Victor Johnson, who suggested that Seigenthaler should "sue the s.o.b. who wrote it" (Seigenthaler). The false information was eventually removed by Eric Newton, a colleague of Seigenthaler's, but the archive of previous edits—an archive that accompanies all Wikipedia articles—still contained the false and libelous information ("Seigenthaler Incident"). Seigenthaler contacted Wikipedia cofounder Jimmy Wales who dispatched a Wikipedia administrator named Essjay to remove the false information from the archives.[1]

Seigenthaler responded to the escapade with a *USA Today* op-ed. He noted that Wikipedia was not the only Web site listing him as being involved in the Kennedy assassinations. A number of mirror sites like Answers.com and Reference.com automatically copy text from Wikipedia, "never checking whether it is false or factual" (Seigenthaler). The entire ordeal reminded Seigenthaler of his mother's advice about gossip:

> When I was a child, my mother lectured me on the evils of "gossip." She held a feather pillow and said, "If I tear this open, the feathers will fly to the four winds, and I could never get them back in the pillow. That's how it is when you spread mean things about people." For me, that pillow is a metaphor for Wikipedia. (Seigenthaler)

In his attempts to chase down the feathers let out by Wikipedia, Seigenthaler found that federal laws make it difficult to trace responsibility to Wikipedia or its writers. Suing "the s.o.b. that wrote it" was not a simple task. This is largely due to section 230 of the Communications Decency Act, which states that "no provider or user of an interactive computer service shall be treated as the publisher or speaker of any information provided by another information content provider." Since the Internet service provider through which Seigenthaler's defamer accessed the Internet was not to be considered the "publisher" of the comments (and thus could not be sued by Seigenthaler), it was not required to release the user's identity. Further, Wikipedia itself falls under the umbrella of protection provided by section 230 and is also not considered to be a "publisher" of content. Such protections meant that Seigenthaler's only legal recourse was to file what's called a John Doe lawsuit in hopes of obtaining a subpoena and tracking down the offending writer, but he was told that he would most likely lose such a suit.

All of this caused Seigenthaler to throw up his hands. In his view, the government was protecting the wrong people: "And so we live in a universe of new media with phenomenal opportunities for worldwide communications and research—but populated by volunteer vandals with poison-pen intellects. Congress has enabled them and protects them" (Seigenthaler). Though section 230 remains in place, Wikipedia did make some changes in the wake of the Seigenthaler incident. Soon after this controversy, Wikipedia stopped allowing anonymous users to create articles. However, "anons" (Wikipedians without usernames but who can be tracked by IP addresses) are still permitted to edit articles (Wales). Such a shift in policy does not prevent a Wikipedian from adding false information to an existing article, and this is because nearly all potential visitors to Wikipedia are part of its "community." Wikipedia's structure remains open to most any writer, and this means that tracing responsibility is extremely difficult. It also means that defining the Wikipedia community is difficult. If anyone can edit any page, the Wikipedia community does not fit our traditional notions of community—a collection of agents working toward a common goal. Furthermore, Wikipedia's penchant for textual noise and its willingness to include a broad range of writers makes it an interesting site of research for rhetoricians interested in the notions of community and responsibility.

Rhetoric has long been understood as a way to build communities that are based on a common set of goals or on a common identity. In some ways, Wikipedia can be viewed as this type of community. Wikipedia has its inner circle—a group many have referred to as a "cabal"—which wields a great deal of power. However, Wikipedia's structure also opens the door to a broad range of writers that have conflicting and competing interests. It is this structure that opens up questions about another notion of community. Certainly, there is an inner circle of Wikipedians that exerts a great deal of control, but this inner circle is constantly complemented and supplemented by the contributions of a vast array of contributors. Thanks to a tool called Wikiscanner, which traces the physical location of Wikipedia editors, we now know that the Vatican, the CIA, Walmart, and various political candidates are members of the Wikipedia "community." With such a messy and cacophonous textual situation, it is difficult to pin down *who* Wikipedians really are. Any attempt to discover the average Wikipedian (and to attach responsibility to that entity) runs the risk of missing an important point: Wikipedia and other electronic communities allow conflicting interests to be in-community with one another. When enemies (say, the Democratic National Committee and the Republican National Committee) can be seen collaborating on a text like Wikipedia, we may need to rethink terms such as responsibility and community.

By inviting such a wide variety of voices to their textual conversation, Wikipedians find themselves in-community with strange bedfellows. This virtual-textual community cannot only be defined as a collection of writers working toward a common goal—the Wikipedia community includes various conflicting and competing interests. It is this peculiar trait that made it so difficult to track down the responsible party in the Seigenthaler controversy. Seigenthaler's frustration that the law protects those posting false or inflammatory information is entirely understandable. Such policies raise difficult questions: Who is responsible for Wikipedia articles? Who should be held liable? Who can be sued? U.S. law protects free expression online, even when it results in situations such as Seigenthaler's, and Wikipedia's unwillingness to ban "anons" shows a similar resistance to quelling such expression. Faced with a choice between free expression and libel, both U.S. law and Wikipedia have tended to protect the former even if it invites the latter. Far from resolving this sticky question of responsibility, I would like to address the question of responsibility through a discussion of how community operates on Wikipedia and on the Web. The question of responsibility is an important one, but virtual-textual communities like Wikipedia have chosen a fairly messy answer to this problem. By inviting a cacophony of writers, Wikipedia has opened the door not only to free expression but also to the possibility of vandalism and libel. Many critics suggest that doing away with anonymity solves this problem, but does tracking a text to its supposed responsible party answer the question of responsibility? Let's return to the Seigenthaler controversy in an attempt to answer this question.

For Andrew Orlowski, a long-time critic of Wikipedia, Wikipedians too often pass the buck when it comes to the question of responsibility. He argues that Wikipedians offered two responses in the wake of the Seigenthaler episode: (1) that no source, Wikipedia included, should be considered the final word on any topic and (2) that Seigenthaler should have corrected the article himself: "The blame goes here, the blame goes there—the blame goes anywhere, except Wikipedia itself. If there's a problem—well, the user must be stupid!" As for the response that Wikipedia, like most other sources, is not to be fully trusted, Orlowski wonders whether such a view requires a constant skepticism bordering on paranoia: "Only a paranoiac, or a mad person, can sustain this level of defensiveness for any length of time" ("There's No Wikipedia").[2] He argues that the second defense—that Seigenthaler should have edited the entry himself—demonstrates that "failure . . . [is] genetically programmed into [Wikipedia's] mechanisms":

> So Wikipedia's second defense rests heavily on the assumption that everyone in the whole world is participating, watching, and writing at every moment of the day . . . a failure to pay attention represents negligence on the part of the complainer. Seigenthaler, the argument goes, was clearly being an idiot when he failed to notice that day's piece of web graffiti. Instead of taking his dog for a walk, or composing an email to his grandchildren, he should have been paying ceaseless attention to . . . his Wikipedia biography. ("There's No Wikipedia")

As for Orlowski, he is not interested in joining the Wikipedia party: "I can't speak for you, but I have better things to do." And this is the response of many Wikipedia critics, though some seem to have different reasons for begging out of editing Wikipedia. When *Wired* blogger Thomas Goetz complained of complicated prose on certain Wikipedia science entries, many Wikipedians asked why he didn't edit the entries himself. He responded in much the same way that Orlowski did: "Sorry, that's not my job" ("Why Does Wikipedia"). He explained that he only edits when the article is within his areas of expertise:

> I do edit when it's something I know about (I've lent a hand to entries on the Replacements, Queen Elizabeth, Petrarch, and metabolic syndrome, among others). But when I look to Wikipedia to learn about something—i.e., when I use it as a reference, not as a "project"—I use it to understand a topic, not to help create the resource. You wouldn't want the ignorant likes of me editing those entries, anyway, right? ("Wikipedians Slash Back!")

Goetz's argument seems fair enough. He's a journalist with a master's degree in public health, and this means he may not be qualified to take responsibility for certain Wikipedia articles. But we are still left with Seigenthaler's question: Who is responsible for Wikipedia? If Goetz is not responsible for articles that are outside of his areas of expertise and if Orlowski has "better things to do," who should shoulder the responsibility?

Orlowski claims to have the answer to this question, as he paints a picture of the person responsible for Wikipedia hijinks: "a picture of the body behind the 'Hive Mind' of 'collective intelligence' begins to take shape. He's 14, he's got acne, he's got a lot of problems with authority . . . and he's got an encyclopedia on dar interweb [*sic*]" ("There's No Wikipedia"). In a separate discussion of Wikipedia, Orlowski repeats this characterization by arguing that "topics are now tightly controlled by a 14-year-old you've never heard of, who has risen to the top of the social backstabbing by seeing off rival 'editors,' by forming cliques and drinking huge amounts of Red Bull" ("Google Kicks Wikipedia"). When speaking to a newspaper reporter about the Seigenthaler incident and the problems of Wikipedia, Wikipedia critic Daniel Brandt paints the same picture: "And a lot of them, they're not only anonymous, but they're teenagers. . . . They get these little ego trips, and they're very irresponsible" (qtd. in Chasnoff). The image of the teenage troublemaker is a popular one that has its roots in the efforts to track down hackers in the 1990s—a witch hunt that Bruce Sterling and others have painstakingly documented. The image of the pimply faced teenager still circulates as commentators envision Web denizens. Recently, that image has taken on a new trait: pajamas. Bloggers have created the portmanteau "pajamahadeen" to describe those who act as gadflies for traditional media outlets.

But in the Seigenthaler controversy, we do not have to rely on the portrait of the teenage punk or the pajama-clad blogger. And this is because the writer of those five false sentences came forward. The responsible party was 38-year-old Brian Chase, who added the text from a computer at Rush Delivery, his place of employment. Daniel Brandt tracked those five sentences to a computer at Rush Delivery by doing some sleuthing and tracing the IP address attached to the Wikipedia edit (Terdiman). Brandt has been a vocal opponent of Wikipedia and its inner circle of editors, which exerts a great deal of control over the text and the community, and his detective work led to Chase providing a written apology to Seigenthaler. In his apology, Chase explained that he thought Wikipedia was a "joke encyclopedia," and he did not figure that anyone would take those five sentences seriously. Seigenthaler spoke to Chase's employers and helped save his job, and this would seem a surprising intervention given the anger that infuses Seigenthaler's *USA Today* op-ed: "I have no idea whose sick mind conceived the false, malicious 'biography' that appeared under my name for 132 days on *Wikipedia*, the popular, on-line, free encyclopedia whose authors are unknown and virtually untraceable" (Seigenthaler). But Seigenthaler is not the only one to have a change of heart upon learning of Chase's identity. Brandt also sympathized with Chase's plight. In an interview after the Seigenthaler affair, Brandt describes Chase as a victim:

> And when this poor guy is trying to send out his resume, and he never gets called back from interviews, how do you know that the people aren't Googling him when they get his resume and saying, "Well, he did this thing." The permanence becomes invasion of privacy even more so than getting your name in the newspaper. (qtd. in Terdiman)

Upon learning who Chase was—a middle-aged middle-manager—Brandt's mission to track down the origin of the five sentences is replaced with concern for the author.

Given the opportunity to hold Chase responsible, these critics turn their critique in another direction—toward Wikipedia. Faced with the *actual* body behind this libelous information, these critics shift their ire back to Wikipedia. When Chase is found to be 38 (rather than 14) and to be wearing business casual rather than pajamas, these critics of Wikipedia don't know exactly what to do. It's as if Chase's body leaves them lacking the expected scapegoat. This, in turn, leads their critique back to Wikipedia. They find themselves able to *identify* with this 38-year-old middle-manager in a way that they can't identify with the 14-year-old punk or a member of the pajamahadeen. These critics took one look at Chase and thought, "He's one of us." This recognition (this *identification*) means that they do not tag him (or, at least, not him alone) with the responsibility. This process of identification is the basis of most any move toward community. That is, any community that forms around an essential identity—an identity of an "us" that is defined against a "them"—completes a circuit of identification. "We" are not "them." This is an extremely difficult (if not, impossible) circuit to break, and it is not always a harmful move. Building community, while always an exclusionary move, is necessary. However, Wikipedia offers a structure that makes for community's constant undoing. By allowing for greater levels of noise than most texts, Wikipedia frustrates attempts to easily define community and responsibility.

Locating the offending Wikipedian in the Seigenthaler controversy did not quench the thirst for a responsible party. Upon discovering the identity of this author—an identity that did not match their expectations—Seigenthaler and others shift the blame back to Wikipedia's "poison-pen intellects." All of this happens because the Wikipedia community is difficult to define. The shifting of blame stems from the discomfort of not knowing who makes up the Wikipedia community. But far from leaving us without any understanding of community, the structure of Wikipedia and of the Web means that the very concept of "community" can be reconsidered. In addition to being something that we build, community is also something that happens over and beyond conscious efforts to consolidate. As Diane Davis and others have argued, rhetoric's propensity for building community is accompanied by its ability to introduce noise into a community's circuits. That is, community building in the name of some essence (for instance, identity or nationalism) can always be supplemented by a discussion of what gets left out of such essential communities. While rhetoric's role in building community has long been recognized, rhetoricians do not always account for rhetoric's noisier role of undoing the perfect circuit of community. Kenneth Burke argued convincingly that a rhetor builds community by building identifications. Through any number of rhetorical devices, one can create a community of listeners/readers, and in creating communities, we have no choice but to exclude. Again, this is not always a bad thing. But we might also provide an account of what Davis calls rhetoric's "*disidentifying* force" (636). The rhetor's job is to complete the circuit and build community; the rhetorician's role is to point out the noise that is always disrupting those circuits.

The noise disrupting the communal circuits of Wikipedia is a result of a structure that invites a broad range of writers, and such noise serves to remind us that identification (that is, community by communion, excretion of various others, community in the name of shared values or identities) is always accompanied by disidentification (that is, the recognition that communities of shared identities are provisional and constantly on shaky ground). Wikipedia's structure makes it extremely difficult to pin down the essence of its community, and because of this it also makes it difficult to track down who is responsible for libel or vandalism on Wikipedia. Answering the question of responsibility simply and reductively runs the risk of ignoring the complexity of texts that invite noise and establishes a "community" that is difficult to define. Pinning responsibility on a pimply faced teenager assumes a coherent community behind the electronic text and ignores the much messier reality—that the Wikipedia community includes the CIA, the FBI, the Vatican, and you.

Notes

1 Interestingly enough, Essjay was later involved in a Wikipedia controversy of his own when it was discovered that he was not the tenured professor of theology he claimed to be. Essjay was actually Ryan Jordan, a 24-year-old from Kentucky with no graduate degrees. The Essjay controversy raised serious questions about Wikipedia's credentials policy. However, for the purposes of the present discussion, we should simply note that Essjay took the necessary steps to remove false information from the archive of the Seigenthaler article.

2 Orlowski's discussion of paranoia should remind us of Lacan's discussions of paranoiac knowledge and the gaze. For Lacan, the gaze is a "seeing, to which I am subjected in an original way" (72). In the act of my looking, I recognize that I am being looked at: "I see only from one point, but in my existence I am looked at from all sides" (72). In addition to Orlowski's critique, Robert McHenry's also reveals this recognition that we are watched from anywhere and everywhere. McHenry, a former editor-in-chief of *Encyclopedia Britannica*, likens Wikipedia to a risky restroom situation:

> The user who visits Wikipedia to learn about some subject, to confirm some matter of fact, is rather in the position of a visitor to a public restroom. It may be obviously dirty, so that he knows to exercise great care, or it may seem fairly clean, so that he may be lulled into a false sense of security. What he certainly does not know is who has used the facilities before him.

Or, presumably, who is using the facilities at the same time. It is in this concern about the others making use of "the facilities" that we see the gaze at work in online spaces. The "edit this page" link at the top of every Wikipedia article serves as a constant reminder of the gaze. As I edit a Wikipedia page, I recognize that I am being seen from anywhere and everywhere. Under the gaze and in the face of a fragmented text that refuses to be still and whole, many critics turn away and look for an opportunity to assert an "I." This turning away provides a fictional comfort that he has averted the gaze for the time being. The "edit this page" link begs readers to intervene right then and there, and it indicates that both reader and text are infinitely exposed. Lacan's notion of a subject constantly looking to reassert its wholeness gives us one way to understand the continued critiques of electronic texts—texts that remind us always and everywhere that we are not whole. I would like to thank Joshua Gunn for helping me think through the implications of the gaze and paranoiac knowledge with regard to Wikipedia and other electronic texts. In fact, Gunn even coined a term—"wikinoia"—that encapsulates this process nicely.

Works Cited

Chasnoff, Brian. "S.A. Man Is Chasing the Secret Authors of Wikipedia." 10 Dec. 2006. *MySA.com*. 31 Aug. 2008 <http://www.mysanantonio.com/news/metro/stories/MYSA121105.01B.wikipedia.320ce32.html>.

Communications Decency Act. U.S. 104th Cong., 2nd sess. GPO, 1996. 31 Aug. 2008 <http://www.fcc.gov/Reports/tcom1996.txt>.

Davis, D. Diane. "'Addicted to Love'; or, toward an Inessential Solidarity." *Journal of Advanced Composition* 19.4 (1999): 635–56.

Goetz, Thomas. "Why Does Wikipedia Suck on Science?" 10 May 2007. *Epidemix.org*. 14 May 2007 <http://epidemix.org/blog/?p=72>.

———. "Wikipedians Slash Back!" 12 May 2007. *Wired Science*. 31 Aug. 2008 <http://blog.wired.com/wiredscience/2007/05/wikipedians_sla.html>.

Lacan, Jacques, and Jacques-Alain Miller. *The Four Fundamental Concepts of Psycho-Analysis*. New York: W.W. Norton, 1981.

McHenry, Robert. "The Faith-Based Encyclopedia." 15 Nov. 2004. *TCS Daily*. 31 Aug. 2008 <http://www.tcsdaily.com/article.aspx?id=111504A>.

Orlowski, Andrew. "Google Kicks Wikipedia in the Googlies." 14 Dec. 2007. *The Register*. 31 Aug. 2008 <http://www.theregister.co.uk/2007/12/14/googlepedia_announced/>.

———. "There's No Wikipedia Entry for 'Moral Responsibility.'" 12 Dec. 2005. *The Register*. 17 Mar. 2008 <http://www.theregister.co.uk/2005/12/12/wikipedia_no_responsibility/>.

"Seigenthaler Incident." 28 Aug. 2008. *Wikipedia*. 31 Aug. 2008 <http://en.wikipedia.org/wiki/Seigenthaler_incident>.

Seigenthaler, John. "Seigenthaler's Op-Eds." 1 Oct. 2005. *Journalism.org*. 6 Feb. 2008 <http://www.journalism.org/node/1673>.

Sterling, Bruce. *The Hacker Crackdown: Law and Disorder on the Electronic Frontier*. New York: Bantam Books, 1992.

Terdiman, Daniel. "Tracking Down the Wikipedia Prankster." 15 Dec. 2005. *ZdNet*. 8 Feb. 2008 <http://news.zdnet.com/2100-9588_22-5996542.html>.

Wales, Jimmy. "Experiment on New Pages." Online Posting. 5 Dec. 2005. *WikiEN-l Listserv*. 21 Apr. 2008 <http://lists.wikimedia.org/pipermail/wikien-l/2005-December/033880.html>.

13

Aesthetics and Rhetoric in *The Oprah Winfrey Show*

Kathleen Dixon

Renato Barilli welcomed the electronic age for what it would bring to rhetoric, shorn in the age of print of two of its canon, memory and delivery.

> Now rhetoric returns also as *actio*, as a mode of delivering words, or managing and acting. It is a *performance*, an action that has a not insignificant degree of well worked out artistry. It is the re-emergence of sounds, and not only of sight, that in fact had accompanied the strong development of rhetoric throughout antiquity. This return is also an attempt on the part of our civilization to . . . recover the sensory dimension, the libidinal erotic pleasure of the word—its "presence," to borrow a term from a scholar close to McLuhan: Walter Ong. (125)

Barilli's words are especially apt for a rhetoric of television. His brief though consequential volume, *Rhetoric*, admires the humanistic and democratic potential of the practice and helps to point the way to what is clearly needed in a rhetoric of the television talk show—a re-conjoining of rhetoric and poetics.

I want to say that specifically *The Oprah Winfrey Show* is in need of this new rhetoric. More than most talk shows, it partakes of artistic and speech genres drawn from an array of media: film, print, radio, the stage, the Internet, and of course, television. A fair amount of the show is devoted to entertainment. Indeed, Winfrey has put a New Age twist on Horace's dictum regarding art (that it exists to delight and to instruct). At Harpo Studios, the staff strive to create programming "to enlighten as well as to entertain" (Farr 14). At least on certain occasions the goal is more or less political: Winfrey wants to persuade audiences to change their beliefs or to take action. This is the realm of rhetoric. But the persuasion transpires by means of an eclectic popular art that "quotes" from television, print, and radio journalism as well as from documentary film and television traditions, including the most recent permutation of the latter, reality TV. Nor does *The Oprah Winfrey Show*, however politically pioneering and "hyper-mediated" (Bolter and Grusin), forsake its "lowly" genre of the afternoon talk show and its middle-class female address. The show's adaptational genius merely combines old and new, always with assiduous attention to audience.

The corpus of episodes of most interest to rhetoric scholars will be those that focus on matters of civic import. During the calendar year 2006, such topics as living on minimum wage, the aftermath of Hurricanes Rita and Katrina, and global warming were examined in hour-long episodes of the show. In this essay, we will look closely at just one of these, a town hall meeting with Frank Rich, author of a book critical of the Bush administration's rush to war in Iraq. *The Oprah Winfrey Show* aired one other town hall meeting in the fall of 2006, featuring Fox commentator and personality, Bill O'Reilly. The show's producers were obviously attempting a balance of political perspectives in booking these two guests.

That is but one indication of the use of an older journalistic rhetoric employed by the show. Winfrey's position as host is frequently cast as that of a neutral party, sometimes in the way of a television news anchor (as in the programs on Hurricanes Rita and Katrina), sometimes as an educator (she's the college professor introducing Al Gore as guest lecturer in the episode on global warming), sometimes as moderator (as in the case of the town hall episodes). In addition to these roles, Winfrey is always simultaneously "Oprah," a popular and entertaining talk show host imbued with the *ethos* she has built over 20 years on television. Her use of the older journalistic rhetoric frequently gives way to the new populist rhetoric that has been steadily gaining influence since the 1970s. The infusion of melodrama (never completely absent from U.S. journalism of any type or historical period) blends well with Winfrey's trademark confessional melodrama and its feminine address.

Linda Williams' melodrama theory enables us to see how the traditionally more masculine sphere of politics and journalistic rhetoric in the manner of Edward R. Murrow can unite with the more feminine, domestic rhetoric of the afternoon talk show. In general, melodrama critics tend to see the genre as expressive of existence in a mass society, perhaps the contemporary substitution for tragedy, which no longer seems plausible in a world where the very concept of nobility seems quaint and irrelevant (Brooks; Singer). Rather than the tragic hero, melodrama foregrounds the victim (often victim-heroes, in Williams' lexicon) and the villain. Excesses of emotions such as grief, fear, and sentimental happiness combine with moral judgment to offer the audience a kind of catharsis and a sense of moral clarity, both highly desirable amid the stresses and confusions wrought by modernity. Melodrama thereby attends to the real and deep-seated needs and desires of the audience. Its aesthetic is embodied in a particular way, putting the victim-hero as well as the audience through thrills and perils, and offering up a satisfying conclusion that punishes the villain and rewards the victim-hero. Williams argues that the excesses of melodrama include what she calls the *pathos* of "prolonged climactic action" (21). The concept of the *pathos* of action gets at the excitement and even exhilaration that the audience experiences in any number of popular filmic texts. A good example is that staple of the masculine blockbuster film, the high-speed car chase.

One doesn't expect a daytime talk show to deploy melodrama in this way, and indeed much of the *Oprah* aesthetic is tamer, befitting the presumptively feminine, middle-class audience. Visually it is a "classy" aesthetic, uncluttered, with classical features of balance and symmetry, a use of rich colors, and careful attention to upscale design. Indeed, a frequent contributor to the show in 2006 was an in-house designer, who oversaw the home makeovers that the show sponsored (an obvious adaptation of another popular television genre). In the 2005–2006 season, *Oprah* also aired an episode in which Winfrey was supposed to have had a guest appearance on *Desperate Housewives,* whose sumptuous visuals *The Oprah Winfrey Show* was able to literally subsume for a day. On other occasions, the show created them outright, as when musical guests give the audience a concert-like performance, replete with an elevated stage, mood lighting, and special effects such as smoke or fog arising from below. In general, the show offers the audience a treat in the form of a retreat, as it were. Time often unravels in the manner of shows like *Desperate Housewives,* which reproduce the leisure of feature films and television soap operas. In relation to some other televisual texts, and particularly in relation to news programming, there is a narrative expansiveness that invites the audience to relax and focus on interior pleasures and intimate fantasies.

But *Oprah* is nothing if not eclectic, even in its own aesthetic. The show's variety is one of its hallmarks. Many episodes are playful and upbeat, and all introductory sequences are lively come-ons designed to incite the audience's imagination and hold its attention. The political rhetoric of Oprah, featured in the episodes under study here, is serious and even sober. Most of the town hall episode depicts Frank Rich and Oprah Winfrey in conversation on the thesis of his book. To be sure, many talk shows offer this fare (e.g., the *Charlie Rose* show), but they do it via public television or during the hours when a low audience share is expected. By contrast, *Oprah* has long attracted a sizeable audience, catering to its tastes and interests while simultaneously attempting to shape them. To pique interest in an episode that is inherently less entertaining than the usual *Oprah* episode, the show seeks out the dramatic and frequently the melodramatic potential of the story line, limned in miniature in the introductory sequence.

In the introductory sequence to the *Oprah* town hall meeting with Frank Rich, we note both the choice of film clips and the fast pace of the editing. Masculine subjects are seen in the halls of power and in the battlefield. Relatively static scenes (including some actual stills, e.g., the president sitting amidst his cabinet) are interspersed with active ones (soldiers running, weapons firing), while some of the stills are imbued with the power of spectacle (e.g., a picture of the World Trade Center towers just after the 9/11 attack). All are joined with dissolves that suggest a running narrative—a story or an argument. Indeed, the images match the script precisely to introduce and illustrate Rich's book and thesis. The cover of the book is zoomed in on and circled by the camera repeatedly as if it were an expressive face, while Winfrey says, "This week, it's number two on *The New York Times* best-seller list,

Frank Rich's new book, *The Greatest Story Ever Sold: The Decline and Fall of Truth from 9/11 to Katrina*, is a controversial and searing indictment of the Bush administration, challenging the reasons America went to war with Iraq." Throughout the introduction (not even a minute long), the camera returns to the book, open, as though the story and images have sprung from its pages onto our television screens. Even the mundane act of book reading can be a melodramatic experience on *Oprah*.

The sound track enhances the melodramatic effect, offering the ominous sounds of a deep and steady drumbeat, booming loud cannon fire at one point, and throughout imitating the kind of suspenseful music found in quasi-journalistic programs like *America's Most Wanted*. Winfrey delivers the voice-over in clear and firm tones, enunciating carefully in the unaccented Standard English required of news anchors, with little of her customary melodramatic emphases. The episode is offered as a form of citizen-inquiry into the issue raised by Rich's book, that is, whether the war was wrongly promulgated by the Bush administration. Yet the melodramatic rhetoric involves the audience in a tangle of feelings—fear, excitement, and anger—that may very likely lead to moral judgment even before the question-and-answer session with Rich begins. The older journalistic rhetoric would eschew this preparation of the audience. But the *Oprah* crew seems to understand that without some kind of interested position, the audience will not be able to achieve the engagement needed for this serious discussion. It takes a lesson from FoxNews (trounced by the liberal documentary *Outfoxed* for its contribution to a biased and spectacle-driven journalism) by attempting to convert a critical book into a melodramatic experience. Yet it manages to do so by avoiding an outright depiction of the Bush administration as villain, the American people (and not, we might notice, the Iraqis) as victim.

This certainly prompts us to consider the relationship between *ethos* and aesthetics. Winfrey's masterful use of melodrama and her televisual stage presence, combined with the equally expert use of film and video techniques employed by her creative staff, provide for the audience the twin experiences of hypermediacy and immediacy (Bolter and Grusin). Winfrey's *ethos* is shaped not only by her long-time presence on the talk show but by her philanthropic enterprises, which are taken up and publicized by the entire institution of the media, particularly through the genre of entertainment news. "Oprah" is indeed a household word, a known quantity that distinguishes itself in a world of "trashy" celebrities as an icon of responsibility.

Even as this icon moves across the television genres, *The Oprah Winfrey Show* itself draws from a multitude of media and genres. Winfrey herself can take on a number of roles to suit the (often hybridized) genre of the show. This is the hypermediacy of Bolter and Grusin, which draws attention to the artifice of the media production. A fair amount of the playfulness of *Oprah* transpires through hypermediacy, as when Winfrey and her "best friend" take off on "Oprah and Gayle's Big Adventure," a cross-country trek that is at least in part an ironic and upbeat replay of *Thelma and Louise* (wink-wink, nudge-nudge; we get to see the dozens of people in Winfrey's retinue in meta-recognition of the constructedness of the program).

The opposite of hypermediacy, immediacy, immerses the audience into an experience that seems to offer them an unmediated participation in the constructed text. Melodrama, as shown above, helps to make such immersion possible. This non-Brechtian form of audience pleasure may have its dangers, as it obscures the constructedness of the text. But equally of concern, in the case of melodrama, is the worry that such texts often encourage the audience to take the position of victim, a position that even the recent history of U.S. jurisprudence has helped to promulgate (Brown). Such a position can act as a refuge for those whose own actions oppress others (Williams).

Neither immediacy nor hypermediacy is inherently critical. Popular art and rhetoric are the responsibility of us all; it may be too much to expect such mainstream programming as *The Oprah Winfrey Show* to charge ahead of everyone else in providing a form of popular art that is also in some fashion a forum for political rhetoric. What scholars can do is to turn their attention to the rhetorical texts themselves, understood as the product of artists with agency—in this case, of talk show hosts, producers, scriptwriters, editors, camera operators, the guests, and the studio audience—in order to understand how rhetoric does its work in our late capitalist times. Jane Shattuc is not wrong when she says that television is the result of industrial production. But that is not all of the story.

Artists and orators of consummate skill have always persuaded audiences to accept particular perspectives on the world, including rather specific political beliefs. Both speak to the needs and desires of their audiences and both often provide them with a pleasurable experience that is part and parcel of persuasion. One understands why, for ease of analysis, Aristotle separated rhetoric from poetics. However, the recent trend of ideological critique in academic circles has claimed both rhetoric and poetics, and sometimes made them seem indistinguishable. Cultural studies is the leader of this approach, and thus we should note with special interest its renewed attention to aesthetics (see especially the Berube collection). Common sense, too, tells us that good orators have always drawn from art and have performed in artful fashion. Rhetoricians may well wish to adopt at least Barilli's perspective, if not his unusually artistic and humane sensibility, in an effort to imagine a robustly sensuous new rhetoric, one that is fully in line with the requirements of the contemporary popular arts. Careful scrutiny of the texts of electronic media make it abundantly clear that today's rhetoricians must also take a lesson from the performances of successful orators, including those of behind-the-scenes artists, if they wish to understand which arguments are carrying the day, and how and why they do.

Works Cited

Barilli, Renato. *Rhetoric.* Minneapolis: U of Minnesota P, 1989.
Berube, Michael, ed. *The Aesthetics of Cultural Studies.* Oxford: Blackwell, 2005.

Bolter, Jay David, and Richard Grusin. *Remediation: Understanding New Media.* Cambridge: MIT P, 1999.

Brooks, Peter. *The Melodramatic Imagination.* Yale UP, 1995.

Brown, Wendy. *States of Injury.* Princeton: Princeton UP, 1995.

Farr, Cecilia Konchar. *Reading Oprah: How Oprah's Book Club Changed the Way America Reads.* Albany: SUNY P, 2004.

Rich, Frank. *The Greatest Story Ever Sold: The Decline and Fall of Truth from 9/11 to Katrina.* New York: Penguin, 2006.

Shattuc, Jane. "Television Production: Who Makes American TV?" *A Companion to Television.* Ed. Janet Wasko. Oxford: Blackwell, 2005: 142–54.

Singer, Ben. *Melodrama and Modernity.* New York: Columbia UP, 2001.

Vester, Linda et al. *Outfoxed: Rupert Murdoch's War on Journalism* (DVD). The Disinformation Company, 2004.

Williams, Linda. *Playing The Race Card: Melodramas of Black and White From Uncle Tom to O. J. Simpson.* Princeton: Princeton UP, 2001.

Textual and Visual Building Blocks
Agency and Social Responsibility in Christine de Pizan's "The City of Ladies"

Julia M. Smith

"For it seems to me that, for now, the walls I have built for you to enclose that City of Ladies must suffice, and they are all finished and plastered. Let my other sisters come forward, and with their aid and counsel may you complete the remainder of the edifice" (Pizan, *The Book* 97). Here, Lady Reason, an allegorical figure in the "City of Ladies," describes how three allegorical figures (Reason, Rectitude, and Justice); the character, Christine; and a community of honorable women worked together within the fifteenth century text of the "City of Ladies." These characters sought to construct a utopian city through textual and visual discourse, where women could live safely away from misogynist attacks. In an era during which misogynist powers— who, because of women's "sinful state"—sought to deny women access to language, Christine de Pizan wrote prolifically and argued on behalf of women and their right to language.

I focus my study on Christine and her manuscript, Harley MS 4431, for two very important reasons. First, studies on Christine and her manuscripts reveal that she had a unique level of authority for a medieval author over the productions of her manuscripts. In particular, Harley MS 4431 is identified as an autograph manuscript. According to Gilbert Ouy and Christine Reno, who examined 20 presentation copies, Christine's manuscripts were written by three scribes: P, R, and X. "The X hand is encountered most often and R and P are found less frequently" (Laidlaw 241). Because scribal hand X is encountered frequently and, at times, appears to make corrections to the other two, Ouy and Reno believed the scribal hand belonged to Christine (Laidlaw 241). Even though this is inconclusive (not enough direct evidence), Ouy and Reno demonstrate that Christine left behind evidence that these manuscripts are her voice, her ideas, and her design. In addition, Harley MS 4431 was "illustrated by the artist known as the *Cité des Dames* Master, who with his associates formed one of the largest and most prolific groups of illustrators in Paris" (Willard 138). This illuminator and his workshop have no recorded names, but instead are labeled by their role in the production of Christine's manuscripts: "The Master of the *Cité des dames*, as Meiss calls him, continued to work for Christine until at least 1411. With his workshop, he was responsible for the miniatures in three separate manuscripts of the *Cité des dames*" (Laidlaw 238). This evidence indicates that Christine had a staff of scribes and made use of specific illuminators to decorate her texts. Even if she did not explicitly have control over all aspects of the production process, she personally knew and interacted with the people who contributed their talents to making her manuscript.

Second, Christine acted with authority and agency as she "debated in a public, written arena with royal secretaries who were all male"; she "names herself as female author"; and her "text explicitly redeploys an essentialism that now works to undermine the authority of males, who have no certain basis for their (derogatory) knowledge about women" (Quilligan 8, 15, 55). In the "City of Ladies," Christine demonstrates an awareness of her own social responsibility to reveal how women have the right to language and to develop their own rhetorical agency through her invention of her own rhetorical agency and her reconstruction of a history of women. Scholars such as Maureen Quilligan and Charity Willard have indicated that without a doubt, the text contributes to Christine's rhetorical agency, her ability to use language to act in the world. Less explored is the degree to which the paratext defined by Gérard Genette in his book *Thresholds of Interpretation* acts as the threshold of the text. The paratext guides the reader; consists of "productions, such as the author's name, a title, a preface," which "are to be regarded as belonging to the text, in any case they surround it and extend it, precisely in order to *present* it"; and functions rhetorically as text and paratext complement each other for that purpose (Genette 1). "The City of Ladies" lends itself to a study of how rhetorical agency is invented and articulated through text and paratext and contributes to our understanding of agency and social responsibility in three ways: (1) it enhances disciplinary understanding of women enacting agency in history, (2) it provides an example of a woman taking on the responsibility to demonstrate women's right to rhetorical agency through her own rhetorical skill, and (3) it sheds light on the relationship between text and image in the invention of agency. In this paper, I argue that Christine designed two miniatures (part of the paratext) for "The City of Ladies" to secure rhetorical agency for herself and other women. These miniatures functioned as agency by, first, evoking the conventions of the period and, second, altering those conventions to invite readers to make new meaning.

I frame my study of Christine de Pizan and rhetorical agency with Karlyn Kohrs Campbell's work on agency, a particularly powerful construct for my presentation because it provides space for both text and paratext and because it grapples with the postmodern moment while simultaneously retaining its applicability for historical studies.[1] In "Agency: Promiscuous and Protean," Campbell defines agency as "the capacity to act, that is, to have the competence to speak or write in a way that will be recognized or heeded by others in one's community" (4). She proposes that

> agency (1) is communal and participatory, hence, both constituted and constrained by externals that are material and symbolic; (2) is "invented" by authors who are points of articulation; (3) emerges in artistry or craft; (4) is effected through form; and (5) is perverse, that is, inherently, protean, ambiguous, open to reversal. (3)

Rhetorical agency occurs when these five definitions work together. Yet these five definitions ought to initially be examined separately to determine how rhetorical agency is produced through multiple points of origin that dialogue with one another through an author or rhetor's skillful crafting in response to a rhetorical situation. This separation allows for "The City of Ladies" to be examined for a variety of social, cultural, and historical layers, which contribute to the construction of agency. So for this paper, I focus on Campbell's discussion concerning the role of artistry in the shaping of rhetorical agency in order to examine how a woman harnessed her rhetorical skill or artistry to navigate multiple points of origin and cultural values instituted by misogynist powers in her work. Christine reveals her artistry or rhetorical skills when she manipulates the visual aspects of the manuscript page or paratexts, specifically the miniatures, so that they demonstrate her agency.

Agency emerges in three ways through artistry: the rhetor's performance as an appropriate response to a rhetorical situation, the repetition of those performances with differences, and the sedimentation of meaning created by repeated performances. Campbell states that artistry is "craft learning . . . learned stochastically through trial and error under the guidance of mentors that emerges ideally as an ability to respond well and appropriately to the contingencies of circumstance" (4). As a rhetor learns the craft of responding well to circumstances, she develops "heuristic skills . . . for which there are no precise or universal precepts, although skilled practitioners are alert to recurring patterns" (12). These responses are style choices that are repeated, and over time skilled scholars can identify emerging patterns. The emerging patterns become "stylized repetition," which are then appropriated and altered (13). As these patterns are repeated, they "fix meaning through sedimentation. Agency equally emerges in performances that repeat with a difference, altering meaning" (13). Therefore, a rhetor who demonstrates her skills as a rhetorician through her strategic responses to different circumstances reveals her rhetorical agency. She must first respond to the situation appropriately with traditional and repeatable style choices. Once she has established her skill, she can make changes to the style choices to articulate new meanings, which gesture to the text and beyond. In "The City of Ladies," Christine articulates her agency as she deftly arranges the paratext through three moves within a folio page: (1) she complies with traditional functions of medieval paratext, (2) she appropriates the traditional use of paratext in order to disrupt them or repeat them with a difference to alter the meaning of the paratext, and (3) she ultimately subverts the paratext so that she layers new meaning through the dialogue between the text and the paratext.

I apply this theoretical framework to two miniatures from Harley MS 4431, where Christine reveals her awareness of her social responsibility to use her agency to speak for silenced women, when she develops her artistry in order to argue for her right and that of other women to agency and language. Specifically, an examination of these two miniatures demonstrates the extent to which the paratext and the miniatures in particular contribute to her rhetorical agency. The first miniature occurs at the beginning of Harley MS 4431 (see figure 1). In the scene depicted, "Christine de Pisan offers her work to Isabel of Bavaria, Queen of France, observed by ladies-in-waiting dressed in the Burgundian manner with very wide and flowing sleeves for their costumes" (Gathercole 13). As the six ladies-in-waiting look on, Christine as the author kneels on the floor before the seated Queen Isabeau and offers the queen a large red velvet book with gold trim. Because of the large red bed and the presence of the fleur-de-lis as decorations on the wall, the setting appears to be the queen's bedchamber. The second miniature, the width of two columns, occupies the top of the first page of "The City of Ladies" (see figure 2 on p. 170). In this miniature, the image of Christine appears in two scenes. On the left side of the miniature, Christine sits within a small architectural structure surrounded by books. By her table stand three crowned women holding different objects. On the right side of the image, the standard depiction of an author at

Figure 1.   Dedication to the Queen, miniature from London, British Library, Harley MS 4431. © British Library Board. All rights reserved, f. 3r (1413-4).

work has changed into one where Christine and one of the crowned ladies engage in the construction of a wall in the midst of a field. Together, these two miniatures symbolically represent Christine as both a scholar and a craftsman, specifically of the "City of Ladies" and by extension, the manuscript.

Christine reveals her artistry by repeating a common type of miniature, the dedicatory miniature, which carries with it specific rhetorical significance. By opening his manuscript with a dedicatory miniature, a medieval male author would typically use the image to rhetorically illustrate how he has received affirmation and authority as a writer from a patron. The author's strategic use of the opening image of the miniature proclaims his skillful artistry, since it demonstrates his ability to make choices that highlight his own agency for his audience. In these presentation manuscripts, the traditional rhetorical performance of the miniatures depicts the writer (usually with indeterminate features) presenting the manuscript to the patron (also symbolically rather than realistically rendered). By using this traditional dedication miniature, the author would choose for the image to visually introduce the writer, the patron, and the historical context of the work to the reader.

As she complies with the practice of introducing herself to her reader using a dedication miniature, Christine makes claims to an agency rooted in her artistry. First, Christine uses this first miniature of the manuscript to confirm her ability to make the skillful rhetorical choice to have herself depicted in the manuscript offering it up to her patron in a scene that implicitly promotes her authority and reveals her agency.

Second, even as she expresses her own rhetorical agency through her compliance with the traditional function of a dedicatory miniature, Christine appropriates and subverts the image in order to expand her agency. Instead of depicting a generic (usually male) author presenting to a patron (usually a figure wearing a crown), the dedication miniature of Harley MS 4431 performs for the reader as a historically accurate representation of the actual historical presentation of the manuscript by a woman to a woman. Christine artfully portrays herself as a historical woman invested with authority by the queen, and she creates a visual text that gestures beyond the image itself to her audience, who can now witness a dedication ritual wherein a woman patron bestows authority onto a woman author. The image (though painted before the actual presentation would have taken place) enacts the actual moment, in which the two women met to perform a ritual, where the patron gives authority to Christine by accepting and paying for the manuscript. As Sandra Hindman in "With Ink and Mortar" states, "One of the extraordinary features of this exquisite miniature is the degree of historical accuracy that it preserves" (462). The image also gestures to historical facts beyond the manuscript itself and humanizes both the queen and Christine into actual historical figures. For example, the queen is depicted with surprising historical accuracy; she sits before Christine in a red and ermine trimmed gown with gold embroidery and her hair is up in a horned headdress (Gathercole 15). The depiction of dress and hair reflect how realistically and historically accurate the miniature

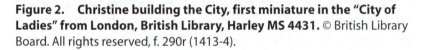

Figure 2.   Christine building the City, first miniature in the "City of Ladies" from London, British Library, Harley MS 4431. © British Library Board. All rights reserved, f. 290r (1413-4).

was rendered. Also, the queen is painted surrounded by furnishings described in the queen's household reports, two dogs in the scene are her favorite animals, and the women with her are dressed just like the historical descriptions of her attendants (Hindman, "Iconography" 103). In this regard, Hindman "confirms the accuracy of Isabeau's likeness" ("Iconography" 103). Christine's rhetorical agency exists through her artistry, since she was able to subvert the traditional role of the dedication miniature into one that acknowledges the author's authority. Specifically, the miniature exhibits the author as a real woman and the dedication ritual as an observable moment for the audience, so that they can witness the authorizing of a woman author to speak.

A similar dynamic occurs in the second miniature. Here Christine complies with traditional expectations of the author composing in order to enact a rhetorical agency that is invented through her skillful use of a miniature to layer new meanings between the image and the text. The scene on the left of the miniature complies with many medieval manuscripts, where the author appears in the act of composing the text. This image speaks to the readers of the text by revealing the presence of the author and symbolically representing his authority. Christine complies with this use of the authorial image by including the depiction of herself at work, which emphasizes her central role in crafting and creating the text. In addition, this miniature dialogues with the text by complying with the scene described. The character, Christine, is depicted sitting at a table in an enclosed structure surrounded by books, which the narrator describes: "one day as I was sitting in my study, surrounded by books on many different subjects, my mind grew weary from dwelling at length on the weighty opinions of authors whom I had studied for so long" (Pizan, *The Book* 3) and "I suddenly saw a ray of light fall on my lap . . . I shuddered then, as if waking from a sleep . . . and as I lifted my head I saw three crowned ladies standing before me, and the splendor of their bright faces shone on me" (6). These allegorical women appear in the miniature wearing traditional symbolic crowns, which represents their royal significance and the importance of their guidance in the text. And each bears a symbol of their allegorical nature, which is also a traditional reiteration of iconography for allegorical figures: a mirror, a measure for grain, and a ruler. Initially, this miniature appears to represent Christine's choice to use the miniature to literally present these three women with objects to signify the cultural values they personify. However, the dialogue between text and image continues when the three allegorical women symbolically extend their authority as Reason, Rectitude, and Justice to Christine the author. By appearing to have the miniature adhere to the text, Christine has the image perform the text, so that her audience can participate in the actions occurring within the text, and the reader can be part of the scene.

However, Christine enhances her agency through her own artistry as a skillful rhetorician through her appropriation and subversion of this authorial miniature by not having it comply exclusively with the meaning in the text. Instead, some of the symbolic elements of the miniature gesture to the other miniatures and to the text, which are in dialogue. Christine's agency is invented from her artistry through the rhetorical choices she makes in creating this dialogue. Rather than have a miniature that stands alone or that only mirrors the text, Christine develops layers of meaning through her appropriation and subversion of different symbolic elements to create new meanings. These three symbolic elements can be identified as strategic rhetorical choices made by Christine to represent different meanings throughout the manuscript: Christine, the character; the book; and the architecture.

First, the figure of Christine appears in all of the miniatures in "The City of Ladies." Her visual representation performs the actions described for Christine, the character, within the text. Christine's rhetorical choice in this instance invites the reader to identify a relationship between the two images of Christine. In fact, in all four miniatures, Christine is identifiable by her garments. She wears a traditional blue and white gown over a violet underrobe and on her head is a white headdress. The two images of Christine from the dedication miniature and from the first miniature of "The City of Ladies" gesture to one another and to the other images of Christine throughout the manuscript, which layers new meaning onto all of the images by signaling Christine as a significant character within the manuscript, who is not only the author, but also a participant in the construction of the City of Ladies in the narrative of the text.

> We three ladies whom you see here, moved with pity, have come to you to announce a particular edifice built like a city wall, strongly constructed and well founded, which has been predestined and established by our aid

and counsel for you to build, where no one will reside except all ladies of
fame and women worthy of praise. (Pizan, *The Book* 10–11)

Through her expert artistry, Christine designated the image that represents her to symbolically depict a woman breaking with traditional roles from
the humanized and historicized image of her in the dedicatory miniature to
the symbolic craftsman and scholar image of her in the first miniature of
"The City of Ladies." This gesture even extends beyond the text to other
depictions of women in miniatures as well. While the iconographic images of
women working in the fields are present in medieval manuscripts, the function of their performance in the miniature here is different. "Women of the
lower classes are shown in the medieval illuminations engaged in all sorts of
field work: harvesting, cutting wheat with sickles, tossing hay, building hay-
stacks, and busy in other agricultural activities" (Gathercole 34). Christine is
not a woman of the lower classes and neither is the allegorical figure who
helps her build. In fact, Hindman argues that the performance in this miniature of women building is exclusively an image of the "City of Ladies." She
states that the performance of "women builders or, if you will, women construction workers—women who, in their fancy clothes, long dresses, and fine
hats, carry heavy stones, mix cement, and spread mortar" was extremely
unusual ("With Ink and Mortar" 472). So, when Christine designates the
miniature to allude to the meanings of the text, she overlays new meaning
onto the text, the image, other images of Christine, and beyond the manuscript to images of women depicted elsewhere.

Second, the image of the book connects the presentation of Harley MS
4431 in the dedication miniature to the books in Christine's study. Through
their presence, the images of the book evoke new meanings. Within the text,
the book symbolically represents the protests against the assault on the community of women. "Let Mathéolus and all the other prattlers who have spoken against women with such envy and falsehood go to sleep and stay quiet"
(Pizan, *The Book* 127). In addition, the image of the book gestures to the text
to indicate that women can and should be educated: "Quintus Hortensius . . .
had a daughter, named Hortensia, whom he loved for the subtly of her
wit . . . had her learn letters and study the science of rhetoric" (153). The
symbolism of producing the book indicates the artistry necessary to construct
the City of Ladies and the text of the "City of Ladies."

> Now take your tools and come with me, go ahead, mix the mortar in
> your ink bottle so that you can fortify the City with your tempered pen,
> for I will supply you with plenty of mortar, and thanks to divine virtue,
> we will soon finish building the lofty palaces and noble mansions for the
> excellent ladies of great glory and fame who will be lodged in this City
> and who will remain here perpetually, forever more. (99)

As described in the introduction to *Women and the Book*, "she is to 'build'
a textual city of women on the Field of Letters, a city of which every stone,
every brick, every tower is an exemplary remarkable woman," and so the

manuscript, "which the reader is holding in his or her hand, *is* the City of Ladies in a material, textual, and metaphorical sense" (Smith and Taylor 14). When she alters the image of the book throughout the manuscript, the image of the books gesture to the other miniatures and the text to layer new meanings associated with authorship, education, and the construction of a space of resistance for women.

Third, the book and the image of architecture represent the act of building "The City of Ladies" described in the text, so that the text and miniatures continue their dialogue. The architecture functions in the miniatures as a frame to indicate a scene (like the dedication miniature) or a separation in the narrative (like the first miniature of "The City of Ladies"). In other words, "the material of the City of Ladies is thus a metaphor for Christine's book, which champions the cause of women. And the frontispiece is conceived as an emblem wherein the process of writing and the product of the book are conceptually merged in the languages of the author and the city" (Hindman, "With Ink and Mortar" 466). The image of architecture also adds new meaning onto the miniature, the city as defense against misogynist attacks, by enacting the description from the text: "therefore you are right, my ladies, to rejoice greatly in God and in honest mores upon seeing this new city completed, which can be not only the refuge for you all, that is, for virtuous women, but also the defense and guard against your enemies" (Pizan, *The Book* 254). The act of building the city does not exclusively perform the text, but rather performs the writing process of composing the text. Both city and manuscript are spaces where women can create a new social order and protect themselves from misogynist attacks. This city (and the manuscript) performs as "a political sphere that afforded the most fluid social possibilities for its citizens" (Kellogg 137). Christine's rhetorical agency emerges from this bridging of performances between the images and the texts. The reader can visualize the actions occurring within the text as well as the actions occurring during the production of the text.

Christine acquires agency from her artistry, her own innate ability to skillfully craft her meaning, and through her rhetorical choices. Each decision she makes dictates the design of the manuscript and the relationship that each miniature has with the text and other miniatures. Her agency emerges as she invites the reader to identify and interpret the layers of meaning within the text, where the miniatures gesture to one another, to the text, and beyond in order to change the meaning of different symbolic acts occurring within the images and the text. These gestures open new venues for spaces of resistance for women by complicating the preexisting meanings of different symbolic images: book, architecture, and author. Christine's agency is articulated through her careful repetition of familiar performative styles within the miniatures, her tailoring of those performances to fit her meanings, and the new layering of meaning that occurs as the visual and verbal texts allude to one another within the space of the manuscript.

This analysis is important because it identifies how a woman can create a space of resistance and articulate her rhetorical agency even against misogynist detractors. Christine took on the responsibility of modeling for women how to develop their own rhetorical agency through the multiple layers of meaning within her manuscripts and her re-visioning of women's histories. Lastly, these multiple sources of agency point to the need to reexamine both the visual and textual aspects of historical rhetoric to construct a fuller picture of agency, particularly in medieval manuscripts.

Note

[1] Even though Campbell's definition of agency comes from a post-structuralist context, I believe this definition can be extended to the early modern period because I, like Campbell, "reject the view that there is a vast chasm separating classical, modern, and postmodern theories" (15). Instead, I believe that "reading and rereading earlier works in light of the insights of more recent theorists, reinventing, if you will, the legacy of the past in ways that fuse these traditions" fits this study (15).

Works Cited

Campbell, Karlyn Kohrs. "Agency: Promiscuous and Protean." 2003. American Rhetoric Society Conference. 24 Sept. 2007. <http://www.rhetoricsociety.org/ARS/pdf/campbellonagency.pdf>.

Gathercole, Patricia M. *The Depiction of Women in Medieval French Manuscript Illumination*. Studies in French Civilization. 17. Lewiston: Edwin Mellon, 2000.

Genette, Gérard. *Thresholds of Interpretation*. Trans. Jane E. Lewin. Cambridge: Cambridge UP, 1997.

Hindman, Sandra. "The Iconography of Queen Isabeau de Bavière (1410–15): An Essay in Method." *Gazette des Beaux-Arts* 6.102 (1983): 102–09.

———. "With Ink and Mortar: Christine de Pizan's *Cité des Dames* (An Art Essay)." *Feminist Studies* 10 (1984): 457–83.

Kellogg, Judith L. "Transforming Ovid: The Metamorphosis of Female Authority." *Christine de Pizan and the Categories of Difference*. Ed. Marilynn Desmond. London: U of Minnesota P, 1998.

Laidlaw, James. "Christine and the Manuscript Tradition." *Christine de Pizan: A Casebook*. Ed. Barbara K. Altmann and Deborah L. McGrady. New York: Routledge, 2003. 231–43.

Pizan, Christine de. *The Book of the City of Ladies*. Trans. Earl Jeffrey Richards. New York: Persea, 1998.

———. *Collected Works*. Harley MS 4431. British Library, London. 2007. Edinburgh University Library. 1 Sept. 2007. <http://www.pizan.lib.ed.ac.uk/maquette.htm>.

Ouy, Gilbert, and Christine Reno. "Identification des autographes de Christine de Pizan." *Scriptorium* 34 (1980): 221–38.

Quilligan, Maureen. *The Allegory of Female Authority: Christine de Pizan's* Cité des Dames. Ithaca: Cornell UP, 1991.

Smith, Lesley, and Jane H. M. Taylor, eds. *Women and the Book: Assessing the Visual Evidence*. Toronto: U of Toronto P, 1997.

Willard, Charity Cannon. *Christine de Pizan: Her Life and Works*. New York: Persea, 1984.

15

The Constitutive Rhetoric of *Common Sense*

David C. Hoffman

"Because the constitutive nature of rhetoric establishes the boundary of a subject's motives and experience, a truly ideological rhetoric must rework or transform subjects," says Maurice Charland in his seminal essay on constitutive rhetoric, "Constitutive Rhetoric: The Case of the *Peuple Québécois*" (148). Here, and at other points in his essay, Charland implies that the most basic feature of constitutive rhetoric is that it interpellates audience members into one or more subject positions, thus "constituting" identities for political ends. For example, the audience of French Canadians addressed by the government of Quebec in the white paper entitled "Québec-Canada: A New Deal" were interpellated into the position of the *peuple québécois* and "constituted such that sovereignty is not only possible, but necessary," according to Charland (146).

As I will demonstrate below, constitutive rhetoric has typically been exemplified by instances in which audiences are constituted so as to partake in some "collective" and "transhistorical" identity, such as "the people of Quebec." Charland argues that collectivity and transhistoricism are necessary "ideological effects" of constitutive rhetoric (139–40). But is it the case that all ideologically useful subject positions are necessarily "collective" and "transhistorical," that every instance of interpellation is necessarily an assimilation to a collective identity? Charland argues that "a theory of constitutive rhetoric leads us to call into question the concept, usually implicit to rhetoric's humanist tradition, of an audience composed of unified and transcendent subjects" (147). But, if it is indeed true that "constitutive rhetoric is part of the discursive background of social life" (147) and that, as subjects, we cannot help but "live inside rhetoric" (147), then must not the subject position of the "unified and transcendent subject," the Enlightenment individual who possesses a universally available power of Reason and natural moral sensibility, also be a product of a constitutive rhetoric?

This work was supported by a grant from the City University of New York (PSC-CUNY) Research Program.

In this paper, I argue that Thomas Paine's pamphlet, *Common Sense*, provides an example of a case where each member of the audience is constituted not as a member of a transhistoric collective, but as an ahistoric individual whose moral and epistemic privilege derives from being at the beginning of the history of the New World. (The New World had a long history before its "discovery," but this is not part of Paine's thinking.) Paine, I argue, does employ constitutive rhetoric in that he interpellates audience members as political subjects. *Common Sense* interpellates readers in two related ways—as *inhabitants of America* and as *individual men* who possess *reason* and "*natural feelings.*" These interpellations exemplify a previously unnoted dimension of constitutive rhetoric, namely, its ability to interpellate audiences into individual as well as collective subject positions. I begin the essay with a brief review of the theory of constitutive rhetoric and then proceed to examine the rhetorical strategy of *Common Sense* within this framework.

CONSTITUTIVE RHETORIC

The root idea of constitutive rhetoric was originally expounded in Michael McGee's "In Search of 'The People': A Rhetorical Alternative." In that essay McGee describes how "the people" are called into being. He cites Ernest Bormann's description of how the advocate "dangles a dramatic vision of the people before his audience. The audience, essentially a group of individuals, reacts with a desire to participate in that dramatic vision, to *become* 'the people' described by the advocate" (239–40). "The people" is, for McGee, a rhetorical construct that creates collectivization as many individuals identify themselves with the group thus designated.

Building from McGee's theory of a collectivizing "people," Charland presented the seminal formulation of constitutive rhetoric in his essay, which was an analysis of the rhetorical strategies of the white paper issued by the Government of Quebec in support of Quebec's political sovereignty on November 1, 1979. Charland draws on Louis Althusser's concept of "interpellation" to extend McGee's ideas as to how "the people" functions as a rhetorical construct: "the collectivized *peuple québécois* are, in Althusser's language, 'interpellated' as political subjects through a process of identification in rhetorical narratives that 'always already' presume the constitution of subjects" (134). "Interpellation" here means the act of addressing a person as a particular type of subject, and thus, in a sense, bringing them into being as such. The paradigmatic example of such an act, used by Althusser himself, is that of a policeman hailing a person with the words "Hey, you there!" instantly activating that person's status as a subject of the state that employs that policeman (174). Charland asks us to imagine, in similar fashion, a "people," constructed with a definite history and destiny, being activated when an audience is addressed as the *peuple québécois*.

Charland styles his expanded theory "constitutive rhetoric" and specifies three "ideological effects" of constitutive rhetoric in his reading of Québécois independence rhetoric. First, a "people," as a collective subject, "transcends the limitations of the individual body and will" (139). Many individuals, in other words, identify themselves with a "people" that is represented as having volitions independent of the individuals who compose it. When Jean-Jacques Rousseau spoke of a "general will" that could be opposed to individual desires (*Social* 2.2 and 2.3), he was creating the sort of ideological effect that Charland describes. Second, constitutive rhetoric posits a people as a "transhistorical subject" (140), a subject that continues to exist down through history despite the fact that the set of individuals who compose it is in flux. The *peuple québécois*, for instance, continues to exist as an entity even though individual Quebecers come and go. Thirdly, constitutive rhetorics produce an "illusion of freedom" (141), speaking of "the people" as a freely chosen entity, even while declaring that they are bound to fulfill a certain destiny, like the *peuple québécois* declaring themselves independent. Thus, for Charland, constitutive rhetoric always interpellates audiences into subject positions that are collective and transhistoric.

Since the framework of constitutive rhetoric was outlined by Charland, it has been used in the analysis of a variety of texts, including television ads (Stein), Puerto Rican political rhetoric (Cordova), and the rhetoric of Abraham Lincoln (Gross) and Martin Luther King, Jr. (Leff and Utley). It has even found application in the study of classical Greek rhetoric (Haskins 104). While not all later applications strictly adhere to the necessity of collectivization within constitutive rhetoric (notably Stein), or to the transhistorical nature of the collective subject, the assumptions have never been explicitly questioned.

McGee, Charland, and most of those who follow them assume that audiences are composed of "individuals" who need to be interpellated into collective positions. But might not audiences often listen to speech from the perspective of some collective identity that they already inhabit, such as American, Democrat, Republican, etc.? Might not the rhetor sometimes be faced with the task of undoing the collective group identifications of audiences by interpellating members into individual subject positions?

An analysis of *Common Sense* within the constitutive framework poses a problem for constitutive rhetoric's traditional assumptions of collectivity and transhistoricism because *Common Sense* tried to undo audience participation in the collective identity of "British subject" and substitute it with the identity of a rational man with "natural feelings" who happens to be an inhabitant of North America. I do not mean to imply that Charland was incorrect in his analysis of the white paper, but only that the rhetorical strategies it employs are not the only possible strategies of constitutive rhetoric. For the constitutive framework to truly be effective in the analysis of American rhetoric, it must come to terms with the constitution of identities that are individual as well as collective, ahistoric as well as transhistoric.

THE CONUNDRUM OF COMMON SENSE

The pivotal role played by Thomas Paine's *Common Sense* (published January 9, 1776) in moving the American people toward accepting the notion that the war with the British that had begun at Lexington and Concord needed to be waged as a war for independence is well established. Space does not permit me to reiterate the case here. Readers interested in a full exposition should refer to Eric Foner's *Tom Paine and Revolutionary America* (71–87), Isaac Kramnick's introduction to *Common Sense*, John Keane's *Tom Paine: A Political Life* (108–37), and Scott Liell's *46 Pages*. My essay "Paine and Prejudice" reviews this scholarship and enumerates five explanations offered by scholars for the success of *Common Sense*: (1) situational factors, such as the fortunate timing of publication, (2) the accessible style of the work, (3) the *ethos* of "manly" firmness Paine projects, (4) the psychological appeal of symbolically killing the king-father, and (5) Paine's synthesis of elements of Rousseau's primitivism and Locke's bourgeois radicalism (Hoffman 377–84). I do not seek to resurrect here the weary question of how *Common Sense* achieved its success. Instead, I ask what sort of subject is hailed by the text. Is it a collective transhistoric "people"? Or is it an independently reasoning individual?

Let us begin by testing the hypothesis that *Common Sense* perhaps does constitute a "people" in the transhistoric collective sense of McGee and Charland. Paine uses the word "people" twenty-four times in the text and appendix of *Common Sense*. Referring to the Penguin Classics edition of *Common Sense*, the word "people" is used on pages 63, 68, 69, 70 (four times), 71 (two times), 74, 75, 76 (two times), 92, 93 (two times), 96, 97 (two times), 98, 99, 104 (two times), 113, and 114 (two times). There are also four uses of the word in the "Epistle to the Quakers," which I have not included in this count. In addition, the verb "peopled" is used twice in the text of *Common Sense*, and I have also left these instances out of the count.

A careful review of the twenty-four uses of "people" in *Common Sense* reveals that, with only a couple of exceptions, Paine uses "people" in a structural sense. "The people" are that part of the society that is other than the government. "The people" are, essentially, those who are governed. The critical reader will naturally want to confirm this assertion for him- or herself in every instance, but let me offer a few examples by way of illustration:

> Absolute governments . . . have this advantage with them, that they are simple; if the people suffer, they know the head from which their suffering springs. (68)

Here's another:

> Some writers have explained the English constitution thus; the king, they say is one, the people another; the peers are a house in behalf of the king; the commons in behalf of the people. (70)

And another (quoting from the Bible):

> And the Lord said unto Samuel, Hearken unto the voice of the people in all that they say to thee, for they have not rejected thee, but they have rejected me, that I should not reign over them. (74)

And finally:

> But the king you will say has a negative in England; the people there can make no laws without his consent. (93)

Not every single usage of "people" in *Common Sense* as clearly refers to that part of the polity that is ruled, but the trend definitely lies in this direction. Exceptions to the rule in *Common Sense* are either illusory or insignificant. On first reading, "It is wholly owing to the constitution of the people, and not to the constitution of the government, that the crown is not as oppressive in England as in Turkey" (71), one may say, "Ah ha! Here is an example of a use of 'people' in the McGee/Charland sense!" But note that, even here, the people are structurally opposed to the crown, and their constitution is a settled fact, not an act that the text is engaging in. The only instances where Paine uses "people" in a way that might be understood as a reference to a transhistorical collective entity with its own volitions are insignificant from the perspective of rhetorical force. For example, while debating the question of whether to build a Navy, Paine said, "We are not the little people now, which we were sixty years ago" (104). This is hardly a grand rhetorical gesture.

Clearly absent from *Common Sense* is any sweeping narrative of the "American people." Does this mean that *Common Sense* does not make use of constitutive rhetoric? No, not if we understand constitutive rhetoric to be any rhetoric that constitutes political subjects through a process of interpellation even if the identities thus constituted are individual and ahistoric.

Paine hails the readers of *Common Sense* in two interconnected ways: He hails them as "inhabitants of America," and he calls them to be good men when he invites each to "put on . . . the true character of a man." I will describe each of these interpellations in turn.

FIRST INTERPELLATION: "INHABITANTS OF AMERICA"

Paine's first interpellation of his audience has its first occurrence in the title itself and will prove to be at odds with the transhistoricism that is supposed to be a necessary characteristic of constitutive rhetoric. Paine called his pamphlet *Common Sense; Addressed to the Inhabitants of America*. This mode of address puts the habitation of his readers ahead of their genetic descent or citizenship. Eight years earlier John Dickinson had addressed his "Letters from a Farmer in Pennsylvania" to "My Dear Countrymen," privileging the political bond of British subjects. Because he is making an argument for independence, Paine naturally cannot hail his audience as British subjects, the collective identity that they had previously shared. Neither does he wish to hail them as citizens of the individual colonies, because this would be divisive rather than unifying. He explicitly speaks against the idea that the colonies are sisters united by the common parentage of England (84). Instead, Paine hails his readers as the *inhabitants* of North America, drawing attention to their habitation of the continent, not their political status.

Paine enlarges on the implications of being an inhabitant of America throughout the pamphlet. The status of Paine's readers as inhabitants of America is first given meaning by the political myth about the origins of government that he unfolds in the first section of *Common Sense*. In this section, Paine asks his readers to imagine "a small number of persons settled in some sequestered part of the earth" (66). These individuals begin in a "state of natural liberty" but are drawn together in order to do what is necessary for survival and comfort. As life becomes easier, they begin "to relax in their duty and attachment to each other" (66). These trespasses necessitate the institution of formal government. From this thought experiment about the origins of government, Paine draws the conclusion that government is "a mode rendered necessary by the inability of moral virtue to govern the world" and also that "the design and end of government" are "freedom and security" (68).

The narrative about the origin of government not only allows Paine to argue that the British government is functioning in violation of government's true purpose, it also implies that Paine's readers, as inhabitants of America, have a better understanding of the true nature of government than would be possible for Europeans, because they are closer to its origin. In the story of the origin of government Paine might appear to come close to speaking of the history of a "people," but note: the story is anonymous and universal. It is not a story of "the American people" but rather a scenario that would unfold with any group of persons in any "sequestered part of the earth" at any time. The key factor in the story is place: presumably any group of people that came to a distant wilderness such as America would have the same experience.

Paine adds another layer of meaning to his readers' status as inhabitants of America in the third section of the pamphlet. The inhabitants of America have in common not a country of origin, but a desire for freedom that drove them to a distant part of the world: "Europe, and not England, is the parent country of America. This new world hath been an asylum for the persecuted lovers of civil and religious liberty from every part of Europe" (84). Furthermore, the fact of living on a large continent with persons arrived from many parts of Europe is said to broaden a person's capacity for friendship and political attachment:

> In this extensive quarter of the globe, we forget the narrow limits of three
> hundred and sixty miles (the extent of England) and carry our friendship
> on a larger scale; we claim brotherhood with every European Christian,
> and triumph in the generosity of the sentiment. (83)

Finally, Paine portrays the American continent as having a great destiny in world history simply by virtue of its size (82, 89, 90–91), its potential to stand apart from the constant and ruinous conflicts of Europe (87), and as a haven for the oppressed (100). The inhabitants of America share in this destiny simply by virtue of living on the continent. In Paine's rhetoric, living in North America gives an instinctive sense of the true purpose of government, an enlarged capacity for tolerance and friendship, and a stake in the destiny of the continent.

When the rhetorical strategy of *Common Sense* is contrasted to Charland's reading of the strategy of the white paper, it becomes clear that Paine is able to create a sense of destiny (Charland's third ideological effect) that is not rooted in the history of a "people," but rather in the situation of a continent. Furthermore, the privileged position of the inhabitants of America depends to a large extent on *not having a collective history.* "Now is the seed time of continental union," in other words, the *beginning* of history. Thus, Paine's interpellation of his audience as inhabitants of America, a continent at the beginning of its history, is at odds with the "transhistoric" character usually associated with constitutive rhetoric.

Second Interpellation: "Put on . . . the True Character of a Man"

If Paine's interpellation of his readers as inhabitants of America is at odds with the "transhistoric" character of constitutive rhetoric, his interpellation of them as individual men endowed with reason and "natural feelings" is at odds with its collectivity. Throughout *Common Sense*, Paine appeals to his readers to search themselves to find the voice of their reason and natural feelings which, if trusted, will lead them to the correct conclusions about American independence. In order to get in touch with reason and natural feeling, readers must put aside distorting attachments and prejudices. (I describe more fully the role of the term "prejudice" in Paine's rhetoric in "Paine and Prejudice.")

Paine makes an explicit appeal that each reader "put on . . . the true character of a man" (more on the gender dynamics operating here follows shortly) at the opening of the third section:

> In the following pages I offer nothing more than simple facts, plain arguments, and common sense; and have no other preliminaries to settle with the reader, than that he will divest himself of prejudice and prepossession, and suffer his reason and his feelings to determine for themselves; that he will *put on*, or rather that he will not put off, *the true character of a man*, and generously enlarge his views beyond the present day. (81–82)

Paine makes similar appeals to *natural feelings* as he disparages the prospect of reconciliation. "Bring the doctrine of reconciliation to the touchstone of nature" (88), he says in one place, and later:

> There are injuries which nature cannot forgive; she would cease to be nature if she did. As well can the lover forgive the ravisher of his mistress, as the continent forgive the murders of Britain. The Almighty hath implanted in us these inextinguishable feelings for good and wise pur-

poses. They are the guardians of his image in our hearts. They distinguish us from the herd of common animals. (99–100)

The "true character of a man" that Paine evokes in these and other passages has at least three determinations: he exhibits civic virtue by confronting prejudice with reason; he is an adult rather than a child; and he owns his feelings of moral outrage. I will develop each of these determinations in turn in the following paragraphs.

Men exhibit civic virtue by confronting prejudice with reason. Civic virtue was a quality central to the *ethos* of classical republican ideology. The case that virtue was a necessary foundation of republican government was made by Montesquieu in the *Spirit of Laws* (3.3, 4.2, and 4.3), a text that greatly influenced American constitutional thought. The notion of civic virtue present in early American republican ideology was "active, self-sacrificial service to the state" that, as feminist historian Ruth H. Bloch states, was "an essentially male attribute" (140) rooted in Roman notions of *virtù*, whose root is *vir* meaning "man," and Greek notions of *areté*, or competitive excellence (on this point also see Pocock 92; Fruchtman 34–35; MacIntyre 114–22). Simply being male did not guarantee a full measure of virtue. Some men are better than others, so virtue needs to be proven in public. Classically, civic virtue could prove itself either through bold military deeds or in great speeches given at critical times. Although, as Bloch argues, the gendered nature of virtue had already begun to shift by the time of the American Revolution, the classical conception of virtue remained a strong current.

Paine puts his own spin on the classical and republican virtue-traditions when he calls his readers to exercise civic virtue by using reason to overcome prejudice and to face the facts in a manly way. When Paine called on his readers to "put on the true character of a man," he meant that they should not be counted among the "men of passive tempers" who "look somewhat lightly over the offences of Britain" (88). Americans needed to awaken from "fatal and unmanly slumbers" (89) and face the gravity of their situation. A passive person rests easy in the arms of comforting prejudices that tell him that Mother England has his interests at heart, that the storm will pass, and all will be well. A virtuous person employs reason to challenge prejudice so as to see things as they really are. For a man to "divest himself of prejudice and prepossession, and suffer his reason and his feelings to determine for themselves" (81) requires an active struggle that is portrayed dramatically by Paine: "And however our eyes may be dazzled with snow, our ears deceived by sound; however prejudice may warp our wills, or interest darken our understanding, the simple voice of nature and reason will say, it is right" (68). As the Romans showed their virtue on the battlefield, Paine calls on his readers to show theirs in an inward struggle against the dangerous comforts of passivity and prejudice.

Men are adults, not children. Not only must Paine's readers actively struggle against prejudice in order to put on "the true character of a man," they need to throw off the sort of dependent attachments that children have. As Robert

Ferguson explains: "For if the truest reader was still at least symbolically the child of a European, the act of reading was calculated to resolve the dependency of that child in the acceptance of adult responsibility" (482).

Paine wants his readers to grow up. He rails against the notion that England is the parent country of America (83–84) and the patriarchal role of the crown, which usurps a place proper to the Almighty (73). To truly be men, Americans must form relationships of mutual respect founded on equality under the law: in one passage Paine recommends that a crown, symbolizing kingship, be placed on the divine law, and then broken up and distributed among the people so that each has a part (98).

Men own their feelings of moral outrage. In a passage already quoted Paine states: "The Almighty hath implanted in us these inextinguishable feelings for good and wise purposes. . . . They distinguish us from the herd of common animals" (99–100). Such feelings represent a natural attachment to what is morally right. Those who lack them, like the man that Paine refers to as the "Royal Brute of Britain," are less than human. Thus, a true man feels moral outrage on appropriate occasions and owns those feelings: "There are injuries which nature cannot forgive."

In sum, when Paine calls on his readers to "put on . . . the true character of a man," he is calling them to exercise civic virtue by unflinchingly facing facts, to be adults by putting aside dependency and forming relations of mutual respect, and to own their natural feelings of moral outrage at what has already been inflicted upon them.

A few words must be said about the gendered nature of Paine's appeals. The passages and discussion above should make clear that, consistent with eighteenth-century notions of virtue and the nature of the sexes, when Paine uses "man" he does in fact mean the male sex. Sixteen years after the publication of *Common Sense*, Paine's friend Mary Wollstonecraft (see Hawke 205) would challenge the notion that activity and reason were qualities more naturally masculine than feminine in *Vindication of the Rights of Woman*. Paine's association with Wollstonecraft suggests that he may have eventually come to see many of those traits he associates with "true men" in *Common Sense* as being available to women as well, but, at the time of writing *Common Sense*, he was certainly far more interested in using the masculine *ethos* of classical republicanism to agitate for independence than in questioning its foundation in nature.

There is a certain resonance between the two ways that Paine hails his readers in *Common Sense*. As "inhabitants of America," they live somewhat apart from the customs and the prejudices of European civilization, and somewhat closer to nature. This closeness to nature makes it more likely that they can feel the "natural feelings" and take on the active and virtuous character of "true men."

Turning back to the framework of constitutive rhetoric, the larger point I wish to make in this analysis is that Paine's appeals to his readers to act the part of true men are definitely instances of interpellation, but they do not attempt to assimilate readers as members of a collective "people." Rather, they ask readers, as individuals, to tap the power of reason and natural feelings available to all men, but which are often buried by habit and prejudice. Thus, these appeals can be understood as constitutive, but not collectivizing. It might be objected that the "universal" nature of the "transcendent subject" that Paine calls his readers to inhabit might in some sense be collectivizing, but to call audience members to tap into the power of reason and the natural feelings that supposedly exist in all men is not the same thing as asking them to see themselves as members of one people as opposed to another. Paine calls his readers to act as individuals against the habits of thought, customs, and prejudices imposed upon them by the social collective.

CONCLUSION

It is my hope that in this essay I have not only shed some light on Paine's rhetorical strategies, but that I have also showed that, although constitutive rhetoric sometimes posits a transhistorical collective subject, it does not necessarily do so. If the basic feature of constitutive rhetoric is the strategic interpellation of audiences into subject positions, then Paine engages in constitutive rhetoric. His rhetoric, however, creates a sense of destiny out of place, not out of history, and a sense of responsibility out of what he takes to be the natural character of individual men, not out of the collective character of a "people."

Works Cited

Althusser, Louis. *Lenin and Philosophy and Other Essays.* Trans. Ben Brewster. New York: Monthly Review, 1971.

Bloch, Ruth H. *Gender and Morality in Anglo-American Culture, 1650–1800.* Ewing, NJ: U of California P, 2003.

Charland, Maurice. "Constitutive Rhetoric: The Case of the *Peuple Québécois.*" *Quarterly Journal of Speech* 73.2 (1987): 133–50.

Cordova, Nathaniel I. "The Constitutive Force of the *Catecismo del Pueblo* in Puerto Rico's Popular Democratic Party Campaign of 1938–1940." *Quarterly Journal of Speech* 90.2 (2004): 212–33.

Ferguson, Robert A. "The Commonalities of Common Sense." *The William and Mary Quarterly* 57.3 (2000): 465–504.

Foner, Eric. *Tom Paine and Revolutionary America.* New York: Oxford UP, 1976.

Fruchtman, Jack, Jr. *Thomas Paine and the Religion of Nature.* Baltimore: Johns Hopkins UP, 1993.

Government of Québec. *Québec-Canada: A New Deal. The Québec Government Proposal for a New Partnership Between Equals: Sovereignty-Association.* Québec: Govt. of QC, 1979.

Gross, Alan G. "Lincoln's Use of Constitutive Metaphors." *Rhetoric and Public Affairs* 7.2 (2004): 173–90.

Haskins, Ekaterina V. *Logos and Power in Isocrates and Aristotle.* Columbia: U of South Carolina P, 2004.

Hawke, David Freeman. *Paine.* New York: Harper & Row, 1974.

Hoffman, David C. "Paine and Prejudice: Rhetorical Leadership through Perceptual Framing in *Common Sense*." *Rhetoric and Public Affairs* 9.3 (2006): 373–410.

Keane, John. *Tom Paine: A Political Life*. Boston: Little Brown, 1995.

Kramnick, Isaac, ed. "Introduction." *Common Sense*. New York: Penguin Classics, 1986.

Leff, Michael, and Ebony A. Utley. "Instrumental and Constitutive Rhetoric in Martin Luther King Jr.'s 'Letter from Birmingham Jail.'" *Rhetoric and Public Affairs* 7.1 (2004): 37–52.

Liell, Scott. *46 Pages: Thomas Paine,* Common Sense, *and the Turning Point of American Independence*. Philadelphia: Running P, 2003.

MacIntyre, Alasdair. *After Virtue: A Study in Moral Theory*. Notre Dame: U of Notre Dame P, 1981.

McGee, Michael C. "In Search of 'The People': A Rhetorical Alternative." *Quarterly Journal of Speech* 61.3 (1975): 235–49.

Montesquieu, Charles de Secondat, Baron de. *The Spirit of Laws*. 1748. Amherst, NY: Prometheus Books, 2002.

Paine, Thomas. *Common Sense*. 1776. New York: Penguin Classics, 1986.

Pocock, J. G. A. *The Machiavellian Moment: Florentine Political Thought and the Atlantic Republican Tradition*. Princeton: Princeton UP, 1975.

Rousseau, Jean-Jacques. *The Social Contract*. 1762. Trans. Maurice Cranston. New York: Penguin Classics, 1968.

Stein, Sarah R. "The '1984' Macintosh Ad: Cinematic Icon and Constitutive Rhetoric in the Launch of a New Machine." *Quarterly Journal of Speech* 88.2 (2002): 169–92.

16

Paternalistic Rhetoric and the American People

Jay P. Childers

By many measures, citizenship, understood as political and civic participation, has declined in the United States over the past half century. This democratic weakening is evident in, among other things, the declining percentage of eligible voters who cast ballots, the reduced numbers of people who join membership-based organizations, and the poor state of civic and political knowledge among today's generations when compared to their elders (Putnam). So bad have things gotten in the United States that one group of political scientists, including Stephen Macedo, Robert Putnam, and Wendy Rahn, recently argued that the American democracy is at risk, and they noted that "although some aspects of civic life remain robust and some citizens still participate frequently, Americans should be concerned about the current state of affairs" (Macedo et al. 1). Many scholars concerned with American democratic practices would agree with this sentiment, but they would not agree on the reasons behind the declining political spirit in the United States. Such reasons range from television to postmaterialism, longer election cycles to suburbanization, and widespread moral weakening to a failing education system.

While all of these culprits may have something to do with the American people's declining political participation, I suggest in this essay that there may very well be another place to point a finger—elite discourse. Specifically, I will argue that a paternalistic rhetoric has emerged in the United States that articulates the interests of today's governmental officials, political elites, and corporate leaders. Paternalistic rhetoric performs this feat, I will show, by calling forth the American people and then constituting them in such a way as to wholly exclude them from the public sphere. To make this argument, I begin by tracing the work of political theorists who suggest that a small group of elites in the United States have begun to engage in governing practices that do not want, nor, more importantly, need, widespread citizen participation. Then, I turn to defining paternalistic rhetoric as a constitutive rhetoric positioned between Edwin Black's second persona and Philip Wander's third persona. And finally I offer three brief examples of how paternalistic rhetorics are articulated by President George W. Bush, one U.S.-based global corporation, and the advertisements of one national nonprofit organization.

THE DECLINING NEED FOR CITIZENS

Several scholars in political science have made the case that a diminished democratic impulse in the United States has emerged in recent decades, an impulse variously labeled: managerial democracy, personal democracy, and inverted totalitarianism. Predicated upon the belief that something close to a true mass participatory democracy once existed in the United States, their argument is not that the American people have become politically apathetic or disconnected on their own. Instead, these scholars suggest the United States' public sphere has been changing from the top down, in voluntary organizations, the federal government, and corporate America.

Theda Skocpol has argued recently, for instance, that

> where once cross-class voluntary federations held sway, national public life is now dominated by professionally managed advocacy groups without chapters or members. And at the state and local levels "voluntary groups" are, more often than not, nonprofit institutions through which paid employees deliver services and coordinate occasional volunteer projects. (7)

Skocpol traces this shift by showing that large national civic organizations and their local chapters have shifted to an organizational model run by administrators and require little more than financial and material resources. As civic organizing has long been understood as a precursor for political engagement in other public affairs, such a shift warrants concern. Skocpol notes this concern when she suggests that "early-twenty-first-century Americans live in a diminished democracy, in a much less participatory and more oligarchicly managed civic world" (11). And this top-down, managed civic world, Skocpol worries, no longer needs widespread membership and citizen mobilization, and worse, no longer wants it either.

While the trend Skocpol documents in the declining membership of civic organizations is alarming, others have raised potentially more dire concerns when they have noted a parallel trend in government. In terms of elections, Steven Schier has recently made an important distinction between the mass *mobilization* political parties used to engage in and the more directed *activation* strategies they now employ to target selected groups. This move toward activation allows, Schier warns, "candidates, parties, and interests to rule without serious regard to majority preferences as expressed at the polls" (9). In *Downsizing Democracy*, Matthew A. Crenson and Benjamin Ginsberg agree and argue that the United States' government itself has increasingly found ways to conduct its business without widespread citizen participation. As Crenson and Ginsberg note rather pointedly, "today's public authorities manage to raise armies, collect taxes, and implement policies without widespread citizen involvement" (21). Instead, today's U.S. federal government treats citizens less often as part of a whole, choosing instead to engage them individually. And they note, "In general, American institutions operate increasingly to disaggregate and depoliticize the demands of citizens. The 'reinvention' of American government has reinvented citizens as 'customers.' . . . It has begun to privatize not only many of its own functions but the public itself" (14).

Taking the notion of a diminished or downsized democracy one step further, Sheldon Wolin has more recently argued that what has happened over the past few decades in the United States should be understood as an inverted totalitarianism. While some may certainly take umbrage with Wolin's use of totalitarianism, he is careful to differentiate it from earlier forms that emerged elsewhere in the twentieth century. What is important for Wolin is the invertedness of today's governing system in which power does not derive from the people. As Wolin defines it, inverted totalitarianism is the name for a political system that is "driven by abstract totalizing powers, not by personal rule, one that succeeds by encouraging political disengagement rather than mass mobilization, that relies more on 'private' media than on public agencies to disseminate propaganda reinforcing the official version of events" (44). This totalizing power and privatization can best be understood, moreover, as a rise of corporate interference in governing processes. As Wolin writes, "corporate power and its culture are no longer external forces that occasionally influence policies and legislation. As these have become integral, so the citizenry has become marginal and democracy more manageable" (131). And as the citizenry has been brushed aside, this has allowed the totalizing private powers to find even more ways to manage society without democracy.

All of these arguments, then, assert the central claim that citizens are growing less and less important to controlling shareholders in government, corporations, national civic organizations, and special interests. In place of a more direct democracy that flourished in the United States between the Jeffersonian revolution of 1800 through the civil rights movement of the 1960s, these scholars argue that a managerial form of governance has emerged that little resembles classical notions of democracy. And here is where these works fall short—they offer up a what (managed democracy) and a why (power) without a how. They fail, that is, to fully account for how the American people have been made willing as of late to give up their democratic inheritance.

These controlling entities (voluntary organizations, the federal government, and corporate America) have, I argue, found a method of helping the American people give up their democratic rights through the articulation of what I call a paternalistic rhetoric, which calls forth the American people in order to exclude them from active participation in the political sphere. In place of traditional forms of mass political participation and self-governance, they have, instead, replaced citizenship with two primary options: donations of money, time, or bodily fluids and volunteerism in loose civic organizations requiring no membership.

PATERNALISTIC RHETORIC ARTICULATED

To develop an explanation of paternalistic rhetoric, it is important to understand it as a constitutive discourse situated between Edwin Black's second persona and Philip Wander's third persona. To do so requires first an acknowledgment that the people, in this case the American people, are a fiction. This is the point that Michael McGee made when he argued that "'the people' are more *process* than *phenomenon*. That is, they are conjured into objective reality, remain so long as the rhetoric which defined them has force, and in the end wilt away, becoming once again merely a collection of individuals" (240, emphasis in original). McGee's point here is not to suggest that individuals living within various contextual boundaries exist only when rhetorically articulated. He argues, instead, that rhetoric offers a process through which these individuals come to identify with one another. And for those doing the constituting, the purpose is not merely to foster group identity but to foster a group identity that best suits the purposes of those in power. As Roderick Hart and his colleagues argue of the American people, "an electorate is not a stable, ontological entity but one 'summoned up' periodically by political actors who define it in order to control it" (108).

The rhetorical critic's job, then, is to find "the people" who are called into being and then identify the constituting patterns that function as a form of control. That is, the rhetorical critic concerned with constitutive discourse must understand the ideological construction of the people. This was Edwin Black's point when he argued that all rhetorical discourse contains within it an implied auditor, or second persona. And Black saw such discourse as ideological when he argued:

> Especially must we note what is important in characterizing personae. It is not age or temperament or even discrete attitude. It is ideology—ideology in the sense that Marx used the term: the network of interconnected convictions that functions in a man epistemically and that shapes his identity by determining how he views the world. (112)

For Black, the second persona was the ideologically constructed ideal audience the rhetor hoped to create through rhetoric. While Black's second persona pointed the critic toward the ideationally constituted audience, Philip Wander noted that discourse does more than attempt to create an audience. In defining who fits the ideal audience, rhetoric also does the work of setting boundaries that keep some, if not many, from identifying with the constituted audience. Wander identified this phenomenon as the third persona, which "refers to being negated" within the text and within societal norms in which texts are produced (206). Wander's third persona defines those excluded from inclusion in the rhetorically constituted audience.

Rhetorical texts do, that is, the double duty of producing an ideal audience and creating ideational boundaries that disenfranchise others. In a democratic public sphere, who is and who is not identified as being "the people" is of the utmost importance, since democracy is predicated upon popular sovereignty and egalitarianism. Ideally, everyone has an equal right to a voice and a place within the public sphere. But the reality of democratic publics is that who actually has a voice and who has access to the public sphere is highly contested. And rhetoric can be the struggle over discursively creating the people in such a way as benefits the rhetor's own interests.

Despite these struggles, it would be wrong to assume that societies do not largely conform to a constitutive identity articulated by a dominant, hegemonic discourse integrally tied to the economic conditions of the society. This is the point Mark Garrett Longaker makes when he argues that hegemonic forces emerge from the connections among "the norms of rhetorical culture" and "a widely accepted political discourse" *and* "other elements, such as a particular variation of capitalism (for instance, Fordism), a particular political party, even a social movement or a spontaneous rebellion" (xv). It is my contention that in recent years such an articulated, hegemonic rhetoric has emerged in the United States at the convergence of the political interests of the dominant political party (Republicans), the prevailing acceptance of neoliberal capitalism, and the changing political structures suited to the needs of corporations and a small group of elites. This rhetoric has, moreover, avoided the complicating tensions between the second persona and third persona by constituting the whole people in order to exclude them completely from the public sphere. That is, it constitutes "the people" writ large in such a way as to exclude them in total. And while this rhetoric articulates the interests of those advancing a managerial or personal democracy, as noted above, I call it a paternalistic rhetoric since it concerns the public sphere, issues of democratic self-governance, and a strong sense of elitist benevolence.

PATERNALISTIC RHETORIC IN ACTION

Paternalism can be defined simply as one's interfering with the freedoms of another out of concern for her well-being, under the assumption that she cannot or will not make appropriate decisions concerning herself and others. When the state takes such intervening actions, it is understood as having made a paternalistic intervention. And while even a democratic society like the United States, which is predicated on liberty and egalitarianism, does occasionally intervene paternalistically in the lives of its citizens, the strong democratic tradition in the United States dating back at least to Thomas Jefferson's election of 1800 has made paternalistic policies less than popular. Indeed, it was Jefferson himself who defended individual liberty against a paternalistic government when writing to Thomas Cooper in 1802: "If we can prevent the government from wasting the labors of the people under the pretense of taking care of them, they must become happy" (1126). And in the pursuit of their own happiness, the American people went on to fight a two century battle for equal rights regarding self-government, a struggle that continues to be waged. Given the American people's democratic history and belief in individual liberties, the emergence of a paternalistic rhetoric is all the more important to note.

As was noted above, a paternalistic rhetoric is one that constitutes the whole in order to exclude the whole. In terms of the American public sphere, paternalistic rhetoric functions as discourse that calls the citizens together as a whole so that they can be excluded from political and civic engagement in the national community. Paternalistic rhetoric accomplishes this by creating or promoting a sense of uncertainty and fear, portraying the people as unable to understand things themselves, offering the rhetorical agent as a benevolent protector, and presenting alternative actions that give the people a false sense of political efficacy. Three brief examples serve to demonstrate how paternalistic rhetoric works in practice. The first example is from George W. Bush, the second from the Exxon Mobil Corporation, and the third from the national Bloodsaves campaign.

George W. Bush

As a paternalistic rhetoric brings to mind the concept of the father, it may be little surprise to find such discourse originating from the president of the United States. The nation's first president is, after all, often called "the father of our nation." But a lot has changed between the time of George Washington and that of George W. Bush, including the emancipation of slaves, the suffrage movement, and the civil rights movement. While Bush's use of a paternalistic rhetoric may seem at odds with the modern nation he found himself governing, Bush's rhetoric, particularly post-9/11, is decidedly paternalistic. His speech, "President Updates America on Operations Liberty Shield and Iraqi Freedom," delivered at a Philadelphia port on March 31, 2003, to members of the U.S. Coast Guard, offers a clear example of Bush's paternalistic rhetoric.

As others have noted at length, Bush was quick to advance his agenda of preventative war through the exploitation of fear in the United States following 9/11. In this particular speech, Bush continues this trend by first reminding the audience of the terrorist attacks of 9/11 and making a reference to Saddam Hussein's production of weapons of mass destruction. In addition, Bush continues to promote a sense of fear by noting, "all Americans understand that we face a continuing threat of terrorism. We know that our enemies are desperate; we know that they're dangerous. The dying regime in Iraq may try to bring terror to our shores. Other parts of the global terror network may view this as a moment to strike, thinking that we're distracted" (par. 21). Having reinforced a sense of fear among the American people, Bush then portrays them as a people who need, above all, protection. In fact, Bush uses the word "protect" in one form or another nine times during his 17-minute speech. Bush argues, moreover, that the Coast Guard should be proud of its ability to "shield your fellow Americans from the danger of this world," and he also notes that it is his administration's job to "use all our power to keep out the terrorists and the criminals so they can't hurt our citizens" (par. 24). The American people, then, are here constituted as a people in need of help, not expected, and indeed unable, to protect themselves.

Second, Bush emphasizes his administration's benevolent role in this protection. Bush creates a sense of benevolence most clearly through his attempt to tie his administration's policies with the core democratic values of the United States. His speech is, for instance, meant to update the American people on two military operations—one named Operation Liberty Shield and the other called Operation Iraqi Freedom. Besides the operational names, Bush more explicitly connects the nation's military engagements in the Middle East to core American democratic values when he calls attention to the speech's setting, Philadelphia, noting that "after all, it was in this place that we first declared our dedication to liberty. We still believe that all men are created equal and have the right to be free" (par. 2). Bush's argument here is meant to justify his administration's actions as benevolently rooted within the ideational framework of American democracy with the use of the ideographic terms liberty, equality, and freedom.

Finally, Bush is clear about who is to take action. Although one might be confused by his multiple uses of collective nouns and pronouns, Bush makes a distinction between the American people, who need protection, and the nation, which takes action. The American people become a they, while the nation becomes a we embodied in the president and his military audience. This is Bush's point when he argues that "there's a lot of room for opportunity for our fellow citizens, people who want to do something for America" (par. 10). Here Bush talks of the American people as outside of the collective "our," and this collective can only be understood as the audience he is addressing and including himself within. Indeed, when Bush suggests that "this nationwide effort is focused on five specific areas" (par. 24), all five areas are ones controlled by the executive branch of government. But if the American people are still seeking a way to help their nation, their government, do its business, Bush offers them one alternative:

> You can volunteer. You can volunteer to help watch neighborhoods. You can volunteer to help neighborhoods become better prepared. You can volunteer for the Red Cross. You could love a neighbor just like you'd like to be loved yourself. It's happening all across America. (par. 10)

The American people, identified as "you" instead of us or we, can become involved in their own self-governing not through self-sacrifice, public deliberation, or other traditional notions of citizen engagement; they can instead find a sense of efficacy in the acts of volunteering and loving their neighbors.

Exxon Mobil Corporation

While Bush's paternalistic rhetoric may come as little surprise to many, another place one can find such discourse is in corporate America. Specifically, the public relations documents and advertising of ExxonMobil, the largest publicly traded oil company in the world and the largest profit maker in U.S. history, offer one clear example of paternalistic rhetoric. Since ExxonMobil, like most large corporations today, does an effective job of synthesizing press releases, advertisements, and corporate speakers under one clear set of messages, I have selected just one corporate speech as emblematic of the rhetorical stance of the company. The selected speech was delivered by Exxon-Mobil Chairman and CEO Rex Tillerson at Boston College's Chief Executives Club on November 30, 2006. While the audience consisted of invited guests, the speech was also open to the press, delivered on a major American university campus, and then posted on ExxonMobil's Web site under the subheading of company news—clearly a speech meant for wider corporate outreach. The speech is not unique or particularly eloquent, but it is important in its banality as it uses, word for word, pieces of the company's larger advertising campaign. Overall, Tillerson's speech focuses on the energy industry's expected growth and, more importantly for this essay, concerns about the environment, a topic that certainly falls within the framework of the American public sphere.

Tillerson begins his speech by presenting the energy demands of the future in strikingly uncertain terms. He suggests that, "by the year 2030—less than twenty-five years from now—the world's energy needs will be almost 50 percent greater than they were last year" (par. 9). And he notes that "in the time it takes me to deliver these remarks, people worldwide will have used over 50 million gallons of oil" (par. 12), which is part of the energy "challenge we face in the future" (par. 14). While this difficult challenge is disturbing enough, Tillerson then turns his attention to the environmental issues surrounding energy consumption and offers an ambiguous view of global warming. Tillerson argues:

> While our scientific understanding of climate change continues to improve, it nonetheless remains today an extraordinarily complex area of scientific study. Having said that, the potential risks to society could prove to be significant, so despite the areas of uncertainties that do exist, it is prudent to develop and implement strategies that address the potential risks. (par. 60)

While this certainly sounds like corporate-speak meant to avoid taking blame for global warming, Tillerson's presentation of the evidence as "an extraordinarily complex area of scientific study" (par. 60) suggests both an ambiguous reality and the implication that the average person simply cannot understand the nuances of the research. Science is, after all, the purview of experts. He echoes this sentiment later in the speech when he calls a large portion of the public dialogue on energy concerns "wishful thinking [that] will only lead us farther away from a long-term solution" (par. 69).

Having presented a scary and uncertain view of future energy consumption and presented the environmental issues as too complex for ordinary citizens to understand, Tillerson then spends much of his time in the final third of the speech showing how ExxonMobil is leading the effort to create a responsible solution to the energy needs of the future. As Tillerson argues that "the solutions to the energy challenges we face will come from this generation's scientists, engineers, managers, and policymakers" (par. 70), he depicts ExxonMobil as at the forefront of the solution. Beyond simply suggesting that his corporation is working internally on climate problems, Tillerson also emphasizes their philanthropic role in the larger national community, specifically through two programs. The first is ExxonMobil's "lead founding sponsor" role in Stanford University's Global Climate and Energy Project (par. 64). The second is the corporation's $42 million in donations to "proven programs nationwide" designed to improve the math and science education of American schoolchildren (par. 74). In the end, with such a benevolent corporate sponsor working to solve the energy challenges of the future with an eye toward helping the environment, the citizen is left with little to do but spend his money on ExxonMobil products and services, so that she might help ExxonMobil reach its destination, which Tillerson suggests is "one where our economy is more competitive, out nation more secure, and our world more prosperous" (par. 78).

Bloodsaves

In September 2004, the American Red Cross, the American Association of Blood Banks, and America's Blood Centers joined forces with The Advertising Council to launch Bloodsaves, a three year public service announcement (PSA) campaign. According to an Ad Council news release, the campaign was "geared towards young adults in an effort to raise awareness about the importance of ongoing blood donation and foster a new generation of lifelong donors" (par. 1). In the campaign's first phase, a series of commercials aired nationwide during times donated by local stations. Each PSA followed the same format, showing a young adult narrating his or her complicated story about trying to make a difference in a local community. Although each representative young adult was successful in bringing about change, the changes subsequently led to more problems and unforeseen complications. The point of the commercials and the slogan was to make young people feel as though, despite the complicated and messy world surrounding political issues, they could still make a difference in the world with very little effort. According to Executive Creative Director of Advertising Kevin Roddy, "young people today feel a certain futility in their ability to affect the world they live in, and we wanted to use that as a leverage point in advertising to show these young adults that giving blood is an easy way to make an incredibly important difference—saving lives." Beyond trying to show young adults that blood donation is relatively easy, the Bloodsaves media campaign also functioned, however, as a paternalistic rhetoric that argued against active citizenship in the larger public sphere. A brief analysis of one of the PSAs demonstrates the familiar pattern of fear and confusion, ignorant citizens, benevolent agent, and alternative action.

The Bloodsaves advertisement, entitled "Charlie," begins with a young, white male explaining how he recently learned that the jeans he bought were made by a child laborer in a foreign country. Upset by this, Charlie then describes his attempts to attack the problem by writing a letter to the company that makes the jeans asking them to stop using child labor, to which the company responds with a letter of thanks for his customer loyalty and a coupon for money off on his next pair of jeans. Troubled, the young Charlie decides to do something more. "So I got smart and wrote letters every day to all the stores that carry the brand asking them to stop supporting the companies that use child labor." These actions, in turn, lead to more letters and more coupons. As Charlie's frustration increases, so does the speed of the commercial: he rapidly outlines the complaint of one of his friends who suggests that all the letter writing is causing trees to be cut down in the rain forest, which is then going to lead to the displacement of indigenous tribes, the spread of rare diseases, and damaging climate change. Just as things seem to be spiraling out of control, the commercial pauses, fades to black, and then the Bloodsaves campaign's tagline appears: "Saving the world isn't easy. Saving a life is. And just one pint of blood can save up to three lives."

In thirty seconds, the Bloodsaves PSA offers the targeted viewer, young adults, a paternalistic rhetoric that de-emphasizes traditional forms of political action. The fallacious slippery slope logic of the PSA suggests, after all, that the young person's attempt to get a company to stop using child labor actually does more harm than good, somehow indirectly leading to major political problems in other parts of the world. Such a complicating view of global politics would certainly raise the fears of the conscientious young adults that might be interested in the PSA's theme. The "Charlie" PSA, moreover, further suggests that he was too naïve to realize the full implications of his letter-writing campaign. Charlie stands in for all young do-gooders, and the implication is that young people in general do not have the appropriate sophistication to navigate the confusing network of global connections now inherent in the public sphere.

Given that the public sphere is so confusing and that Charlie, an average young adult, does not have the ability to understand complicated political issues, the Bloodsaves campaign offers an alternative political action. It suggests to the viewer that if she wants to make a difference in the world, she should abstain from getting directly involved in the public sphere and simply give blood instead. As the blood is not given directly from one individual to another, the conscientious young adult is left to trust the benevolent group of blood organizations joined together in the Bloodsaves campaign to give her blood to someone who needs it, feeling in the end that she has saved a life (or three).

Conclusion

Democratic citizenship takes work. It requires sacrifice predicated on trust and a real sense of efficacy. In today's large nation-states, it is also a sleight-of-hand trick through which the people are given the sense of being in charge through the system of representation. Political theorist Danielle Allen has recently noted this when she argues that

> Democracies inspire in citizens an aspiration to rule and yet require citizens constantly to live with the fact that they do not. Democracies must find methods to help citizens deal with the conflict between their politically inspired desires for total agency and the frustrating reality of their experience. (22–23)

Rhetorically, these methods for helping citizens cope have been accomplished by asking the American people to sacrifice, to work together, and to labor more vigorously. They have always, that is, been encouraged to believe that popular sovereignty was a reality. Generations of civic education curricula have been based on such beliefs. While the U.S. government, American corporations, and various social movements and special interest groups may find it advantageous to keep the people out of politics, one would think the American people would be unwilling to give up the belief that they live in a democracy predicated on popular sovereignty and requiring mass participation.

Today, however, many in the United States do seem willing to treat politics and the public sphere as ancillary to their own lives. And this willingness seems to be finding some encouragement from a number of elite interests. As the examples above demonstrate, a new discourse has emerged that bypasses the traditional call to citizen action and instead treats citizens paternalistically. This paternalistic rhetoric works by hailing the people as concerned citizens and then tells them, politely, to step out of the way so that others can take care of things for them. This is achieved, as I have shown, by creating or promoting a sense of fear and uncertainty that advances a view of the people as unable to tend to their own governance. In place of the people, paternalistic rhetoric offers up benevolent elites and organizations who work on behalf of the people. And in place of traditional forms of citizen action, paternalistic rhetoric then reduces political and civic participation to donations, consumerism, and volunteering. In the end, paternalistic rhetoric functions paternalistically in that it encourages the people to give up on one of their most cherished democratic liberties—self-governance.

I do not mean to overstate the case of paternalistic rhetoric, but it should not be understated either. Encouraging citizens to donate, spend money, and volunteer moves citizens one full step away from political and civic participation. Donating money (or blood?) may feel efficacious, but once the money has been given, how it is spent is left to organizational leaders, who often label themselves today as CEOs and CFOs. Spending money does much the same thing. Shopping at an environmentally friendly company may feel better to the consumer, but it then leaves decisions about how best to improve the environment to corporations whose philanthropic endeavors may be more about good public relations than attempting to find sound solutions to complex political issues. And as some scholars have recently argued, volunteering today does not require the sacrifices of organization membership of decades past and does not, therefore, produce the same levels of social capital necessary for a vibrant public sphere (Blyth, Saito, and Beikas 52). What is at stake in identifying and criticizing paternalistic rhetoric as it is currently articulated by hegemonic forces in the United States, then, is democracy itself. So long as the people are paternalistically asked to step aside, a relatively small group of people will make governing decisions about the public sphere on, in the best scenario, the people's behalf, or, in a more troubling alternative, their own behalf. For rhetorical scholars then, being attentive to paternalistic rhetoric in our research and pedagogy is one step toward fighting back against such antidemocratic practices. Another responsibility we have is to create and foster more democratic rhetorics.

Works Cited

Advertising Council. "Leading Blood Groups Continue Successful Bloodsaves Campaign with Launch of Animated Superhero . . . 'The Red Defender.'" 22 Aug. 2006. <http://www.aabb.org/Content/News_and_Media/Press_Releases/pr060822.htm>.

Allen, Danielle S. *Talking to Strangers: Anxieties of Citizenship since* Brown v. Board of Education. Chicago: U of Chicago P, 2004.

Black, Edwin. "The Second Persona." *The Quarterly Journal of Speech* 56 (1970): 109–19.

Blyth, Dale, Rebecca Saito, and Thomas Beikas. "A Quantitative Study of the Impact of Service-Learning Programs." Ed. A. S. Waterman. *Service-Learning: Applications from the Research.* Mahwah, NJ: Erlbaum, 1997. 39–56.

Bush, George W. "President Updates America on Operations Liberty Shield and Iraqi Freedom." 31 Mar. 2003. <http://www.whitehouse.gov/news/releases/2003/03/20030331-4.html>.

Crenson, Matthew A., and Benjamin Ginsberg. *Downsizing Democracy: How America Sidelined Its Citizens and Privatized Its Public.* Baltimore, MD: Johns Hopkins UP, 2002.

Hart, Roderick P. et al. *Political Keywords: Using Language That Uses Us.* New York: Oxford UP, 2005.

Jefferson, Thomas. *Thomas Jefferson: Writings.* Ed. Merrill D. Peterson. New York: Library of America, 1984.

Longaker, Mark Garrett. *Rhetoric and the Republic: Politics, Civic Discourse, and Education in Early America.* Tuscaloosa: U of Alabama P, 2007.

Macedo, Stephen et al. *Democracy at Risk: How Political Choices Undermine Citizen Participation, and What We Can Do About It.* Washington, DC: Brookings Institution P, 2005.

McGee, Michael C. "In Search of the 'People': A Rhetorical Alternative." *Quarterly Journal of Speech* 61.3 (1975): 235–49.

Putnam, Robert D. *Bowling Alone: The Collapse and Revival of American Community.* New York: Simon and Schuster, 2001.

Schier, Steven E. *By Invitation Only: The Rise of Exclusive Politics in the United States.* Pittsburgh: U of Pittsburgh P, 2000.

Skocpol, Theda. *Diminished Democracy: From Membership to Management in American Civic Life.* Norman: U of Oklahoma P, 2003.

Tillerson, Rex W. "Understanding Our Shared Energy Future." 30 Nov. 2006. <http://www.exxonmobil.com/Corporate/news_speeches_20061130_RWT.aspx>.

Wander, Philip. "The Third Persona: An Ideological Turn in Rhetorical Theory." *Communication Studies* 33 (1984): 197–216.

Wolin, Sheldon S. *Democracy Incorporated: Managed Democracy and the Specter of Inverted Totalitarianism.* Princeton: Princeton UP, 2008.

PART III

Shaping Histories and Envisioning Futures

17

Rustic Experience and the Rhetorical Work of National Park Architecture

Gregory Clark

Rhetoric works in many ways. Our study of the nature and functions of rhetoric has moved beyond the spoken and written word into visual, aural, and spatial realms, acknowledging that our nonverbal as well as verbal experiences can be rhetorical. We are now beginning to understand ourselves as immersed in rhetoric. As Richard Weaver put it, we are "caught up in a great web of inter-communication and inter-influence" where we must "speak as rhetoricians affecting one another for good or ill" (1360). True, but we're also rhetoricians when we're not speaking. That great rhetorical web Weaver described is woven of a variety of communicative strands of which written and spoken language are but a few. So we who study rhetoric are learning something about the extent to which people affect and are affected by others for good or ill *without* words—about the extent to which the wordless elements of our experience can do rhetorical work. Language is indeed, as Weaver claimed, inherently sermonic. But so are many other things.

My project here is to describe one of those other sermonic things by recounting a particular situation in which buildings and landscapes were rendered rhetorical. During the first half of the twentieth century, the U.S. National Park Service (NPS) used structural and landscape architecture to compose a particular kind of rhetorical experience for those who would visit the spectacular natural places it was charged to administer. In terms of a specific rhetorical purpose, the NPS designed its buildings and their grounds in the national parks to prompt in visitors particular attitudes—attitudes that might lead to actions of what we would now call environmental responsibility.

RHETORIC, ATTITUDES, AND THE NATIONAL PARK SERVICE

From the day of its organization, the NPS was engaged in both preservation and presentation of the lands it administered as a matter of mission. And that mission was, primarily, a rhetorical one. That is, the statutory charge given to the NPS was to preserve and protect the exceptional natural places in the United States that had been designated national parks against the settlement and development that were proceeding unrestrained across the continent. The purpose of that preservation and protection was to provide the public with ample opportunities to access and use those places for their recreation. What made this dual project of preservation and public presentation rhetorical is the particular kind of recreation those parks were intended to provide, a project envisioned most clearly by Frederick Law Olmsted, the landscape architect whose ideas about parks and natural public spaces—realized most famously in New York City's Central Park—shaped the national park movement. Olmsted, writes Joseph Sax, "based his theory of recreation on what he called 'a faith in the refinement of the republic'" (76) and encouraged landscape and building designs in America that "would reflect the aspiration of those who believed that an experience of quiet solitude in a setting of untrammeled natural scenery could attract and stir the contemplative faculty in even the most ordinary citizen" (75). The NPS was charged with enabling this rhetorical work.

This general idea that contemplative time in spectacular natural places would render individuals more refined as citizens had been an American assumption since the mid-nineteenth century, when Western lands that were considered exceptional began to be nominated for federal protection and development as public retreats. Implicit in that idea is an aesthetic project with rhetorical purpose. As it was organized in 1916, the NPS set about putting that project into coordinated practice. As Olmsted's ideas suggest, the felt and sensed quality of visitors' experiences in these places was a high priority for the new NPS because providing the American public with a particular kind of experience in nature was at the heart of its charge. This charge followed from a romantic conception of nature that developed during the nineteenth century as natural resource development, manufacturing, and a very dirty sort of urban life expanded unconstrained across the United States. So early on the NPS established development policies intended to provide the public with experiences that would subordinate all tourist development in the parks to the beauty of nature. Primary among those policies was the design standard that became known as "NPS Rustic."

That standard emerged formally soon after the NPS was organized in 1916, a time when the lofty mission of America's national parks was being challenged by the material realities of rapidly increasing tourism. An early and general version of that lofty mission had been expressed in the mid-nineteenth century by the painter George Catlin, who proposed in his *Letters and Notes on the Manners, Customs and Conditions of the North American Indians* that American lands "of pristine beauty and wildness" be preserved "and [held] up to the view of her refined citizens and the world, in future ages" as "a *nation's Park*, containing man and beast, in all the wild and freshness of their nature's beauty!" (263). By the turn of the twentieth century that mission had matured and was being rendered practical. As President Theodore Roosevelt expressed it in 1903 in reference to Yellowstone as he laid the cornerstone for that park's monumental entry arch,

> this Park was created, and is now administered for the benefit and enjoyment of the people. The government must continue to appropriate for it, especially in the direction of completing and perfecting an excellent system of driveways. But already its beauties can be seen with great comfort in a short space of time and at an astonishingly small cost, and with the sense on the part of every visitor that it is in part his property; that it is the property of Uncle Sam and therefore of all of us. The only way that the people as a whole can secure to themselves and their children the enjoyment in perpetuity of what the Yellowstone Park has to give, is by assuming the ownership in the name of the nation and jealously safeguarding and preserving the scenery, the forests, and the wild creatures. (Whittlesey and Schullery 13)

Immediately after its inception, then, the NPS began to put that project of safeguarding and preserving into practice in all the parks, a considerable task because the existing parks had been administered by a variety of government agencies that had not attended to the rhetorical work of those lands. An NPS history of NPS Rustic design describes the earliest concessioners that followed the first tourists into the parks as largely unregulated—their buildings were rough and improvised and the quality of their services often marginal. The wealthy railroads that replaced those early entrepreneurs built grand hotels, providing tourists with opulent buildings and grounds that "tended . . . to ignore the natural setting." But the railroads' architects soon found that tourist facilities designed to fit into their spectacular settings by featuring local materials and handwork that served to blend a structure into its environment better pleased their patrons (Tweed, Soulliere, and Law 3–4). NPS architects also recognized that such "natural" design principles that the railroads were beginning to develop would serve tourist needs without detracting from the natural beauty that prompted the tourism in the first place, which initiated a creative collaboration with the railroads' architects. NPS Rustic evolved in this interaction of commercial and conservationist interests, and it did so rapidly. By 1918, the second full year of NPS operation, the service was able to issue this "Statement of Policy" regarding park development:

> In the construction of roads, trails, buildings, and other improvements, particular attention must be devoted always to the harmonizing of these improvements with the landscape. This is the most important item in our programs of development and requires the employment of trained engineers who either possess a knowledge of landscape architecture or have a proper appreciation of the aesthetic value of park lands. (qtd. in Tweed, Soulliere, and Law 23)

The design principles that became known as NPS Rustic carefully subordinated human habitation to the natural setting and attempted to combine aesthetic values and practical work. It is that combination that made the buildings and landscapes rhetorical. Essentially, NPS Rustic was a rhetorical aesthetic that provided visitors in these natural places with a particular quality of experience while at the same time accommodating their practical needs—it offered the experience of subordinating themselves for a time, and contentedly so, to the beauty of nature. The buildings and landscapes that followed from these principles were intended to prompt in visitors an attitude toward nature that was respectful and even, as I will explain, reverent. The rhetorical project of NPS Rustic was abandoned after World War II as rapid expansion of the park system made construction of such buildings and landscapes too expensive for the NPS to sustain. At this point in its history, the NPS formally adopted new design policies favoring modernist principles that mirrored the urban and suburban aesthetics of postwar America where people traveled not by railroad but in their own automobiles.

Until then, though, NPS Rustic principles guided the construction of lodges and cabins, roads and bridges, trails and picnic areas, and even toilets in American national parks. These design principles rendered each of the national parks rhetorically a scene in Kenneth Burke's sense of that term. "From the motivational point of view there is implicit in the quality of a scene the quality of the action that is to take place within it" (*Grammar* 6–7). When Burke embarked on his project of redefining the rhetorical in reference to the experience of identification, he did so to demonstrate, as he put it, "how a rhetorical motive is often present where it is not usually recognized or thought to belong" (*Rhetoric* xxxi). And a rhetorical motive is indeed present in places, particularly in carefully designed places. That is because places prompt identifications, identifications comprise attitudes, and attitudes are at the root of the rhetorical. Indeed, an explanation Burke once offered of the rhetoricality of lyric poetry applies as readily to these designed places. The lyric, he noted, "*strikes an attitude.*" That is because "a lyric may be, on its face, but a list of descriptive details specifying a scene . . . [but in their function] these images are all manifestations of a single attitude" ("Eye-Poem" 25–26). So, I suggest, is a designed place like those that followed the principles of NPS Rustic.

The single attitude that is manifest in places designed using those principles is, I believe, what philosopher Paul Woodruff calls "reverence." To explain that statement, I want first to describe this idea of reverence and its rhetorical work. Then I'll summarize the principles that guided NPS Rustic design and explain how they worked rhetorically to prompt visitors to attitudes of reverence. To make things clear, and perhaps more interesting, I'll conclude by showing how this rhetorical aesthetic was put into practice early in the twentieth century in a new national park called Zion.

REVERENCE AND RHETORIC

Woodruff's argument is that reverence is an essential civic virtue in any community and particularly in a democratic one. Defined as "the well-developed capacity to have feelings of awe, respect, and shame when these are the right feelings to have" (8), Woodruff's reverence is a public expression of a common attitude that provides an essential bond among citizens. It is their shared acknowledgment of, and respect for, "something that reminds us of human limitations" and that binds people together (65). That something may be justice, it may be divinity, it may be life itself. Whatever the object of reverence, it prompts a shared attitude that enables individuals to experience their moral common ground. As they do so, they find that the object of their common reverence also demarcates the boundaries of that common ground, boundaries that reverence reminds them each individually not to cross.

Reverence is an individual virtue. A virtue is, for Woodruff, "a capacity, cultivated by experience and training, to have emotions that make you feel like doing good things" (62). Such a definition is easy to attach to the more specific notion of a civic virtue—of individual virtues collectively held. Important here is the idea that a virtue is a capacity for feeling, for feelings that do motivating—and, thus, rhetorical—work. The Aristotelian notion of epideictic rhetoric deals with the prompting of such virtues. The epideictic project, as Gerard A. Hauser succinctly describes it, involves enabling "virtue to make its appearance in civic life" (14). That appearance, or display, is rhetorical because, in the familiar phrase from Perelman and Olbrechts-Tyteca, it "strengthens the disposition toward action by increasing adherence to the values it lauds" (50). But Hauser is more specific, writing that "the shared testimony of audience members both certifies the reality of this excellence as a civic virtue while joining community members with bonds of affiliation to the celebrated values and deeds" (19). In reference to reverence, those bonds emerge when people find themselves sharing an experience that prompts in them similar feelings of awe, respect, or—in the negative case—shame.

Paul Woodruff describes reverence as standing "in awe of something" (117). "You feel, when you are in awe," he continues, "that you are human, that your mind is dwarfed by what it confronts, that you cannot capture it in a set of beliefs, and that you had best keep your mouth closed and your mind open while awaiting further disclosure" (147). It is the attitude that follows from those feelings that is the rhetorical consequence of an experience of reverence. And to provide such an experience, one that would produce such a consequence, was precisely the project of NPS Rustic design. National parks require structures and associated development to enable visitors to access and temporarily inhabit them. When those structures and that development are designed to provide a mode of habitation that keeps visitors aware, first and foremost, of the primacy of the natural grandeur surrounding them, those visitors are prompted by the experience of being there to feelings of awe and respect for nature, and even, perhaps, some shame at how nature is treated in places other than these.

THE NPS RUSTIC AESTHETIC

What, then, is NPS Rustic design? The most succinct description I have found is in the preface to an NPS handbook published in 1935 that featured what were considered the best design practices of, in the words of the volume's title, *Park Structures and Facilities*. The description appears in the foreword, authored by the director of the NPS:

> In any area in which the preservation of the beauty of Nature is a primary purpose, every modification of the natural landscape, whether it be by construction of a road or erection of a shelter, is an intrusion. A basic objective of those who are entrusted with development of such areas for the human uses for which they are established is, it seems to me, to hold these intrusions to a minimum and so to design them that, besides being attractive to look upon, they appear to belong to and be a part of their settings. (1)

But the NPS architect who actually pulled the handbook together, Albert Good, introduced those design principles with considerably more color. In his introduction—titled "Apologia"—he wrote this: "Lamentable is the fact that during the six days given over to Creation, picnic tables and fireplaces, foot bridges, toilet facilities, and many another of man's requirements were negligently and entirely overlooked," leaving it to us now "to supply these odds and ends undone when the whistle blew on Creation." Hampered by the reality that "structures, however well designed, almost never truly add to the beauty, but only to the use, of a park of true natural distinction," we can at least remember that "if the trespass is unavoidable, it can be done with certain grace" (3). Good goes on to explain that this "certain grace" should involve "the use of natural materials in proper scale, and . . . the avoidance of rigid, straight lines, and over-sophistication, [giving] the feeling of having been executed by pioneer craftsmen with limited hand tools" in order to achieve, in Good's simple concluding statement, "sympathy with natural surroundings and with the past" (2–3).

This is a prescriptive statement that describes the practices of the western national parks where these principles had guided building and landscape design for two decades. In each of those parks, NPS Rustic had assumed a local form—using local materials that would reflect the particular landscape and designs that would express both the natural and human history of the particular place. In each case, though, a national rhetorical project had been advanced. The notable articulation of that project is another of Olmsted's. In 1865, the state of California was given by the federal government a charge to preserve and present to the public the Yosemite Valley. In a ceremony observing that gift held on the floor of that valley, Olmsted—who had been selected to lead the project—argued that a nation recovering from civil war needs public access to places where citizens can retreat to experience a "union of the deepest sublimity with the deepest beauty of nature, not in one feature or another," an experience not available "in any landscape that can be framed by itself, but all around and wherever the visitor goes" (8–9). That is, an experience made available only by inhabiting such a place.

This statement—made fifty years before the NPS was organized—called upon the country to use its natural landscapes to enable for its citizens what amounts to common experiences of reverence. It called for provision of public access to the unique and spectacular American places where divergent and diverse people could encounter for themselves, yet together, the feelings of awe, respect, and even shame that would renew their commitments to their common project of democratic life—the project that was, itself, a primary object of reverence in America. Inherent in Olmsted's call was a mandate to government to provide the public with opportunities to inhabit temporarily places where such a union of natural sublimity and beauty remains intact.

NPS RUSTIC IN ZION NATIONAL PARK

Southern Utah's Zion Canyon was made a national monument in 1909 and a national park in 1919. Soon after that, an architect employed by the Union Pacific Railroad Company began working with the NPS on the project of

> making this park, along with the neighboring parks of Bryce Canyon and the North Rim of the Grand Canyon, comfortable for the tourists the railroad was bringing in. That architect, Gilbert Stanley Underwood, had been employed by the railroad to develop accommodations in the parks that would "evoke imaginative associations and dramatiz[e] the scenery." (Zaitlin 20)

That charge, enacted in an ongoing process of negotiation between the railroad's commercial purposes, the design principles insisted upon by the NPS, and Underwood's own aesthetic sensibility, resulted in Zion's characteristic expression of NPS Rustic.

Underwood first designed the Zion Lodge, a complex of low buildings tucked under towering cliffs (see figure 1). At its center was the lodge building itself, which contained a lobby, a restaurant, and a gift shop. Guest rooms were located in separate cabins spread out on either side among newly planted trees. Native stone that resembled the rubble at the base of the cliffs dominated the buildings: the architectural center of the lodge was its four stone columns, and of the cabins their massive chimneys. Walls were made of local, rough-sawn lumber with a "studs-out" construction reminiscent of the granary buildings of the region's Mormon farms, some of which remained in the valley. At the same time, Underwood designed the "Zion Inn," which functioned as the office and cafeteria for a development of lower-priced rustic cabins available at the entrance to the park. His biographer describes the design of these buildings as a "lighter rustic" than that developed in other parks like Yellowstone or Yosemite, reflecting the mass and verticality of the canyon, but using its desert materials to express the more open topography.

Figure 1. Zion Lodge, 1930s. Colored Lantern Slide. National Park Service Historic Photograph Collection.

The lodge burned down in 1966 but the deluxe cabins (see figure 2) and the Zion Inn (see figure 3)—now the Zion Nature Center—have been restored and remain.

Through the 1920s and into the 1930s, Underwood designed a wide range of other structures for Zion National Park, including checking stations, ranger stations, ranger residences, employee dormitories, shops and garages, trails, bridges—including the North Fork Virgin River Bridge that is still in use—and, of course, toilets. In 1987, park officials nominated many of those that remain for the National Register of Historic Places. The nomination form included the following general description of NPS Rustic as it was put into practice in Zion: "The intent of the style was to design buildings which would not intrude upon the natural scenic beauty and which would blend with the natural terrain by use of building materials and massing similar to the natural materials found in the park" (*Multiple Resources* Item 8 page 8).

Elsewhere in the nomination is this further statement about Zion's particular version of these principles that works as a summary description of its combined aesthetic and rhetorical function:

> The style's tenets were an intensive use of hand labor, rejection of regu-
> larity and symmetry in building materials, and acceptance of the premise

Figure 2. Deluxe Cabin, Zion Lodge, Spring 2008. Photograph by author.

Figure 3. Zion Inn (now the Zion Nature Center). Spring 2008. Photograph by the author.

that a structure employing native building materials blended best with the natural environment. Properly executed, "NPS-Rustic" . . . structures achieved sympathy with their natural surroundings and the past. (*Multiple Resources* Item 8 page 4)

Figure 4. North Fork Virgin River Bridge, Zion National Park. Spring 2008. Photograph by the author.

I can push that last statement a bit further. Aesthetically, well-executed NPS Rustic structures achieve that sympathy and, as they do so, rhetorically display it as a prompt to an attitude. It is in this inviting and even compelling display of an attitude of sympathy for its natural and cultural context—a display of reverence, essentially—that an NPS Rustic structure finds its rhetorical power.

INHABITING REVERENCE

In his introduction to *Rhetorics of Display*, Lawrence Prelli suggests that "what appears or looks to us as reality is constituted rhetorically through the multiple displays that surround us, compete for our attention, and make claims upon us" (1). As a child, I thought a lot about displays. My father designed and installed the window displays in the clothing store he operated. Each of the large display windows on the front of that store was a transparent fourth wall of an elegant and interesting little room that was inhabited by mannequins dressed in beautiful clothes. My dad made each of those windows a life-sized model of the reality that his store offered to provide to passers-by, a model that invited them into the store. While the window displays didn't *state* that invitation, it was nonetheless conveyed by the beauty of the display itself. That beauty is what prompted those passers-by to imagine themselves inhabiting the alternative reality presented in those windows, a reality they could readily acquire for themselves inside the store.

This was advertising, after all, and so clearly rhetorical as it attempted to get people to buy what the store had to sell. But it is important to note the content of that rhetorical appeal. The window display didn't work to *persuade* people to come into the store and buy. Rather, it *presented* them with a reality with which they could, in Kenneth Burke's sense of the term, identify. And they identified with the reality in the window when they imagined themselves inhabiting its beauty—the clothes, their inviting context, and the attitudes they all expressed. In identifying themselves with those attitudes, they would find themselves wanting to buy for themselves at least some elements of what they found displayed there.

As Prelli suggests, we are surrounded by displays. Indeed, he adds, "rhetorics of display are nearly ubiquitous in contemporary communication and culture, and thus have become the dominant rhetoric of our time" (2). Such displays make powerful claims upon our attention, as he notes, but more importantly they can make almost irresistible claims upon our attitudes and our aspirations. As Burke taught us, rhetoric works most powerfully upon us when it invites us to inhabit for ourselves the alternative identities and, therefore, realities that it presents. When we inhabit those identities, even temporarily, we experience the attitudes and aspirations that follow from them. It is this understanding of the nature and function of rhetoric that helps us understand why it is important to attend to the kind of rhetorical work that NPS Rustic design enabled national parks to do. Such rhetorical work is, indeed, ubiquitous.

The rhetorical, for Burke, involves one working to "form attitudes or induce actions" in another (*Rhetoric* 41). In that particular statement from *A Rhetoric of Motives*, Burke was describing the rhetorical work of words. But the larger context of that statement is a book that begins with this summary of its project: to show "how a rhetorical motive is often present where it is not usually recognized or thought to belong" (xiii). One of those places where rhetorical motives are present and yet not usually recognized or thought to belong is, in fact, *places*—physical places that one can actually enter and, for a time, inhabit. And it is clear from its founding documents and the policy practices of its first forty years that the work of the NPS to protect and provide access to the national parks is primarily rhetorical. A study of NPS Rustic design in national park buildings and landscapes can explain some of the ways that such rhetorical work is done.

In terms of the NPS language I quoted above, structures and landscapes designed according to NPS Rustic principles "achieved sympathy with their natural surroundings and the past," and as they did so they displayed an attitude that might lead those who identified themselves with it to compatible actions. Essentially, NPS Rustic design made remote and spectacular places that had been designated national parks available to tourists in ways that provided them with strategically composed experiences of nature. This experience—enabled by roads and trails, lodges and cabins, signs and toilets—was one of practical convenience: visitors were able to inhabit these places temporarily without significant effort or discomfort. But the design of these accommodations made a visit to these places an experience of respectful, even reverent, habitation. Visitors were directed by design into an alternative way of life that subordinated them and their projects to the sublimity and beauty of nature. For them the experience of being in the place was replete with lessons about reverence for the natural world. Such lessons did not preclude the development or domestication of nature. But they did instruct the public in attitudes of reverence for nature, attitudes that might have eventually prompted them to their own efforts to preserve and protect it.

Works Cited

Kenneth Burke. "An Eye-Poem for the Ear, with Prose Introduction, Glosses, and Afterwords (Eye-Crossing From Brooklyn to Manhattan)." *Late Poems, 1968–1993: Attitudinizings Verse-Wise, While Fending for One's Selph, and in a Style Somewhat Artificially Colloquial.* Ed. Julie Whitaker and David Blakesley. Columbia: U of South Carolina P, 2005: 3–28.

———. *A Grammar of Motives.* Berkeley: U of California P, 1969.

———. *A Rhetoric of Motives.* Berkeley: U of California P, 1969.

Catlin, George. *Letters and Notes on the Manners, Customs and Conditions of the North American Indians.* London, 1844.

Hauser, Gerard A. "Aristotle on Epideictic: The Formation of Public Morality." *Rhetoric Society Quarterly* 29 (Winter 1999): 5–23.

Multiple Resources for Zion National Park: National Register of Historic Places Inventory—Nomination Form. Zion National Park, Utah, 1987.

Olmsted, Frederick Law. *Yosemite and the Mariposa Grove: A Preliminary Report (1865)*. El Portal, CA: Yosemite Association, 1995.

Park Structures and Facilities. Washington, DC: National Park Service, U.S. Department of the Interior, 1935.

Perelman, Chaim, and Lucie Olbrechts-Tyteca. *The New Rhetoric: A Treatise on Argumentation*. Trans. John Wilkinson and Purcell Weaver. Notre Dame: U of Notre Dame P, 1969.

Prelli, Lawrence J., ed. *Rhetorics of Display*. Columbia: U of South Carolina P, 2006.

Sax, Joseph. "America's National Parks: Their Principles, Purposes, and Prospects." *Natural History* (October 1976): 59–87.

Tweed, William, Laura E. Soulliere, and Henry G. Law. *National Park Service Rustic Architecture: 1916–1942*. National Park Service. Western Regional Office. Division of Cultural Resource Management. February 1977.

Weaver, Richard. "Language is Sermonic." *The Rhetorical Tradition: Readings from Classical Times to the Present*. 2nd ed. Ed. Patricia Bizzell and Bruce Herzberg. Boston: Bedford/St. Martin's, 2001: 1351–60.

Whittlesey, Lee H., and Paul Schullery. "The Roosevelt Arch: A Centennial History of an American Icon." *Yellowstone Science* (Summer 2003): 1–24.

Woodruff, Paul. *Reverence: Renewing a Forgotten Virtue*. New York: Oxford UP, 2001.

Zaitlin, Joyce. *Gilbert Stanley Underwood: His Rustic, Art Deco, and Federal Architecture*. Malibu, CA: Pangloss P, 1989.

18

Eugenics, Nazism, and the Sinister Science of the Human Betterment Foundation

Kathleen A. Swift

The term "genocide" was coined by Polish prosecutor Raphaël Lemkin during the Second World War to provide a legal term for the brutal race hygiene policies of the German Third Reich (Black 402). Interestingly, the same root word "gene" used in "genocide" was previously employed by Francis Galton to form scientists' term for technologies of human breeding he dubbed "eugenics," or the science of the well-born. Scientists such as Galton, Huxley, and Davenport would spawn an international forum for improving human heredity known as the eugenics movement in the early twentieth century. Premised on the biologically determined nature of human beings, and the belief that, thus, race and mental hygiene could solve social problems, the eugenics movement set an inexorable course for the death camps of Nazi Germany.

Most would agree that the promotion of a responsible rhetoric requires a basic understanding of the rhetorical histories that have brought us to this point. How did the U.S. eugenics movement present social reforms at a time of broad territorial expansion, massive immigration, and historical confrontation with other races, religions, and cultures? How does eugenic rhetoric continue to influence modern-day debate over immigration restriction, population control, family planning, and genetics? What can be learned about the responsibilities of rhetoric through a rhetorical analysis of the eugenics movement? My paper seeks to address these questions by applying a Burkean analysis to the motives underlying the shift in eugenic discourse in the period leading up to and after WWII.

American eugenicists were behind three major policy initiatives during the early twentieth century. For example, they maintained that the "race suicide" of Anglo-Americans could be prevented through laws prohibiting interracial marriage. Eugenicists campaigned for immigration restriction quotas to stem the tide of foreign genes into the U.S. gene pool. Perhaps their most controversial measure called for the compulsory sterilization of all those of unsound body or mind. Eugenicists believed that sterilization protected society from the "menace" of the insane and feebleminded through the practice of mental hygiene. That the targets of mental hygiene largely constituted the socially marginalized only served as further evidence of their "social inadequacy." To quell criticisms of California's strict sterilization laws, a Pasadena eugenics organization called the Human Betterment Foundation undertook an ambitious study of the results of California's experimental program in order to document the "physiological and mental effects of sexual sterilization" on mental patients (Harry H. Laughlin Papers, D-2-3:24).

The technical papers of E. S. Gosney and the Human Betterment Foundation (HBF), as well as the California Institute of Technology historical files on Biology Division, serve as the basis for my analysis of the transition in eugenic rhetoric in the 1930s and 1940s. These technical papers demonstrate the gradual morphing of eugenic discourse as the HBF evolved from a hereditarian rhetoric predicated on strict biological determinism to a socio-scientific rhetoric that finally acknowledged social and psychological factors in human development. When the HBF closed its doors in 1942, it would give rise to a successor organization called EngenderHealth (Valone 41). The HBF's transition from compulsory sterilization to voluntary sterilization in the form of EngenderHealth represents one important aspect of the shift in eugenic discursive strategies at the conclusion of the war.

Founded by E. S. Gosney, a wealthy Pasadena businessman worried about the devolution of the American gene pool, the HBF employed Paul B. Popenoe to study the problems associated with the differential fertility rate of the insane and feebleminded. The HBF insisted that compulsory sterilization was neither mutilation nor punishment. It sought to quell criticisms of sterilization by publishing authoritative, scientific reports demonstrating the benefits of sexual surgery for mental patients, their families, and society, and to encourage wider application of eugenic sterilization at the state, national, and international level. By 1979, California's Department of Mental Health had sterilized at least 20,000 patients.

Many eugenicists adhered to socially conservative theories of race, religion, class, and sex. The HBF's technical reports provided scientific evidence that dysgenic births were largely the fault of the infirm, the indigent, immigrants, women, Catholics, and racial minorities. The HBF went on to publish its reports in such medical journals as the *Journal of the American Medical Association*, the *American Journal of Obstetrics and Gynecology,* and the *Journal of Heredity* (*Collected Papers*). It also brought out three books on the subject.

One of these books was used by Hitler's Third Reich to buttress and expand upon Germany's developing race hygiene programs (Kühl 25). German officials praised the work of Gosney and Popenoe and in particular their book, *Sterilization for Human Betterment*, citing it as a "valuable contribution" to Germany's national hygiene legislation (E. S. Gosney/HBF Papers, Box

8.13). That HBF eugenic programs were initially paralleled by Nazi eugenic programs is more understandable when considered in "light of the fact that Hitler's national hygiene legislation, whose preliminary targets were also mental patients and the physically disabled, began 'after careful study of the California experiment under Mr. Gosney and Dr. Popenoe'" (E. S. Gosney/ HBF Papers, Box 5.15).

As new discoveries in genetics dispelled older theories of biological inheritance, eugenicists found themselves at an impasse in the nature versus nurture debate. Sterilization came under increasing attack as Mendel's principle of genetics replaced Galton's biometric model. Eugenicists found they could no longer justify mandatory sterilization based on strict genetic determinism. This ideological crisis was further compounded by the revelation of Nazi race hygiene atrocities at the conclusion of the war. Eugenicists viewed with rising alarm the erosion of their scientific ethos. Gosney and others realized it was necessary to disassociate themselves from their former Nazi colleagues and the controversy surrounding forced sterilization if they wished to regain their standing as technocratic experts for the public good.

The traditional eugenic historiography suggesting that eugenics either "declined" or "reformed" in this period misses the deliberate modification of eugenic rhetorical tactics as eugenicists strove to regain their former scientific legitimacy. Indeed, the use of conscious rhetorical tactics endowed hereditarian ideologues with a near protean ability to reinvent their basic premises. In a memorandum assessing the eugenic conundrum for "the Rockefeller interests," Fredrick Osborn argued that the "'rediscovery of Mendel . . . and the marvelous development of a science of genetics in the succeeding years distracted attention from the social and psychological studies necessary for a broader base in eugenics'" (qtd. in Mehler 117).

Realizing they could no longer qualify eugenic social improvement based on strict genetic determinism, eugenicists turned instead to the human sciences as the new paradigm for social improvement. The socio-scientific emphasis on the individual meant that eugenicists who had formerly fought for compulsory sterilization switched instead to voluntary sterilization as the more politically expedient of the two. Toward that end, eugenic sterilization campaigns changed rhetorical emphasis from the benefits to society in limiting dysgenic births to the benefits to the individual in practicing reproductive choice through sterilization and birth control (Mehler 279). This shift in eugenic strategy is illustrated by the HBF's gradual transformation into EngenderHealth, a modern-day family planning and reproductive health organization working in third-world countries.

When Gosney passed away in 1942, many of the HBF's sterilization articles and reports were initially turned over to its sister organization, the New Jersey Sterilization League (Association). In 1964, the league became the Association for Voluntary Sterilization (AVS). The transfer of records, staff, and membership from the HBF to the AVS is indicative of the tactical move to reformulate compulsory sterilization as voluntary sterilization and, ultimately, a palatable form of birth control. Starting in the 1980s, the organization went through a series of name changes, becoming, first, the Association for Voluntary Surgical Contraception and, finally, EngenderHealth (Valone 41). Such name changes are indicative of the widening scope of socio-scientific population control and family planning programs as they have evolved from the national to the international level.

In 1974, Henry Kissinger wrote the summary for National Security Study Memorandum 200, identifying population growth in developing countries as a concern to "U.S. security and overseas interests" (National Security). Two years prior to that, the U.S. Agency for International Development made a grant to AVS to increase access to voluntary sterilization through the dissemination of its programs and services abroad (Association). In its current incarnation as EngenderHealth, the HBF's successor continues to work in Bangladesh to reduce poverty via fertility control, as it is one of thirteen countries whose population growth has been identified as a U.S. security interest. The fact that nonwhite and indigent people seem, again, to be the targets of U.S. sterilization programs is in itself telling, especially in light of the rhetorical elasticity of eugenic ideology from the past to the present.

Burke warns against the peddling of social improvement schemes that "provide a non-economic interpretation of economic ills" for being, in essence, "snake-oil" ("Rhetoric" 219). The continued eugenic focus on the birth rate of minorities and the poor is such an instance of this. By employing the scene/act ratio of Burke's dramatist pentad, it becomes clear that one of the underlying motives of eugenicists is to deflect attention from historical and economic realities (scene) by insisting that the real source of the problem lies in the fecund instincts of the underclass (agent) (Burke, *Grammar* 17). Eugenicists rely on a simplistic Malthusian premise dictating that the proliferation of the poor and the nonwhite lies at the root of world poverty. This effectively diverts scrutiny from the preexisting socioeconomic order into which they are born into in the first place. Burke observes that "a malaise which gets its neurotic intensity from the social structure is . . . thought to be explainable obstetrically" (*Rhetoric* 82). He further notes that eugenics is essentially an argument of convenience, for in attacking a group of people as the cause of economic misery, it generally leaves the attacker in the advantageous position of controlling the sum of economic resources, having once reduced (or eliminated) the offending population ("Rhetoric" 219).

What is more, Burke claims that by failing to distinguish dialectical realities at the crux of social relations, those who would sell snake-oil as a social panacea only aggravate the situation. He states that "emotional trickeries that shift our criticism from the accurate locus of our trouble" are never a solution "since the factors pressing toward calamity remain" ("Rhetoric" 230).

The HBF's transition from eugenic sterilization to voluntary sterilization is indicative of the new rhetorical strategy of post-WWII eugenicists as they sought to regain their credibility as technocratic experts for the public good. The rhetorical history of the HBF reveals that what some historians have insisted is the post-WWII transformation from "mainline" to "reform" eugenics is, in fact, the ideological transition from *hereditarian* to *socio-scientific* eugenics in order to maintain the viability of a eugenic technocracy in the face of the discredited science of its former political initiatives.

The responsibilities of rhetoric in current debates over fertility control and the limits to population growth demand a basic understanding of the eugenics movement. The technocratic *topoi* linking EngenderHealth, the Human Betterment Foundation, and Nazi race hygiene programs imply a rhetoric of motives that casts a long shadow over considerations in family planning and population control. Without the countervailing balance of an informed and responsible public rhetoric, the sinister shadow of eugenics will continue to cast an ominous pall over international policies of family planning and population control.

If we take away nothing else from a rhetorical analysis of the eugenics movement, it should be just one critical question: Exactly *whose* population is on the table in discussions of population control?

Works Cited

Association for Voluntary Sterilization. Social Welfare History Archives. 2002. Regents of the University of Minnesota and the University Libraries. 8 Nov. 2007. <http://www.special.lib.umm.edu/swha/>.

Black, Edwin. *War Against the Weak: Eugenics and America's Campaign to Create a Master Race*. New York: Four Walls, 2003.

Burke, Kenneth. *A Grammar of Motives*. Berkeley: U of California P, 1969.

———. "The Rhetoric of Hitler's Battle." *The Philosophy of Literary Form*. Berkeley: U of California P, 1973. 211–31.

———. *A Rhetoric of Motives*. Berkeley: U of California P, 1969.

E. S. Gosney/HBF Papers. Institute Archives, California Institute of Technology. Pasadena, California.

Harry H. Laughlin Papers. Special Collections, Truman State University, Pickler Memorial Library. Kirksville, Missouri.

Human Betterment Foundation. *Collected Papers on Eugenic Sterilization in California: A Critical Study of Results in 6,000 Cases*. Pasadena: Human Betterment Foundation, 1930.

Kühl, Stefan. *The Nazi Connection: Eugenics, American Racism and German National Socialism*. New York: Oxford UP, 1994.

Mehler, Barry Alan. *A History of the American Eugenics Society, 1921–1940*. Diss. U of Illinois at Urbana-Champaign, 1988. Ann Arbor: UMI, 1988. 8823199.

National Security Study Memorandum 200. 7 Aug. 2008. Wikipedia. 6 Sept. 2008. <http://en.wikipedia.org/w/index.php?title=National_Security_Study_Memorandum_200&oldid=230489679>.

Valone, David A. "Foundations, Eugenic Sterilization, and the Emergence of the World Population Control Movement." *Philanthropic Foundations and the Globalization of Scientific Medicine and Public Health*. Ed. Benjamin B. Page and David A. Valone. Lanham: UP of America, 2007. 35–43.

Synecdoche as Figure of the Holocaust

Richard Glejzer & Michael Bernard-Donals

Daniel Mendelsohn's memoir, *The Lost: A Search for Six of the Six Million*, was published in 2006. In many ways it is like other memoirs written after the Holocaust by children and grandchildren of survivors who are looking for remnants of their families, or for the European past from which their families, and their families' stories, originated. It begins with a tableau of the author's youth, his certainty that his family is somehow different and has a past that the family itself doesn't wish to discuss, and follows the author's journey of discovery, both of who he is and of his family's buried past. And yet the book is different from many other memoirs, both in its length and its method: the author, beginning with those childhood memories of his family in suburban New Jersey and photographs of those relatives who were lost in the destruction of the years 1933–1945, undertakes a journey that brings him to Europe, Australia, and central Asia, sometimes alone and sometimes in the company of those who, like the author, also have a connection to the town of Bolechow in Poland.

What Daniel Mendelsohn finds, both through his physical search for his family and through the writing of his memorial narrative, is not a past, or a narrative of history, that explains what happened to his grandfather's family. Quite to the contrary, and quite literally, he finds a hole, a hole in the ground in Poland that may or may not have been his family's final hiding place during the war. More importantly—and this is the point of departure for this essay—he finds another hole, a *figural* one, that functions as a void at the center of history, not just Daniel Mendelsohn's history but the history of the Jews of Poland and their destruction at the hands of the Nazis. We'll argue here that the book is, in fact, one long series of digressions in which the author bounces from fragment to fragment, story to story, leading not so much to a solution to the problem with which he began—what happened to my grandfather, and what is his relation to me—but to the conclusion that the writing of history makes palpable the unavoidable loss of events at the hands of any narrative that would attempt to name it. To put this another way, Daniel Mendelsohn's book writes the loss, rather than the recuperation, of history.

FIGURES OF LOSS, FIGURES OF HISTORY

Daniel Mendelsohn's memoir throws into relief a problem—a rhetorical problem—announced thirty years ago by Hayden White in a series of books (including *Metahistory* and *Tropics of Discourse*). That problem is that history is underwritten not by events but by the structures of figure. As White puts it in *Metahistory*, any approach to history, the events whose effects the historical agent and, later, the writer, attempt to grasp, "depends, ultimately, on the pre-conceptual and specifically poetic nature of their perspectives on history and its processes" (4). This doesn't mean that events themselves don't happen, or that they don't matter; they do. White's point, though, is that *history itself*—its events—doesn't have a structure: only the *language* through which events *become* history does. It is that structure to which historians and writers must turn for an explanation for how history works. White enumerates the four principal tropes through which history is made evident—metaphor, metonymy, synecdoche, and irony—and it is these figures from which historians derive their modes of "telling" history, and from which history itself originates.

We rehearse White's early theoretical position here because Mendelsohn's memoir—and memoir is unquestionably a historical mode of writing—complicates not only White's catalogue of historical tropes but, in so doing, also complicates how we think of the event of history. More particularly, White's consideration of trope as the undercarriage of history becomes more complicated because the event, the Holocaust, makes itself visible largely through absence. We want to pay specific attention to the relation, in White's scheme, between metonymy and synecdoche, figures of relation based on contiguity. If metaphor, in the typical classical scheme, can be thought of as a figure based on similarity—in which the terms placed into relation are different in kind (the typical example is "love is a rose," in which the two objects are of different orders and the relation is based on a relation of that difference)—metonymy and synecdoche are figures in which the terms in the relation are parts of some whole (again, the typical example, this time from Aristotle, is the reference to ships by the term "sail"). Put more simply, metonymy and synecdoche both express part-whole relations. The difference between the two, then, is that in metonymy, "one can simultaneously distinguish between two phenomena and reduce one to the status of a manifestation of the other" (*Metahistory* 35), in which the part is seen as the effect of the whole, or in which it is the patient of an agent. Synecdoche, by contrast, is a part-whole relation that is expressed through quality rather than cause-effect, where the whole "is qualitatively different from the sum of the parts" (35). In fact, in White's scheme, synecdoche could better be expressed as a part-for-part substitution, in which the associative relation *implies* a whole rather than expresses it as part of the substitutive relation.

We typically understand the work of Holocaust representation as met-onymic: it is through the fragments of memory and of the material leavings of history (its documents, photographs, artifacts, and oral or written testimo-nies) that we can work backwards to the event as a whole. We can do this because we understand the fragments as effects of events, and so we can trace them back to the cause, or (to use the language of Hayden White) the docu-ment left by the eyewitness or the narrative produced by the one who was there is seen as the manifestation of the event that produced the need for sto-ries in the first place. This, it seems to us, has typically been the method of historians of the Holocaust since Raoul Hilberg's *The Destruction of the Euro-pean Jews* and of memoirists and diarists since Anne Frank and Abraham Lewin.[1] What's so interesting about Mendelsohn's memoir, however, is that although its surface structure appears to be metonymic, and while Mendel-sohn himself attempts to assert a metonymic structure, it ends up functioning through synecdochic substitution, in which narrative after narrative, memory after memory, and photograph after photograph—in spite of assertions to the contrary—eventually and finally *defer* that causal relation, suggesting not so much a whole that might anchor the fragments, but a hole, a void at the heart of the narrative, one that causes the events being narrated to become unmoored, constantly deferred, until it's no longer clear just what happened. Mendelsohn's narrative, in other words, finds that it finally cannot speak the name of the event, the historical cause of foundation of the story, to which all of the various narrative bits can refer; instead, it skips from fragment to frag-ment, eventually finding that there's nothing *there* to which the narrative can finally be tied. In this sense, the part becomes patient to the void and demands part after part to defer a fall into chaos.

What we'll do in the remainder of this essay is suggest how Mendel-sohn's approach to the problem of history (the problem of finding an ade-quate figural means by which to represent the vexed events of the past) veers between metonym and synecdoche and finally resolves itself—though it's hardly a resolution—in the latter figure, and to suggest, through the recent historical work of Jan Gross, which also depends upon the material leavings of history and the narratives that can be forgotten from them, how synecdo-che tends to emerge from even those historical narratives that hew most closely to metonym. We'll conclude by arguing that synecdoche, not meton-ymy, is the principal founding trope of Holocaust representation and Holo-caust history, sometimes in spite of the historian's aim.

METONYMY

Mendelsohn's narrative begins by establishing a clear metonymic chain between his personal family history, Jewish history, and the Holocaust, each narrative strand promising to weave a coherent whole with what happened to Shmiel, his wife, and his children at the center. Mendelsohn establishes the totality of the family as patient to the various stories that inform his familial identity. In fact, even before the book's first part, titled "Bereishit, or, Beginnings (1967–2000)," Mendelsohn charts Shmiel Jäger's family tree, tracing out the family lines, including the lines of Shmiel and his four daughters and also of Abraham, his grandfather, eventually leading to himself, Daniel, at the bottom with his three brothers and sister. The family tree marks a whole even if pieces of information are missing or unknown: under the marriage between Elkune Jäger (b. 1867, d. 1912) and Taube Mittelmark (b. 1875, d. 1934) is Shmiel (b. 1895, d. 1943?). The question mark here marks a gap in what Mendelsohn knows about his family tree, but it does not undermine the whole of the tree. There is a discreet place for Shmiel and his daughters' stories in this tree waiting for an answer about their fate. The tree itself offers the promise of metonymy, that the parts themselves indeed add up to form a coherent whole and even if some information might be missing, the whole remains the product of the parts.

Likewise, Mendelsohn begins his narrative with a focus on how various stories all metonymically intertwine to form one history. From the very beginning, Mendelsohn frames his search for his family's story in terms of his grandfather, who Mendelsohn remembers as painfully bound to the unknown fate of his brother Shmiel and his family.

> It was hard for me, when I was a child and first started hearing that refrain about Shmiel and his lost family, to imagine what exactly that meant. Even later, after I was old enough to have learned about the war, seen the documentaries, watched with my parents the episode of a PBS series called *The World at War* that was preceded by a terrifying warning that certain images in the film were too intense for children—even later, it was hard to imagine just how they had been killed, to grasp the details, the specifics. When? Where? How? With guns? In the gas chambers? But my grandfather wouldn't say. Only later did I understand that he wouldn't say because he didn't know, or at least didn't know enough, and that the not knowing, in part, was what tormented him. (8)

Mendelsohn rehearses many of the stories that his grandfather does tell him, their relationship being bound up with the telling of these stories over the years. And it is this one story that his grandfather does not tell him—because he does not know it—that likewise torments Mendelsohn. The story of Shmiel becomes the missing piece to this relationship with his grandfather, a piece that although unknown persists in its knowable remains. Mendelsohn's text begins with this metonymic claim that the story must be tellable in part because its absence is so palpable. The grandfather is tormented, says Mendelsohn, not because there is no story, but because he does not know it. And thus the answer is seemingly simple in the abstract if not in practice: find out what happened to Shmiel. It is with this promise of metonymy that Mendelsohn begins his journey to find out what happened to Shmiel and his children—where, when, and how they perished.

But very quickly the simplicity of metonymy's promise is deferred as he encounters conflicting narratives that muddle the simple questions that drive his search. The story that might remove the question mark after Shmiel's name constantly shifts throughout the text, often leaving Mendelsohn on the brink of chaos. Often enough, a given piece of the story is not enough to address his central question as to what happened to his Uncle Shmiel and his wife and children, and metonymy fails. At times, Mendelsohn overtly acknowledges the discrepancies between the event's wholeness and those specifics or details that refuse to substantiate history. Mendelsohn writes, "I had wanted the details and the specifics for the *story*, and had not—as how could I not, I who never knew them, who had never had anything *but* stories?—really understood until now what it meant to be a *detail*, a specific" (502, emphasis in original).

The detail that Mendelsohn contemplates here is the place of Shmiel and Frydka's death: the base of a tree in a garden outside of the house where they were hidden in a basement until an informant turned them in to the Gestapo. His search through details, specifics from numerous sources, culminates in this garden when he realizes the significance of where he stands:

> As I stood in this most specific place of all, more specific even than the hiding place, that place in which Shmiel and Frydka experienced things, physical and emotional things I will never begin to understand, precisely because their experience was *specific* to them and not me, as I stood in this most specific of places I knew that I was standing in the place where they had died, where the life that I would never know had gone out of the bodies I had never seen, and precisely because I had never known or seen them I was reminded the more forcefully that they had been specific people with specific deaths, and those lives and deaths belonged to them, not me, no matter how gripping the story that may be told about them. (502)

But after coming through 500 pages of different parts of Shmiel's story, some overlapping with others, some false, some only half true, Mendelsohn takes this one specific place, this one detail that marks the place of death, as standing in for all other details, a part that bears the other parts. On the one hand this final spot addresses the question mark after Shmiel's name in the family tree. But on the other hand, this one story is no more valid than any of the others. And although Mendelsohn jumps to the metonymic conclusion that the narrative is complete (that is, although he attempts to anchor the story metonymically), the wholeness of his story is suspect since the other parts of the narrative are left unsettled. It is in fact a *synecdochal* substitution— a part for what's missing—that thus undermines the possible metonymic claim—part for whole. And at this moment metonymy has been replaced by synecdoche, the part no longer standing in for a whole but rather for other parts that all attempt to fill up a much greater hole.

And it is in this place where Mendelsohn's story ends, appearing satisfied with this one part now standing in for a w-h-o-l-e. But the part is insufficient to the whole since it only subjectifies itself as a part: why does this part—this one place—bear such a reference? Why not the place below the floorboards in the house where his relations hid day after day? Even as Mendelsohn chooses one part above others, the movement toward such a claim is metonymically insufficient to stand in for the whole of his narrative. Put another way, why does Mendelsohn continue to pursue the veracity of the witnesses who lead him to this particular hole in the ground, but then stop his questioning when the old Ukrainian woman points to the garden with that one tree as the place of Shmiel and Frydka's death? Why shift from the instability of synecdoche to the promised coherence of metonymy at this point and not others?

SYNECDOCHE

What Mendelsohn tells us is that the garden is *the* place because it marks the point from which all other details emanate: Shmiel and Frydka are "specific people with specific deaths." The deaths of Shmiel and Frydka make all the journeys necessary. In other words, Mendelsohn—like other Holocaust writers, historians, and memoirists alike—is at pains to find some explanatory coherence, and ultimately some point of origin (an originary event, in Walter Benjamin's terms), that would finally anchor all of the other digressions and all of the other incoherences and blind alleys in the story, that would finally allow him to say, "Here is what makes the story make sense," and here is where the search can come to a close. But instead, what Mendelsohn finds is that each death marks not a whole life but rather a *hole,* not some point of reference to which all other parts both point and take their origin, but simply an array of events, and a maelstrom of destruction, in which each death is individual and horrifyingly singular. This part-for-part-for-part synecdochic relation, one that points to the *absence* of any unifying or coherent narrative, intrudes into metonymic relation, and the writer, Mendelsohn, is forced to figure out what to do in confronting this void. Mendelsohn writes,

> There is so much that will always be *impossible to know,* but we do know that they were, once, themselves, *specific,* the subjects of their own lives and deaths, and not simply puppets to be manipulated for the purposes of a good story, for the memoirs and magical-realist novels and movies. There will be time enough for that, once I and everyone who ever knew everyone who ever knew them dies; since as we know, everything, in the end, gets lost. (502)

For the narrative to end, for history to begin, and for Mendelsohn and the reader to *understand* the narrative *as* history, Mendelsohn finds that he has to just stop the story—and this is as good a place as any.

What Mendelsohn has to say about history itself only reiterates this problematic tension between the *whole* (that originary, and explanatory, coherence that provides a kind of anchor for the parts, the bits and pieces of Mendelsohn's, and any historian's, view of the past) and the *hole* (the recognition that there is, in fact, no coherence in the events themselves, and that the events of history simply *happen,* that they are themselves not meaningful). It makes all the more apparent the very vexed relation between metonymy's reliance on a part that is the *effect of a whole* (where pieces of stories give rise to a history that forms a whole and can be told) and synecdoche's insistence of the part as the *effect of the hole or void* (where pieces only mark an absence that resists such knowing or telling). Towards the end of his book, as he closes in on the house that may or may not have been the final hiding place of Shmiel and Frydka, Mendelsohn sees his journey as a demonstration of the workings of history, suggesting "that what we had achieved, what we had experienced, finally, during the course of all our searching, was precisely what history is" (485). He takes this even further, merging the choices that he has made on his search with the choices others made over 50 years ago, seeing history both in its completeness (metonymy) and also its random chaos (synecdoche):

> There is the hardwired impulse to go back for one last look; there is the thing that will make a person turn left rather than right, approach this woman in the street but not that man in order to ask a question about the location of a house or a road; there is the thing that makes you decide one night, as you are carrying a package of food to the hidden Jewish girl whom you love, that it is dark enough that you don't have to conceal the package under your coat; there is the impulse that causes the neighbor who sees the youth carrying the package to wonder, for the first time, why this boy comes every night to this street, that house; there are the whole vast histories of temperament and psychology in all their incalculable but ultimately concrete and knowable minutiae, the tiny things that make you decide to pursue a conversation with an old Ukrainian woman for precisely thirty-two minutes rather than, say forty-seven minutes, with the result that you arrive at a house of an old Ukrainian man just as he is leaving for his job at church, rather than a quarter of an hour later, at which point, because of a whole vast series of other factors and considerations, hunger, the hot sun, exhaustion, you may have decided that enough was enough, *genug is genug*, and let's just drive back to L'viv. (485)

Mendelsohn's book—and finally history—rests in this oscillation precisely because the whole is inadequate to its parts, because history or the whole story does not supply the cause for any of these specifics. In the end, the only alternative is "genug is genug," enough is enough, and the alternatives are to surrender to the despair of chaos, or give in to the desire for the whole (the story) history and simply cut the story short and manufacture a narrative of coherence that will, nonetheless, not stand up to the maelstrom.

CONCLUSION: SYNECDOCHE AS FIGURE OF THE HOLOCAUST

If our argument about Mendelsohn's memoir is right—and if, in turn, Hayden White's understanding of rhetorical figure as foundational for history and historical writing is also right—then it stands to reason that history, as that which is written about the events of the past, also functions (figurally) in ways similar to Mendelsohn's memoir. It would be worth the time, we think, to reexamine other historical accounts of the Holocaust—particularly

those whose authors specifically make claims about their historical coherence—to see the extent to which the synecdochic mode intrudes upon and
interrupts metonymic or metaphoric claims for history. We think that what
such analyses will yield is the slippage from metonym to synecdoche that
we've argued Mendelsohn's account makes visible is likewise visible—and
inevitable—in the work of those of historians. Anyone who attempts to grap-
ple with the fragmentary leavings of the event will find that the material detri-
tus of history—and the narratives constructed to make sense of them—lead
as much to a void, a hole in history, as they do to a narrative understanding of
it. To conclude this essay (and to briefly test our hypothesis, as it were), we
turn to a recent and salient example of historical writing whose aim is quite
specifically to construct a narrative of coherence—of finding a historical
cause that can provide an explanation for a number of horrifying, singular
deaths—and that was in its turn called into question because it disobeyed
another, competing coherent and explanatory narrative.

Jan Gross's influential and highly provocative account of the extermina-
tion of the Jews of Jedwabne, Poland, in 1942, during the early stages of the
Nazi sweep eastward into the Soviet Union, was published in 2001. The
book—*Neighbors: The Destruction of the Jewish Community in Jedwabne, Poland*—
relies on documents found in old Soviet archives recently opened at the end
of the cold war and upon the testimonies of survivors and eyewitnesses taken
immediately after the war and well afterwards. The question Gross is
attempting to answer is, "What happened, in June of 1942, that resulted in
the town's Christian population's massacre of the town's Jewish population?"
And, like Mendelsohn's book, it functions by means of figures of substitution.
Fragments—individuals' recollections of the events to which they were privy,
historical documents noting the events in the town during those days in early
June 1942, and the evidence found at the site of the massacre itself—are
related not by their similarity to other events during the war, but by their contiguity: this person's killing of that Jewish neighbor is related to that person's
recollection of what happened that day, the bullet cartridges found at the site
of the barn in which the majority of Jedwabne's Jews were burned alive are
related to the documentary evidence of which guns were fired, and so on.[2]

But what is also clear about Gross's account, like Mendelsohn's memoir,
is that it cannot sustain the metonymic account it tries to provide for the
events of the massacre, and it is interrupted by synecdochic deferral. Each
eyewitness—like Jakov Piekarz or Szmul Wasersztajn—has only his or her
memories. Whether it is the burning of their neighbors and family members
or the horrifying narrative account of it that disturbs their sense of history, or
their membership in the collective "we" of Polish identity, or simply their
own memories, those events have had the same effect as staring into the sun.
They've been blotted out from the narrative that would integrate them into
history, as their neighbors have been blotted out. And when Antoni Niebrzydowski tells an interviewer, a few years after the massacre, what happened,
he says that he issued kerosene to his brothers at his warehouse. Then, he

goes on, the brothers "brought the eight liters of kerosene that I had just issued to them and doused the barn filled with Jews and lit it up; what followed I do not know" (Gross 48). Perhaps he doesn't know; but he saw. It would be easy to say he doesn't know because it is simply too horrible to remember. In fact, what Antoni Niebrzydowski saw is lost to knowledge altogether, though his testimony of what occurred ("they bought the eight liters of kerosene") is deferred by another memory, which is in fact not a memory at all ("what followed I do not know"), and cannot be corroborated by others who were there. The desire to impose a metonymic relation of cause and effect, and part to whole, is foiled by the event itself, and provides—as figural evidence—the synecdochic *hole* into which the events plunge. Giambattista Vico, whose work on history is seen as precursor to that of contemporary theorists of historical writing, was also highly conscious of the figural dimension of our understanding of the past, particularly a catastrophic one. Of Vico's use of synecdoche, White writes that the figure "moves from the most particular idea to the most general, which results in the 'elevation' of particulars into universals, of parts into wholes" (*Tropics of Discourse* 207). And yet, what we see in this passage in Gross's book, and what we see time and time again in Mendelsohn's, is that the particular is *not* elevated to the universal at all, but is linked in a series of repetitions to other particulars, and the whole— "what followed I do not know." The events of the massacre at Jedwabne remain altogether lost, both to memory and to history, as the 1600 Jews of Jedwabne are also altogether lost.

So what does this analysis of synecdoche as a figure of Holocaust history tell us about the relation of history and rhetoric? At the conclusion of an essay on history and the Holocaust, "Historical Emplotment and the Problem of Truth," Hayden White recommends that the historian engage in what he calls an "intransitive" mode of writing, in which "the subject is constituted as immediately contemporary with the writing, being effected and affected by it" (49), in which an "order of experience beyond (or prior to) that expressible in the kinds of oppositions we are forced to draw (between agency and patiency, subjectivity and objectivity, literalness and figurativeness, fact and fiction, history and myth, and so forth) in any version of realism" is eschewed (49). We would argue, in fact, that the deferral of synecdoche—the relation of part to part, fragment to fragment—has the effect of intransitivity about which White writes, because it makes visible not the whole of history, but history's void, the absence of its events that causes the writer, and the writing of history, to become both a part of, and apart from, the history about which he writes. Daniel Mendelsohn recognizes, near the end of his book, that what startled his relatives in suburban New Jersey when he was a child was that his face, and the face of Shmiel, were thought to be uncannily similar, if not the same. It was that same startling recognition—that Daniel was seen as a repetition of the one who was lost, but that Daniel is an *impossible* double of his lost relative—that forces him to see that the relation of contiguity that he was so frantically trying to set up in the memoir may well be impossible, because the universal to which those fragments were related is also altogether lost. It is the uncanny repetition—a repetition of Daniel's face as the face of the lost ancestor, one that makes evident the loss of the latter at least as much as it makes evident the continuity (and contiguity) of the former—that interrupts his relatives' easy association of Daniel for Shmiel, and points not to a coherence, a *whole*, to which both can be linked, but a *hole*, a loss or void, that makes any link impossible to sustain.

What this suggests about rhetoric's relation to history is that, at least in the modernist mode—"a style developed in order to represent the kind of experiences which social modernism made possible" (52), including the experience of systematic annihilation not only of a people but also of the very events to which those people could testify, and which those people could remember—it is not metonymy but rather *synecdoche* that is very much the fig-ural foundation of any history of the Holocaust. As much as the historian's aim (as much as the memoirist's or the novelist's) is to provide a kind of coherence to hold the details of the narrative together so that we can derive some explanation for the events and, in the case of the Holocaust, their apparent disorder, it is that very disorder that imprints itself on those accounts as synecdoche and makes plain—even if only momentarily—the void that undoes the coherence and leads writers like Mendelsohn to stop the narrative and its semblance of order in its tracks. What ultimately matters most, and what ultimately becomes visible, is the *displacement* rather than what's displaced, and what we learn about rhetoric—in fact, what we re-learn about rhetoric, for this is what Aristotle said over two thousand years ago about rhetoric's status as a *dunamis*—is that figure marks the making (and unmaking) of the event as much if not more than it marks the event-as-repre-sentation, that it divulges the substitution involved in figure as much if not more than it makes clear the substance of the relation itself. What drives Mendelsohn's narrative, like other representations of the Holocaust, is the constant *displacement of representation*, the displacement of the facts of history. In spite of metonymy's promise for a coherent whole of history, synecdoche works to make most visible the hole of history and ultimately casts a reflec-tion back upon figure itself.

Notes

[1] For a discussion of the diary of Abraham Lewin, see Michael Bernard-Donals' "History and the Disaster: The (Im)Possibility of Writing the Holocaust." For a discussion of Anne Frank's diary, see Susan Bernstein's "Promiscuous Reading: The Problem of Identification in Anne Frank's Diary."

[2] A fuller account of Jan Gross's analysis of the massacre in Jedwabne can be found in chapter 5 of Michael Bernard-Donals's *An Introduction to Holocaust Studies: History, Memory and Representation.*

Works Cited

Benjamin, Walter. *Illuminations.* Trans. Harry Zohn. New York: Schocken, 1968.

Bernard-Donals, Michael. "History and the Disaster: The (Im)Possibility of Writing the Holocaust." *Clio* 30.2 (Winter 2001): 143–68.

―――. *An Introduction to Holocaust Studies: History, Memory, and Representation*. Upper Saddle River, NJ: Prentice Hall, 2006.

Bernstein, Susan David. "Promiscuous Reading: The Problem of Identification in Anne Frank's Diary." *Witnessing the Disaster: Essays on Representation and the Holocaust*. Ed. Michael Bernard-Donals and Richard Glejzer (Madison: U of Wisconsin P, 2003): 141–61.

Gross, Jan. *Neighbors: The Destruction of the Jewish Community in Jedwabne, Poland*. Princeton: Princeton UP, 2001.

Mendelsohn, Daniel. *The Lost: A Search for Six of the Six Million*. New York: Harper Collins, 2006.

White, Hayden. "Historical Emplotment and the Problem of Truth." *Probing the Limits of Representation*. Ed. Saul Friedlander. Cambridge: Harvard UP, 1998.

―――. *Metahistory: The Historical Imagination in Nineteenth-Century Europe*. Baltimore: Johns Hopkins UP, 1975.

―――. *Tropics of Discourse: Essays in Cultural History*. Baltimore: Johns Hopkins UP, 1986.

20

The Arabs Did Not "Just" Translate Aristotle
Al-Farabi's Logico-Rhetorical Theory

Maha Baddar

> Many of the matters that Aristotle aims to teach in his books become dif-
> ficult for us to understand at these times. The reason is that many of the
> expressions he used and which signify well and are generally known mat-
> ters to people of his language do not signify in our language the same
> meanings. . . . Moreover, many of the examples he used were well known
> to the people of his time. But these same examples changed in his coun-
> try as well as in ours. . . . Furthermore, many of the topics that were
> investigated in the past are considered strange at the present time. That is
> why those who want to teach these matters from Aristotle's books, be
> they individuals or nations, must substitute the awkward or strange or
> unknown things with things that are known and acceptable to people at
> the present time.
>
> —Al-Farabi[1]

A few years ago, I had the opportunity to sit in on a graduate seminar in
feminist rhetoric at one of the top programs in our field. In the two-and-a-
half-hour meeting, the professor spent about 35 minutes lecturing on the history of rhetoric, summarizing the standard range of historical epochs from
the "Dark Ages" to the "Enlightenment" and emphasizing the role rhetoric
played in religious discourse along the way. The Muslim Arabs were mentioned a few times in that lecture, noting for instance that the period between
600 and 700 CE saw the rise of Muslim Arabs, that Asians, Arabs, and
Vikings were forces that made Europe unstable in the 900s, and that in 962
the pope made peace with the emperor of Germany and united Italy and Germany against forces in Asia and the Muslim Arabs.

Overlooking the intellectual contributions of the Arabs during this time
period while only highlighting their role as a military nuisance is problematic, and is, unfortunately, an example of what history of rhetoric classes gen-

erally have to offer about the medieval period. Studying the work of philosophers such as al-Kindi, al-Farabi, Ibn Sina (known in the West as Avicenna), and Ibn Rushd (known in the West as Averroes) will provide rhetoricians with a more comprehensive understanding of the history of *Western* rhetoric by tracing its development in different centers such as Baghdad and Cordoba. This knowledge will not only fill a huge gap in the history of rhetoric as currently studied, but will also provide an invaluable example of the dialogic nature of knowledge and the roles of context, audience, and purpose in the reshaping of a received body of knowledge, the phenomenon of creating a new product out of an old one.

This paper calls attention to an all-too-easily accepted attitude in current scholarship and advanced rhetorical history pedagogy that proffers an Orientalist view of Arabic philosophy as essentially imitative—except when it is arcane and mystical. Using an analysis of al-Farabi's theory of rhetoric as a case in point, I challenge this attitude by showing that al-Farabi's book on rhetoric is more than a mere summary of Aristotle's *On Rhetoric*, as the introduction by Salim to the Arabic edition states (5). After reviewing the Orientalist trend in Western scholarship on Arabic philosophy, I provide a brief introduction to al-Farabi's life and main influences on his thought before moving on to my three main points about al-Farabi's contributions to rhetorical theory: his understanding of rhetoric as a logical art, how logical and rhetorical terms acquired new meanings when translated from Greek to Arabic, and the rhetorical nature of al-Farabi's own work in adapting Platonic and Aristotelian models to suit a monotheistic audience. Emphasizing a dialogic approach to comparative rhetorical study, I wish to show how al-Farabi used different parts of Aristotle's *Organon* to create a unique theory of rhetoric that was appropriate to his context in tenth-century monotheistic Baghdad.

Orientalist Attitudes toward Medieval Arabic Philosophy

In an article on the historiography of Arabic philosophy published in the *British Journal of Middle Eastern Studies*, Dimitri Gutas defines an Orientalist attitude as "a certain nineteenth century picture of the natives of the 'Orient'—and in our case, of the Semite Arabs—held by Westerners: mystical, sensual, otherworldly, non-rational and intensely interested in religion" ("The Study of Arabic" 8). Gutas argues that this cultural predisposition determined the questions that the West asked about the Orient; in other words, it determined the West's research agenda. The prevalent attitude that Islamic philosophy either was a mere replica of the Greek or, when it was original, that it dealt predominantly with nonrational issues such as mysticism and religion was a self-fulfilling prophecy. Gutas provides a long list of examples, ranging from the late nineteenth century to the mid-eighties of the twentieth, of Western scholars misinterpreting the original content of Arabic philosophy in order to fulfill their own Orientalist fantasies. The perspective that medieval Arab scholars were little more than recorders of the vanishing Greek tradition is evidenced, for example, in the work of T. J. De Boer and Van den Bergh (Gutas, "The Study of Arabic" 10). Similarly, Ian Netton cautions against regarding the influence of Greek thought on Arabic philosophers such as al-Farabi as the only dimension of these scholars' thought and rejects the "'Orientalist' paradigm that saw Islamic philosophy as nothing more than an amalgam of Greek thought" (85). Netton criticizes the "exotic paradigm," which depicts medieval Arabic court life as echoing the *One Thousand and One Nights*, as "a naïve model" (19), emphasizing that, instead, rigorous intellectual activity was taking place at the medieval caliphal courts.

With advances due in part to the effects of postcolonial and cultural studies, current Western scholarship on the subject of Arabic philosophy has begun the work of acknowledging the contributions and innovations of medieval Arabic philosophy. The scholars involved in this undertaking (Hallden, Anderson, Gutas, Reisman, Haddad, Fakhry, and Netton) agree that there are massive gaps in current scholarship. Haddad cautions against a "partial vision of history . . . and a selective adoption of the contributions of thinkers" and recommends that the interaction among Greeks, Oriental Christianity, and Islam be "reexamined with open mindedness, sympathy, objectivity and daring attitudes" (10). Fakhry warns that

> it is not sufficiently realized by most students of the history of philosophy in the Middle Ages that the "Little Renaissance" in thirteenth century Europe was triggered by the Latin translations of the writings of al-Farabi, al-Ghazali, Ibn Sina, abu-Ma'shar, and Ibn Rushd, with the subsequent revival of Aristotelianism, the cornerstone of Latin scholasticism. (*Short* 4–5)

Gutas emphasizes that "one can justly claim that the study of post-classical Greek secular writings can hardly proceed without the evidence in Arabic which in this context becomes the second classical language, even before Latin," while also acknowledging the difficulties involved in the process because of the numerous gaps in the literature: "I am conscious of the difficulty of this undertaking both in terms of the intractable and complex source material, and in terms of the relative novelty and delicacy of the subject" ("The Study of Arabic" 7–8). Because of the continuous discovery of Arabic manuscripts and the lack of scholarly analysis of these works, Netton describes the "epistemological assessment of the Islamic scene [as] both profoundly difficult, and paradoxically, structurally possible" (35).

AL-FARABI'S LIFE AND PHILOSOPHY

Abu-Nasr Muhammad al-Farabi was born around 870 CE. Though his family was from Farab in Turkestan, al-Farabi studied Arabic grammar and logic in Baghdad, the capital of the Islamic empire at the time. In his introduction to al-Farabi's *Kitab Ara' Ahl al-Madina al-Fadila* (*The Opinions of the Inhabitants of the Virtuous City*), Albert Nader cites thirteenth-century biographer Ibn-Khallikan, who tells us that al-Farabi was known in philosophical circles as the second master after Aristotle, the first master (12). According to Ibn-Khallikan, al-Farabi mastered several languages in addition to Turkish and Arabic. He studied logic under Abu Bishr Matta Yunus in Baghdad and Yuhanna ibn-Haylan in Harran (13). His instructors also included Isra'il Quwayri and Ibrahim al-Marwazi (Fakhry, *Al-Farabi* 2). Netton describes al-Farabi's life as "the product of a highly eclectic milieu where al-Farabi, the student of a Nestorian Christian, Yuhanna ibn Haylan, among others, inhabited the court of the Shi'ite Sayf al-Dawla [in Damascus]" (7).

By the time Aristotle's works reached al-Farabi in Baghdad, they had undergone several centuries of studying and reinterpretation. Following the Alexandrian tradition, the *Organon* included the *Rhetoric* and *Poetics*, as well as Porphyry's *Isagogue*, a factor that has major implications for the repurposing of rhetoric in the Arabic tradition. As a member of the Baghdad Peripatetic school, which followed in the tradition of the Alexandrian school and focused on studying logic, al-Farabi was familiar with the *Organon* and had access to works, such as the *Prior* and *Posterior Analytics,* that had been newly translated into Arabic. Moreover, unlike earlier Syro-Christian members of the Alexandrian school who were not allowed to study the second half of the *Prior Analytics* or any of the *Posterior Analytics*, the Baghdad Peripatetics had no such restrictions. Scholars suggest that al-Farabi's corpus can be divided into three categories: introductory works to the study of philosophy, commentaries and paraphrases (where his logical curriculum resides), and original works that adopt a syncretic approach to all aspects of philosophy (Reisman 54–55).

In addition to its grounding in Aristotelianism, al-Farabi's curriculum was also rooted in Neoplatonism, and he relied heavily on the works of Plotinus and Proclus in creating his theory of emanation. In this system, laid out in detail in *The Opinions of the Inhabitants of the Virtuous City*, there is a hierarchy of ten intellects, each imparting being on the other in a descending order. The last of these, the Active Intellect, is the link between the divine world and the sublunar world, known in al-Farabi's view as the world of generation and corruption. This hierarchy of celestial intellects finds its parallel in al-Farabi's classification of human intellect and directly informs his theory of logic and the central role of rhetoric therein (al-Farabi, *Kitab Ara' Ahl*).

Though the role of monotheistic religions is usually downplayed in the literature describing influences on al-Farabi's work, there is evidence to suggest that his background in Islam and Christianity (he studied logic under Christian scholars) influenced the way he reinterpreted many of the Aristotelian and Neoplatonic concepts that came down to him, a factor that contributes considerable originality to his philosophical thinking. For example, he describes the Aristotelian First Cause in terms of God, the Active Intellect in terms of the angel of revelation in Islam, and the philosopher in terms of a prophet in the first chapter of *Kitab Ara' Ahl:*

> Then it is this man [the philosopher] who receives Divine Revelation, and God Almighty grants him Revelation through the mediation of the Active Intellect. . . . Thus he is, through the emanation from the Active Intellect to his Passive Intellect, a wise man and a philosopher and an accomplished thinker who employs an intellect of divine quality, and through the emanation of the Active Intellect to his faculty of representation a visionary prophet: who warns of things to come and tells of particular things which exist at present. (245)

It is open to interpretation here whether al-Farabi was trying to reinterpret religion in terms of Greek philosophy or the opposite, reinterpreting philosophy in terms of religion.

Rhetoric for al-Farabi: A Logical Art in the Arabic Tongue

Not all of al-Farabi's works have been edited in the original Arabic, let alone translated into other languages. Moreover, there is a state of confusion in the literature about which of his works are extant and which are not. Al-Farabi's book on rhetoric is a case in point.[2] The book, *Bibliography*, is labeled as "not extant" in Rescher's *Al-Farabi: An Annotated Bibliography*, published in 1962 (43), even though the manuscript was discovered in 1960 (Langhade and Grignashi 4). The book was edited by Mohamed Salim in the original Arabic in 1976 and was translated into French in 1971 by Langhade and Grignashi. No English translation of the book has yet been attempted.

This section is an overview of al-Farabi's book on rhetoric. It highlights how al-Farabi's rhetorical theory is not an imitation of Aristotle's. Instead, it shows how the presence of rhetoric in the *Organon* redefined rhetoric and its purposes for al-Farabi and his school.

A close look at the title of al-Farabi's book on rhetoric, *Kitab fi al-Mantiq: Al-Khataba* (*A Book on Logic: Rhetoric*), shows a clear deviation from Aristotle and illustrates the repurposing of rhetoric as a logical art. Moreover, the definition of rhetoric in the opening sentence of the treatise is one suited to its presence in the *Organon*: "Rhetoric: a syllogistic art whose purpose is persuasion in all of the ten categories. The persuasion that takes place in the hearer's soul is the ultimate goal of the actions of rhetoric" (7). The references to the syllogism and the categories both reflect the repurposing of rhetoric as a logical art in al-Farabi's curriculum. This repurposing includes the transformation of rhetoric from a practical art with the three uses that Aristotle assigns it to a theoretical epistemological one: it has a place in a hierarchy of logical arts that, in their turn, correspond to a hierarchy of human intellects. As such, it is not only a means of conveying knowledge (acquired through other means, as Aristotle would have it), but also a tool for acquiring knowledge, albeit not the most sophisticated one.

Being the fourth in a hierarchy of five syllogistic arts, al-Farabi transforms rhetoric beyond the Aristotelian model into a component of an epistemological structure whose aim is acquiring and communicating knowledge in a manner that accommodates the different capacities of the human intellect (demonstration, dialectic, sophistic, rhetoric, and poetics). For example, philosophers, by virtue of their superior intellectual abilities, are able to arrive at knowledge (which in al-Farabi's scholarship means learning the causes of things both in the sublunar and divine worlds) through demonstration, the highest of the logical arts. According to al-Farabi, the ability to arrive at such knowledge is a gradual one that necessitates going through the other, less sophisticated means—including rhetoric. Rhetoric has an additional role, as well: it is used by philosophers to instruct the masses. In al-Farabi's own words, in *Didascalia in Rhetoricum*:

> And the proverb of Plato, which he posited in his book, the *Republic*, about the cave and how man leaves and then returns to it, is especially suited to the order which Aristotle posited for the parts of logic. For he begins with the lowest opinions, namely those that pertain to many things (pluribus), and then does not cease to proceed gradually, step by step, until he ascends to the most perfect of the sciences. Then he begins to descend through those gradually, until he arrives finally at the lowest, least, and more vile of [the sciences]. (qtd. in Black 117)

The ascent in this passage indicates that rhetoric, the art whose subject matter is opinion, is a component of the hierarchy of syllogistic arts required to arrive at true knowledge via demonstration. The second role of rhetoric is as part of the descent process: the philosopher's task of communicating the knowledge that he acquired through demonstration to the masses in a manner that is suited to their inferior intellect. For al-Farabi, then, rhetoric is a logical art in its own right as well as a general method of instruction used in other arts, and this view is a clear transformation from the Aristotelian focus on the practical uses of rhetoric for ceremonial, forensic, and legislative purposes, and as only a means of instruction of the knowledge arrived at through dialectic. Moreover, while Aristotle pairs rhetoric and dialectic (probably because both of them deal with opinion), al-Farabi does not shy away from pairing rhetoric and demonstration, now that rhetoric is a member of the same hierarchy. Al-Farabi's rhetorical theory cannot, therefore, be studied in isolation from his larger logical curriculum that, in its turn, is directly related to his theory of how knowledge is acquired and the different kinds of intellect.

Because of the role that rhetoric plays in this highly complex epistemological structure, both as a logical art in its own right and as a method of instruction to the masses, a close look at al-Farabi's definition of persuasion, a definition that Aristotle never offers (Black 104), is relevant here:

> Assent takes place when nothing else is possible—this is knowledge. Per-
> suading in the art of rhetoric is similar to instruction in the demonstrative
> arts, and persuasion is the equivalent of the knowledge acquired by the
> learner (as a result of learning). Listening to the speaker, and deliberating
> and speculating over what he says is the equivalent of knowledge. The
> noun "persuasion" is derived from being satisfied with something (as in
> satisfaction and economy), even when it is possible to have more. People
> are inclined when they encounter each other over dealings concerning
> their livelihood to believe each other in what they are talking about, and
> they refer to what others say calling this meaning knowledge. (9)

In this passage, the parallel relation created by al-Farabi between assent in
demonstration and persuasion in rhetoric is evidence of the cognitive dimension that rhetoric acquires in the Farabian curriculum as a result of its presence in the *Organon*. The reference to "people" and "livelihood" here is a
reference to the subject matter of rhetoric, namely, opinion that has, by virtue
of its being widely circulated, been elevated to the status of knowledge.

Al-Farabi offers a similar definition of persuasion as based on opinion in
Didascalia in Rhetoricum:

> But the persuasive is that to which the soul acquiesces in such a way that
> the assent of the soul (*assenus anime*) is given that something is thus, with-
> out its contradictory; but its contradictory exists along with it, and the
> soul easily admits it, except that the mind inclines to the one contradic-
> tory rather than the other. (qtd. in Black 111)

In this passage, al-Farabi adds another quality to the understanding of persuasion: the hearer knows of the existence of opposition and decides to
believe what the rhetor is saying anyway. This state of consciousness is
another quality of rhetoric as an epistemological art and will be discussed further in the following section on the Arabic translation of the enthymeme.

The epistemological quality of rhetoric in al-Farabi's scholarship is also
clear from his lengthy discussion of the different types of human knowledge
in *Kitab al-Khataba*. In addition to mentioning opinion as the subject matter
of rhetoric, he proceeds to compare opinion to certainty (9); describes the
propositions that are based on opinion as either necessary or possible (10);
contrasts the syllogism to innate knowledge (13–15); discusses the properties
of certainty (16) and opinion (16–20); proceeds to a discussion of doubt (21);
and defines rhetoric and dialectic as methods to verify opinion by examining
the existence of opposition to it (21). All of these are points related to the
nature of knowledge and the degrees of certainty associated with each kind.

The role of the rhetor undergoes major transformation in the Farabian
curriculum. Al-Farabi's ruler in *Kitab Ara' Ahl* is a philosopher-prophet who
should have a long list of qualities, including eloquence: "[The ruler] should
have a fine diction, his tongue enabling him to explain to perfection all that is
in the recess of the mind" (247–49). Al-Farabi's representative of the highest
intelligence in the intellect hierarchy *must* be eloquent; eloquence isn't just a

techne, a practical skill that a rhetor is trained in to resolve matters at the senate or the courthouse. The connection between the perfect representation of a sound mind in the character of the philosopher-prophet and eloquence is a direct reference to the role rhetoric plays as a cognitive art, and is related directly to the connections that al-Farabi makes in the *Ihsa' al-'Ulum* (*Enumeration of the Sciences*) between articulate speech and the ability to make sound decisions as characteristics of logic.

The inclusion of the *Rhetoric* and the *Poetics* in the *Organon*, which the Baghdad Peripatetics inherited from the Alexandrian school, has serious implications for the way rhetoric was repurposed as well as the way logic itself was redefined by the Arabic philosophers. Deborah Black reminds us that the

> suggestion that the *Rhetoric* and the *Poetics* embody a logical teaching, which [their inclusion in the *Organon*] clearly implies, necessitates a radical rethinking of the character and aims of these two Aristotelian texts. Perhaps more importantly, an expansion of the scope and contents of the *Organon* implies an expansion of the realm of logic itself. (1)

The epistemological qualities that rhetoric acquires as a logical art, the redefinition of persuasion, and the transformation in the subjectivity of the rhetor are some examples of how al-Farabi's work on rhetoric illustrates Black's statement. The fact that al-Farabi's scholarship was conducted in Arabic and that he wrote for an Arabic audience are additional factors that contributed to the uniqueness of his theory of rhetoric.

GREEK TERMS, ARABIC TRANSLATION[3]

Because of the fact that al-Farabi was writing in Arabic, he not only uses translations of Greek terms, but also examines the different meanings that these terms have in the Arabic language, meanings that these terms did not necessarily have in the original Greek. As a result, key terms such as logic, persuasion, and enthymeme acquire new connotations in not only al-Farabi's logical curriculum, but also the entire Arabic tradition that built upon his work.

In *Ihsa' al-'Ulum*, al-Farabi lists three meanings of the Arabic word for logic: *mantiq*, as derived from the root *nutq*. The first meaning is the "voiced utterance by which the tongue expresses what is in the consciousness" (78).[4] The second is "the utterance that is in the soul, or the intelligibles that are expressed by words" (78). The third meaning reflects the traditional meaning of logic: "an innate psychological power which distinguishes humans from animals. Through this power, humans acquire the intelligibles, sciences, and arts . . . and distinguish between good and bad actions" (78). According to al-Farabi, logic provides rules for external and internal utterances, as well as rules for "the third utterance," which enables humans to make sound choices (78–79). The emphasis on utterances in al-Farabi's logical curriculum adds a communicative dimension in an otherwise purely intellectual field.

Another term whose Arabic translation al-Farabi examines is persuasion (see the definition of persuasion in the previous section). He combines two synonyms of the Arabic word, *qana'a*, in it: persuasion and being satisfied with something with the possibility of having more. This is a curious decision that is complicated by the fact that the second meaning is culturally based. The decision reflects an attempt on al-Farabi's part to create a philosophical lexicon rooted in the Arabic language, and, because he does so, new connotations are added to the philosophical concepts that they did not possess in the original Greek.

Like his reworking of the concepts of logic and persuasion discussed above, al-Farabi's discussion of the enthymeme is another case of a Greek term acquiring new connotations when translated into Arabic. Al-Farabi uses the Arabic word *damir* to refer to the enthymeme. He explains his choice by noting that the use of the enthymeme (*damir*/ضمير) contracts (*yadmor*/يضمر) one of its propositions (*Kitab al-Khataba* 26). While the translation seems successful based on the meaning of the enthymeme as a truncated syllogism in Aristotle, al-Farabi doesn't stop there. He uses another synonym of the Arabic word *damir*, conscience, to add another dimension to the meaning of enthymeme that it did not have in Greek. Al-Farabi adds this meaning to the enthymeme, explaining that the omission takes place because of the previous knowledge of the omitted proposition in the conscience of the hearer (26). For al-Farabi, therefore, an enthymeme is not simply a truncated syllogism, because a syllogism can lose one of its premises and still be called a syllogism:

> When one uses demonstrations and dialectical syllogisms in addressing [others] and in writing, most of the time each of these suppresses one of its premises, for the sake of brevity, or because what is suppressed is extremely obvious to the audience. But these are not called enthymemes. (qtd. in Black 160)

Instead, what distinguishes an enthymeme from a syllogism is the fact that the omission is key to its persuasiveness (*Kitab al-Khataba* 31). Al-Farabi clarifies this rather vague claim in a later section: it is the *reason* behind the omission that makes an enthymeme an enthymeme. Al-Farabi provides two technical reasons that would make the omission of the major proposition an enthymeme: either there is opposition for this proposition or the proposition is a lie and its omission will contribute to giving the enthymeme the appearance of truth (44–45). This definition illustrates not only the rather low position that rhetoric holds in the logical hierarchy, but also the lower status of the masses in the intellectual hierarchy.

The meaning of the enthymeme as a reflection of the conscience of the masses has another implication for al-Farabi: that a rhetor must appeal to her audience in terms that they can comprehend. He explains that including both propositions would not be persuasion but certitude, a domain that the masses do not have access to. He emphasizes the importance of communicating with one's audience by using methods that both the speaker and the audience (and opponents) share. He compares the strategy of utilizing methods that are inaccessible to the audience to using a weapon in wrestling in an attempt to show that using the syllogism with an audience that cannot process it is cheating (Black 162).

THE RHETORICAL NATURE OF AL-FARABI'S OUEVRE

Audience awareness and *kairos* are issues that arise not only in al-Farabi's theory of rhetoric, but also in the way he practices rhetoric to appeal to an Arabic readership located in a different time and place than the Greek audience of the material he was reworking. As I have shown so far, al-Farabi Arabicizes the terminology he uses to appeal to an Arabic readership in the case of logic, persuasion, and the enthymeme. Moreover, throughout his corpus, al-Farabi replaces Greek examples with Arabic ones. When he does use foreign examples, he uses those that he knows his audience can grasp. The epigraph of this article explains in al-Farabi's own words his views on accommodating one's audience and his awareness of the inaccessibility of knowledge once it has been moved in time and place.

Al-Farabi practices what he preaches. For example, in explaining the Aristotelian concept of accidents in *The Opinions*, he uses the Arabic name Zayd in sentences such as "Zayd walks" (qtd. in Haddad 51). When he uses foreign names, he uses ones with which he knows his audience is familiar. In his treatise on rhetoric, *Kitab al-Khataba*, al-Farabi makes several references to Galen. At first glance, this might seem strange: Aristotle could not have used Galen in his own treatise, and al-Farabi prefers using Arabic examples. However, an understanding of the cultural context of Baghdad at the time explains that Galen would have been a familiar name. Al-Farabi's lifetime marks the end of a two-century translation movement where medicine (and the work of Galen especially) was heavily translated and commented on. Galen's name, therefore, would have been familiar to al-Farabi's circle and among his readers (for an account of the translation movement, see Gutas, *Greek Thought, Arabic Culture*).

In addition to his conscious use of familiar names, the way al-Farabi defines the role of logic, perhaps the most important term in his scholarship, is heavily context based. Al-Farabi's immediate context included the major debate between logicians and grammarians about the importance of studying the imported, foreign discipline of logic. Al-Farabi's theory of Arabic grammar is rooted in a contemporary debate between the logician Abu Bishr Matta b. Yunus and the grammarian al-Sirafi. The former argued for the universal use of logic as a metalanguage, while the latter refused this view, claiming that the Arabs did not need a foreign science because they had Arabic grammar to aid them in avoiding methodological errors (Reisman 66). Being a student of the former, al-Farabi predictably viewed logic as a universal tool that aids the human intellect, regardless of the language used, in acquiring truth and avoiding error. Grammar, on the other hand, is language specific:

> Our purpose is the investigation of the art of logic, the art which includes the things which lead the rational faculty towards right thinking, wherever there is the possibility of error, and which indicates all the safeguards against error, wherever a conclusion is to be drawn by the intellect (*al-'aql*). Its status to the intellect (*al-'aql*) is the status of the art of grammar in relation to language, and just as the science of grammar rectifies the language among the people for whose language the grammar has been made, so the science of logic rectifies the intellect (*al-'aql*), so that it intellects only what is right where there is the possibility of error. (qtd. in Netton 55–56)

The close parallel between grammar and logic reflects his consciousness of the debate and his attempt to resolve it in light of his expertise in both fields.

CONCLUSION

Al-Farabi's treatise, *Kitab al-Khataba*, is based on Aristotle's work, and it covers concepts that come up in Aristotle's *On Rhetoric*, such as analogy, examples, emotional and ethical appeals, and types of audience. In a dialogic fashion (cf. Bakhtin), however, al-Farabi expands the Aristotelian theory of rhetoric to not only include subjects that Aristotle covers in other "logical" works, but also redefine some of the Greek terms for an Arabic audience, providing rhetoric with newer epistemological and communicative attributes.

Al-Farabi's scholarship reflects the complex rhetorical nature of his work. Knowledge and logic are directly related to communication. His classification of the arts of discourse is rooted in an awareness of the importance of context and audience in the transferring of knowledge. Moreover, al-Farabi's adaptation of Greek thought and terminology are signs of a rhetorically savvy philosopher who is aware of how changes in geographical, historical, religious, and cultural contexts can affect the reception and assimilation of imported knowledge.

Rhetoric is not only covered in al-Farabi's treatises explicitly on the subject, but also comes up throughout his corpus: he mentions it in the *Ihsa' al-'Ulum*, *Kitab al-Huruf* (*Book of Letters*), and the *Kitab Ara' Ahl al-Madina al-Fadila*. As one of the earlier and most influential medieval Arabic philosophers, al-Farabi's work influenced many Arabic philosophers who came after him. Ibn Sina and Ibn Rushd's treatises on rhetoric are based on al-Farabi's scholarship, for example.

This paper is a humble attempt to start a conversation in comparative rhetoric that focuses on medieval Arabic scholarship. Extensive medieval Arabic scholarship is already taking place in fields such as philosophy, history, and near eastern studies. This scholarship hints at the important role that rhetoric played in this scholarship, but does not delve deeply into studying rhetoric. It is our responsibility as rhetoricians to take the initiative and examine these treatises, as well as examine the larger role that rhetoric played in the philosophical scholarship of Arabic philosophers. It is also imperative that serious translation projects of rhetorical treatises be commissioned and supported by our field.

Notes

[1] MS 812 in Hamidiyyeh, qtd. in Haddad 19.
[2] *Kitab al-Khataba* is an abbreviated version of al-Farabi's *Kitab fi al-Mantiq: Al-Khataba,* which I will use throughout this paper.
[3] This heading was inspired by Gutas' *Greek Thought, Arabic Culture.*
[4] Haddad translates this first kind of logic as articulate speech.

Bibliography

Adamson, Peter, and Richard C. Taylor. *The Cambridge Companion to Arabic Philosophy.* New York: Cambridge UP, 2005.

Al-Farabi, Abu-Nasr. *Ihsa' al-'Ulum.* Ed. Uthman Amin. Cairo: Anglo-Egyptian Library, 1968.

———. *Kitab al-Huruf.* Ed. Mushen Mahdi. Beirut: Dar el-Mashreq, 1970.

———. *Kitab Ara' Ahl al-Madina al-Fadila.* Trans. and ed. Richard Walzer. Oxford: Clarendon, 1985.

———. *Kitab fi al-Mantiq: Al-Khataba.* Ed. Mohamed M. Salim. Cairo: Dar al Kutub, 1976.

Alon, Ilai. *Al Farabi's Philosophical Lexicon.* 2 vols. Wiltshire: Aris and Philips, 2002.

Aristotle. *On Rhetoric: A Theory of Civic Discourse.* Trans. George Kennedy. New York: Oxford UP, 1991.

Bakhtin, Mikhail. "Discourse in the Novel." *The Dialogic Imagination: Four Essays by M. M. Bakhtin.* Ed. Michael Holquist. Austin: U of Texas P, 1981. 259–422.

———. "From *The Problem of Speech Genres.*" *The Rhetorical Tradition: Readings from the Classical Times to the Present.* 2nd ed. Ed. Patricia Bizzell and Bruce Herzberg. Boston: Bedford/St. Martin's, 2001. 1227–45.

Black, Deborah. *Logic and Aristotle's* Rhetoric *and* Poetics *in Medieval Arabic Philosophy.* Leiden: E. J. Brill, 1990.

Dickins, James. *Thinking Arabic Translation: A Course in Translation Method: Arabic to English.* New York: Routledge, 2002.

Fakhry, Majid. *Al-Farabi, Founder of Islamic Neoplatonism: His Life, Works and Influence.* Oxford: One World, 2002.

———. *A History of Islamic Philosophy.* 3rd ed. New York: Columbia UP, 2004.

———. *A Short Introduction to Islamic Philosophy, Theology, and Mysticism.* Oxford: Oneworld, 1997.

Gutas, Dimitri. *Greek Thought, Arabic Culture: The Graeco-Arabic Translation Movement in Baghdad and Early 'Abbāsid Society (2nd–4th/8th–10th Centuries).* New York: Routledge, 1998.

———. "The Study of Arabic Philosophy in the Twentieth Century: An Essay on the Historiography of Arabic Philosophy." *British Journal of Middle Eastern Studies* 29.1 (May 2002): 5–25.

Haddad, Fuad S. *Alfarabi's Theory of Communication.* Beirut: American U of Beirut P, 1989.

Hallden, Philip. "What is Arab Islamic Rhetoric? Rethinking the History of Muslim Oratory Art and Homelitics." *International Journal of Middle Eastern Studies* 37 (2005): 19–38.

Langhade, J., and M. Grignashi. *Deux Ouvrages Inedits sur la Rhetorique.* Beyrouth: Dar el Mashreq, 1971.

Morris, Pam, ed. *The Bakhtin Reader: Selected Writings of Bakhtin, Medvedev, and Voloshi-nov.* London: E. Arnold, 1994.

Nader, Albert, ed. Introduction. *Kitab Ara' Ahl al-Madina al-Fadila.* By Abu-Nasr al-Farabi. Beirut: Dar el-Mashreq, 1986.

Netton, Ian Richard. *Al Farabi and His School.* New York: Routledge, 1992.

Peters, F. E. *Aristotle and the Arabs: The Aristotelian Tradition in Islam.* New York: New York UP, 1968.

Reisman, David C. "Al Farabi and the Philosophical Curriculum." Cambridge Companions Online: Cambridge UP, 2006.

Rescher, Nicholas. *Al-Farabi: An Annotated Bibliography.* Pittsburgh: U of Pittsburgh P, 1962.

———. "Al-Farabi on Logical Traditions." *Journal of the History of Ideas* 24.1 (Jan.–Mar. 1963): 127–32.

Said, Edward W. *Orientalism.* New York: Pantheon Books, 1978.

Salim, Mohamed M., ed. Introduction. *Kitab fi al-Mantiq: Al-Khataba.* By Abu-Nasr al-Farabi. Cairo: Dar al Kutub, 1976.

Sheikh, M. Said. *Ancient World.* The Hague: Martinus Nijhoff, 1974.

———. *Islamic Philosophy.* London: Octagon P, 1962.

The Cynic

Charles Johnson

The ruler of the world is the
Whirlwind, that has unseated Zeus.

—*The Clouds,* Aristophanes

If you listen to those who are wise—the people who defended my teacher at his trial before the state killed him—they will tell you that the war destroyed the golden days of our city. The Corinthians, fearing our expansionist stance and growing power, convinced the Spartans to make war against us. Our leader, Pericles, knew we were stronger at sea than on shore. So he had all the inhabitants of Athenian territory in Attica huddle inside the fortifications of the city, which left the lands of the rich to be ravished by our enemies. He gambled that after this sacrifice our swift and deadly ships, triremes outfitted with three banks of oars, would wear the Spartans down in a war of attrition. His plan might have worked. But at the outset of the war, a plague fell upon Athens, laying waste to those crowded in the city and, if that weren't bad enough, Pericles himself died the following year. With his death, demagogues like the young general Alcibiades seized power in the Assembly. They convinced the voters to abandon our defensive strategy and launch an attack on Syracuse in faraway Sicily. This ill-advised military adventure drained the manpower and treasure of the polis, our city-state. Within two years, "the hateful work of war," as Homer might have put it, had wiped out our ships and ground forces. However, this was just the beginning of what we later learned was the spell of chaos cast upon us by the goddess Eris.

The war dragged on for another ten years, dividing us, disenchanting our civic life. No one could stop the growing hatred of the poor for the rich, or the bitterness in those wealthy families who lost their crops year after year. The rich began to plot against the regime, against rule by the people, and against the Assembly, which had conducted the war in a dark comedy of miscalculations and decisions based on collective self-delusion.

When our defeat finally came, after a demoralizing 27 years, everyone knew it was the end of the empire, that we had unleashed the furies, and entered a time of dangerous extremes, a long-prophesied Iron Age. Crime, fraud, and violence increased. Many Hellenes started to feel that the gods, like Zeus and Athena, were either fictions or helpless to affect our lives. The gossamer-thin foundation of laws and traditions our fathers and forbearers had lived by (especially our devotion to sophrosyne or moderation) seemed arbitrary. The faith in a moral order that unified us during our Golden Age was no longer possible. Almost overnight loyalty to our sea-girt city-state reverted to family, tribe, and clan. A new breed of citizen was born: cold, calculating, and egotistical men like Jason in Euripides' *Medea*, devoted not to civic duty but to the pleasures of food, drink, sex, and, most of all, power. These new men, who believed might was right, like Thrasymachus, saw "justice," "honesty," and "loyalty" as ideas created by and for the weak. A new level of nastiness, incivility, and litigation entered our lives. Of these men, Thucydides said, "The meaning of words had no longer the same relation to things, but was changed by them as they thought proper. Each man was strong only in the conviction that nothing was secure. Inferior intellects generally succeeded best. For, aware of their own deficiencies and feeling the capacities of their opponents, for whom they were no match in powers of speech and whose subtle wits were likely to anticipate them in contriving evil, they struck boldly at once."

Now, such new men needed new teachers, ones who were very different from the wonderful man who taught me. These teachers, foreigners, sprang up like Athena from the head of Zeus, and came from places like Corinth and Ceos. They were called Sophists, and for a nice purse of drachmae, they instructed children of the rich in clever, honey-tongued rhetoric and perfumed lies designed to soothe the mob and sway the members of the factious Assembly. Prostitutes, my teacher called them, because he charged no fee. The most famous of these was Protagoras, who argued that everyone knew things not as they are but only as they are in the moment of his perception. "Man," he said, "is the measure of all things," and by this he meant nothing was objective: all we could have were opinions, and so each citizen was his own lawgiver. (And, as you know, opinions are like assholes: everybody has one.) In my youth, then, at this hour in history, in the wreckage of our society, it came to pass that common values had all but vanished. Truth was relative to each man. And nothing was universal anymore.

But the greatest, most unforgivable crime of my countrymen was, if you ask me, the killing of my teacher for refusing to conform to the positions of the political factions. His accusers—Anytus, Meletus, and Lycon—called him an atheist, a traitor, and a corrupter of youth. Then they brought him to trial, and I shall remember for all my days what he said in his defense: "Gentlemen, I am your grateful and devoted servant, but I owe a greater obedience to God than to you. I shall go on saying, in my usual way, my good friend, you are an Athenian and belong to a city that is the greatest and most famous in the world for its wisdom and strength. Are you not ashamed that you give your attention to acquiring as much money as possible, and similarly with reputation and honor, and give no attention or thought to truth and understanding and the perfection of your soul?"

He could have fled the city, escaping injustice with the help of his students. Instead, and because he could not imagine living anywhere but Athens, he drank the chill draught of hemlock.

To this very day, I regret that I could not be at his side when he died. I was sick that evening. But since his death, which wounded us all, I have tried everything to honor him. I feel like a son whose father has died too soon, right when he is on the verge of being mature enough to say something that might interest him. Sometimes I would see or hear something I wanted to share with him only to realize he was gone for the rest of my life. For years now I've carried on dialogues with him in my head, talking into the darkness late at night, saying aloud—perhaps too loudly—all the things I wanted to tell him, apologizing for things I failed to say, often taking his part in our imaginary conversations until my five slaves, who are like family to me, started looking my way strangely. I didn't want anyone to think I had wandered in my wits, so I began quietly writing down these dialogues, adding more speakers in our conversations where he is always the voice of wisdom. That is how I want to remember him. Yet, and still, his death left a scar on my soul, and a question that haunts me day and night: how can good men like Socrates survive in a broken, corrupt society?

There was one man who seemed as bedeviled by this question as I was. I can't say we were on the same friendly terms as Damon and Pythias, though sometimes he did feel like a brother—one who infuriated me because he said my lectures at the Academy were long-winded and a waste of time. He was not, I confess, my only critic. My teacher's other students think my theories are all lunacy and error. They see my theory of eternal Ideas existing beyond this imperfect, shadowy world as being nothing more than my cobbling together the ideas of Heraclitus (who saw only difference in the world and denied identity) and Parmenides (who saw only identity and denied the existence of change). In their opinion, I've betrayed everything Socrates stood for. They hate my view that only philosopher-kings should rule. Antisthenes has always been especially harsh toward me, treating me as if I am as cabbage-headed as a Boeotian, perhaps because he, and not I, was present at Socrates' side when he passed away. Years ago, he had his own school. In his teachings he rejected government, property, marriage, religion, and pure philosophy or metaphysics. Rather, he preached that plain, ordinary people could know all that was worth knowing, that an ordinary, everyday mind was quite enough. He taught in a building that served as a cemetery for dogs. Therefore, his pupils were called cynics ("dog-like"), and among the most earthy, flamboyant, and, I must say, scatological of his disciples was the ascetic Diogenes.

For an ascetic, he was shamelessly Dionysian, and without an obol or lepton to his name; but Diogenes was also a clown with hair like leaves and tree bark, gnarled root-like hands, and eyes like scars gouged into stone. He made a virtue of vulgarity, wore the worst clothing, ate the plainest porridge, slept on the ground or, as often as not, made his bed in a wine-cask, saying that by watching mice he had learned to adapt himself to any circumstance. Accordingly, he saw animals as his most trustworthy teachers, since their lives were natural, unselfconscious, and unspoiled by convention and hypocrisy. Like them, he was known for defecating, urinating, masturbating, and breaking wind in public. He even said we should have sex in the middle of the marketplace, for if the act was not indecent in private, we should not be ashamed of doing it in public. Whenever he was praised for something, he said, "Oh shame, I must be doing something wrong!" Throughout Athens he was called The Dog, but to do him justice, there was a method in his madness. For example, his only possessions were his staff and a wooden bowl. But one afternoon Diogenes stumbled upon a boy using his hands to drink water from a stream. Happily, he tossed his bowl away, and from that day forward drank only with his bare hands.

Thus things stood in postwar Athens when one day The Dog decided to walk around the city holding a lighted lantern. He peered into all the stalls of the marketplace, peeked in brothels, and when someone asked what he was doing, replied, "I'm looking for an honest man." His quest brought him to the Academy, where I was lecturing. As I placed several two-handled drinking cups before my students, I could from the corner of one eye see him listening, and scratching at dirt in his neck creases, and sticking his left hand under his robe into his armpit, withdrawing it and sniffing his fingers to see if he needed a bath. I sighed, hoping he'd go away. I turned to my students and told them that, while there were countless cups in the world, there was only one idea of a cup. This idea, the essence of cupness, was eternal; it came before all the individual cups in the world, and they all participated imperfectly in the immortal Form of cupness.

From the back of the room, Diogenes cleared his throat loudly.

"Excuse me," he said, "I can see the cup, but I don't see cupness anywhere."

"Well," I smiled at my students, "you have two good eyes with which to see the cup." I was not about to let him upstage me in my own class. Pausing, I tapped my forehead with my finger and said, "But it's obvious you don't have a good enough mind to comprehend cupness."

At that point, he sidled through my students, put down his lantern, and picked up one of the cylices. He looked inside, then lifted his gaze to me.

"Is this cup empty, Plato?"

"Why, yes, that's obvious."

"Then," he opened his eyes as wide as possible, which startled me because that was a favorite trick of my teacher, "where is the emptiness that comes before this empty cup?"

Right then my mind went cloudy. My eyes slipped out of focus for a second. I was wondering how to reply, disoriented even more by the scent of his meaty dog breath and rotten teeth. And then Diogenes tapped my forehead with his finger, and said, "I believe you will find the emptiness is here." My students erupted with laughter, some of them even clapping, when he, buffoon that he was, took a bow. (That boy from Stagira, Aristotle, who was always questioning me, and expressed the preposterous belief that the ideas must be in things, laughed until he was gasping for breath.) "I think your teacher's problem," he told them, "is that he'd like to run away from the messiness of the world, to disappear—poof!—into a realm of pure forms and beauty, where everything has the order and perfection of mathematics. He's a mystic. And so—so dualistic! He actually wants certainty where there is none."

"What," I said, "is wrong with that? Things are terrible today! Everyone is suing everyone else. There's so much anger and hatred. No one trusts anyone anymore!"

Again, his eyes flew open, and he winked at my students, raising his shoulders in a shrug. "When have things not been terrible? What you don't see, my friend, is that there are only two ways to look at life. One, as if nothing is holy. The other, as if everything is."

Oh, that stung.

All at once, the room was swimming, rushing toward me, then receding. I felt unsteady on my feet. Now my students would always tap their heads and giggle when I tried to teach, especially that cocky young pup Aristotle. (I think he'd like to take my place if he could, but I know that will never happen.)

"In my opinion," I said, "only a fool would carry a lantern in the day time. Why don't you use it at night like a sensible man would?"

"As a night light?" He raised his eyebrows and bugged out his eyes again. "Thank you, Plato. I think I like that."

All I could do was dismiss my students for the rest of the day, which The Dog had ruined. I pulled on my cape and wandered through the marketplace until darkness came, without direction through the workmen, the temples of the gods, the traders selling their wares; among metics and strangely tattooed nomads from the steppes who policed our polis; past the theater where old men prowled for young boys whose hair hung like hyacinth pedals; and soldiers sang drinking songs, all the while cursing Diogenes under my breath because the mangy cur was right. He was, whatever else, more Socratic than Socrates himself, as if the spirit of my teacher had been snatched from the Acherusian Lake, where souls wait to be reborn, and gone into him to chastise and correct me from beyond the grave, reminding me that I would always be just an insecure pupil intoxicated by ideas, so shaken by a world without balance that I clung to the crystalline purity of numbers, the Apollonian exactitude and precision of abstract thought. Where my theories had denied the reality of our war-shattered world, he lapped up the illusion, like a dog indifferent to whether he was dining on a delicacy or his own ordure.

Tired, I decided to return home. And it was when I reached the center of town that I saw him again. He was still holding high that foolish lantern and walking toward me with a wild splash of a smile on his face. I wanted to back away—I was certain he had fleas—or strike him a blow for humiliating me, but instead I held my ground and said crisply, "Have you found what you're looking for yet?"

"Perhaps," he said, and before I could step back, he lifted my chin with his forefinger and thumb toward the night sky. "What do you see? Don't explain, look."

It was the first night of a full moon, but I hadn't noticed until now. My mind started racing like that of a good student asked a difficult question by his teacher. I recalled that when Democritus tried to solve the mystery of the One and the Many, he said all things were composed of atoms, and that Thales believed that everything was made of water, and that Anaximenes claimed the world's diversity could be reduced to one substance, air. Oh, I could plaster a thousand interpretations on the palpable orb above us, but at that moment something peculiar took place, and to this day I do not understand it. I looked and the plentitude of what I saw—the moon emerging from clouds like milk froth—could not be deciphered. Its opacity outstripped my speech. I was ambushed by its sensuous, singular, and savage beauty. I felt a shiver of desire (or love) rippling through my back. For a second I was wholly unconscious of anyone beside me or where I was.

As moonlight spilled abundantly from a bottomless sky, as I felt myself commingled with the seen, words failed me, my cherished opinions slipped away in the radiance of a primordial mystery that was as much me as it was the raw face of this full-orbed moon, a cipher so inexhaustible and ineffable it shimmered in my mind, surging to its margins, giving rise to a state of enchantment even as it seemed on the verge of vanishing, as all things do— poleis and philosophical systems—into the pregnant emptiness Diogenes had asked me to explain. A sudden breeze extinguished the wick inside his lamp, leaving us enveloped by the immensity of night. There, with my vision unsealed, I felt only wonder, humility, and innocence, and for the first time I realized I did not have to understand, but only to be.

All I could do was swallow, a gulp that made The Dog grin.

"Good." He placed one piebald paw on my shoulder, as a brother might, or perhaps man's best friend. "You didn't dialogue it to death. I think I've found my honest man."

Loyalty Oaths and the Letter of the Law
Rhetoric, Resistance, and Responsibility

M. Karen Powers

When a loyalty oath is introduced in the atmosphere of a witch hunt, those who sign are swearing not to the text of the oath, but to a subtext. Loyalty is sworn not to the body politic, but to the political whims of those who have called for the oath to be signed. . . . I will not swear allegiance to witch hunters.

—Elissa Guralnick,
Professor of English, University of Colorado, 2005 (qtd. in Talbott)

In the wake of the terrorist attacks on September 11, 2001, public universities across the United States have resurrected dormant loyalty oaths or have implemented others newly written by state and federal agencies. By my estimation, nearly two-thirds of the states now require employees—including university professors at public institutions—to sign loyalty oaths and/or security questionnaires disavowing ties to terrorist associations and activities. The government's renewed program to solicit pledges of allegiance from myriad public workers in the name of security is one consequence of this bleak moment in recent U.S. history, but the far-reaching repercussions this agenda might entail for the practice of democracy and academic freedom have yet to garner adequate public or scholarly attention. One implication of particular concern arises from the link between the current proliferation of loyalty oaths and the concomitant resurgence of a fervent and narrow wartime nationalism. At a time when xenophobia often passes for patriotism, loyalty oaths are advocated as a means to preserve the nation and thereby ensure citizen safety. When oaths are duly cast as discursive security mechanisms, they reciprocate by exacerbating a national discourse that tends to conflate globalization and terrorism.

If post-9/11 ideologies of nationalism, globalization, and security intersect in distinctive ways to fuel the most recent spate of loyalty oaths, the rhetoric that comprises such oaths is nonetheless disquietingly familiar. The first decade of the twenty-first century invokes the specter of the late 1940s through the 1950s, when "more than 40 states passed laws requiring loyalty oaths from their public employees" and "[a]bout 13.5 million Americans signed loyalty oaths as a condition of employment" (Ross). These historical patterns are not coincidental, nor are they inconsequential. The civil liberties at risk now are precisely those that galvanized some faculty members at the University of California to resist the reduction of debate and dissent in 1949–1950 when a revised loyalty oath incited controversy. Caught in the grip of rampant anticommunist legislation, thirty-one academics, holding ranks from lecturer to professor, defied the letter of the law by refusing to sign an addendum requiring them to swear that they did not belong to the Communist Party.

The addendum was attached to the university's existing pledge. This long-standing oath, which exacted the standard promise to support state and federal governments, did not occasion notable protest until it was tailored in ways that legitimated red scare politics. The new and, for some, intolerable language introduced by the thirty-four-word addendum raised much larger issues than support for communism, or any other political faction for that matter. Those few words transcended the specific time and place of the debate by precipitating reconsiderations of not only the addendum and the existing oath it altered, but also of the intrinsic ideas inscribed by the language of both. In essence, the addendum brought scrutiny to bear on the very notion of an oath and its multiple and complex rhetorical functions in a political system promising government by the people. Despite risking "pain of dismissal," the nonsigners rejected the offending words on ethical and political grounds; at the same time, they challenged the board of regents' authority to define "loyalty" in ways they considered antithetical to their constitutional liberties (Gardner vii). The ensuing recriminations, which "convulsed the largest university in the nation and one of the world's leading centers of letters and science," culminated in the dismissal of thirty-one University of California faculty members and jeopardized foundational tenets of democracy and academic freedom in ways that continue to resound more than fifty years later (vii).

This decisive dispute's key argument about the meaning of "loyalty" remains inextricably interwoven into the disparate and shifting interpretations of "democracy" and "academic freedom" that even now define and animate the contemporary U.S. university. As even a cursory examination of the 1949–1950 conflict in California implies, signing—or refusing to sign—a loyalty oath constitutes a profoundly rhetorical act, especially in times of intense political upheaval such as the two historical moments I consider here, the middle of the twentieth century and the beginning of the twenty-first century. In the discussion that follows, I juxtapose the State of California oath with the State of Georgia oath, which also emerged mid-twentieth century and continues to exist. I suggest that these loyalty rhetorics, seemingly particular to specific sites and a certain era, are instead broadly representative in the sense that they do not stand as solitary texts but function in rhetorical tandem with other texts and across history to perform definitive cultural work. To that end, I reread these documents and their histories to suggest ways loyalty oaths, orchestrated in the name of American democracy, lend themselves, paradoxically, to antidemocratic conscription.

My overarching purpose for examining these texts, their subtexts and contexts, and their lingering influences on the present-day university is to enact one type of rhetorical responsibility. I propose a line of inquiry critical to the current era and map one trajectory with these questions: In what ways does the increasing prevalence of loyalty oaths and security questionnaires contribute to the fraying of academic freedom at this historical moment? What strategies for contravention might rhetoricians learn from past efforts to resist loyalty oaths that have been deployed to suppress dissent and circumvent democracy? Admittedly, an interested analysis of just two oaths provides provisional and partial answers, at best. On the other hand, I argue that past and present oaths like these are powerful rhetorical mechanisms that mark local sites of a recurring national campaign—not to secure public safety, as typically touted—but to safeguard antidemocratic agendas by preempting or mitigating dissent.

When demarcated by these questions and concerns, the oaths function as a palimpsest on which definitions of "loyalty" have been written, partially erased, and overwritten. And, when reread within the theoretical framework Naomi Wolf constructs in *The End of America,* these historical artifacts present a crucial concern at this unstable juncture in U.S. democracy: the prospect that loyalty oaths are functioning in concert with other nationalist dictates to foment what Wolf terms an impending "'fascist shift'" (21). Wolf describes this shift as an "antidemocratic ideology that uses the threat of violence against the individual in order to subdue the institutions of civil society, so that they in turn can be subordinated to the power of the state" (21). She is troubled by what she sees as "structural echoes," the historical residue of past antidemocratic regimes that now appears disturbingly obvious in the United States (10). Her description of dictators across the historical continuum "invoking emergency decrees to close down civil liberties" brings to mind the USA PATRIOT Act, while their interest in "creating military tribunals" finds a parallel in secret prisons such as Guantánamo (10). Her delineation of how past dictators have invested in "criminalizing dissent" is particularly pertinent, since it elucidates the distinct possibility that loyalty oaths validate and advance just such a project (10). Deciphering these structural echoes, Wolf enumerates "ten steps that are taken in order to close down a democracy or crush a prodemocratic movement, whether by capitalists, communists, or right-wing fascists" (11). Such assaults on democracy are also marked by telling and indelible traces left by loyalty oaths, and, as the controversy at the University of California attests, their rhetorical complicity is sobering.

THE UNIVERSITY OF CALIFORNIA
LOYALTY OATH (1949–1950)

[N]owhere and never has there been a guaranty that an oath formula imposed on, or extorted from, the subjects of an all-powerful state will, or must, remain unchanged. The contrary is true. All oaths in history that I know of, have undergone changes. A new word will be added. A short phrase, seemingly insignificant, will be smuggled in. The next step may be an inconspicuous change in tense, from present to past, or from past to future. The consequences of a new oath are unpredictable. It will not be in the hands of those imposing the oath to control its effects, nor of those taking it, ever to step back again.

—Ernst H. Kantorowicz,
Professor of History, University of California, 1949

Fear of communist infiltrators precipitated by the developing cold war prompted the objectionable addendum to the University of California loyalty oath. The final revision that appeared in June of 1949 retained the long-standing and largely uncontested pledge to support state and national constitutions but added these words: "I am not a member of the Communist Party, or under any oath, or a party to any agreement, or under any commitment that is in conflict with my obligations under this oath" (Stewart 145). As David Stewart, a professor embroiled in the debate, explains, "In addition to the traditional oath included in the Constitution of the State of California . . . and gladly taken already, University employees were suddenly required to swear to a codicil . . ." (20). From Stewart's perspective, "The whole controversy . . . arose over thirty-four words, or if the small change of articles, conjunctions, and prepositions be not counted, over about half that number" (20). Without question, these few words launched one of the most well-known and acrimonious of debates, to date, about loyalty oaths.

Although these particular words ignited the controversy, the addendum alone was not solely responsible. The added words did not signify in isolation but collaborated with existing texts and within a rapidly shifting political context that Geoffrey Stone calls "the anti-Communist onslaught" to cast a pall over democracy and academic freedom (420). As he notes, the University of California was among "[s]cores of colleges and universities [that] fired hundreds of professors because of their actual or suspected, past or present, membership in the Communist Party" (422). At the same time, the California incident is particularly illustrative because it demonstrates how thirty-four words that emerged within the context of a sharply narrowed nationalism, owing to anticommunist sentiment, as well as within the contexts of the original pledge and a previous draft of the addendum, appropriated and redefined the traditional oath. On the surface, the addendum does not appear so extraordinarily stirring as to initiate a controversy that still shadows the history of higher education, although, to be sure, the label "communist" rankled deeply in that era. A closer look, however, shows how the addendum not only launched an argument that dismantled the accord that had existed when the original pledge was "gladly taken," but also demonstrates how profoundly and irrevocably it altered the meaning of the original pledge (Stewart 20).

The regents' first attempt to mold the constitutional oath initiated tensions with this language: "I do not believe in and am not a member of nor do I support any party or organization that believes in, advocates or teaches the overthrow of the United States Government by force or violence" (Stewart 145). Stewart describes a "special meeting of the Academic Senate" to discuss this draft, noting that there remained "much unity of feeling" and "general expression of loyalty and of willingness to take the constitutional oath" (28–29). Significantly, faculty members continued to "have no objection to reaffirming their loyalty to the state and nation," as long as their "request that the special addition 'be deleted or revised in a manner mutually acceptable to the regents and the members of the Academic Senate'" was granted (29). The regents complied with the request and supplanted the first draft that required faculty members to promise they would not overthrow the government with the final addendum that required them to swear they were not members of the Communist Party. The explicitly discordant words such as "overthrow," "force," and "violence" were deleted. Regardless, the collective connotation of those words that whispered "sedition" and "subversion" continued to augment the addendum, leaving an ideological residue that added weight to the document's thirty-four words.

The force of these words, both those written, as well as those written and erased, raised the specter of strictures on academic freedom that charged the atmosphere within which the second and final version of the addendum appeared. This text infused the traditional pledge with a new and different meaning by pronouncing that "support for the Constitution of the United States and the Constitution of the State of California" entailed the indiscriminate rejection of one political party and all persons associated with what was at the time a legal entity. Thus, swearing to the first part of the pledge, to support the constitutions, had meant being "party to [an] agreement" and "under [a] commitment" to protect the rights to civil liberties requisite to democratic constitutions. But swearing to the second part, the addendum, to wholly disavow the Communist Party by order of the state, was "in conflict with [these] obligations." The regents' revision of the addendum, if intended as a conciliatory gesture, did little to assuage the risk it posed for academic freedom. As one faculty member asserted in his letter of resignation, "I cannot accept the recent so-called 'compromise' with the Regents, for, to me, it is a compromise with totalitarianism" (Stewart 151).

In a statement to the president of the university, another faculty member criticized what he termed the regents' "dictatorial power," insisting that "loyalty to the United States cannot be extorted by threat or intimidation. The line between democracy and totalitarianism remains indelible so long as allegiance to the State or Nation is not exacted by external compulsion" (Stewart 150). For him, and presumably the other dissenters, the regents' aim to alter the oath was adversative to democracy and thus unconscionable. Further, the regents' definition of "loyalty" that infused their attempt to align the university and its faculty with prevailing antidemocratic ideologies was equally untenable. This professor voiced the dissenters' convictions when he went on to say, "The action of the Regents . . . constitutes, in my opinion, a denial of the very democracy we cherish and hold dear. It seeks to extract by force an expression of loyalty which is essentially un-American. America will not be saved by methods borrowed from Fascism and Communism" (150). Signing this pledge, one fraught with irreconcilable contradictions, meant signaling support for a dramatically changed and disturbingly antidemocratic national political agenda. A nonsigner who resigned rather than take the new oath wondered, "Do those who have signed such a document realize they have *contributed* to the furtherance of totalitarianism?" (151). For the nonsigners, affixing their signatures to the new oath represented signing away the very civil liberties they believed imperative to the U.S. university and a democratic nation.

Significantly, the thirty-one professors who resisted did not act in defense of the political ideology specifically named. These nonsigners, although subsequently fired, were not accused of communist membership or of harboring such sympathies, each having been previously deemed by the "Academic Senate Committee on Privilege and Tenure to be a competent scholar, an objective teacher, and untainted by disloyalty to the country" (Gardner 3). They challenged the regents because, in their shared view, the oath no longer supported but rebuked state and national constitutions, the very documents most integral to democracy and necessarily the rightful subject of debate and dissent in a free society. This oath reified rather than resisted the national witch hunt that targeted educational institutions, especially, and the allegedly seditious intellectuals with subversive ideas who were sheltered there. Ironically, although the thirty-one dissenting professors were fired for their refusal to sign an oath that rejected communism, in actuality, their dismissal transpired as a result of their steadfast defense of democracy.

The eight primary reasons the nonsigners gave for their opposition to signing the oath explicitly reflect their joint refusal to sanction overarching antidemocratic strictures such as government control and suppression of dissent. Stewart explains that "many professors believed that the oath constituted a political test for membership in the faculty and was therefore contrary, certainly to the spirit, and probably to the letter, of the articles in the state Constitution under which the University operates" (22). The nonsigners also dismissed as indefensible the regents' assumptions about "guilt by association" (22). They could not countenance the possibility that "people were to be convicted and punished merely because they kept disreputable company, not because they themselves had actually committed any offense or had even been shown likely to commit an offense" (22). The related assumption that all members of the Communist Party deserved condemnation was resisted by the nonsigners as a virulently "un-American practice, and a dangerous one [that] should be vigorously opposed from its very beginning" (22–23).

Concern for university welfare was another pivotal reason fueling the resistance; the regents were viewed as exerting their power to "destroy any effective faculty autonomy, and thus gain direct control of the University in a way not warranted by the spirit of the Constitutional Act or by tradition" (Stewart 24–25). The issue of academic tenure impinged on the decision, as well; the oath was regarded as "open[ing] the way for the imposition of any kind of tyrannical requirement upon the Faculty, on penalty of being dismissed without even a hearing" (25). All eight reasons for refusing to sign the oath hinged on the protection of civil liberties within democracy and the attendant rights to academic freedom. This intricate, esteemed, and inextricably interconnected complex of ideas and ideals was simply explained in one sentence: "The imposition of the oath . . . struck directly at Freedom by setting up a field within which thought was no longer free" (25).

THE STATE OF GEORGIA'S LOYALTY OATH, SECURITY QUESTIONNAIRE, AND ACADEMIC BILL OF RIGHTS (2004)

> We learned . . . something about how suspicion arises, and mistrust, and fear. Of men whom we had known for twenty years we heard it said, "You can't be sure of him!" Before then these were only things we had read about in books as having happened years ago or in other countries.
>
> —George R. Stewart,
> Professor of English, University of California, 1950

The infamous "year of the oath" that shook the foundations of the University of California stands as a historical backdrop for the University System of Georgia loyalty oath and security questionnaire, a document that emerged from the same era in U.S. history and continues to exist in its 1950s edition. Considered outside the context of the security questionnaire to which it is attached, the oath echoes its California counterpart in the standard call for support of state and national constitutions:

> I, _____, a citizen of _____ [State] and being an employee of the University System of Georgia and the recipient of public funds for services rendered as such employee, do hereby solemnly swear and affirm that I will support the Constitution of the United States and the Constitution of the State of Georgia. (Georgia Board 2)

The Georgia text diverges dramatically from the California text, however, when the security questionnaire that establishes the primary rhetorical bent of the Georgia document is considered. If the addendum that redefined California's constitutional oath was injurious to academic freedom and democracy, Georgia's security questionnaire perhaps presents an even more potent threat to those vital underpinnings of the contemporary university.

In a sense, Georgia's loyalty oath hardly exists apart from the questionnaire. Not only does the latter text appear first on the two-page document, it also fills the entire first page and commands two-thirds of the space on the second page, where the loyalty oath is tacked onto the end. The questionnaire clearly dominates the document, if not simply by virtue of the amount of visual space it claims, then certainly with its language. The gamut of inflammatory words and phrases that shadowed the infamous loyalty controversies of the 1940s and 1950s freight this contemporary document: "sedition," "subversive," "force," "violence," and "overthrow of the government" (Georgia Board 1). These volatile terms mark a distinct contrast with the California oath, which avoided such explosive language. Moreover, when that oath was challenged, the regents' revision included a retraction of the most explicitly provocative phrase, "overthrow of the United States Government by force or violence," even if they could not so easily revoke the idea.

The Georgia questionnaire signals no concession to lessons learned from historical struggles like the one at the University of California, although the Georgia document emerged in 1949—the very year the California controversy challenged suspect meanings of "loyalty" that were embedded in mandated pledges of support for state and national governments. In 1949, "the Georgia General Assembly passed a law requiring all faculty members in the state to sign an annual loyalty oath and fill out a one-time security questionnaire when they were initially hired" (Georgia Conference). In 1953, "Governor Talmadge declared the questions concerning memberships in certain organizations null and void," yet those questions remained on the form in 2008 (Georgia Conference). The current loyalty oath and security questionnaire evinces no recognition of court decisions in its own state in the early 1960s, ruling that "loyalty oaths were vaguely worded and that security questionnaires were too invasive" (Georgia Conference). Nor does the document offer a glimmer of acknowledgement that "from 1946 to 1954, there was a steady erosion in the support of civil liberties among those individuals and institutions we rely upon most to preserve and protect freedom of expression—the press, intellectuals, liberal politicians, lawyers, courts, and educators" (Stone 419).

In fact, the unabashed declaration in the first line of the security questionnaire discursively aligns the text with the antidemocratic viewpoints that characterized the era:

> NOTICE TO EMPLOYEES: The Sedition and Subversive Activities Act of 1953 (Ga. Laws, 1953), as amended, requires each employee to complete and sign, prior to his/her employment by the State of Georgia, a questionnaire which is designed to establish that there are no reasonable grounds to believe that he/she is a subversive person. (Georgia Board 1)

The undercurrents of suspicion that inflect the timbre of the opening line continue in the second:

> A subversive person is defined as one who commits acts, advocates, or teaches the overthrow of the government of the United States or government of the State of Georgia by force or violence or who is a knowing member of a subversive organization. (1)

The questionnaire then asks, in even more chillingly recognizable language:

> Are you now or have you been within the last ten (10) years a member of any organization which to your knowledge at the time of membership advocates or has as one of its objectives, the overthrow of the government of the United States or the government of the State of Georgia by force or violence? (1)

If a signer of the questionnaire dares answer "yes" to this query, and "the employing authority deems further inquiry is necessary," the person has "an opportunity . . . to present evidence," presumably in her/his own defense (1). This scenario, seemingly implausible in the United States in 2008, mirrors programs in the late 1940s that hauled suspicious federal employees before loyalty boards under President Truman's Executive Order No. 9835 (Stone 344). Stone describes the particular historical context and national climate strongly supported by the language of Georgia's archaic oath and questionnaire:

> The Cold War, which followed hard on the heels of World War II, marked perhaps the most repressive period in American history. In an aggressive effort to uncover subversion, the federal government initiated abusive loyalty programs, legislative investigations, and criminal prosecutions of the leaders and members of the Communist Party of the United States. (12–13)

The force of history is clearly evident in the questionnaire's current language, which moves beyond intimidating to almost menacing. The loyalty lexicon that it favors remains so explicitly redolent of anticommunist panic and rampant McCarthyism that unfounded accusations of political disloyalty inevitably loom. It is this historical context that breathes particular contemporary meanings into Georgia's loyalty oath and security questionnaire. The rhetorical capabilities this document has at its command are problematic, especially in this Deep South state at this post-9/11 moment.

The very words "Are you now or have you ever been" intimate residual risks that shade this infamous question for academics in Georgia, especially given the March 22, 2004, adoption of SR 661, titled the Academic Bill of Rights at Georgia Private and Public Universities (ABOR) (Georgia General, "Adopted"). This version of the ABOR, like the thus-far-failed federal version, aims to commend "academic freedom as indispensable to the American university," and asserts that "the concept of academic freedom has been premised on the idea that human knowledge is the pursuit of truth, [and] that there is no humanly accessible truth that is not in principle open to challenge" (Georgia General, "Adopted"). David Horowitz, the ABOR's primary advocate, describes the resolution's purpose differently. He reasons that the aim is to "enumerate the rights of students to not be indoctrinated or otherwise assaulted by political propagandists in the classroom or any educational setting" (B12). Horowitz offers no definition of "political propagandists," but an earlier draft of the ABOR perhaps sheds some light on the politically conservative perspective he represents.

This version of the ABOR suggests that the resolution was written, at least in part, to oversee the humanities, the social sciences, and the arts. Considered together, the introduced and adopted versions of the ABOR raise concerns about the definition of academic freedom operating at this rhetorical site at this time. Significantly, the draft first introduced to legislators cautioned that "curricula and reading lists in the humanities, the social sciences, and the arts shall respect the uncertainty and unsettled character of all human knowledge in these areas and provide students with dissenting sources and viewpoints" (Georgia General, "Introduced"). No other disciplines—other than those that tend to attract the highest percentage of liberals or leftists—were mentioned. No other fields—other than those more open to a range of political perspectives, more likely to eschew traditional understandings of "knowledge," and more willing to flout boundaries drawn by conservative political agendas—were mentioned. If indeed, "human knowledge is a never-ending pursuit of truth, . . . there is no humanly accessible truth that is not in principle open to challenge, and . . . no party or intellectual faction has a monopoly on wisdom," the impulse to single out only some of those "intellectual factions" for special surveillance, whether the words naming the unsettled areas were nullified or not, suggests a troubling bias (Georgia General, "Introduced").

The draft language that called to accountability the humanities, the social sciences, and the arts does not appear in the adopted version of the ABOR, but, like the first draft of the California addendum, although the words were deleted, the presumption that generated the language in the first place is less easily rescinded. It is not inconceivable, then, that a professor attached to these already-suspect disciplines, especially one who openly endorses an antiwar perspective in the current political climate that favors loyalty oaths as security mechanisms, might unwittingly invite the state's description of a "subversive person" (Georgia Board 1). Defined as "one who commits acts, advocates, or teaches the overthrow of the government of the United States or the government of the State of Georgia by force or violence or who is knowingly a member of a subversive organization," the "subversive person" is not invulnerable to co-optation and redefinition to suit a particular political agenda (Georgia Board 1). Granted, considerable rhetorical tailoring would be required to transform Horowitz's "political propagandist" into the state's "subversive person" (B12). But Wolf describes a national climate amenable to such a project: "State legislators in the United States are putting pressure on regents to put pressure on academics who criticize the Bush agenda—another tactic with historical antecedents" (107). Positing the possibility that "subversive person" could be redefined to suit a campaign to close down democracy is perhaps not overly alarmist, given that in a fascist shift "certain subjects become too charged to address, or begin to be avoided altogether, because addressing them carries possible criminal penalties" (Wolf 134). It is likely no coincidence, then, that the very disciplines that tend to take up "certain subjects" and submit them to analysis and critique are the very ones that the ABOR targeted for surveillance in 2004.

Although the ABOR is a resolution and provides no enforcement mechanism, it nonetheless exists as a visible and trenchant reminder to academics and other public employees of the State of Georgia's political position. The state is rhetorically equipped to assume the authority to demand compliance with its antidemocratic dictates when the governing body's ABOR is coupled with its security questionnaire and loyalty oath. Most likely, these texts work together to bolster the current conservative rereadings of both state and national constitutions to which academics in Georgia must pledge their allegiance. The ABOR claims the power of recommendation only, but the security questionnaire and loyalty oath provide rhetorical strategies to sidestep that limitation and identify subversives if and when necessary. Conceivably, liberal arts professors in the state of Georgia could be accused under the rubric stipulated in the ABOR, tried under the definitions of the security questionnaire, and dismissed from their jobs with loyalty oath rhetoric.

Given the history of government coercion in which the Georgia document is embedded, the fiery rhetoric it continues to flaunt, and the forthright affront to democratic principles it represents, the stunning lack of controversy about the state's loyalty oath and security questionnaire—a document egregiously indicative of the post-9/11 agenda to watch, to control, to silence—is surprising. And given Annette Kolodny's recent and compelling argument that reiterates others to insist that "both tenure and academic freedom are in crisis again," the current paucity of public and scholarly protest about loyalty oaths in general moves beyond surprising to disquieting (23). Like the California oath, the Georgia security questionnaire is in coalition with other texts and subtexts that variously lend it meaning. Both documents are illustrative of a distinctly political—if arguably fascist—discourse of oaths, pledges, and security questionnaires, all of which coalesce into a complex rhetoric of loyalty that has long been woven into the fabric of the nation and into American institutions of higher education. The version that infused the University of California after World War II prompted rancorous debate and stalwart resistance, while another version that continues to pervade public universities in Georgia has generated insufficient discussion and opposition. If the alarm Wolf raises rings true, if indeed "some Americans, especially civil servants and members of the military, risk losing their jobs if they take up the patriot's task and speak out," the burgeoning presence of loyalty oaths in universities across the nation necessitates vigorous rhetorical resistance in this post-9/11 era (154).

THE RESPONSIBILITIES OF RHETORIC (2008)

I am calling your attention to important lessons from history about how fragile civil liberties are, and how quickly freedom can be lost.

—Naomi Wolf, Author and Political Activist, 2007

According to Wolf, "clear lessons from history" predicted in 2007 that "White House spokespeople would begin to use terms such as *treason, espio-*

nage, subversion, and *aiding the enemy* to describe criticism, press scrutiny, dissent, and even simple departure from alignment with White House goals" (14–15). A rhetorically transparent document such as Georgia's security questionnaire signals its ready complicity to take part in agendas that aim to criminalize dissent and justify antidemocratic policies. Oaths that adopt the tone of California's prior to the objectionable addendum seemingly stand in contrast, the indeterminate word choice less immediately alarming. Yet, as history attests, this latter category of oath is equally poised to participate in antidemocratic agendas when a fresh "set of assaults suddenly pushes the nation into a new and degraded reality" (14).

Although the loyalty lexicon favored in the Georgia text likely strikes an unfamiliar chord, those explosive terms often relegated to historical conflicts now considered resolved, the language preferred by the California oath is almost certainly recognizable. Given the prevalence of epideictic rhetoric, such as the Pledge of Allegiance that children continue to recite in schools across the nation, this oath is perhaps read in the current political milieu as a harmless recitation, at worst, and a patriotic display of national unity, at best. Or perhaps the quieter threat represented by this type of oath goes largely unnoticed, for, as Wolf observes, "Most of us have only a faint understanding of how societies open up or close down, become supportive of freedom or ruled by fear, because this is not the kind of history that we feel, or that our educational system believes, is important for us to know" (4).

One category of oath considered here obliges citizens to swear loyalty with deceptively innocuous promises to support constitutions. Another threatens potentially disloyal citizens with intimidating language. Both, however, suggest ways oaths might be (re)written or (re)interpreted to enlist other rhetorical artifacts in the performance of new cultural work—such as easing into place massive political change. The potential to subvert democracy resides ever present in both texts, if "in every fascist shift, more and more kinds of speech and protest become cast as 'treason,' 'terrorism,' 'subversion,' 'espionage,' or 'sabotage'" (Wolf 133). As the California controversy exemplifies, the omission of the most incendiary terms from oaths fails to render the text impervious to dangerous revisions and reinterpretations. Fifty years ago, as well as at the present moment, swearing to support state and national constitutions invariably means swearing to support changeable, unpredictable, and ultimately unknowable subtexts and contexts—even swearing to support antidemocratic efforts, as history attests.

Gardner's prescient words written in 1967 about California speak to Georgia and to the whole of the United States even now: "While the University of California loyalty oath controversy is inextricably a part of the legal, political, and educational history of mid-twentieth century America, the issues which constituted the conflict remain essentially unresolved and promise, perhaps more firmly than before, to erupt again into public debate" (viii). His words speak to rhetoric especially, our discipline long assuming the responsibility to press critical questions about democracy, academic freedom, civil liberties, public discourse, and civic participation. Resounding with urgency, his words are relegated to the past at democracy's peril. To dismiss loyalty oaths and security questionnaires—both those riddled with menacing words such as "sedition" and "violence," and those rife with disconcerting ideas in the guise of patriotic pledges to constitutions—is to risk "clos[ing] down our experiment in democracy in ways that would look very American and familiar, but still leave us less than free" (Wolf 149).

In this first decade of the twenty-first century, rhetoric is responsible for making inquiries into how loyalty oaths operating at specific times and places, such as the post-9/11 United States, might lend themselves to "new laws or new interpretations of existing laws" (Wolf 134). Rhetoric is responsible for mounting vocal challenges to laws such as those requiring new or altered pledges of loyalty that "seek to establish new categories of offenses that criminalize citizens' ideas, actions, or speech" (133–34). Rhetoric is responsible for monitoring changes to all legislation pertaining to academic freedom, since, as Wolf points out, "Often the laws that criminalize dissent in a fascist shift are enacted quietly" (139).

Above all, rhetoric is responsible for gleaning lessons in responsibility from the historical model left by the nonsigners of the California loyalty oath in 1949–1950. The thirty-one faculty members who resisted the profoundly antidemocratic "'sign-or-get-out'" law did so "in terms of next month's bills, or the daughter to be kept in college, or the payments on the house and the baby due in the summer, or the ever-recurrent thought, 'At my age, could I get another job?'" (Stewart 9). Despite experiencing firsthand what Wolf terms "the threat of violence against the individual," a tactic she considers paramount to a fascist shift, the nonsigners nonetheless stood firm on principle to defend not only academic freedom but also the full repertoire of foundational democratic principles on which the contemporary university depends (21). If the University of California, as one among many "institutions of civil society," was eventually and evidently "subordinated to the power of the state" (Wolf 21) during a grim era, the nonsigners left a legacy of resistance that, more than half a century later, provides a paradigmatic and eminently hopeful rhetoric of contravention at this not dissimilar historical moment.

Works Cited

Gardner, David P. *The California Oath Controversy.* Berkeley: U of California P, 1967.

Georgia Board of Regents. "Loyalty Oath." Revised 1999. 28 Sept. 20008. <http://www.busfin.uga.edu/forms/security_oath.pdf>.

Georgia Conference of the American Association of University Professors. Georgia Institute of Technology. 28 Sept. 2008. <http://www.library.gatech.edu/archives/finding-aids/display/xsl/MS033>.

Georgia General Assembly. Senate Resolution 661. Academic Bill of Rights at Georgia Private and Public Universities; observance. 3 Feb. 2004 (Introduced). 28 Sept. 2008. <http://www.legis.state.ga.us/legis/2003_04/versions/sr661_As_introduced_LC_18__2.htm>.

————. Senate Resolution 661. Academic Bill of Rights at Georgia Private and Public Universities; observance. 22 Mar. 2004 (Adopted). 28 Sept. 2008. <http://www.legis.state.ga.us/legis/2003_04/versions/sr661_Adopted_Senate_5.htm>.

Horowitz, David. "In Defense of Intellectual Diversity." *Chronicle of Higher Education* 13 Feb. 2004: B12–13.

Kantorowicz, Ernst H. *The Fundamental Issue: Documents and Marginal Notes on the University of California Loyalty Oath.* San Francisco: Parker Printing, 1950.

Kolodny, Annette. "Tenure, Academic Freedom, and the Career I Once Loved." *Academe* 94 (2008): 22–26.

Ross, Michael E. "Free Speech Concerns in Colo. Campus Spotlight." 16 Mar. 2005. 28 Sept. 2008. <http://www.msnbc.msn.com/id/7047993>.

Stewart, George R. *The Year of the Oath: The Fight for Academic Freedom at the University of California.* New York: Doubleday, 1950.

Stone, Geoffrey R. *Perilous Times: Free Speech in Wartime from the Sedition Act of 1798 to the War on Terrorism.* New York: W.W. Norton, 2004.

Talbott, Clint. "Swear Loyalty or Be Fired." *Daily Camera* 26 Feb. 2005. 28 Sept. 2008. <http://209.157.64.200/focus/f-news/1351914/posts>.

Wolf, Naomi. *The End of America: Letter of Warning to a Young Patriot.* White River Junction, VT: Chelsea Green, 2007.

Scholarship of Engagement
Both a *New Name For* and a *Challenge To* the Work of Rhetoric

Richard C. Gebhardt

> Let us . . . consider The Responsibilities of Rhetoric. How can the study and practice of rhetoric contribute to social progress? What does rhetoric offer as means of understanding and coping with globalization . . .? What do rhetorical studies have to offer in a presidential election year when political discourses and popular fundamentalisms are polarizing, confrontational, divisive? How do new media affect civic participation and the conduct of argument . . .? How can rhetorical studies contribute to scientific exchange, technology transfer, and risk management—all in the interest of public . . . good . . .?
>
> —From the 2008 RSA Conference Call

For well over a decade, a new expectation has been evolving for faculty: to be engaged with challenges and issues facing society and to make such engaged activity the object of research and publication. This expectation reflects ideas from *Scholarship Reconsidered* (Boyer) and *Scholarship Assessed* (Glassick, Huber, and Maeroff), from Ernest Boyer's 1996 article "The Scholarship of Engagement," and from many higher education reports and conferences intended to promote increasing engagement of universities with their communities and regions, and beyond.

Much of this new expectation centers on engaged activity by institutions, faculty, and students—service learning is a prime example—whether or not that activity results in research or publications. But the scholarship of engagement movement is not really about engaged activity of the kind that, typically, would be included in the service or teaching sections of a merit review or promotion file. Rather, it seeks to integrate the faculty member's roles as scholar, teacher, and citizen. Eugene Rice, for instance, sees scholarship of engagement promoting "a broader definition of scholarship" in which "the four primary dimensions of scholarly work—discovery, integration, teaching, and engagement—are fundamentally interrelated" ("Future" 307). And Kelly Ward emphasizes that this integration is necessary for higher education to address broad social issues and serve the public good. For an institution "to serve the public good, an integrated view of faculty work is necessary" ("Rethinking" 231). So Ward writes that "to fulfill the goals of the scholarship of engagement, scholars must link their teaching, research, and service to community problems, challenges, and goals, whether the community served is the department, the university, the town, state, nation, or the global community" (231).

ENGAGED SCHOLARSHIP IN RHETORIC AND COMPOSITION

Clearly, concern for the public good is nothing new for a field that from ancient times has prepared people for effective citizenship and that, today, is involved in writing instruction, leadership of first-year writing and WAC/WID programs, the preparation of teachers for America's schools, and community outreach and service-learning programs. In fact, we can see evidence of this kind of engagement of our field in the theme-setting conference call for the 2008 Rhetoric Society of America meeting. It implies that "The Responsibilities of Rhetoric" include contributing "to social progress," providing "means of understanding and coping with globalization," helping address "political discourses and popular fundamentalisms [that] are polarizing, confrontational, divisive," and promoting "scientific exchange, technology transfer, and risk management—all in the interest of public . . . good." Clearly, too, the efforts of rhetoric faculty in pursuit of such goals frequently lead to refereed publications in which authors describe and theorize their work. Indeed, many women and men in quite a few areas of rhetoric and composition now are doing—and long have done—engaged scholarship. Likely, you sense this intuitively, as I did even before a 2007 sabbatical research project led me to appreciate the amount, and especially the variety, of engaged scholarship in rhetoric and composition.

The previous paragraph's sketch of the engagement of our field and its publications suggests a positive or optimistic future for rhetoric and composition in an era of engagement. From this perspective, engaged scholarship may be a new name for what many rhetoric and composition faculty do: a badge we can display to our benefit on campuses where scholarship of engagement is emphasized in budgeting and personnel decisions. Working from this optimistic perspective, I think that rhetoric and composition faculty should use the engaged nature of our field to our advantage, where and when we can, and that our professional organizations should do the same—as the Rhetoric Society of America seems to be doing when it emphasizes the responsibilities of rhetoric in its 2008 conference and in this book.

Engaged Research in the Scholarship of Engagement Movement

This optimistic view of rhetoric and composition in our era of engagement depends on a sense of engaged research broader than the definition most often used in the scholarship of engagement movement. Like many faculty, I see engaged scholarship centered on a broad ideal—exploring current problems, addressing social issues, advancing the public good. This ideal is important for the scholarship of engagement movement, something rooted in Ernest Boyer's 1996 statement that "the scholarship of engagement means connecting the rich resources of the university to the most pressing social, civic, and ethical problems" ("Scholarship of Engagement" 19). Or as *Scholarship Assessed* put it, "the scholarship of application . . . moves toward engagement as the scholar asks, 'How can knowledge be responsibly applied to consequential problems?' " (Glassick, Huber, and Maeroff 9).

Besides trying to apply knowledge responsibly to "pressing social, civic, and ethical problems," the scholarship of engagement movement calls for extensive, thoroughgoing collaboration of the university-based scholar with other stakeholders in the research. For example, a Bowling Green State University scholarship of engagement document grounded in committee review of some thirty sources sees scholarship of engagement as helping "solve pressing public problems and contribut[ing] to the public good" through "a true collaboration with community partners who help define the problem, develop plans to address it, and play an important role in assessment" (Report 3). *Engaged Scholarship: A Guide for Organizational and Social Research* describes it as "a participatory form of research for obtaining the different perspectives of key stakeholders . . . [in order] to obtain and be informed by the interpretations of others about *each step of the research process*: problem formulation, theory building, research design, and problem solving" (Van de Ven 265, emphasis added). And Eugene Rice emphasizes that engaged scholarship "involve[s] *sharing the results* of such work with the wider community as well as academic colleagues" ("'Scholarship'" 28, emphasis in original).

This dominant definition of research in the scholarship of engagement movement suggests a less positive view of how rhetoric and composition may fare in an era of engagement. It emphasizes both the focus of research—things of significance in community settings where there are identifiable people with whom to collaborate—and the methodology. Of course, much good work is being done in our field that fits within this definition of engaged research. During my review of engaged scholarly publication in rhetoric and composition, I came to call this Explicit Engaged Scholarship—for instance, community-based research that reflects the spirit of Ellen Cushman's title "The Rhetorician as an Agent of Social Change." But other rhetoric and composition faculty work to study or address critical social issues without using anything like the collaborative, social sciences approach of the dominant definition. And, as the sketch of rhetoric's responsibilities found earlier suggests, our field has a wide-ranging agenda for engaged research. Besides Explicit Engaged Scholarship centering in the community, three other categories of engaged work show up in the publications of our field—what I call Background Engaged Scholarship, Broad Engaged Scholarship, and Public-Writing Engaged Scholarship ("Composition"). Even without details, these labels suggest my point. Of the four broad kinds of engaged scholarship I see in rhetoric and composition, only one has an explicit connection to the dominant definition of research used by scholarship of engagement advocates.

I used the word "advocates" deliberately. For scholarship of engagement is part of an activist movement that seeks to change the nature of faculty work—integrating the faculty roles of teacher, researcher, and citizen—and to increase all kinds of engagement of the university with the community and society at large. The activism shows in books and reports with titles like *Higher Education for the Public Good* (Kezar, Chambers, and Burkhardt), *Establishing Universities as Citizens* (Rothman), *Engaging Departments* (Kecskes), *Faculty Priorities Reconsidered* (O'Meara and Rice), and *New Times Demand New Scholarship*. Works like these provide thoughtful discussions about engagement by scholars and academic leaders strongly committed to it. They also offer approaches intended to promote a culture of engagement on individual campuses and across American higher education. For example, James Votruba writes, "*Institutional resources need to be reallocated* in order to support the scholarship of engagement," and that "faculty . . . reward systems should be redesigned" since "*without proper incentives, faculty are unlikely to change their ways*" (39, emphasis added). And Eugene Rice writes, "We have a rare opportunity to *shape* a new generation of faculty or . . . *choose a new configuration* of academic staff [that has] the potential for greatly enhancing the substance and effectiveness of the scholarship that a changing society requires" ("The Future" 304, emphasis added).

RECONSIDERING ENGAGED SCHOLARSHIP

Such top-down efforts to change campus culture often trigger faculty suspicion and resistance, but my intent is not to attribute dark motives to the efforts of individuals and organizations to make American higher education more engaged. Key to the engagement movement, after all, is something I have been advocating for nearly twenty years—expanding the idea of scholarship in faculty work and rewards (e.g., see "Avoiding"). Still, I am concerned about how narrowly scholarship of engagement often gets defined, and about what this may mean for a field in which so many faculty are doing substantial engaged research that does not fit within the dominant definition of the scholarship of engagement movement. Since this situation poses a considerable challenge to the work of rhetoric and how that work is regarded and rewarded, we should seek a broader, more inclusive idea of engaged scholarship that does not exclude out of hand much good work by rhetoric and composition faculty.

As a start, we should not accept uncritically—or let our departments adopt without vigorous debate—narrow definitions of engaged scholarship. "Community," for instance, is a broader idea within the engagement movement than it may seem in passages being considered for quotation in personnel documents. Rather than being limited to the area immediately surrounding a college or university, "community is broadly defined to include audiences external to the campus" (Clearinghouse). And the campus itself may be part of "community" when—as many in rhetoric and composition do—faculty engage their scholarly expertise beyond their own departments (see Ward, *Faculty* 127, 112–15). Even within a narrower, beyond-the-campus definition, the growing emphasis on "the public good" and "civic education" within the engagement movement points toward a national or even international idea of community—and, of course, toward issues with much relevance to the work of rhetoric.

Second, we should be aware that the dominant definition of engaged research, collaborating with people in the community from the definition of the research problem through the reporting of results, is not the only methodology for engaged research. Indeed, one frequent publisher within the movement writes that "*traditional research* can (and often does) meet community needs and support the advancement of the public good. This takes place through knowledge production (*regardless of whether it was accrued through community collaboration* . . .) that contributes to the public good" (Ward, "Rethinking" 221, emphasis added).

Finally, with perspectives like these in mind, we should advocate in our journals, within our professional associations, and among colleagues at our institutions for a broader idea of engaged scholarship: one that does not presume a geographical region close to campus or specify a single kind of research to be conducted in collaboration with community stakeholders, but one that encourages faculty to bring the full array of rhetoric and composition research approaches to bear on issues and problems important to society and its future. And when our national organizations speak out about the significant engagement of rhetoric and composition, as the Rhetoric Society of America is doing with its emphasis on the *responsibilities* of rhetoric, we should lend our support to their efforts and invoke them as we work toward an inclusive view of engaged scholarship.

Works Cited

Boyer, Ernest L. "The Scholarship of Engagement." *Journal of Public Outreach* 1.1 (1996): 11–20.

———. *Scholarship Reconsidered: Priorities of the Professoriate*. Princeton: Carnegie Foundation for the Advancement of Teaching, 1990.

Clearinghouse for the Scholarship of Engagement. "What Is the Scholarship of Engagement?" 5 May 2008. <http://schoe.coe.uga.edu/about/FAQs.html>.

Cushman, Ellen. "The Rhetorician as an Agent of Social Change." *CCC* 47.1 (Feb. 1996): 7–28.

Gebhardt, Richard C. "Avoiding the 'Research versus Teaching' Trap: Expanding the Criteria for Evaluating Scholarship." *The Politics and Processes of Scholarship.* Ed. Joseph M. Moxley and Lagretta T. Lenker. Westport, CT: Greenwood, 1995. 9–17.

———. "Composition Scholarship and the Scholarship of Engagement." Conference on College Composition and Communication. New Orleans. 4 Apr. 2008.

Glassick, Charles, Mary Taylor Huber, and Gene I. Maeroff. *Scholarship Assessed: Evaluation of the Professoriate.* San Francisco: Jossey-Bass, 1997.

Kecskes, Kevin, ed. *Engaging Departments: Moving Faculty Culture From Private to Public, Individual to Collective Focus for the Common Good.* Bolton, MA: Anker, 2006.

Kezar, Adrianna, Tony Chambers, and John Burkhardt, eds. *Higher Education for the Public Good: Emerging Voices from a National Movement.* San Francisco: Jossey-Bass, 2005.

New Times Demand New Scholarship: Research Universities and Civic Engagement. Report of the 2005 Tufts University Conference on Research Universities and Civic Engagement. 14 Jan. 2008. <http://www.compact.org/initiatives/research_universities/conference_report.pdf>.

O'Meara, KerryAnn, and R. Eugene Rice, eds. *Faculty Priorities Reconsidered: Rewarding Multiple Forums of Scholarship.* San Francisco: Jossey Bass, 2005.

Report of the Standards Committee on the Scholarship of Engagement. Aug. 2005. Bowling Green State University. 3 Feb. 2008. <http://www.bgsu.edu/downloads/bgsu/file13272.pdf>.

Rice, R. Eugene. "The Future of the Scholarly Work of Faculty." *Faculty Priorities Reconsidered: Rewarding Multiple Forums of Scholarship.* Ed. KerryAnn O'Meara and R. Eugene Rice. San Francisco: Jossey Bass, 2005. 303–12.

———. "'Scholarship Reconsidered': History and Context." *Faculty Priorities Reconsidered: Rewarding Multiple Forums of Scholarship.* Ed. KerryAnn O'Meara and R. Eugene Rice. San Francisco: Jossey Bass, 2005. 17–31.

Rothman, Michael, ed. *Establishing Universities as Citizens: Towards the Scholarship of Engagement.* Indianapolis: Indiana Campus Compact, 1998.

Van de Ven, Andrew H. *Engaged Scholarship: A Guide for Organizational and Social Research.* New York: Oxford UP, 2007.

Votruba, James. "Organizational Change." *Establishing Universities as Citizens: Towards the Scholarship of Engagement.* Ed. Michael Rothman. Indianapolis: Indiana Campus Compact, 1998. 38–39.

Ward, Kelly. *Faculty Service Roles and the Scholarship of Engagement.* ASHE-ERIC Higher Education Report 29.5. San Francisco: Jossey-Bass, 2003.

———. "Rethinking Faculty Roles and Rewards for the Public Good." *Higher Education for the Public Good: Emerging Voices from a National Movement.* Ed. Adrianna Kezar, Tony Chambers, and John Burkhardt. San Francisco: Jossey-Bass, 2005. 217–34.

Gender Equity in the Rhetoric Society of America

Cheryl Geisler

When considering issues of academic advancement, most of us turn our eyes to our local institutions, the universities and colleges that pay our salaries and shape our working hours spent in teaching and service. Indeed when we speak of "moving through the ranks," we picture in our minds movement in our home universities. Consistent with this focus on the university as the core institution responsible for academic advancement, the National Science Foundation (NSF) has, since 2001, invested significant resources in thirty-two universities to "support academic institutional transformation to promote the increased participation and advancement of women scientists and engineers in academe." These NSF Advance Institutional Transformation Awards challenge universities to find ways to change policy and change culture. Since 2006, as part of my university's NSF-supported effort, I have become increasingly aware of the many ways in which our local institutions can either help or hinder the advancement of women.

The Rhetoric Society of America (RSA) is an example of a second kind of institution that has a bearing on our lives as academic professionals, a professional society that works at a national level and addresses itself in large part to their third leg of our working lives, our scholarship. The responsibility of professional societies in creating and maintaining the discipline-specific collegium that sustains our scholarly work is well defined. The RSA, like other professional societies, takes at least some responsibility for the mechanisms by which new members are recruited and trained in rhetorical studies. It subsidizes student membership. It provides forums through which potential members can interact with more senior colleagues over important issues. And, most recently, it has created summer institutes to provide more in-depth training to new members on a wide variety of scholarly topics.

The RSA, also like most professional societies, oversees many mechanisms through which the work of continuing members is evaluated and recognized. Through its peer-reviewed conference programs and journals, it ensures that the best work is disseminated. Through its awards, it rewards strong scholars and projects. Indeed, through these efforts it mints the coin of the realm in academic advancement, those entries into our curriculum vitae that home institutions count toward tenure and promotion.

The RSA also plays a role in academic advancement through many more informal mechanisms. Through conferences such as this one, it sustains the collegial network that sparks our creativity and structures our opportunities. Out of these networks come the editorial boards and journal reviewers who step forward to ensure our scholarly standards. Links in this network, direct or once removed, form the basis for the external letters of review most universities expect in promotion and tenure cases. When we write in such letters that, "Though I do not know the candidate personally, we are well aware of her solid contributions . . ." or "I have had the pleasure of following his career over the past few years and consider him to be one of the rising stars . . ." it is this collegial network that enables us to make such statements. Indeed, if the RSA and other professional societies were to disappear tomorrow, not many years would need to pass before such assessments would become nearly impossible to write. This is just one example of the way in which local university advancement systems are intertwined with professional societies.

Despite their obviously central role in academic advancement, however, the impact of professional societies on how women advance through the ranks is not well understood. Nor do we have clear ideas about the appropriate level of responsibility that professional societies should have for ensuring gender equity. The purpose of this essay, then, is to provide some important background for this discussion by looking at three areas. First, we will briefly review the overall situation for academic women. Second, we will look at the specific situation for women in the RSA. And finally, we will suggest some basic categories for the kinds of activities that the RSA might undertake in response to this situation.

Gender and Academic Advancement

The balance of gender in the academy, like the shift in the national workforce generally, is a relatively recent phenomenon. Between the end of World War II and the mid-1960s, the percentage of doctorates going to women was a stable 11 percent. After 1965, it rose rapidly to 35 percent at which point, in the 1980s, it leveled off. In the 1990s the percentage began rising once more, steadily increasing to 40 percent by 1996 (National Research Council) and to 47 percent by 2002 (Loeb).

The increase in earned doctorates going to women in humanities has followed this general pattern, but had reached parity (50 percent) earlier, at least by 1996. In earned doctorates in speech/rhetorical studies, women have been outpacing men since 1993 when women earned 54 percent of the doctorates; by 1996, the percentage was 59 percent.

When we look at these senior ranks nationally, we find that despite the increasing numbers of women earning doctorate degrees, the number of women at the senior level in the academy has remained quite low. According to the American Association of University Professors (AAUP), which has been monitoring the representation of women in the ranks for many years, only 20 percent of academic women had reached the rank of full professor in 2007–2008 while nearly 40 percent of men have done so (30). That is, a woman is less than half as likely to have reached the rank of full professor as her male colleague.

A comparable discrepancy exists in what my colleagues and I have called the 13+ Club, the cohort of faculty who are 13 or more years since advanced degree (Geisler, Kaminski, and Berkley). When monitoring of the 13+ Club first began at Rensselaer Polytechnic Institute in 2001, women were 2.3 times more likely to remain unpromoted as men in the club; by 2004, this index had dropped to 2.1 and by 2007, it had dropped again to 1.7. In 6 years, then, one university saw the discrepancy in promotion to full professor improve by more than 25 percent.

ACADEMIC ADVANCEMENT IN THE RSA

Turning to the RSA itself, we look at an analysis taken from the membership rolls as they existed on January 1, 2006. Of the 727 members on that date, the 433 who held faculty positions in the United States were selected for examination. Excluded were those who were students (279), international (13), or unclassified (2).

A sample of the data used for analysis in shown in table 1. In addition to name (Cheryl Geisler), these rolls contained information about institutional affiliation (Rensselaer), which was used as a starting point for a Web-based search to establish current rank (professor) and a search through dissertation abstracts to establish date of degree (1986) and then to calculate years since degree in 2006 (20). Information was completed for 93 percent of the selected RSA members, for a total of 403 members, who were included in the analysis that follows.

Table 1.   Sample Data Entry

Name	Institution	Rank	Place of Degree	Year of Degree	Years since Degree in 2006
Cheryl Geisler	Rensselaer	Professor	Carnegie Mellon	1986	20

The analysis shows, to begin with, that the gender balance of the RSA membership has reached parity. Of the 403 members in 2006, 205 were men and 198 were women. In terms of overall representations, then, RSA membership mirrors representation in the academy, which reached parity by 2007–08 (AAUP).

Disparities arise, however, when we look at representation in the senior ranks. Figure 1, for example, shows how the academic ranks of men change with increasing years since degree. In the 13+ Club (the area to the right of the vertical line), only 31 percent of the men have not reached the rank of full professor. That is, fully two-thirds of these men have been promoted to full professorship. Figure 2 shows comparable data for women. Here we see that fully 53 percent of the women have not reached the rank of full professor, more than half. Overall, then, in the 13+ Club in the RSA, women are 1.7 times more likely to remain unpromoted than men.

This overall picture of disparity needs to be tempered, however, by a recognition that conditions have changed over time. As the National Research Council data on earned doctorates reviewed earlier suggests, the representation of women among doctoral degree holders has changed dramatically over the last 60 years. Figure 3, which shows the gender composition of the six degree cohorts active in the RSA in 2006, confirms that this has been true for the members of the RSA as well.

In figure 3, the grey line indicates that for the first 30 years since degree, the size of the degree cohorts among the men has been fairly constant, on average 43 members. More specifically, when we look at the men of the RSA, we see roughly equal degree cohorts, including 44 newly minted assistant professors (0–6 years out), 46 mid-career faculty (6–12 years out), and 41 and

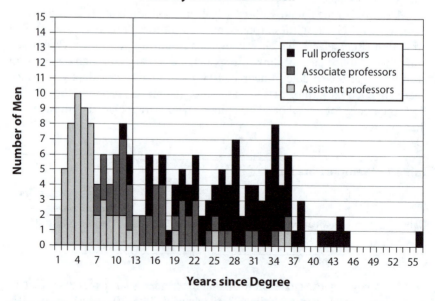

Figure 1.   Number of men at each rank at increasing years since terminal degree.

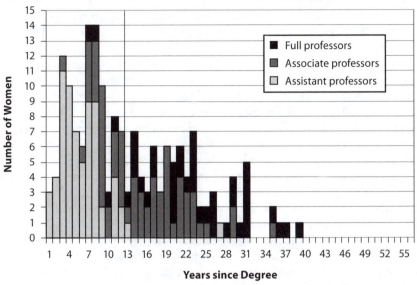

Figure 2. Number of women at each rank at increasing years since terminal degree.

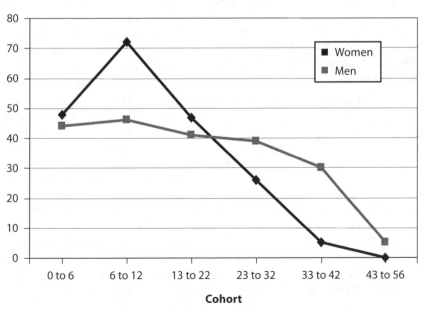

Figure 3. Size of degree cohorts in the RSA membership.

39 senior faculty respectively in the two 10-year cohorts making up the younger generations of the 13+ Club (13–22 years out and 23–32 years out). Only when we reach the two cohorts with the greatest longevity (33–42 years out and 43–56 years out) do we see a decline in cohort size (to 30 and then to 5), due at least in part to members' retirement.

The story for the women of RSA is quite different (as shown by the black line in figure 3). In the two most senior cohorts, of those who graduated before 1974 (33–42 years out and 43–56 years out), women are almost absent (5 and then 0). But, in the middle cohorts, those who completed dissertations before 1993 (13–22 years out and 23–32 years out), the size of women's degree cohorts roughly equals men's. And finally, in the mid-career cohort, those who competed degrees between 1994 and 2000 (6–12 years out), the size of the women's cohort is actually significantly larger than that of the men. Interestingly, with the most junior cohort, those completing since 2000 (0–6 years out), the cohort sizes of men and women return to near comparability.

These very different patterns in the size of degree cohorts is important to recognize for it creates what Hargens and Long have called demographic inertia. Because of the historical overrepresentation of male faculty among the cohorts with the greatest longevity, these demographers point out, nearly a generation will have to pass before the changes in gender balance at the degree-granting stage could be reflected in the gender composition of the academy, especially among senior ranks.

The data in table 2 suggest that we are part way through this generational change. Here we see the rates of nonpromotion to full professor compared for the three degree cohorts making up the 13+ Club. The third column gives the index or differential in rate of nonpromotion for women compared to men. No comparison has been given for the cohort 43–56 years out because no women are in this group. For the next most senior group, 33–42 years out, we see that the discrepancy in rates of non-promotions is far worse than for the RSA as a whole. That

Table 2. Rate of Nonpromotion for Men and Women in the 13+ Club by Degree Cohort

	Women	Men	Index
13–22	0.68	0.59	1.2
23–32	0.31	0.15	2.0
33–42	0.20	0.07	3.0

is, women in this generation are fully three times more likely to remain unpromoted to full professor than their male colleagues. In the next degree cohort, 23–32 years out, this discrepancy is reduced, but still substantial: Women are twice as likely as their male colleagues to remain unpromoted. But by the time we get to the youngest cohort in the 13+ Club, those 13–22 years out, we are approaching, though still not at, parity. Women are 1.2 times more likely than their male colleagues to remain unpromoted.

PROFESSIONAL SOCIETY RESPONSE

At this point in our history, then, the RSA appears to be at a crossroads in terms of achieving gender equity in the senior ranks. The current demographic momentum has begun to reduce gender disparities, but complacency should not deflect us from considering ways in which the RSA could and even should work to promote greater equity. But what can a professional society do in terms of gender equity? What have other professional societies been doing?

To begin to address this question, table 3 shows a sample of organizations within professional societies whose main purpose is to foster the advancement of women in their disciplines. With the exception of the Coalition of Women Scholars in the History of Rhetoric and Composition, most of these organizations operate in the sciences where the lack of women is seen

Table 3.   Organizations within Professional Societies Who Work for the Advancement of Women in Their Disciplines and Some of Their Efforts

Association for Women in Science http://www.awis.org/	• For fee professional coaching service for those considering a career transition, advancement issues, or work-life balance
Coalition of Women Scholars in the History of Rhetoric and Composition http://www.cwshrc.org/	• Annual conference
Committee on the Status of Women in the Economics Profession http://www.cswep.org/	• Awards for women researchers • Professional development seminars • Mentor travel fund • Summer fellowship
Women Chemists Committee of the American Chemical Society http://membership.acs.org/W/WCC/	• Yearly letter writing to encourage nominations of women for society awards • Travel awards • Professional development sessions at conferences
Women in Cell Biology, Standing Committee of the American Society for Cell Biology http://www.ascb.org/index.cfm?navid=89	• Annual award to women researchers • Career lunch table to provide informal mentoring • Professional development workshops • Speaker service
Women in Cognitive Science http://www.womencogsci.org/	• Travel awards to women to travel to conferences or to meet with senior collaborators • Mentoring awards to members with a demonstrated record of nurturing young women faculty • A study of letters of recommendation

as a national crisis. And, for the most part, their efforts are "fix the women" efforts that use education and resources to better equip women to pursue their careers. Some of these efforts include providing grants for travel to conferences, holding professional development workshops at conferences, and giving awards to young women researchers.

A few efforts are aimed at more systemic change in the society itself. The annual letter writing campaign by the Women Chemists Committee of the American Chemical Society encourages the nomination of women for society awards and therefore attempts to counterbalance the bias that often leads to women being overlooked. The award by the Women in Cognitive Science to members who have a strong record of mentorship reaches out to reward members for activities that make a significant contribution to women's advance but are often overlooked.

These few efforts suggest that much remains to be done—indeed, that the RSA has the opportunity to become a national model for a professional society addressing issues of equity. The appointment in 2008 of the Task Force on Gender Equity is a first step in this direction. And as the RSA moves forward to consider the task force recommendations, we should keep in mind three ways in which systemic change should be undertaken:

1. *Changes in the infrastructure of the RSA* to actively monitor progress, do outreach, and develop programs that will reduce disparities and improve equity.

2. *Changes in the networks of the RSA* to address the structural disadvantages so often limiting members' advancement—particularly the isolation of the sole rhetorician and the pressure of administrative burdens.

3. *Changes in the norms of leadership in the RSA* to actively promote and reward involvement of more senior members in the career development of its pre- and post-tenure members.

Changes in infrastructure, changes in networks, changes in norms: these are the kinds of changes that will be systemic, that go to the heart of what the RSA is and wants to become, that hold the promise of making academic advancement for all its members more transparent and fair.

Works Cited

American Association of University Professors. *Where Are the Priorities? The Annual Report on the Economic Status of the Profession 2007–08.* 21 May 2008. <http://www.aaup.org/NR/rdonlyres/C98CAC79-4E8A-42B8-B034-BACF37E6DF03/0/zreport.pdf>.

Geisler, Cheryl, Debbie Kaminski, and Robyn A. Berkley. "The 13+ Club: A Metric for Understanding, Documenting, and Resisting Patterns of Non-Promotion to Full Professor." *The National Women's Studies Association Journal* 19.3 (2007): 145–62.

Hargens, L. L., and J. S. Long. "Demographic Inertia and Women's Representation among Faculty in Higher Education." *Journal of Higher Education* 73.4 (2002): 494–517.

Loeb, Jane W. "The Status of Female Faculty in the U.S.: Thirty-five Years with Equal Opportunity Legislation." *Management Revue* 17.2 (2006): 157–80.

National Research Council. *Summary Report 1996 Doctorate Recipients from United States Universities.* Washington, DC: National Academies P, 1998. 21 May 2008. <http://www.nap.edu/catalog.php?record_id=9530>.

National Science Foundation. ADVANCE: Increasing the Participation and Advancement of Women in Academic Science and Engineering Careers. 21 May 2008. <http://www.nsf.gov/funding/pgm_summ.jsp?pims_id=5383>.

PART IV

Preparing Students to Live in a Rapidly Changing World

I Told U So
Classical and Contemporary *Ethos* and the Stabilization of *Self*

Nathaniel A. Rivers

I begin this essay with a brief literary indulgence. *The Happy Hypocrite: A Fairy Tale for Tired Men,* by Max Beerbohm, serves to open this discussion of *ethos* and its relationship to notions of the self in the way the story works to challenge models of *ethos* as the presentation (or the masking) of a stable self. Read as rhetorical theory, Beerbohm's tale theorizes *ethos* as the cultivation of self through (or within) interaction with others.

The Happy Hypocrite is the story of a man, Lord George Hell, who, at the beginning of the tale, has a terrible reputation. Indeed, the narrator spends several pages recounting Lord George Hell's *ethos* and its emergence from "all the sins of his lordship's life" (Beerbohm 10). While the title of the story might suggest some ironic commentary on the perils of hypocrisy, the narrator offers a somewhat counterintuitive questioning of the virtue of candor—a virtue (closely paralleling authenticity) generally offered as the counter to the vice of hypocrisy. For Lord George, the narrator confesses, was quite candid and authentic with respect to his sins.

In the course of the story, Lord George, struck by Cupid's arrow, falls in love with a dancer named Jenny Mere. When Lord George proposes to Mere he is rejected and told that his face, while it *may* mirror true love, also reflects the world's vanity (Beerbohm 19). In other words, Jenny Mere does not trust his face. Instead, she wants only the man "whose face is wonderful as the faces of the saints" (19). Lord George's next move is to visit Mr. Aeneas, a maker of masks, in the hopes of acquiring a mask that mirrors only true love. At the shop, Lord George is told the story of Apollo and the mask that was made for him by his brother Vulcan in the hopes that Apollo, the sun god, could also watch the earth at night. Here, we see masks first as disguises for true and singularly authentic selves, and then realized as the cultivation of other, equally authentic selves. The sun *becomes* the moon. Fitted with his own mask, the mask of true love, Lord George likewise "felt he was a new man indeed" (33). And though the mask was perfect, he was ashamed that "he should so cheat the girl he loved. Behind that fair mask there would still be," he thought, "the evil face that had repelled her" (37). "His face was evil because his life had been evil" (37–38).

Conveniently, the now masked Lord George quickly reencounters Jenny Mere who is then immediately struck by Cupid's arrow herself, falls in love with Lord George, and agrees to marry him, remarking, "Surely . . . you *are* that good man for whom I have waited" (Beerbohm 39, emphasis added). Having secured the heart of his beloved, Lord George felt a pain from behind his mask. At that moment, he decided, "He would atone. He would shun no sacrifice that might cleanse his soul" (46). He would give up gambling, move away from the vanity of the city, give to charity, and begin his life anew with Jenny Mere. Applying for a marriage license shortly thereafter, Lord George was required to sign his name. "What name would he assume? Under a mask he had wooed this girl, under an unreal name he must make her his bride" (48). And with the license signed, Lord George Hell *became* George Heaven.

All was well, but still Lord George feared he would be discovered as an imposter, as a fake, as inauthentic. Nevertheless, reconciled that he must wear the mask forever, "it seemed to become an integral part of him, and, for all its rigid material, it did forsooth express the one emotion that filled him, true love" (Beerbohm 52). Then came the day when the happy couple inevitably had to venture into the city to shop, and, once there, Jenny noticed "a strange woman smiling" at her (56). The woman, of course, was the scorned lover of Lord George Hell who knew full well who he was underneath the mask she knew he wore. Terrified when confronted, Lord George denied knowing her and pleaded to be left alone. But she insisted otherwise: "Bid him unmask for me," she demanded of Jenny. The scorned lover then pounced at the mask trying to remove it. "There was a loud pop, as though some great cork had been withdrawn" (61). The scorned lover looked swiftly at the now unmasked Lord George and saw that, "staring back at her, was the man she had unmasked, but, lo! His face was even as his mask had been. Line for line, feature for feature, it was the same. 'Twas a saint's face" (62).

Ethos remains, as it was for Lord George, a topic of constant consternation to those in rhetoric and composition; how is such a diffuse concept to be defined and how is any version of *ethos* to be taught? Part of our difficulty seems to lie in the unstable nature of the term itself—an instability reflected in the numerous ways *ethos* has come down to us through the history of rhetoric: as character, as authority, as the mask, as sinister showmanship. Another crucial component of our dis-ease with *ethos* is the instability that it embodies as a rhetorical concept in its connection to notions of the self (connections that are at the center of this essay). If our impulse as a field leads us to certain notions of the self (or practices of the self) will we see a concomitant shift in the way *ethos* is theorized, defined, and taught?

My contention is that classical and contemporary notions of *ethos* work (intentionally or not) to stabilize a specific notion of the self—the self as singular, insulated, and authentic. I want to lay out a critique of this construction of *ethos*, present in Aristotle and in many contemporary composition textbooks (one of which I discuss below), in an effort to begin exploring other constructions that are more reflective of rhetorical notions or conceptions of "self," that is, of a self that *emerges* in the moment of contact and through the conversation. Looking first at discussions of *ethos* in a contemporary textbook, and then at descriptions of *ethos* in Aristotle, I hope to explicate the implied or assumed notions of the self (and its relation to the rhetorical situation) inherent in these discussions. I then move to complicate this notion of the self, looking at Andy Clark's recent exploration of cognitive science in *Being There* and *Natural-Born Cyborgs* and what notions of the self these works offer us. Finally, I want to indicate the implications for *ethos* and rhetorical instruction that might result from Clark's notion of the self, touching briefly on the work of Debra Hawhee. I argue, "finally," that *ethos* can (or ought to) be a way to theorize what could be called *self-cultivation*. *Self-cultivation* forwards the idea that selves are not *stable through* discourse but *constituted in* it. "Cultivate" also suggests the layers of agency at work in such an endeavor. We do not invent or discover our *ethos*, but cultivate it from within a matrix of other forces and agents.

The *self*-stabilizing *ethos* that I am working against is exemplified by several popular textbooks. In these pedagogical tools, *ethos* is primarily taught as authority and credibility. In this, I see these textbooks privileging a fairly logocentric view of *ethos*. This logocentrism, however, is not for its own sake. Such a *logos*-driven view of rhetoric still privileges a problematic view of truth as stable and knowable, and, more importantly, for my purposes, of the self as singular, insulated, and authentic. *Ethos* becomes, then, merely a tool for revealing this stable self strategically to an audience. Rhetoric, presented this way, runs the risk of being merely a way to get what one wants (the classic pejorative take) and not an activity at the heart of who one is and might become. Thus, I offer this argument, as well, in the hopes that we can come to offer first-time students of rhetoric a stronger version of it: a rhetoric introduced and endorsed as the means by which students engage others in emerging as themselves.

As I have indicated, much of what I am claiming for such textbooks appears unintentional, as many recent textbooks (including the one I discuss) complicate rhetorical theory with respect to other areas of rhetoric and composition: for instance, in what counts as composition or as an argument. Additionally, much of the scholarship of the authors of these textbooks runs counter to the assertions their textbooks make. My critique here is focused on the point of first contact between students and rhetoric, which is, for many, the composition textbook, rather than what the author might say elsewhere. I am concerned, then, with the terms used to introduce rhetoric generally and *ethos* particularly.

Timothy W. Crusius and Carolyn E. Channell, in the fourth edition of *The Aims of Argument*, argue, "A good argument will always *reveal* the writer's values, intelligence, knowledge of the subject, grasp of the readers' minds and concerns, and so on" (274, emphasis added). This brief quote, part of the authors' discussion of *ethos*, is a good example of what I am describing. The self here is *revealed* by the argument; *ethos*, in their words, is "*self*-presentation" (273). The writer's values, intelligence, etc., are all apparently stable, and *ethos* becomes the tool of revealing the writer's self as stable—a way of bringing a stable "I" to a group of stable "Yous." Additionally, it is assumed that readers' "minds" and "concerns" are capable of being grasped, ahead of time, by the speaker. Crusius and Channell promote an explicitly Aristotelian argument for rhetoric when they write:

> The study of rhetoric, therefore, includes both what we have already defined as reasoning and ways of appealing to an audience. These include *self-conscious* efforts to *project oneself* as a good and intelligent person as well as efforts to connect with an audience through humor, passion and image. (5, emphasis added)

All in all, we have an insulated self in an apparently stable rhetorical situation; the challenge for the student is discovering the appropriate course to follow. This is a prime example of a description of *ethos* that stabilizes rhetorical work and the self that engages in it. And more often than not, the preferred strategy for this work of *ethos* is the establishing of authority and credibility.

When *ethos* is defined as authority and credibility there is not only an overdeterminism of *ethos* by *logos*, there is also a problematic use of the terms *author*ity and credibility. It seems far too often to mean a stable author (the student) maintaining a credible (or authentic) self in the production of an argument. Not only does such a view of *ethos* cut-off more *pathos*-driven configurations of *ethos*, such as familiarity and identification, it also elides the ways in which the audience itself constructs the *ethos* of the speaker (even Aristotle opens the door for this in his very attempt to control *ethos* as constructed by the argument at hand, and not by any previous ways the audience may have perceived the speaker). The self that is speaking remains stable and insulated—it is not constructed *with* others but merely assessed by them—and it is the speaker or writer's job to present an appropriate authority for that self. While Crusius and Channell discuss *ethos* as self-presentation, they also, even if unintentionally, theorize *ethos* as self-preservation.

This, in several ways, reflects the Platonic and Aristotelian roots of much composition instruction. Indeed, the above textbook, like many textbooks, relies on Aristotle's taxonomies in laying out *rhetoric* for students. It seems that borrowing the terminology makes it hard to avoid picking up the philosophy.[1] In what many take to be Aristotle's definitive statement on *ethos*, he writes:

> [There is persuasion] through character whenever the speech is spoken in such a way as to make the speaker worthy of credence; for we believe fair-minded people to a greater extent and more quickly [than we do others] on all subjects in general and completely so in cases where there is not exact knowledge but room for doubt. And this *should* result from the speech, not

from a *previous opinion* that the speaker is a certain kind of person; for it is
not the case, as some of the technical writers propose in their treatment of
the art, that fair-mindedness [*epiekeia*] on the part of the speaker makes no
contribution to persuasiveness; rather, character is almost, so to speak, the
controlling factor in persuasion. (38, emphasis added)

There are three specific points (or moves) in this passage that I want to
briefly highlight. The first, and perhaps most revealing, is Aristotle's use of
the word *should*. In this specific context it is used to indicate that *ethos* should
be located in the *logos*, in the argument itself. As Kennedy reminds us, Aristotle has in mind here the specific speech situation of an Athenian jury, the size
and procedures of which meant the jury *could not* know the character or *ethos*
of the plaintiff ahead of time. What is important to recognize is that it is this
ethos, disconnected from its historical context, that regularly appears in contemporary textbooks. This is all standard fare for Platonic rhetoric, as well. In
the larger scene, however, this *should* broadcasts the moral imperative also at
work in Aristotle. It is not enough that he claim that *ethos is* located in the
text; he goes the additional step of making it an *ought*.

But of course this *should* covers more than just where *ethos* should be
located; it covers as well where it *should not* be. Aristotle's imperative that
ethos should not come from "previous opinion" is my second focal point. In
his efforts to stabilize *ethos* as something done *by* the speaker *for* or perhaps *to*
the audience, it is quite reasonable for him to prescribe that it should not
come from the audience ahead of time—that would be something the *audience* does *to* the speaker. If "previous opinion" is allowed to shape *ethos* then
immediately the whole strategy is thrown into disarray. The self presented by
ethos is no longer singular, insulated, and authentic; it is now contaminated
by the audience. Again, order is assured (in the rhetorical situation and in the
self), for us, by Aristotle's "should not."

Aristotle's final move in this brief passage, and my third focal point, is his
claim that *ethos* is "the controlling factor in persuasion." This is a compelling
statement; it is certainly one that I generally agree with. However, on the
heels of and as a part of Aristotle's broader treatise on rhetoric, and in light of
much contemporary rhetorical education, it remains difficult to accept. It
places the writer or speaker completely in control of a passive audience (once
you have found the way they are yours). *Ethos* is powerful as a means of persuasion—it is not merely carried to an audience, but constructed with them.
This is the notion of *ethos* as self-cultivation that I am working toward. I do
not mean to suggest that there is no agency, but that any one agent both
engages and emerges from a complex network of other agents. The work a
rhetor does is neither pure invention nor pure discovery, but instead the work
of cultivating a self from within this network. Aristotle's *ethos*, operating to
stabilize the occasion and assure success, elides much of the complexity of
the self and of any situation, and cuts off the possibility of a more robust
notion of the self and its distributed sources. In presenting such an attractive
and stabilizing *ethos*, do we ourselves risk presenting *ethos* as a rhetorical silver

bullet that, if made strong enough, authoritative enough, can penetrate all audiences defenseless against it? What I am coming to suggest is that we need to think of not only *ethos* as a performance of the self, but of self as a performance as well, not existing prior to, but only in interaction. *Ethos* is not added to a stable self, but emerges in the ethical cultivation of unstable, compromised selves that exist between and among the speaker and the audience.

Of course, one of the profoundest difficulties of a project such as this is explicating a notion of self, and arguing that *ethos* is connected to *self* to begin with. Such a task is important, nevertheless, because the greatest risk in Aristotelian *ethos* is the philosophy of self that is carried with it. What I have been attempting to argue is that any description of *ethos* necessarily assumes some notion of the self and that any notion of the self is necessarily reflected in how one approaches *ethos*. What I am further suggesting is that we teach an *ethos* that is in line with more rhetorical and less foundational conceptions of self. Cognitive scientist Andy Clark's notion of the soft self (as one constructed socially and environmentally) is such a rhetorical construction. In contrast to the sealed notion of self embodied in Aristotle, Clark presents a leaky self. We are, Clark argues, "hopelessly cognitively compromised" (*Natural* 140).

Clark's notion of the "soft self" challenges us to reconsider *ethos* as stable, as self-authored, and as a sole product of the individual rhetor. We might see how Aristotle is on to something like this when he explores how structures such as age and the law create a menu of characters from which to choose, but he seems to miss or ignore how character, like the self itself, is created in the exchange. Clark's notion of the self, however, is one of incredible seepage (a strikingly un-Platonic notion). It is a self open to constant change. It is a self that annexes more and more external elements in coalitional processes of control sharing. It is here where Clark gives voice to the "role of context, culture, environment, and technology in the constitution of individual human persons" (*Natural* 139). The seepage of all these elements in and out of human skin and skull, what Clark calls "mingling," "is the truest expression of our distinctive character as a species" (139). The self, in Clark, and in others, is seen as rhetorically cultivated.

In this view, the self, like order, as Derrida admonishes, is not assured (5). *Ethos* is always a gamble (as any politician attempting to connect with voters can testify); it is inherently unstable (any stable *ethos* is only accessible via prophesy after the fact). This is why teaching *ethos* as a tool, as a deliberate choice between masks that are placed over an authentic self, but never seen as another authentic self, is problematic. Only from an Aristotelian or Platonic standpoint, where the truth is reasonably assured, and where the means to that truth are visible if only we have the light to see them, is *ethos* seen as a mask for an authentic self, as a tool or map to persuading the audience. But from a fuller, perhaps more sophistic rhetoric, *ethos*, character, the mask, can all be seen as variously authentic cultivations of self that happen in the process of engagement with the audience. In *The Happy Hypocrite* Lord George cultivates himself as the good lover *in* loving Jenny Mere. As Debra Hawhee argues in *Bodily Arts*, while discussing *mtis* and Odysseus, "Odysseus' various disguises do not function to 'conceal' some hidden 'identity,' . . . rather, the disguises *become* his identity" (52). Odysseus, Hawhee argues, "is always becoming something else" (52). This is a notion of the self (one that finds a home in the work of Andy Clark on the "soft self") that I find helpful in laying out other approaches to *ethos*.

What happens, then, to *ethos* when the *self* as a stable, consistent, and individuated starting point becomes untenable? When *ethos* rests on *authority* it rests solely on the author, the stable self who constructs the argument. When *ethos* is softened, made em*pathetic*, we can see it less as a tool or a strategy, or even as the pejorative mask, and more as emergent in the argument, in the act of persuasion, in the conversation itself, where *ethos* is distributed across the author, the audience, and the situation. None of this is to say that the rhetor (or the rhetor in training) takes no part in the construction of an *ethos*. Lord George does do his level best to make himself the good lover. It does mean, however, that *ethos* can no longer be a disguise picked out of time. Nor does it mean that *ethos* is a costume given to the rhetor by the audience; Clark's self experiences seepage in *both* directions, in *and* out. And as Jim Corder suggests, while acknowledging that authors are in many ways projections of their readers, "I think that . . . authors . . . leave trails for us" (311).

Hawhee writes, constructing an embodied *kairos*, "as with *mtis*, kairotic impulses can therefore be habituated or intuitive—bodily, even—and are not limited to a seat of reason or conscious adherence to a set of principles" (70). We can, and do, like Lord George, become the masks we wear. In place of a theory of *ethos* that stabilizes a supposedly singular, insulated, and authentic self, what I am suggesting is an intuitive and timely *ethos* that is not learned as a means to control persuasion but rather as a way of negotiating rhetorical situations through the timely and contingent cultivation of selves. An *ethos* not of self-preservation but of self-cultivation.

Note

1 A note on my (mis)use of Aristotle. My critique here is not so much focused on the limitations of Aristotle's *ethos* for contemporary situations (such a critique would be, to a certain extent, unfair), but with what I feel are common understandings of Aristotle that I find problematic or limiting. The same is true of translations of Aristotle. Regardless of the contextual inaccuracies of translations of Aristotle, we all share common translations of his work. Whether Aristotle, in Kennedy's translations, means "should not" as *we* do, *we all* share, roughly, the same understanding of the hortatory "should not" in *our own* context. And it is out of this contemporary context that textbooks are written.

Works Cited

Aristotle. *On Rhetoric*. Trans. George Kennedy. New York: Oxford, 1991.

Beerbohm, Max. *The Happy Hypocrite: A Fairy Tale for Tired Men*. New York: John Lane, 1906.

Clark, Andy. *Being There*. Cambridge: MIT P, 1998.

————. *Natural-Born Cyborgs*. Oxford: Oxford UP, 2003.

Corder, James. "Hunting For *Ethos* Where They Say It Can't be Found." *Rhetoric Review* 7.2 (1989): 299–316.

Crusius, Timothy W., and Carolyn E. Channell. *The Aims of Argument: A Brief Guide.* 4th ed. New York: McGraw Hill, 2003.

Derrida, Jacques. *Archive Fever: A Freudian Impression*. Chicago: U of Chicago P, 1996.

Hawhee, Debra. *Bodily Arts: Rhetoric and Athletics in Ancient Greece*. Austin: U of Texas P, 2005.

Kennedy, George. *Classical Rhetoric and Its Christian and Secular Tradition from Ancient to Modern Times*. 2nd ed. Chapel Hill: U of North Carolina P, 1999.

Coming to Terms with Analogy
Generativity and Constraint in the Work of Nagaoka, Gamow, and Freud

Joseph Little & Lisa Jane Kabasin

Analogy has long been recognized as a vehicle of serious thought, a vehicle of insight in the context of invention. It enables us to see an object in a particular light, focusing our attention here rather than there, there rather than here: on the particular, on the general, on the static, on the dynamic, on something else altogether. This is no Emersonian project of transparency and infinitude, no hyperbolic dream of being nothing and seeing all. With analogy, it seems we all agree, figure can become ground, and ground figure, but, as Kenneth Burke pointed out long ago, something is always brought to the fore, and something else suppressed.

Science-minded scholars of analogy typically address the issue of analogy's selectivity by concerning themselves with whether the analogy helped the scientist "get it right," whether the particular light thrown by the analogy led to ontologies we believe in today or whether it led the rhetor astray. Thus, we read of James Watson and Francis Crick's fortuitous framing of the microsome as a small quantity of RNA enveloped in protein (Judson 318), Crick's subsequent misstep in predicting a comma-free genetic code (Gross, *Rhetoric* 29), and Hantaro Nagaoka's getting it both right and wrong when he claimed that the atom behaved like Saturn and its satellites (Little, "Analogy"). Some scholars have sought out the moral or social consequences of analogy's role in the creation and suppression of knowledge, as in Nancy Stepan's superb essay on the biosocial analogy between race and gender, an analogy that worked to legitimize race, class, and gender inequalities in the late nineteenth century.

In this essay, we move the discussion in another, less veritistic direction by elaborating on two neglected dimensions of analogy's selectivity, two contours of all rhetorical situations informed by analogy. The first centers on the idea that analogies are generative to different degrees, that in the juxtaposition of two distinct domains of knowledge, usually called the base and target domains, the number of candidate correspondences called to mind by the rhetor and audience depends on the analogy at hand. Analogies are selective in their constitution of objects, as Leah Ceccarelli ("Neither") has expertly illustrated, yet they are more than that: *In situ* they can be characterized by the number of correspondences they generate, the very signs that mediate the process of selectivity. Put simply, some analogies are more prolific than others or, to borrow from Mario Bunge, more fertile. For better or for worse, they offer more inventional pathways than other analogies, and it is this variation in fertility that constitutes an important feature of rhetorical performance, rarely discussed save Lionel Wee's acknowledgement that the choice of a base domain impacts the degree of inventional complexity available to the rhetor.

Second, we want to foreground the idea that the correspondences generated by the analogy can constrain the rhetor to different degrees depending on the situation at hand. Nearly all humanities scholarship on analogy tacitly advances the notion that rhetors are at liberty to draw from analogy only those correspondences that serve their purposes (Little, "Analogy"). While we agree with Keith Gibson that rhetors have no ultimate assurance that an audience will interpret an analogy in accordance with their intent, a large body of social scientific research strongly suggests that audiences do tend to infer many of the same commonalities from an analogy in a given rhetorical situation and, what is more, they tend to agree on the relative importance of those commonalities (Thagard et al.; Gentner and Jeziorski; Gentner; Gentner, Holyoak, and Kokinov; Clement and Gentner).

Some rhetorical scholarship has followed suit: Because the audience will likely call to mind a common set of correspondences, as Little argues elsewhere ("Analogy," "Role"), rhetors are compelled to address those correspondences or risk having their argument perceived as incomplete and their *ethos* as right-thinking individuals called into question. In short, there is an *orthos logos* to the moment, a tacit sense of "right reasoning" understood by the audience, which contributes to the "productive tension" across rhetor, text, and audience recently acknowledged by John Angus Campbell and Ryan Clark. Investment in analogy can constrain rhetorical options by all but demanding the acceptance of certain claims and the rejection of others, or, in the case of a mildly constraining set of correspondences, it can simply afford a variety of optional ideas for strategic uptake at the rhetor's discretion. Whereas generativity addresses the number of correspondences sponsored by the analogy, constraint inversely addresses the degree to which the rhetor can afford to ignore them without compromising the suasory power of the performance.

In *Shaping Science with Rhetoric*, Leah Ceccarelli demonstrates a "new critical practice" of reading scientific texts, a triangulation of sorts that balances her close reading against historical context and intertext. Her practice adds "a level of rigor and precision," she argues, "that is lacking in the more standard close reading method of rhetorical criticism" (171). It is in that same spirit, though by different means, that below we analyze three cases of analogy operating in science. It is our attempt to show how the concepts of generativity and constraint enable a more specific, more precise, and ultimately more contestable conversation regarding the effects of analogy on rhetorical performance. Encouraging students to consider the number of candidate correspondences sponsored by an analogy, as well as the variation in inventional fertility across analogies, moves the discussion beyond the limiting assumption that analogy functions collectively in a given rhetorical situation. It enables students to see how each correspondence, or subset of correspondences, has the potential to serve a distinct rhetorical end and thus affect the scientist in palpable ways. Encouraging students to consider a rhetorical situation from the perspective of constraint offers entrance to larger issues of audience, agency, *orthos logos*, and *logos* in relatively palpable ways.

NAGAOKA'S SATURNIAN THEORY

A staccato of discoveries in the late 1890s—most notably, the electron, radioactivity, and X-rays—compelled even the most intransigent *fin-de-siècle* physicist to concede that the atom was not basic but composite, not the elementary unit of Newton's day but an aggregate of still smaller particles whose properties would likely explain the latest empirical findings emanating from laboratories across Europe. The atom had a structure, and it was the nature of that structure that physicists were pressed to invent.

The long-term mission of explaining a host of natural phenomena in terms of subatomic particle interaction demanded not only the rigor and precision typically associated with scientific activity, but also an unusual level of creative thinking, for in the early 1900s, neither electricity nor spectral emissions were well understood, and the cause of atomic weight remained a mystery (Yagi 29). The wealth of spectroscopic data emerging from Germany and England enabled ballpark claims about several atomic properties; however, many fundamental issues, such as the size of the atom and the motion of the electron within it, were far from resolved (Heilbron 112). Nature was indeed "pushing back," but not in ways that physicists interpreted as instrumental to the adjudication of competing theories.

Enter Hantaro Nagaoka, who, on December 5, 1903, presented his Saturnian theory of atomic structure before the Physico-Mathematical Society of Tokyo. Drawing from James Clerk Maxwell's analysis of the dynamics of Saturn's rings, Nagaoka proposed an atomic system consisting of a large number of small, high-velocity particles of equal mass—electrons in his thinking—revolving at equal angular intervals around a large central particle of much greater mass. While attracted to the central particle by a force inversely proportional to the square of the distance, the revolving particles repel each other by the same inverse-square relationship, thus creating a dynamic system that is generally stable against small, inevitable disturbances while predictably unstable against larger ones. In good hypothetico-deductive form, Nagaoka estimated the empirical implications of his proposed structure and found promising experimental fit.

Relative to the cases discussed in the following sections, the Saturnian analogy was highly generative, delivering seven structural correspondences to Nagaoka's inventional space:

REVOLVE AROUND (satellites, Saturn)
REVOLVE AROUND (electrons, central particle)
DISTANCE (satellites, Saturn)
DISTANCE (electrons, central particle)
ATTRACTS (Saturn, satellites)
ATTRACTS (central particle, electrons)
VARIES INVERSELY PROPORTIONAL [DISTANCE^2 (Saturn, satellites), ATTRACTS (Saturn, satellites)]
VARIES INVERSELY PROPORTIONAL [DISTANCE^2 (central particle, electrons), ATTRACTS (central particle, electrons)]
DISPLACES RADIALLY (external force, satellites)
DISPLACES RADIALLY (external force, electrons)
DISPLACES ANGULARLY (external force, satellites)
DISPLACES ANGULARLY (external force, electrons)
DISPLACES NORMALLY (external force, satellites)
DISPLACES NORMALLY (external force, electrons)

The first four worked in unison to sponsor a highly constrained set of claims about the geometry of the atom, namely that electrons revolve around a central particle owing to an attractive force inversely proportional to the distance. It was a geometry Nagaoka could not afford to ignore, and it separated him from his colleagues on a variety of important issues, including nuclear compatibility (for a detailed account, see Little, "Analogy").

At the time, the electron was known to be negatively charged and constituent of even the smallest atom, yet the atom was known to be electrically neutral. Therefore, competitive theorists had to develop plausible conceptions of positive charge to counterbalance the effect of electrons within the atom. The resulting conceptions varied considerably, but no one except Nagaoka envisioned the positive charge in the form of a massive central particle. For Nagaoka, this was not a matter of choice, not a case of analogy functioning heuristically in the context of invention. Practically speaking, he could not have done otherwise. To advocate a Saturnian theory without the analog to Saturn, which once assumed became the only logical choice for the source of the positive charge, would have undermined the cogency of his theory at its most fundamental level. This sort of constraint on Nagaoka, this need to negotiate an *orthos logos* brought to the moment by the analogy, represents a contour of his rhetorical situation that was largely absent in his colleagues'. Indeed, the analogy offered Nagaoka *a priori* justification for a variety of initial claims, but it came at the cost of a certain amount of inventional freedom, which ultimately worked in his favor: Upon his startling discovery of the nucleus in 1911, Ernest Rutherford (688) singled out Nagaoka for having predicted the central particle in his Saturnian theory nearly a decade earlier.

It was in the remaining three correspondences that Nagaoka's theory gained much of its explanatory power, largely owing to the concept of relative stability in three dimensions. Nagaoka's theory is, after all, a theory of dynamic equilibrium: Stability is not achieved by way of electrons coming to rest—as in static theories of atomic structure—but by way of electrons finding their way into stable orbital motion. With such motion comes the possibility of displacement or disruption in three dimensions, which offered Nagaoka three plausible *topoi* for explaining empirical results in terms of the fundamental properties of stable atoms: electrons accelerating and decelerating along the orbital path (angular displacement), electrons moving closer to and farther from the central particle (radial displacement), and electrons moving above and below the orbital path (normal displacement). Although static theories may have had the benefit of appearing simple or elegant in certain cases—James Jeans' comes to mind—the notion of a stable atom as an ensemble of particles at rest afforded few structural options for explaining the regularity of spectral emissions from stable atoms. Sometimes, static theorists invented additional terms to achieve the structural complexity needed for adequate explanatory reach (cf. Carazza and Robotti). Not so for Nagaoka: In the "ready-made" *topos* of normal displacement—a concept completely unavailable to static theorists—by assuming a large number of electrons oscillating with a particular frequency about their average path, Nagaoka was able to derive an equation whose graph coincided with the wealth of empirical evidence for the regularity of band spectra; in the *topos* of angular displacement—again, unavailable to static theorists—he found a similar qualitative explanation for the regularity of line spectra.

In broad strokes, when discussing the regularity of spectral emissions, Nagaoka focused on the small, inevitable disturbances of the revolving particles in the normal and angular planes, mild but patterned oscillations that occurred without compromising the overall stability of the system. What is more, to account for radioactivity, he focused on the system's general instability against larger, less predictable displacements in the same planes and the likely ejection of high-velocity particles when the displacements reached rupturing amplitudes. Important to the purpose of this paper is the fact that Nagaoka's neglect of the *topos* of angular displacement did not draw criticism from the physics community, not even from the harsh G. A. Schott, which illustrates the ancillary relationship of the DISPLACES correspondences to Nagaoka's argument. Suggested but not entailed by the other correspondences, and therefore unlikely to be perceived by the audience as integral to the overall cogency of the argument, all three correspondences were available independently for Nagaoka to employ or ignore at his full discretion, enabling him to achieve the desired level of structural complexity for his theoretical undertaking.

GAMOW'S LIQUID DROP THEORY

In 1928, when the rest of the world was focusing on the atom, George Gamow turned his attention to the nucleus. Like Nagaoka, Gamow enjoyed considerable latitude in his theorizing, the empirical record offering little more than a sketch of this atom within an atom. In the seventeen years since Rutherford's discovery, physicists had identified the nucleus as the source of alpha and beta radioactivity; they had also calculated its radius—at least for hydrogen and helium—to be around 10^{-12} centimeters (Pais 230; Gamow, *My World Line* 59). However, these were the days before the discovery of the neutron—the "prehistory of nuclear physics" as Hans Bethe would call it (qtd. in Segre 240)—and therefore the nucleus was understood as a collection of positively charged alpha-particles, He^{2+}, themselves aggregates of still smaller protons and electrons (van den Broek).

A Leningrad graduate student working first in Goettingen and then in Niels Bohr's legendary Blegdamsvej institute only months after Bohr and Werner Heisenberg's development of the Copenhagen interpretation of quantum mechanics, Gamow became intrigued by the curious force holding the intranuclear alpha-particles together at very short distances. Unlike the atom, the nucleus seemed to exhibit a sort of outer wall, a barrier or wrapper that the alpha-particles could not easily penetrate (Stuewer). Sometime in 1928, the similarity between this binding force and the surface tension acting on a drop of water—a topic Bohr himself had dedicated much time to—struck Gamow, and in his 1929 talk before the Royal Society of London and more fully in his *Proceedings* paper of 1930 he developed this insight into the liquid drop theory of nuclear structure.

Gamow was quick to point out that surface tension is not a fundamental force but an effect of a relatively uniform distribution of particles with short-range attractive forces between them. Particles located deep within the distribution, be it a water drop or nucleus, are surrounded by neighboring particles and thus bound by the short-range attractive forces acting on them from all sides, whereas particles located at the surface only have neighboring particles and thus short-range attractive forces acting on the inward side. The net effect of this asymmetry is an inward pull of the surface particles toward the center of the distribution, a binding effect known as surface tension. Therefore, we can characterize the liquid drop analogy as mildly generative, creating three correspondences for Gamow's theoretical work:

SURFACE TENSION (water drop)
SURFACE TENSION (nucleus)
UNIFORM DENSITY (water drop)
UNIFORM DENSITY (nucleus)
ATTRACTS AT SHORT RANGE (water molecule, water molecule)
ATTRACTS AT SHORT RANGE (nuclear particle, nuclear particle)

The relationship among the correspondences, however, is anything but mild: Essentially, Gamow's subscription to the SURFACE TENSION correspondence logically demanded his acceptance of the other two correspondences, much like the relationship among the first four correspondences in Nagaoka's case.

Unlike Nagaoka, however, Gamow had no ancillary set of correspondences, no pathways of potential inquiry to pursue or neglect at his discretion. The liquid drop analogy was an all or nothing approach that demanded a small but very clear set of assumptions regarding the geometry of the nucleus, and his investment in it had the important effect of eliminating any consideration of a dynamic nuclear equilibrium. Enamored by the success of planetary atomic theories such as Nagaoka's and Bohr's, many physicists turned to the atom as a model for the nucleus. This resulted in the emergence of a variety of shell theories that envisioned nuclear particles revolving around the nuclear center akin to electrons around the nucleus, which implicated a whole host of variables—a particle's charge, mass, and quantum state to be sure—in even the most basic calculations. (Although quantum mechanics does not require the notion of orbiting electrons, many physicists still used that language and other references to electronic motion when attempting to visualize the atom. It was a point of frustration for the acerbic Wolfgang Pauli [qtd. in Segre 130], who in 1924 remarked, "Weak men, who need the crutch of defined orbits and mechanical models, can think of my rule as saying that electrons with the same quantum numbers would have the same orbits and therefore collide with one another.") Gamow necessarily sidestepped these complexities, his analogy requiring him to assume that the distance between neighboring particles and therefore the binding energy per particle—that is, the amount of energy required to bind each particle to its neighbors—were constant, a scheme wholly incommensurate with shell predictions at the time. This led Gamow to conclude on analogical grounds, with strong experimental fit, that stable nuclei exist in static rather than dynamic equilibrium, which freed him from considering variations in charge, mass, and quantum state—all constants in his thinking—in his theoretical work. In this way, the analogy lent to his theory a profound conceptual and mathematical simplicity—an unmistakable elegance—by way of extinguishing a variety of *topoi* that occasionally muddled his colleagues' work.

FREUD'S CLARK LECTURE

Hysteria had been studied since the eighteenth century, advances having been made by Franz Mesmer, Marquis de Puysegur, and, most notable in reference to Sigmund Freud, Jean Charcot. Charcot, a renowned neurologist and early mentor of Freud, scandalized the scientific community by arguing, in the words of Howard Kendler, that the "ability to be hypnotized is a symptom of hysteria, and that hysteria is a product of a hereditary disorder of the central nervous system" (228). One of Charcot's protégés, Pierre Janet, was the first to introduce the term "subconscious" into the scientific lexicon, a term Freud referred to as the "unconscious" and used extensively in his studies of psychoanalysis. Another contemporary of Freud, Hermann von Helmholtz, believed that the workings of the unconscious were implicated in the performance of intellectual feats, which bolstered Freud's growing belief in the power of the unconscious (Kendler 229). Also in the nineteenth century, Eduard von Hartmann compiled his popular piece, "The Philosophy of the Unconscious," in which he "postulated unconscious mental forces, blind impulses of will, that were constantly in conflict with the conscious forces of reason" (230). These ideas foreshadowed Freud's later views of the unconscious. It is also important to note Nietzsche's influence on Freud's later contributions to psychology. His ideas of the unconscious and, as Kendler (230) put it, "disturbing memories being forced out of the unconscious" set the stage for Freud to invent his notions of the unconscious and repression, which ultimately combined to form psychoanalysis.

Without a doubt, Freud's pioneering work paved the way for the many successes of his followers. However, Freud's path itself was bumpy, to say the least. Criticisms of his writings were considerable. Putnam, writing just after the Clark lectures, noted in reference to the general opinion of Freud's writings, "Its vast literature—well known to be of great importance—was repulsive and should not be seen on our shelves" (372). Yet Freud slowly gained followers. "There is an audience," noted Putnam in 1910, "small, perhaps, but constantly increasing to which the researches of a band of workers, of whom Freud is one, strikingly appeal" (373).

At the same time that Freud was coming into his own, Clark University was celebrating its twentieth anniversary. To mark the occasion, the president of the university, Dr. G. Stanley Hall, extended an invitation to Freud to hold a series of lectures. Freud's theories of psychoanalysis were already known to a certain extent; however, these lectures would be the first time the issues of psychoanalysis and sexuality would be covered comprehensively. The lectures were also important because they marked the first time Freud addressed an American audience, a unique mixture of those experienced in early psychoanalysis and those for whom Freud's theories were entirely new. Realizing this, Freud stated early in his opening remarks: "It is not without satisfaction that I have learnt that the majority of my audience are not members of the medical profession. You have no need to be afraid that any special medical knowledge will be required for what I have to say" (4). Although there is no extant list of attendees (Patterson 218), it is certain that Dr. Hall was present, bringing with him a host of his contemporaries. Also in attendance were Franz Boas, James Putnam, William James, the noted anarchist Emma Goldman, and reporters from the Worcester *Gazette* and *Telegram* as well as the Boston *Transcript*. It seems that Freud geared his lectures toward those audience members whose psychological convictions were still fresh and tentative enough to enable them to consider new ideas. This focus on ease of understanding sets the stage for our investigation of his explanatory use of analogy.

Freud used several analogies to explain his theories of hysteria and repression in the lectures. These analogies seem to be Freud's way of creatively addressing the audience in such a way that they would understand his relatively complex theories. Patterson notes that, "throughout the Clark lectures, Freud depended on analogy as his chief means of argumentation" (222). However, while Freud's analogies are central to his goal of promoting understanding, they are not the basis for his argument, nor did they serve an epistemic function in the invention of hysteria or repression. Unlike the cases of Nagaoka and Gamow, and *contra* Patterson, Freud's analogies served an explanatory or pedagogical function. In the beginning of his first lecture, for example, Freud used a material analogy to enable his audience to visualize the symptoms of hysteria. He equates a hysterical patient with a Londoner who pauses to outwardly weep at the sight of memorials commemorating tragedies long since past (12–13). We can characterize the correspondences of this mildly generative analogy as follows:

MNEMIC SYMBOL OF PAST TRAUMATIC EVENT (London monument)
MNEMIC SYMBOL OF PAST TRAUMATIC EVENT (hysterical symptom)
ABNORMAL ATTACHMENT TO EVENT (mourning Londoner)
ABNORMAL ATTACHMENT TO EVENT (hysteric)

It is not that the hysterical symptoms cause negative emotion as the monument causes negative emotion; rather, the hysterical symptom is a symbol of a past traumatic experience—more precisely, an amnesia, a "gap in memory," as Freud later explains—just as the London monuments are symbols of past traumatic experiences. In their behavior, the hysteric and the mourning Londoner alike demonstrate an abnormal attachment to the past, a fixation that results in their neglecting "what is real and immediate," to borrow again from Freud (13). In short, Freud used the analogy to encourage his audience to visualize how a hysterical person clings in an unhealthy way to an event. However, important to the purpose of this paper is the fact that never again does talk of London monuments enter into his lecture.

Freud used an extended analogy to explain his theory of repression and the physician's task of curing a neurotic patient, which implicated his ideas of the conscious and unconscious. In his self-proclaimed "rough analogy" (23), Freud allows the lecture hall enveloping his audience to play as backdrop and his audience to play a role as well. He describes an individual within the audience who is thrown out of the lecture because of a series of unruly outbursts. For the purpose of our exploration, we will call him Gus. Gus is forced to stay out of the lecture hall, thanks to a barricade of chairs disallowing the option of reentry. After some time, Gus makes a commotion outside, which eventually leads to a peace-making mission. Gus is coaxed out of his erratic behavior by the president of Clark University and, after promising to behave himself, he is allowed to return. We can characterize the correspondences of the first half of this highly generative analogy as follows:

SOURCE (Gus' disruption in lecture room)
SOURCE (painful memory)

REACTION (Gus is thrown out of lecture room)
REACTION (painful memory is repressed)
LOCATION (lecture room, outside of lecture room)
LOCATION (conscious mental state, unconscious mental state)

In short, Freud invents the story to illustrate via analogy the process, consequences, and ultimate curing of repression, mapping material spaces to the conscious and unconscious mind. After introducing the analogy, he continues to draw from it to further describe how the neurosis affects the individual and how a physician aids in treatment. Freud notes the continuous character of his analogy by remarking: "rather than giving a complicated theoretical account, I will return here to the analogy which I employed earlier for my explanation of repression" (25), effectively handing the audience a familiar notion they can expand upon. Also, Freud's statement, "rather than giving a complicated theoretical account," underscores the explanatory and distinctly nonepistemic function of analogy in Freud's mind. It is neither the foundation nor the main focus of Freud's theories, but a pathway to understanding.

The second half of Freud's (25) analogy proceeds as follows:

EFFECT OF REACTION (Gus' shouting and banging interferes with lecture)
EFFECT OF REACTION (unconscious painful memory interferes with conscious mental state)
TREATMENT (Dr. Hall persuades Gus to behave himself; Gus is readmitted)
TREATMENT (psychoanalyst coaxes painful memory back into conscious mental activity)
OUTCOME OF TREATMENT (peace resumes in lecture room)
OUTCOME OF TREATMENT (peace resumes in conscious mind)

Here, Freud is arguing that neurotic patients repress uncomfortable events. These events cause trauma to the unconscious, which leads to problems in the conscious. Freud illustrates the role of intervention to show that a third party is almost always necessary to allow the neurosis to escape the grasp of the unconscious mind.

Freud's analogy, while highly generative, posed no constraint over his rhetorical situation. It was a fiction that he could revise to suit his explanatory needs; as an explanatory analogy and not at all a part of his own inventional work, he could discard it at any time without jeopardizing the integrity of his theory (though indeed at risk of jeopardizing the success of his lecture). In this way, Freud stands in stark contrast to Nagaoka and Gamow, for whom analogy was the *ansantz*, the device of initial orientation in their theoretical work. As such, they were accountable to the analogy in ways that Freud was not.

CONCLUSION

The historiography of rhetorical studies of analogy can be read as one of increasing analytic specificity. Early studies by John Angus Campbell and Alan Gross, which in their macroscopic conception of analogy imbued it with a seemingly ineffable quality, have been complemented by more resolved studies that take as their unit of analysis not analogy *per se* but the specific correspondences made possible by it. This has owed primarily to our willingness to draw upon the advances of related fields. In 1983, cognitive scientist Dedre Gentner's structure mapping theory offered rhetoricians an alternative unit of analysis in the form of the analogical correspondence. A decade earlier, however, correspondence-level studies of analogy could be found in the general science and social science literature. The neuroscientist Marty Sereno's "Four Analogies Between Biological and Cultural/Linguistic Evolution," published in the *Journal of Theoretical Biology* in 1991, stands as a superb example of the power of such refined analysis—as well as an implicit endorsement of the value of rhetoric situating itself within the larger purview of science studies. In the rhetoric of science, studies by Heather Brodie Graves and Keith Gibson come to mind as exemplars in this tradition; in fact, it was Gibson's recent pedagogical urging that provided the exigence for the present essay. "[S]tudents will be better scientific communicators," he implores, "if we can teach them to think *specifically* about the uses of inductive reasoning. . . . [W]e can, therefore, do our students a great service by including discussions of analogy, example, and metaphor in our classes" (217, emphasis added).

We offer the concepts of generativity and constraint as vehicles for helping students (and scholars) think more specifically about the dynamics of analogy in scientific discourse. Encouraging students to consider the number of candidate correspondences sponsored by an analogy, as well as the variation in inventional fertility across analogies, moves the discussion beyond the limiting assumption that analogy functions collectively in a given rhetorical situation. It enables students to see how each correspondence, or subset of correspondences, has the potential to serve a distinct rhetorical end. In the case of Nagaoka's seven correspondences, the first four worked together to underwrite a set of interrelated claims about the geometry of the atom, the remaining three serving as individual, optional *topoi*. In contrast, and speaking to Wee's earlier point about the relationship between base domain and inventional complexity, Gamow's analogy generated a mere three correspondences, all working together to sponsor a simple nuclear geometry that eschewed from further consideration a variety of otherwise reasonable *topoi*. In broad strokes, we might say that Nagaoka's analogy served as a sort of floodlight on his inventional space, and Gamow's had the focusing effect of a spotlight. In the case of Freud, the analogies were not part of his inventional activity; serving as an explanatory device for a relatively popular audience, they inhabited the traditional role of a passive option to be enlisted or discarded at the discretion of the rhetor.

Whereas Nagaoka and Gamow drew from well-known base domains of considerable specificity—Saturn for Nagaoka, hydrodynamics for Gamow—and therefore induced a relatively rigorous *orthos logos*, Freud invented a fictional story involving Gus to enable his lay audience to understand the technical material at hand through the language of everyday experience. Accordingly, Freud enjoyed the luxury of full agency over the analogy because he was at liberty to invent the story to best serve his rhetorical purpose, and of course he could discard it at any time. Contrastive cases like these offer students clear examples of the varying degrees of rhetor-audience negotiation underlying rhetorical situations, a dynamic easily overlooked in the classically informed composition or technical communication classroom.

Students' ability to articulate these fundamental differences is integral to their understanding of the nuanced relationships that can exist between analogy, invention, and knowledge production; equally important—and increasingly important as rhetoric of science situates itself within the larger milieu of science studies—is the potential for such concepts to enable students to link broader historical, sociological, and philosophical characterizations of scientific activity to specific discursive typifications. Well known to historians of science, for example, is Gamow's deftness in distilling complex physical problems to their essential concepts, his "ability to observe the essence of a matter through a mass of details," as Stanislam Ulam explained in the preface to Gamow's autobiography (vii). In the case of his theory of nuclear structure, Gamow's penetrating insight, his "cutting through to the heart of things" (vii), owes substantively to his choice of analogy and the effects of its individual correspondences on his inventional options, which is precisely the kind of connection that students of rhetoric and technical communication are uniquely positioned to make.

Bibliography

Bunge, Mario. "Analogy in Quantum Theory: From Insight to Nonsense." *British Journal for the Philosophy of Science* 18 (1968): 265–86.

Burke, Kenneth. *Language as Symbolic Action: Essays on Life, Literature, and Method.* Berkeley: U of California P, 1966.

Campbell, John Angus. "Charles Darwin and the Crisis of Ecology: A Rhetorical Perspective." *Quarterly Journal of Speech* 60 (1974): 442–49.

———. "The Invisible Rhetorician: Charles Darwin's 'Third Party' Strategy." *Rhetorica* 7 (1989): 55–85.

———. "The Polemical Mr. Darwin." *Quarterly Journal of Speech* 61 (1975): 375–90.

———. "Scientific Revolution and the Grammar of Culture: The Case of Darwin's *Origin*." *Quarterly Journal of Speech* 72 (1986): 351–76.

Campbell, John Angus, and Ryan Clark. "Revisioning the Origin: Tracing Inventional Agency Through Genetic Inquiry." *Technical Communication Quarterly* 14 (2005): 287–93.

Carazza, Bruno, and Nadia Robotti. "Explaining Atomic Spectra within Classical Physics: 1897–1913." *Annals of Science* 59 (2002): 299–320.

Ceccarelli, Leah. "Neither Confusing Cacophony nor Culinary Complements." *Written Communication* 21 (2004): 92–105.

———. *Shaping Science with Rhetoric.* Chicago: U of Chicago P, 2001.

Clement, Catherine, and Dedre Gentner. "Systematicity as a Selection Constraint in Analogical Mapping." *Cognitive Science* 15 (1991): 89–132.

Emerson, Ralph Waldo. *Nature and Selected Essays.* New York: Penguin, 2003.

Freud, Sigmund. *Five Lectures on Psycho-Analysis.* New York: W. W. Norton, 1990.

Gamow, George. "Mass Defect Curve and Nuclear Constitution." *Proceedings of the Royal Society of London, Series A* 126 (1930): 632–44.

———. *My World Line: An Informal Autobiography.* New York: Viking, 1970.

Gentner, Dedre. "Structure Mapping: A Theoretical Framework for Analogy." *Cognitive Science* 7 (1983): 155–70.

Gentner, Dedre, Keith Holyoak, and Boicho Kokinov, eds. *The Analogical Mind: Perspectives from Cognitive Science.* Cambridge: MIT P, 2001.

Gentner, Dedre, and Michael Jeziorski. "The Shift from Metaphor to Analogy in Western Science." *Metaphor and Thought.* 2nd ed. Ed. Andrew Ortony. Cambridge: Cambridge UP, 1993. 447–80.

Gibson, Keith. "Analogy in Scientific Argumentation." *Technical Communication Quarterly* 17 (2008): 202–19.

Graves, Heather Brodie. *Rhetoric In(to) Science: Style as Invention in Inquiry.* Cresskill, NJ: Hampton, 2005.

Gross, Alan G. *The Rhetoric of Science.* 2nd ed. Cambridge: Harvard UP, 1996.

———. *Starring the Text: The Place of Rhetoric in Science Studies.* Carbondale: Southern Illinois UP.

Heilbron, John Lewis. "A History of the Problem of Atomic Structure from the Discovery of the Electron to the Beginning of Quantum Mechanics." Diss. University of California, Berkeley, 1964.

Judson, Horace Freeland. *The Eighth Day of Creation.* New York: Simon and Schuster, 1979.

Kendler, Howard H. *Historical Foundations of Modern Psychology.* Pacific Grove, CA: Brooks, 1987.

Little, Joseph. "Analogy in Science: Where Do We Go From Here?" *Rhetoric Society Quarterly* 30 (2000): 69–92.

———. "The Role of Analogy in George Gamow's Derivation of Drop Energy." *Technical Communication Quarterly* 17 (2008): 220–38.

Nagaoka, Hantaro. "Kinetics of a System of Particles Illustrating the Line and the Band Spectrum and the Phenomena of Radioactivity." *Philosophical Magazine* 7 (1904): 445–55.

Pais, Abraham. *Inward Bound: Of Matter and Forces in the Physical World.* New York: Oxford UP, 1988.

Patterson, Gordon. "Freud's Rhetoric: Persuasion and History in the 1909 Clark Lectures." *Metaphor and Symbolic Activity* 5 (1990): 215–33.

Putnam, James J. "Personal Impressions of Sigmund Freud and His Work." *Journal of Abnormal Psychology* 4 (1910): 372–79.

Rutherford, Ernest. "The Scattering of Alpha and Beta Particles by Matter and the Structure of the Atom." *Philosophical Magazine* 21 (1911): 669–88.

Segre, Gino. *Faust in Copenhagen: A Struggle for the Soul of Physics.* New York: Viking, 2007.

Sereno, M. I. "Four Analogies Between Biological and Cultural/Linguistic Evolution." *Journal of Theoretical Biology* 151 (1991): 467–507.

Stepan, Nancy L. "Race and Gender: The Role of Analogy in Science." *Isis* 77 (1986): 261–77.

Stuewer, Roger H. "The Origin of the Liquid-drop Model and the Interpretation of Nuclear Fission." *Perspectives on Science* 2 (1994): 76–129.

Thagard, Paul, Keith J. Holyoak, Greg Nelson, and David Gochfeld. "Analog Retrieval by Constraint Satisfaction." *Artificial Intelligence* 46 (1994): 259–310.

van den Broek, A. J. "Intra-atomic Charge." *Nature* 92 (1913): 372–73.

Wee, Lionel. "Constructing the Source: Metaphor as a Discourse Strategy." *Discourse Studies* 7 (2005): 363–84.

Yagi, Eri. "On Nagaoka's Saturnian Atomic Model (1903)." *Japanese Studies in the History of Science* 3 (1964): 29–47.

Textual Machinery
Authorial Agency and
Bot-Written Texts in Wikipedia

Krista Kennedy

In her 2007 *Rhetoric Society Quarterly* essay on automation and agency, Carolyn Miller explored the consequences of allowing bots to grade compositions written by human students. Her conclusions extend previous conversations in the field that describe agency as bifurcated and illusory. In this brief essay, I draw on her work along with other rhetoricians and legal scholars to explore some of the implications of using bots to write and edit texts in Wikipedia. Most particularly, I'm interested in the question of whether or not a machine that writes can be considered an author in either a legal or theoretical sense. This question has concerned intellectual property specialists since at least 1969, when a paper on the subject by Karl Milde appeared in the *Journal of the Patent Office Society*,[1] and it's an increasingly relevant topic these days as our mundane textual environments become ever more automated.[2]

BACKGROUND

The capital-A Author looms as a construct for so many of us who study rhetoric and writing, if for no other reason than our common concerns about plagiarism and tenure publication requirements. When we consider the Author, dead or alive, the creature we typically refer to is the Poetic Author, creator of original compositions. In this construct, the notion of *originality* is central: it is vital that the work be fresh, inventive, and unusual within its cultural context, lest it lose its cultural value or even become vilified as plagiarism. It must also typically be the product of an individual mind. With the last decade's turn to the examination of authorship in digital environments, we've tended to rely more frequently on the continental critique of authorship, applying more distributed concepts such as the death of the author or the Author Construct to networked environments. This works, more or less,

303

but a strictly postmodern stance also potentially brushes aside some central questions about authorial agency and responsibility, as Cheryl Geisler ("Teaching") and Michael Leff and Andrea Lunsford have suggested. The fact remains that actual people—and entities, in the case of bots—create actual texts, even if these agents do so in radically distributed, collaborative, and sometimes automated ways.

The technological affordances of digital collaboration are not the only factors that impact the construction of authorship; genre does as well. Studies of authorship very often take for granted the assumption that we can safely apply our preferred version of the Author Construct across any genre or form of text. Our work, then, often suggests this same Author can be found in any number of textual genres, both poetic and pragmatic. It also assumes that authorial agency remains static across genres, rather than fluctuating according to situation, as Karlyn Kohrs Campbell suggests when she describes agency as "protean, ambiguous, open to reversal" (2). This poses a number of problems for scholars of scientific and technical communication, which is often produced in collaborative and unsigned ways, although the issue is beginning to be addressed in the case of the scientific author.[3] Still, we've not looked deeply into the matter of reference texts, particularly those that purport to cover the broad scope of the Enlightenment project—that is, encyclopedias and dictionaries.

The construction of encyclopedias requires a unique mode of composition that focuses on collecting other texts, assessing their quality, splicing the best information from each together with the most recent data and, in the process, transforming the results into a new text. This composition process more closely resembles what I've come to call *textual curation* than our Romantic idea of original composition. Our canonical, unified Author doesn't easily map to this form of composition, but this difficulty doesn't mean that such texts don't have an author. Rather, it means the encyclopedic author demonstrates a different sort of agency and responsibility.

WIKIPEDIA

These factors are compounded when we consider them within the radically open, densely networked digital environment of Wikipedia. The study of authorship in Wikipedia must deal with a variety of complications posed by the affordances of wiki applications. As rhetoric and writing scholars already know, the technological structure of wikis, as well as their *ethos* of openness, affords nearly instantaneous collaboration by anyone with sufficient access, literacy skills, and leisure time. This results in co-extant texts of primary articles, and their related prior versions, article discussions, and page histories, all simultaneously written in real time by anonymous and pseudonymous authors. Interestingly, it must also account for robot-written texts—that is, texts written and edited by bots, which are programs or scripts that effect change without the aid of human decision-making processes.

Bots are the unspoken textual curators of Wikipedia. Perhaps the most well-known of these bots is the RamBot, named after its creator, Wikipedian Derek Ramsey. In operation since October 2002, it has created articles on every U.S. city by inserting census information in a predetermined textual format. It has also been updated with functionality to improve existing entries with some intelligence (User:Rambot). SpellBot, another prominent bot in the project, corrects common typos, and an army of other bots insert interwiki links, tags, and redirects as well as perform general maintenance tasks such as resetting sandboxes and reverting pages that have been vandalized (Wikipedia:Bot). These compositional tasks were formerly the exclusive domain of humans, who were expected to use their critical judgment and authorial agency to responsibly attend to these duties.

Bots are quarantined, tracked, and approved by the Bot Approvals Group, which imposes strict policies because of the peculiar agency bots demonstrate. As the Bot Guidelines note, "since bots are potentially capable of editing far faster than humans can, have a lower level of scrutiny on each edit than a human editor, may cause severe disruption if they malfunction or are misused, and are held to a high standard by the community, high standards are expected before a bot is approved for use on designated tasks" (Wikipedia:Bot). The Wikipedia policy on bots makes a strict distinction between the human user who creates a bot and the bot itself. Bots are required to have their own names and user pages. (Hence, RamMan's bot's user name is RamBot.) Their scripts must be able to leave notes and comments akin to the ones human users leave when making an edit . . . that is, an automatically logged signature and a cordial description of the changes made. (Cordiality is a basic requirement for bot approval.) An unsupervised bot can wreak havoc in the text and leech unnecessary resources from the infrastructure. In order to prevent these blunders, strict rules govern their editing speed. A bot performing high-priority tasks is permitted to edit once every four seconds; lower-priority task bots may edit every ten seconds. Lower speeds are required during typically high-use periods: Wednesdays, Thursdays, and between 1200 and 0400 UTC on any given day.

When we outsource these more mundane textual tasks to bots, should we then consider them as authors when we scroll through the list of authors on an entry's history page? Was the article on, say, Darwin, Minnesota, drafted by humans or by bots if 17 of its 32 edits are bot-generated? Bots are very much products of their creator's intentionality; indeed, they owe their existence to intention and the fulfillment of it. With that in mind, we might suggest that rhetorical agency lies in the creator of the bot, who demonstrated intentionality by writing the program. Still, the writer of the program is not necessarily the writer of the text that his program eventually creates.

As Miller has pointed out, agency has been previously attributed to AI programs and expert systems ("Expertise" 208). One might object to applying this notion to the case of Wikipedia bots, pointing out that these particular bots work in the service of agency rather than the other way around. They are written into being and permitted to exist and work purely in service of the task they perform; for example, they do not perform the sort of complex decision-making behavior that expert systems like air traffic control systems exhibit. Rather, they make very limited decisions as to whether or not they will perform a given task, such as reverting a vandalized page, or as to whether or not a particular word is a typo that should be fixed. None of them are meant to pass a Turing test, although they are required to leave notes that meet human standards of politeness and match human syntax. They are clearly not sentient in the ways that we normally think of agents, but they do perceive their environment and initiate action with it. They also clearly do effect change both within the texts and sometimes within the broader scope of the project, as when Wikipedia rather suddenly expanded to cover thousands of towns. When we look at a Wikipedia entry, it is not immediately apparent which edits were made by humans and which were made by bots. Which sort of writer contributed which text can only be discerned by a careful reading of the page's history. These small writing machines are in fact intelligent agents, in however basic a way.

These bot-generated texts demand that we reconsider commonplaces about the attribution of rhetorical agency as well as the ways it is split from the agent. Previous discussions in our field about agency have argued as to whether or not we should make a distinction between agent and agency and not necessarily assume that one automatically comes with the other. Geisler ("How" 9) noted this as a prominent strand of inquiry at the 2003 Alliance of Rhetoric Societies conversations on agency, and Christian Lindberg and Josh Gunn explore it more fully in their response to her synopsis. What happens to the conventional rhetorical account of agency, they ask, "if it starts out by presuming that the agency possesses the agent, as opposed to the agent possessing agency as an instrument or substance?" (97). This is the sort of bifurcation of agent and agency that we see in robot-written texts. We might well say that agency possesses the bot-agent, not the other way around. If that's the case: is there an author of the bot-written text? Perhaps so, when we apply both the theoretical and pragmatic senses of agency. But what about when we consider agency in the legal sense of authorship?

LEGAL PRECEDENTS

Under U.S. copyright law, anyone who modifies a text—who contributes an original expression of an idea—is an author. Does this mean that entry-writing bots are authors? According to the law, no, for reasons primarily related to agency. Legal authorship status requires both responsibility and demonstrable decision-making agency, as illustrated in the Ninth Circuit Court opinion on *Aalmuhammed v. Lee*. As most readers will remember, Spike Lee cowrote, directed, and produced the movie *Malcolm X* in 1991. During his preparation for the starring role, Denzel Washington contracted with Jefri Aalmuhammed as a subject-matter expert on both Malcolm X and Islam.

Aalmuhammed reviewed the script and suggested a number of significant revisions, most of which concerned religious and historical accuracy in the scenes of Malcolm X's conversion and subsequent hajj, or pilgrimage, to Mecca. Judge Kleinfeld's opinion in the case notes the plaintiff submitted evidence that he "directed Denzel Washington and other actors while on the set, created at least two entire scenes with new characters, translated Arabic into English for subtitles, supplied his own voice for voice-overs, selected the proper prayers and religious practices for the characters, and edited parts of the movie during post production" (*Aalmuhammed v. Lee*). Aalmuhammed subsequently sued for coauthorship credit on the grounds that his contributions constituted authorship. The court ruled that the status of "coauthor" required not only a mutual initial intention to enter into joint authorship but also that both parties have superintendence, or decision-making authority. In other words, demonstrable agency concerning decisions is a central, defining facet of authorship. In the case of *Malcolm X*, only Lee, the director, had such agency. In other words, while Aalmuhammed was indisputably an *agent* within the larger *Malcolm X* production, he did not possess sufficient *agency* to be legally considered a coauthor. This bifurcation of agent and agency is in line with the previously noted theoretical arguments.

A similar bifurcation is evident in work-for-hire doctrine, which returns to one of our central concerns about impetus. As Andrew Wu points out in a 1997 article on computer-generated works, concerns about bots' lack of impetus—that is, the ability to induce the motivating factor in producing the work—is consistent with the reasoning for work-for-hire doctrine (164). The 1976 Copyright Act grants authorship rights to the employer for works produced under specific contractual conditions based on the reasoning that the employer is the motivating factor in producing the work (17 USC 101). In exchange for providing impetus, the work environment, and whatever support is needed, the employer assumes ownership of the resulting work. The decision-making agency that the worker demonstrates in the process of actually creating the work is deemed inconsequential in this contractual situation. In much the same way, the work of bots, motivated and supported by humans, could easily be considered simply work-for-hire, if a bot were considered hirable. Hiring implies entering into a contract, which implies that both parties possess sufficient agency and responsibility to make a contractual agreement. For now, our culture and economies deny attribution of such agency to machines (Miller, "What" 152).

CONCLUSION

The law has a long-standing precedent of both honoring and ignoring authorial agency demonstrated by individual working authors. The Romantic, poetic author is accorded full control of her creative work until 70 years after her death. Authors of more mundane texts rarely enjoy the same privileges (whatever the broader implications of such far-reaching privileges might be). We would hardly impose this stance in our own classrooms, claiming that the university owns student writing because it provides the motivation and support for it.

Instead, we recognize more and more that writing happens as an interactive process that involves exchanges between multiple agents, texts, and influences. It is, as a number of rhetorical scholars have suggested, a *performance* that also includes the added factors of audience and interactivity (see Jarratt; Leff; Leff and Lunsford 55; Miller, "What"). The Encyclopedic Author must constantly negotiate all of these factors while performing the task of textual curation. This element of performance is perhaps particularly explicit in the swirling, constantly moving text that is Wikipedia, where the writer becomes the audience and vice versa and back again; where meta-discourse about the text occurs simultaneously with the text; where a bot begins an entry and humans build it out, only to have their typos edited by another bot. In a textual situation like this, agency occurs somewhere in what Miller has called the "kinetic energy" of all these exchanges ("What" 146). At this point in the life of the project, the impetus for contributing is mutable. This sense of energy and flux is particularly suited to the encyclopedic form, which is driven by an ever-broadening and deepening quest for knowledge. The Wikipedia "author" is becoming the purest sort of textual curator, shaping and showcasing what already exists—no longer fitting our construction of The Author but becoming a newly identifiable creature.

Notes

[1] See also Butler and Farr for early and late 1980s perspectives on the subject.
[2] Examples of everyday automated textual environments include search engines, digital forms, spell check, indexing tools, and computer viruses.
[3] See Biagioli and Galison's anthology *Scientific Authorship: Credit and Intellectual Property in Science*.

Works Cited

Aalmuhammed v. Lee. 202 F.3d 1227. Ninth Circuit Ct. 2000.

Biagioli, Mario, and Peter Galison, eds. *Scientific Authorship: Credit and Intellectual Property in Science*. New York: Routledge, 2002.

Butler, Timothy. "Can a Computer be an Author? Copyright Aspects of Artificial Intelligence." *Comm/Ent Law Journal* 4.4 (1982): 707–47.

Campbell, Karlyn Kohrs. "Agency: Promiscuous and Protean." *Communication and Critical/Cultural Studies* 2.1 (2005): 1–19.

Farr, Evan H. "Copyrightability of Computer-Created Works." *Rutgers Computer and Technology Law Journal* 63 (1989): 63–79.

Geisler, Cheryl. "How Ought We To Understand the Concept of Rhetorical Agency? Report from the ARS." *Rhetoric Society Quarterly* 34.3 (2004): 9–17.

———. "Teaching the Post-Modern Rhetor: Continuing the Conversation on Rhetorical Agency." *Rhetoric Society Quarterly* 35.4 (2005): 107–113.

Jarratt, Susan C. "A Matter of Emphasis." *Rhetoric Society Quarterly* 36.2 (2006): 213–19.

Leff, Michael. "Up from Theory: Or I Fought the Topoi and the Topoi Won." *Rhetoric Society Quarterly* 36.2 (2006): 203–11.

Leff, Michael, and Andrea Lunsford. "Afterwords: Dialogue." *Rhetoric Society Quarterly* 34.3 (2004): 55–67.

Lindberg, Christian, and Joshua Gunn. "Ouija Board, Are There Any Communications? Agency, Ontotheology, and the Death of the Humanist Subject, or, Continuing the ARS Conversation." *Rhetoric Society Quarterly* 35.4 (2005): 83–105.

Milde, Karl F., Jr. "Can a Computer Be 'An Author' or an 'Inventor'?" *Journal of the Patent Office Society* (1969): 378.

Miller, Carolyn R. "Expertise and Agency: Transformations of Ethos in Human-Computer Interaction." *The Ethos of Rhetoric.* Ed. Michael Hyde. Columbia: U of South Carolina P, 2004. 197–218.

———. "What Can Automation Tell Us About Agency?" *Rhetoric Society Quarterly* 37.2 (Spring 2007): 137–57.

User:Rambot. Wikipedia. 7 Apr. 2008. 14 May 2008. <http://en.wikipedia.org/wiki/User:Rambot>.

Wikipedia:Bot Policy. Wikipedia. 11 May 2008. 14 May 2008. <http://en.wikipedia.org/wiki/Wikipedia:Bots>.

Wu, Andrew J. "From Video Games to Artificial Intelligence: Assigning Copyright Ownership to Works Generated by Increasingly Sophisticated Computer Programs." *AIPLA Quarterly Journal* 131 (1997): 133–78.

28

The Rhetoric of the Graphic Novel

Kathryn E. Dobson

It has been more than two millennia since Aristotle advised rhetors to persuade an audience by verbally bringing a thing before the eyes, a maneuver graphic novels perform quite well; little surprise, then, that rhetorical theory might be used to explain how comic books convince the reason and move the passions. Other extensions of rhetorical theory to comics seem equally intuitive: we readily draw upon concepts such as selection, presence, arrangement, and style; terministic screens and identification; and narrative rhetorics from Booth or Fisher or Genette. These familiar rhetorical tools capture much about the rhetoric of the graphic novel, just as they capture rhetorics in a number of other media. But as has been found with other new media, the very medium of comics—that is, its special fusion of the verbal and the (usually hand-produced) visual—may force a rethinking of old tools and invite us to take new approaches.

It may matter, in the end, that comics are comics. This paper seeks to illuminate some ways that the medium of comics itself enables a particular rhetoric and, perhaps, complicates existing rhetorical precepts. To borrow from Marshall McLuhan, my purpose is to asses how the medium is, or at least mediates, the message.

The current project has its inception in watching students engage with and respond to serious comics like Joe Sacco's *Palestine* and Marjane Satrapi's *Persepolis*, progeny of Art Spiegelman's *Maus*. When college students claim that these books help them better understand the Middle East, when they confess that they have never before understood the least thing about the Arab–Israeli conflict (indeed, have felt entirely outside of that discussion), it seems mistaken to explain their engagement with the dismissive comment that comics are an "easy read."

It is inaccurate to characterize a book like *Maus*, or many other serious comics, as "easy." Books that take seriously such topics as September 11, the Arab–Israeli conflict, the Iranian revolution, the Holocaust, Hiroshima,

I would like to acknowledge the assistance and collaboration of Linda C. Macri in crafting the larger panel presentation for the RSA conference. The remarks presented here are my own.

queer identity, spina bifida, epilepsy, autism, incest, cancer, and adolescent anomie are not easy books, nor are today's long-form comics simple. In privileging "difficult" texts and theorists, we may under-value and under-investigate the phenomenon of ease in reading and writing. Prior engagements with aspects of "reading ease" have offered rhetorical studies a wealth of information about style and delivery. We should keep that truth in mind as we consider the lessons comics might have to offer rhetoricians.

When people try to explain why comics communicate so successfully, they tend to offer the following three points, none of which adequately explain the phenomenon:

1. Sequential format lends itself to teaching.

2. Comics are motivating.

3. Comics are simple.

The formula deserves scrutiny. First, because purely verbal text is also sequential, sheer sequentiality is not a sufficient explanation. Second, to say that comics are "motivating" is a bit circular. Moreover, many graphic narratives fail to move or engage readers, which suggests that the format itself is not inherently "motivating" unless the specific performance does something *else* well at the same time. Finally, simplicity and ease make many kinds of texts fail utterly for adolescent and adult readers. For instance, while *Reader's Digest* redactions and illustrated children's books are "easy," they do not seem to provoke quite the same motivated, engaged response as today's serious graphic novel. Thus, it seems worthwhile to examine what *aspects* of simplicity support the formation of reader interest in and engagement with comics. Finally, though comics do simplify particular aspects of texts—for instance, the word-to-page ratio is almost necessarily lower—those simplifications do not necessarily make the comic itself easy or simple. Rather, they make comics highly rhetorical.

The claim that comics motivate readers dates back to the early heyday of the comic book, when 1940s-era educators feared that comics would undermine literacy. Among the few defenders, there emerged a consensus around two profound conclusions about the difference between comics and the non-pictorial text: Kids like to read comics, and they actually remember what they read. Two articles published in the *Journal of Educational Sociology* in the 1940s reported on empirical studies that posttested adolescent readers after one group read a story presented in comic book form and the other read a nonpictorial account of the same story (Sones; Hutchinson). The comics readers scored distinctly higher in reading comprehension and retention. Subsequently, when the groups were reversed and the posttest repeated, the group that began with the nonpictorial version made a significant forward leap after reading the comic, but the group that began with the comic made only modest additional gains by reading the purely verbal text. Similar results were found in a 2007 study (Mallia) that tested reading recall, text comprehension, and "imaginative engagement" after students read a comic about the national history of Malta.

In the decades between these studies, Will Eisner's instructional comics on preventive maintenance won head-to-head usability tests when compared to other instructions written by the military's engineers (Andelman 85). Serialized as the Army's 1940s era publication *PS Magazine*, Eisner's comics won adherents among military enlisted, to the consternation of military engineers. Eisner would depict his Beetle Bailey-looking GIs removing parts or adding oil, but in place of the engineers' technical explanations, the caption referred to "grease jobs" or (elsewhere) "cleaning the crud out of the engine." According to Andelman (84–85), the engineers thought that Eisner's humble phrases and crude visuals could not possibly convey adequate mechanical understanding. In the usability tests they demanded, they wanted to beat Eisner's comics, so it seems likely they put forward their most user-friendly instructions. They lost.

Figure 1.   Joe Dope, from *PS Magazine* 18 (1954): 832–33, by Will Eisner. Permission granted by Virginia Commonwealth University.

Nevertheless, in 1994, James Hartley, a specialist in designing instructional text, was still repeating the dictum in which comics served mostly to motivate (slow) readers:

> Clearly the affective role of instructions is to the fore in comic strips: their aim being to attract and motivate less-able learners. . . . The general picture that emerges . . . is that cartoons often enhance motivation, but they do not often increase comprehension. (87–88; qtd. in Mallia)

Although I would challenge Hartley's conclusion that cartoons do not increase comprehension, he is correct to note that research into the efficacy of comics as instruction has been inadequate. Yet faculty in physics and literature (Versaci; Kakalios) have reported improvements in subject comprehension when students engaged the concepts and texts via comics. If comprehension improved largely as a matter of motivation, it is still worth understanding how and when to harness the motivating capacity of comics. That is, rhetoricians might benefit from understanding why comics "work" for certain audiences and purposes and whether rhetoric, broadly, can benefit from such an inquiry. Such an inquiry might help us better understand the ways that particular discourses raise barriers or lower resistance to particular subjects. For instance, if it is truly "just" affect that helped Eisner prevail in usability tests, rhetoricians should learn why comics produce a pleasant or engaging affect and whether that affect extends to comics about difficult subjects.

I have not yet formulated full answers to these questions, but I believe that an approach one might broadly class as rhetorical phenomenology offers some important insights to how readers encounter comics. I will try to suggest how modes of encounter may make comics "easy" for readers to read— that is, may lower certain forms of resistance and enlist participation, engagement, and even immersion—as readers "come to grips with" comics, to echo Merleau-Ponty's terminology. I start from the presumption that comics provide a particular way for consciousness to be present to its objects (Merleau-Ponty, *Phenomenology* 29). That analysis includes examining what it is the reader perceives on the page, as well as what is absent, since comics is an art of gutters and redactions. My goal here is to demonstrate that such an approach offers an important complement to current comics scholarship and to suggest some of the questions rhetoric should be asking about discourses that lower barriers.

ENTERING THE LIFEWORLD: *ETHOS* AND THE GRAPHIC NOVEL

As Linda C. Macri has argued, comics gain a particular *ethos* from their status as a rebel genre—outlaw, underground, unapproved. In her comment on the *ethos* of the graphic novel, we turn to the broader, culturally more familiar meaning of *"ethos"* in place of the rhetorician's familiar triumvirate of *phronesis, arête*, and *eunoia*. As Michael J. Hyde's *The Ethos of Rhetoric* suggests, perhaps rhetorical studies have always suffered by losing the larger meanings of the term. Hyde, in approaching Aristotelian *ethos* via Heidegger's concept of *ethos* as a dwelling place, argues for the existence of an "architectural element" in rhetoric (xii). That is, if the Greek *ethos* shares a root with words for "homes" and "places of dwelling" (as in the study of ethology and ethnography), we might best understand rhetorical *ethos* as a process of world building and place shaping, as an invitation to readers to "dwell together" in and with the author-text. The problem of rhetorical *ethos* becomes not simply to craft adequate authority and value for an argument's warrants, but rather to build the kind of space—moral, tonal, aesthetic—that an audience will momentarily indwell and, further, one that supports the author's rhetorical objectives.

Such an architectural element may well permeate all rhetoric, but I want to argue that graphic narrative, perhaps more than purely verbal forms of rhetorical discourse, especially demands an architectural concept of *ethos*. As in film, in graphic narrative visual choices create atmosphere and, with varying success, build a world for the viewer to enter or, at least, to entertain its implications. The *ethos* of a graphic novel emerges, then, from a panoply of textual choices. These include: the ways comics panels are framed and pages constructed (irregular and angular panels in complex relationships? superhero splash pages?); the kinds of events that are felt to "happen" in the gutters (the spaces between panels); and the sense-crossing synaesthesia that turns a comic's visually busy noise (or its calm quiet) into the text's aural atmosphere. It emerges, perhaps most evidently, from the voice of both the narrator and the "graphiator" (the personality of the drawing "voice"), including the nature of the artist's line and its affective, conventional, and historical implications. In some cases, it emerges even from textural choices about the quality of the paper and ink, the gloss of the design, or the choice to craft a Web comic. As readers encounter these various choices, many of which provide atmospheric cueing, the text demands a series of cognitive performances about the kind of world—or dwelling place—the reader is invited to enter.

For most readers, the graphic novel's atmospheric cueing represents one of the types of "ease" that characterizes the medium. Readers enter the graphic novel's tonal, atmospheric world—or, rather, to allow that world to enter *them*—without parsing massive additional verbiage. To a significant extent the sheer visuality of the medium provokes the reaction. As Olga Belova remarks, "The reader simply opens himself up to the object and sensitizes himself to what the object has to express. This relation can be described as chiasmic (Merleau-Ponty, 1968) in that one holds and lets oneself be held at the same time, allows dispossession without considering it as a loss of defeat" (99). For a great number of individuals, a purely verbal rhetoric is slower to provoke this "chiasmic" response, this dispossession.

Admittedly, some readers find comics bewildering in their visual complexity, a complexity I have heard them characterize as a kind of "noise." The gestalt of the page—which some comics scholars call the *"mise-en-page"*—compels their attention, yet they feel pulled in various directions and fragmented by its divisions. Such readers may experience themselves as constantly at-choice. They ask, "What do read I first, the words or the images?" For these readers, the graphic novel never becomes, in Poulet's sense, subjective. In their encounter with an off-putting busyness and noise, the comic's lifeworld remains for them inert on the page.

To succeed with readers, a successful graphic novel must invite readers into a lifeworld, one that—if the teenagers reading serialized Japanese manga (comics) in the aisles at Barnes & Noble are any proof—transports readers to some kind of cognitive "elsewhere." The question for further research is what types of rhetorical "dwelling places" are particularly productive in serious comics. Setting aside those readers for whom *no* graphic novel becomes subjective, we might begin to ask these questions: What forms of *ethos* in graphic novels provide the greatest likelihood of a "truth experience" for readers, an assent that reaches beyond mere intellection? At what point does a dwelling place become so engrossing that sensation overwhelms other forms of response?

It seems likely that sheer verbal barrage in nonpictorial texts, particularly in a scholarly register, ensures that for some readers the text never becomes "subjective." That is, concepts hardly move beyond the status of being objects on a page, never becoming imaginatively vivid or producing anything like a truth experience. Weaknesses in literacy can inhibit subjective experience of texts (as can weaknesses in comics literacy), but the problem is surely not limited to this single source. It emerges, too, from a role disparity that prevents certain readers from comfortably entering the "dwelling house" of that discourse. For them, to become absorbed by the discourse, to enter it fully, would require of them a shift of attentions and affects so significant as to rearrange the very self. By contrast, readers of serious comics may find themselves invited to "come as they are," more able to adopt the readerly roles the text contemplates for them, to participate in its lifeworld, and to experience the text subjectively.

Will Eisner's preventive maintenance comics offer an illustration. Beyond providing his readers the sheer fun of entering what Macri calls comics' "rebel intertext"—the entertaining interplay of mainstream message with underground messaging—Eisner's *PS Magazine* chose visual and verbal stylings that connected to the daily life of the enlisted man. They addressed the enlistee-mechanic in his guise as both mechanic and enlistee, not as the idealized Mechanic addressed by the Army's engineers. Eisner's instructional comics thus found their reader at his most relaxed and comfortable self. Turned the other way around, as the enlisted man approached Eisner's preventive maintenance comics, he found himself performing a familiar and enjoyable "I." The magazine thus created an encounter, an indwelling in an imaginatively vivid and welcoming world, where the man who would perform the maintenance spent time with the technical knowledge he would need to perform it. Encountered in connection with the life the GI really lived, that knowledge became more subjectively real.

But to successfully provoke such a coexistence between the reader and the material in comics form required Eisner to achieve something more imaginative than sheer dumbing down. Rather, to cultivate an engaging dwelling place for readers to encounter the text, the author's rhetorical choices must permit readers to venture there without losing their self-respect. In Eisner's case, the magazine needed to *like* the American GI; because it did, he liked it right back.

By contrast, the authors of *Macedonia*, Harvey Pekar, Heather Roberson, and Ed Piskor, fail to merge graphic elements into a sufficiently inviting textual world. As one reviewer writes, the book is "cumulatively too dry and overwhelming for all but the most wonky reader to absorb" (Olsen). In writing about this Balkan state's peace process, the creators of *Macedonia* have not rendered the text's image-world nearly as salient as the text's verbal track. Although *Macedonia* provides readers with scenery, character, and action, they fail to carry their weight at either the atmospheric or story level, leaving too much of the work to the purely verbal track. In a McLuhanian sense, this over reliance on the verbal track "hots up" a typically "cool" medium.

The hotting up interferes with the typically lo-fidelity, absorbing life-world of comics; there is neither opportunity nor incentive to enter—to "ind-well"—the world it depicts. The case is a curious one principally because there is no lack of artistic acumen, storytelling skill, or comics know-how among the collaborators. Indeed, on prior occasion Piskor has produced outstanding illustration to accompany Pekar's famously angsty musings. Thus, the collaborators' failure to use image, sequence, and juxtaposition to create an atmosphere relevant to the story, or to convey important details, leaves the impression of a cynical attempt to cash in on readers' taste for graphic novels on serious subjects.

Some reviewers have attributed *Macedonia*'s failures to the book's linguistic difficulty. As one reviewer notes, "The book is textually dense, even in terms of Pekar's oft dialog-heavy work, and while some readers' complaints about an advanced vocabulary level hardly pertain to the majority of the

Figure 2.   From *Macedonia* by Harvey Pekar and Heather Roberson and Ed Piskor, illustrator. Copyright © 2007 by Harvey Pekar LLC and Heather Roberson. Used by permission of Villard Books, a division of Random House, Inc.

book, there are a few occasions in which it would certainly help to grasp the meaning [of] 'hegemony' . . ." (Heater). But the successful graphic adaptation of the *9/11 Commission Report* demonstrates that linguistic difficulty is not, truly, the problem encountered in *Macedonia*. The authors of the graphic *9/11 Report,* Jacobson and Colon, took their language directly from the independent commission's report, producing a book that scores at the eleventh grade reading level, far higher than the average newspaper. Yet the book has been a major commercial success, and it is engrossing as a comic book. Ironically, the book's "Fog Index" and Flesch-Kincaid scores—two measures of reading difficulty—indicate that the adapted *9/11 Report* is more difficult than 96 percent of comic books and, strikingly, more difficult than 40 percent of *all* books sold on Amazon.com. Nevertheless, the book sells well, ranking thirty-sixth of all September 11 books sold on Amazon (as of May 2008). These various figures suggest that linguistic difficulty alone does not doom a graphic narrative, provided that textual choices work syncretically to produce a compelling world for readers to enter.

WHAT ARE YOU LOOKIN' AT?

I return, though, to the question of what it is we *perceive* when we pick up a graphic novel. It is inaccurate to say that we "read" the comic as we read a nonpictorial text. The two activities are distinct: One cannot make a successfully Braille version of a comic. Yet we also do not *gaze* as we do with painting; the comics image rarely rewards quite such rapt attention, and the *mise-en-page* both fractures the gaze and pulls us forward to the next image. We also do not *watch* comics as we watch TV, or sit back to passively *see*, as most say we do with film. Rather, I would suggest that comics require us to adjust the nature of our visual attention, at turns *looking, watching, seeing, glancing,* and occasionally *gazing*. Comics require us to engage not just one mode of looking, but various kinds of looking as the eye and the attention shift focus across the page. Yet, at the same time, the form of visual attention is one of incaution, of permission *to* glance without threat of repercussion. He who loses the thread easily returns to prior pages and, with the aid of frames and visuals previously glanced, quickly finds it.

To be at grips with comics is, furthermore, to accede to the patterns of visual attending they command. One might imagine here Burke's suggestion that assent to form is assent to content. With comics, in a manner very much akin to music and to the cadences of oral rhetorics, readers assent to rhythms that are managed by the timing device of the frame. Readers accede, too, to the gestural implications of the author-artist's lines, lines that offer not photography's stasis but drawing's movement. My argument, in short form, is that the physicality of drawing leaves its traces in the images, giving comics more of the embodied quality of speech than one finds in sanitized, typewritten text. Indeed, precisely to bring readers into contact with an embodied voice, Art Spiegelman deliberately preserved poor panel edging in *Maus*, an artistic "error" that usually counts as poor draftsmanship. I suspect that this gestural quality in comics connects readers' own bodies more intimately to the ideas they "read" on the page.

The *voice* of comics works not only through line but also through strategic absence. An art of redaction, comics *strips*. These redactions make comics one of McLuhan's "cool" media, low-fidelity and unsaturated. The reader must fill in the blanks in the panels and gutters as well as the images themselves. In other words, it matters not just that comics are a visual medium, but a visual medium of a particular sort, one that invites readers to lean forward and look rather than to sit back and see. The comics author—whether working in long or short form—engages in decoding and recoding, determining what to make figure and what to make ground, identifying the panel that crystallizes an emotional state or closes off an event-arc. As Pascal Lefevre argues, "Unlike films or stage plays, comics can only represent fragments of events (and objects). A comic has to suggest a whole sequence of events by representing only some single significant actions" (section 2). The reader undertakes the rest of the work, filling a great many gaps and contributing significant cognitive labor to make a comic signify. In the *9/11 Report*, hundreds of words about Zacharias Moussaoui become a quick visual representation of a figure engaged in an action. Clearly, the decrease in verbiage makes processing comics faster than processing sheer text.

However, if all visual redactions were created equal, a schematic of a car's electrical system should be just as accessible as an Eisner preventive maintenance comic. And that is clearly not true. As John Berger noted in *Ways of Seeing*, we never just look at something, but are "always looking at the relation between things and ourselves" (9). Advancing this insight, Sturken and Cartwright argued in their 2001 book *Practices of Looking* that images invite particular kinds of seeing.

In part, the power comes from the "friendliness" of the cartoon style historically associated with comics. By friendliness, here, I mean to indicate that certain line-drawing styles—typically, clear lines with graceful arcs and orderly, balanced lines—offer readers a kind of calm and avoid the nerve-jangling challenge presented by other comics artists (e.g., Lynda Barry, Bill Griffith, or R. Crumb). For its simplicity and underelaborated grace, Charles Schulz's *Peanuts* might be read as exhibiting a kind of meditative or Zen quality (McCloud). Working in the opposite direction, we might imagine the downside to producing how-to manuals in comics styles that suggest a less steady hand, a less certain direction, and a less unified and solid line. In the Army publications, comics drawn with the exaggerated, grotesque, and shaky line of Bill Griffith's existential *Zippy the Pinhead* would very likely have undermined the preventive maintenance program. (Imagine the angst-ridden mechanic!) Styles that lack clear, simple lines and that capture the hesitations of the hand—a metonymy of our weak grasp on the world, where we move ahead without ease—may well trouble the mechanic-reader's sense of calm, ease, and control. As the machines become more real, and the mechanic strangely more particularized, the possibility for crisis increases. Further, such complicated lines would introduce a distracting hermeneutic impulse, ultimately interfering with the preventive maintenance process Eisner and the Army sought to ease.

But even in more serious styles of comics, the art style is quite different from the sterile, alienating voice of the engineer's drawing of the departmental photocopier, which presents the item with unselective detail that is relevant mostly to the engineer—preserving with exactness the thicknesses of the washers and the bolts and the springs. It is a drawing that constructs its reader also as an engineer, an identity most of us do not easily adopt. The entire angle of vision is foreign to me, and foreign to the task I must undertake. Engineers know equipment as a designed object; the mechanic knows it as a broken item that must be engaged. A comics version of instructions to fix machinery tend to emphasize those contours helpful to identifying the relevant portion of the item and manipulating it, not for manufacturing it or securing a patent. The strategic absences of comics proclaim, implicitly, that there is a whole host of physical information that the reader need not know. The friendliness of the line elides mechanical specificity likely to be overly specific and alienating.

This logic extends to graphic novels more broadly, including texts such as *Persepolis, Palestine*, and the graphic adaptation of the *9/11 Report*. For some readers, these books represent a first accessible entrée to a particular subject matter. For those who assumed that the subject matter, at its very core, allowed it to be known only through particular verbal forms—scholarly discourse and (stuffy) documentaries—the discovery of a comics (re)presentation means not only finding an unusual textual format, but also finding that the subject's nature is different from what was presumed. Its basic shape, the reader now sees, has contours of a variety that interests that reader.

WHY DON'T YOU JUST TAKE A PICTURE? COMICS AS THE UN-PHOTO

Finally, to understand the particular rhetoric of comics requires us to distinguish them from other forms of visuality, most notably the photograph. Photography, naturalistic photography in particular, creates the sense that the viewer is in perceptual contact with the world and insists on the ontological actuality of the things we see. This actuality includes those things made visually central as well as the indiscriminate surplus of reality that surrounds the viewer, which Walter Benjamin calls the "optical unconscious" of photography. Comics, by contrast, provide readers with a *fiction* of seeing. Even in serious nonfiction comics, readers are aware that they are seeing a mediated representation, not the actual thing itself. As Stanley Cavell argues in *The World Viewed: Reflections on the Ontology of Film*, it is the nature of photography to imply that the thing it images exists without me, whether or not I look.

Moreover, there is a frozenness and stillness about the photographic image, in which the moment imaged is ontologically past/passed; the viewer is temporally foreclosed and separate from the image in the photo. In comics, by contrast, line can seem alive and even moving; the moment, happening; and absences require the reader-viewer to fill in the underelaborated spaces for the drawing to achieve its meaning.

Of course, in both photography and comics, the viewer's mind must *think* the image, and both types of image provoke between a separation and a merger between image and viewer. To borrow Georges Poulet's formulation, though, with comics the "usual sense of incompatibility between my consciousness and its objects" subsides (55). The images in comics, and the pictures themselves, quickly relinquish their existence as real objects. Sketches on a page, they "do not seem radically opposed to the me who thinks" (55). Consequently, comics become more of a happening-now, compared with photography's viewed-now-but-happened-then.

I believe that the difference in photos and drawings extends even to photos of machinery, especially when taken for purposes of instruction. In *PS Magazine*, Eisner limited the number of photos and, when he presented them, added both word balloons and over-drawing that altered the edges and thus, fundamentally, the feel of the photographic image. The sterile and complete (perfective) image of the machine is invaded by lines that designate and comment. The image is remade, on the viewer's behalf, its stubbornly real irrelevancies fading as demarcations focus the viewer's attention.

The distinction between photography and comics becomes yet more pressing when it comes to the difference between drawings and photos of the Face. I'd like to illustrate the distinction with some images from Ann Marie Fleming's graphic memoir, *The Magical Life of Long Tack Sam*. Fleming juxtaposes photos and cartoons to tell the story of her grandfather, a famed Chinese acrobat. Image choices make *Long Tack Sam* read more like a documentary in print; indeed, the favorable reviewers on Amazon.com and Goodreads.com announce themselves as fans of the author's eponymous film documentary and praise the book in largely historical terms. One reader calls it an "archivist's dream," and another praises its "scrapbook" feel. Even those who liked the book enough to write about it confess that it is "a little tough to read" (Tanner) and note that the format "doesn't do any favors for cohesion" (Goodreads.com).

I would suggest that Fleming relies significantly on the syntax of comics—the use of panel and gutter, the serial juxtaposition of frames with word and image to tell a story—but only partially on its phenomenology. The book's proliferation of photos, including historical photos, gives the book a historical temporality from which we readers are necessarily excluded, just as one tends to be excluded from the temporality of another person's scrapbook. *Long Tack Sam* doesn't supply readers with much opportunity to put ourselves into its images. Though the reader is the one who thinks the images encountered in its pages, the persons imaged there feel distinctly separate from the me-who-thinks. There is a strong sense of division between consciousness and its objects. And where Fleming reduces that division in the book's occasional cartoon-filled sequences (which begin to shift the story toward a happening-now), her introductions of photographed faces are jarring, the surplus reality of the photographed face producing a visceral shock. The historical particularity of its many faces jars us out of the absorption produced by the book's comic-strip stretches, a rhetorical difference that—depending on the author's purposes—is not necessarily a rhetorical harm.

While a photo may well flatten out faces, reducing the complexity of their address, it does yet capture the face's stubborn reality. By contrast, a comics version of that face, even one drawn with a realist aesthetic, necessarily per-

Figure 3.   Fleming intermixes cartoons with realistic and historical photographs. From *The Magical Life of Long Tack Sam* by Ann Marie Fleming, copyright © 2007 by Anne Marie Fleming. Used by permission of Riverhead Books, an imprint of Penguin Group (USA) Inc.

forms various types of emptying. The surplus that typically overflows in photography is avoided. The ontological status of the face and the Other it presents is shifted: the drawing does present another being, but it is a being drawn for us. Consequently, a graphic novel such as *Palestine* (see figure 4) simultaneously brings images of others before the eyes yet relieves readers from encountering the face. Rather, we encounter on the *concepts* of visible strain and aging pain.

Figure 4.   One of many haunting faces of Palestinian elders. From the graphic novel *Palestine*. © Joe Sacco. Permission granted by Fantagraphics Books.

This intuition about the differences between photographed and drawn faces appears to be confirmed in recent fMRI studies (Peters). As photos are replaced with cartoons of decreasing specificity, brain activity recedes in the fusiform face area and lateral occipital gyrus, the areas used for face recognition, and dramatically so on the left side. At a certain level of abstraction, passive viewing of face drawings produces the same response as the viewing of house drawings (Peters). In other words, drawn at increasing levels of abstraction, the human face becomes just another object. In certain serious comics, such as Debbie Drechsler's *Daddy's Girl*, a cartoonish graphic novel in which sexual molestation takes place between and above the panels, or in Joe Sacco's story arc about torture, "Moderate Pressure II," the redaction of comics may offer a combination of visuality and relief from seeing real photos of trauma. Thus, by offering a fiction of seeing, comics may paradoxically avoid the desensitizing consequence of realist representations of evil. Readers encounter the stories in a visual medium, but they simultaneously see and do not see.

CONCLUSION

In the end, it does matter (rhetorically) that comics are comics. Comics permit the serious graphic novel to offer readers conceptually rich stories without solely relying on the verbal track, instead communicating parts of the story through visual cueing, line style, panel rhythm, and page layout, features that bring readers into particular patterns of attending. Further, as a "cool" medium, comics engross readers by requiring them to fill in blanks left by the medium's constituent redactions and gaps, thus reducing (for many readers) the sense of distance between their consciousness and its objects. Space between the image and the me-who-thinks is minimal.

At the same time, those redacted images offer readers a fiction of seeing. The graphic novel captures many benefits of visual representation, in particular the concreteness of images and the reader's natural empathy and identification with human faces, including facial expressions of emotion. There is a visceral difference between reading about a person's fear versus seeing the look of fear on a face. Yet while presenting persons and places more concrete and visible than mere words on a page, comics relieve the reader from seeing actual human faces in pain, in fear, in abjection. The serious graphic novel thus benefits from visuality while avoiding the surplus reality carried by photographs, as well as the distance (historical, ontological) between the self and the photographed face.

Finally, the serious graphic novel permits readers to encounter political, social, and/or historical concepts in a medium that licenses a kind of visual browsing, a form of attending that implies something unexpectedly relaxed about the subject matter. In place of academic and policy discourse's single-channel torrent of highly demanding verbiage, readers of these graphic novels discover in serious topics meanings that can be approached without having to don the persona of an academic or a policy wonk.

Perhaps this means that comics really are "easier" than their purely verbal counterparts. If so, that ease deserves further investigation by rhetorical theorists. If the permission to browse and glance, if the reliance on visual rhythms and atmospheric cueing, permit more readers to encounter important, demanding subject matter, that truth reveals something important about how people process discourse and, thus, about the effects or prudence of particular rhetorical choices. The questions are worth asking not only because we encounter an increasingly multimodal world, but also because democracies demand rhetorics that engage a broad array of readers in political and social analysis. When only the most sophisticated processors of verbal texts engage such pressing problems, societies suffer. As Will Eisner once helped the U.S. Army understand, when experts persist in offering only technical or scholarly explanations, a great deal of machinery can break down.

Works Cited

Andelman, Bob. *Will Eisner: A Spirited Life*. Milwaukie, OR: M Press, 2005.

Aristotle. *On Rhetoric: A Theory of Civic Discourse*. Ed. and trans. George Kennedy. New York: Oxford UP, 1991.

Belova, Olga. "The Event of Seeing: A Phenomenological Perspective on Visual Sense-Making." *Culture & Organization* 12.2 (June 2006): 93–107.

Benjamin, Walter. "Little History of Photography." Trans. Edmund Jephott and Kingsley Shorter. *Selected Writings*. Vol. 2. Ed. Michael W. Jennings, Howard Eiland, and Gary Smith. Cambridge: Belknap P of Harvard UP, 1999. 507–30.

Berger, John. *Ways of Seeing*. London: Penguin, 1972.

Burke, Kenneth. *A Rhetoric of Motives*. Berkeley: U of California P, 1969.

Cavell, Stanley. *The World Viewed: Reflections on the Ontology of Film*. Cambridge: Harvard UP, 1979.

Drechsler, Debbie. *Daddy's Girl*. Seattle: Fantagraphics, 2008.

Eisner, Will. *PS Magazine*. United States Army. Virginia Commonwealth University Digital Collections. <http://dig.library.vcu.edu/cdm4/index_psm.php?CISOROOT=/psm>.

Fleming, Ann Marie. *The Magical Life of Long Tack Sam*. New York: Riverhead Trade, 2007.

Goodreads.com. Review of *The Magical Life of Long Tack Sam*. <http://www.goodreads.com/review/show/17812349>.

Hartley, James. *Designing Instructional Text*. London: Kogan Page, 1994.

Heater, Brian. Rev. of *Macedonia*. *The Daily Crosshatch*. 18 July 2007. <http://thedailycrosshatch.com/2007/07/18/macedonia-by-harvey-pekar-et-al/>.

Hutchinson, Katharine H. "An Experiment in the Use of Comics as Instructional Material." *Journal of Educational Sociology* 23.4 (1949): 236–45.

Hyde, Michael J., ed. *The Ethos of Rhetoric*. Columbia: U of South Carolina P, 2004.

Jacobson, Sid, and Ernie Colon. *9/11 Report*. New York: Hill & Wang, 2004.

Kakalios, James. "Adding Pow! to Your Physics Class with Comic-book Lessons." *Curriculum Review* 42.2 (October 2002): 14–15.

Lefevre, Pascal. "Narration in Comics." *Image & Narration* 1 (Aug. 2000). <http://www.imageandnarrative.be/narratology/pascallefevre.htm>.

Macri, Linda C. "The Rhetoric of the Graphic Novel." Rhetoric Society of America, Seattle, WA. 24 May 2008.

Mallia, Gorg. "Learning from the Sequence: The Use of Comics in Instruction." *ImageText* 3.3 (2007): 27 pars. <http://www.english.ufl.edu/imagetext/archives/v3_3/mallia/>.

McCloud, Scott. *Understanding Comics*. New York: Harper, 1994.

McLuhan, Marshall. *Understanding Media*. Cambridge: MIT P, 1994.

Merleau-Ponty, Marcel. *Phenomenology of Perception*. London: Routledge, 2002.

———. *The Visible and The Invisible*. Evanston: Northwestern UP, 1968.

Olsen, Erik. Rev. of *Macedonia*. *Blog Critics Magazine*. 17 July 2007. <http://blogcritics.org/archives/2007/07/17/1339402.php>.

Pekar, Harvey, Heather Roberson, and Ed Piskor. *Macedonia*. New York: Villard, 2007.

Peters, R. J. et al. "Psychophysics and Physiology of Figural Perception in Humans." <http://ilab.usc.edu/rjpeters/pubs/arvo2000/>.

Poulet, Georges. "The Phenomenology of Reading." *New Literary History* 1 (1969): 53–68.

Sacco, Joe. *Palestine*. Seattle: Fantagraphics, 2002.

Satrapi, Marjane. *Persepolis*. Vols. I and II. New York: Pantheon, 2004.

Sones, W. D. "The Comics and Instructional Method." *Journal of Educational Sociology* 18.4 (1944): 232–40.

Spiegelman, Art. *Maus*. Vols. I and II. New York: Pantheon, 1986.

Sturken, Marita, and Lisa Cartwright. *Practices of Looking*. New York: Oxford UP, 2001.

Tanner, Matt. "Interview: Ann Marie Fleming, *The Magical Life of Long Tack Sam,* Author, Artist, Filmmaker." *SMITH* (10 Oct. 2008). <http://www.smithmag.net/ memoirville/2007/10/05/interview-ann-marie-fleming-the-magical-life-of-long-tack-sam-author-artist-and-filmmaker/>.

Versaci, Rocco. "How Comic Books Can Change the Way Our Students See Literature: One Teacher's Perspective." *English Journal* 91.2 (2001): 61–67.

29

The Earth Liberation Front's (ELF) Failed Diatribe of Sacramental Arson

Mark Meister & Curt Gilstrap

Bound by a strong sense of morality, participants in moral confrontations often resort to diatribes intent on offending the opposing moral view. Generally associated with discursive rhetoric, the diatribe is a rhetorical strategy in "which participants protect their most precious beliefs by expressing their perceptions in the faults of the other" (Freeman, Littlejohn, and Pearce 318). During the height of its notoriety prior to 9/11, the Earth Liberation Front's (ELF) faith and environmental advocacy was concerned with the courtly customs of revolution and the conversion of the sinful through a fiery baptism that often included arson. To demonstrate this faith, ELF disciples torched symbols of industrial culture, including SUVs, biotechnology laboratories, and construction sites from 1997–2001. The rhetorical power of arson is a highly ritualized performance of sacramental faith that illustrated the ELF's advocacy on behalf of the Earth. For the ELF, belief in the sacredness of the Earth's gravamen provided opportunities for stylistic demonstrations of faith and fortitude, embodied by arson, because the Earth remains an altar-like scene appropriate for sacrifice and salvation. Through arson, ELF fire-starters potentially demonstrate piety toward natural law and provide criticism toward industrial capitalism, not through offensive and shocking language, but rather through fire. As smoke and fire consume the SUV dealership, the resort condominium construction site, or the genetic labs at universities, arson seemingly highlights and communicates ELF beliefs through nontraditional discursive forms.

For the Greek Cynics—historically recounted through their most popular embodiment, Diogenes—the diatribe involved orchestrated public performances that highlighted the ironic and satirical nature of a society. In ancient Greece, the diatribe functioned as a *public* criticism of how public institutions threatened individual freedoms. The intent of Diogenes and other Greek

Cynics was to shock the public, to unveil the absurdity of public life. Arguably, "members" of the ELF are present-day Cynics, who articulate their criticism of modern industrial culture through the public performance of arson. But unlike the diatribes of the ancient Cynics, the ELF diatribe incorporates the direct and shocking rhetoric of arson, all the while extolling caution and anonymity. Whereby the ancient Cynics did not mask their diatribes, the ELF used arson for purposes other than extolling cultural change to reinforce the mystery of their piety.

This study of the symbolic uses of arson offers historical and contemporary insights into the rhetorical processes through which arson facilitates protest and resistance as a diatribe. This essay does not focus on audience reception of ELF sponsored arson, but rather how nondiscursive forms such as arson rhetorically reflect stated ELF beliefs. Building on DeLuca's ideographic and articulation analysis of environmental protest events, this study expands social movement theory beyond its discursive, leader-centered, and organizational emphasis (DeLuca 25). This essay begins broadly by profiling the rhetorical and cultural significance of arson. Additionally, a profile about social movement theory and the role of the diatribe previews a discussion of ELF-sponsored arson as a visual diatribe. Michael Osborn's notion of "depiction" is key to understanding the nondiscursive rhetoric of arson in moral confrontation (79). Arson symbolically depicts a radical commitment, as described by James Darsey: "to be restored to grace, the people must experience a revival of *pathos*, a resurrection from their spiritual death" (25–26). Moreover, this analysis extends Theodore Windt's discussion of diatribe by addressing how arson in ELF protest rhetoric fails as a diatribe for its critique of industrialized culture (2).

FROM FIRE TO ARSON

Broadly conceived, arson is the planned and orchestrated use of fire for malicious reasons. Arson is considered immoral because it intentionally inflicts damage. The Arson Prevention Bureau defines arson "as any willful or malicious burning or attempt to burn, with or without intent to defraud, a dwelling house, public building, motor vehicle or aircraft, personal property of another, etc." (1). The criminality of arson focuses on performed intent—the use of fire for purposes not naturally or accidentally occurring. Fire is a natural element existing in nature, while arson is the intentional use of fire by humans for other purposes.

Fire is an element of nature with which humans have long been fascinated despite its use in criminal arsons. Fire, even when distinguished from arson, is a powerful cultural symbol. Eco-theologian Benjamin Farley argues that the "Big Bang" theory of creation powerfully symbolizes fire as the primary giver of life (8), while anthropologist Carl Sauer illustrates how fire has long been a tool for modifying the environment. Sauer notes that humans "learned early that fire aided in collecting food, both plant and animal, and thus began the practice of setting fire to vegetation" (4). Burning became an integral maneuver for cultivation and the conversion of wetlands into agricultural-based systems. Even today fire remains a prominent tool for reshaping and redefining nature for human purposes. Presently, fire is used extensively to manage ecosystems. Historically, fire has enabled human occupation and use of the Earth (Pyne, *World Fire* 12).

Moreover, fire symbolically illustrates human evolution from primate to civilized being. Besides Pyne's historical work, Lévi-Strauss discusses a foundational relationship between humans and fire. In his book, *The Raw and the Cooked*, Lévi-Strauss focuses on cultural myth. In particular he notes how the role of fire transformed humanity from a "raw" nature based on ignorance and barbarism to a "cooked" state—a process that, he argues, marks the emergence of civility and industry (45). Herein, fire symbolically signifies change, a desire for rhetorical transcendence in the Burkean sense. The metaphor of fire, note Dale Hardy-Short and Brant Short in their analysis of the 1988 Yellowstone fires, is associated with death and rebirth; an association that typified "the human capacity, or need, to reconstruct chaotic images in fundamentally human terms" (125).

The symbolic relationship between fire and a variety of religious themes (sacrifice, baptism, rebirth, redemption, hell, etc.) is culturally significant. Fire purifies, and like its antithetical construct of water, it cleanses and transforms us sacramentally into grace-filled followers. In the Judeo-Christian tradition, fire is a prominent symbol of transformation and a vehicle of divine grace. Tamar Katriel points out that in Israel, fire is a "key symbol" serving to ground modern Judaism (456). In the New Testament, disciples of Christ received the Holy Spirit in the forms of "tongues of fire." "Baptism by fire" provides disciples with the needed grace for transforming the "uncleansed." From the Aztecs to the Stoics, from the Christian apocalypses to the Nordic *Ragnorok*, the myth of a world-beginning or world-consuming fire is nearly universal. Human domination of the Earth began with fire, ushering in an anthropocentric (human-centered) vision of use-value and utilitarianism that pervades how we presently view nature.

As for malicious intentions, arson resonates with the innate fire-human relationship and often facilitates a moral focus. Because fire is an important aspect of a culture's collective memory, it serves as a reminder of morality (Sauer 4). From early sparks of lightning igniting primitive forests to present-day news reports recounting the torching of SUVs at a Pennsylvania automobile dealership, fire has blazed a path from symbolic significance to moral rhetorical significance. Fire has changed how we use the Earth and its resources, and, as Gilbert White points out, fires are an "interaction of human, physical, and biological systems and are never wholly the work of man or wholly the undisturbed processes in the environment" (3). Noting that fire is "as much cultural as natural," Stephen Pyne argues, "Remove fire from a society, even today, and both its technology and its social order will lie in ruins. Strip fire away from language, and you reduce many of its vital metaphors to ash"

("Consumed" 83). Such totalizing of social, technological, cultural, and moral influence inevitably facilitates the rhetorical motives of arson.

Given the complex relationship between fire, culture, and morality, arson becomes a kind of rhetoric in times of moral conflict and distress. Psychologists argue that the tendency to use arson is not only a product of deviant personalities; this fiery behavior also issues forth from cultural and moral influences. Recent psychological research explains arsonists' desire to start fire. Lewis Lowenstein notes that family problems, personality problems, and personal turmoil often encourage people to start fires (109). Acts of arson have been called "symbolic suicide attempts" by psychiatrist Ehrig Lange (304), while criminologist Leon Pettiway argues that the desire for revenge is a contributing factor among "fire-starters" (172). Interestingly, evidence within the psychiatric community suggests a "communicative" function to arson. Jeffrey Geller argues that "communicative arson" expresses a "desire, wish, or need by pathological fire-starters" (77).

Clearly, however, the transformation from fire to arson depends on human intent. Arson, as a weapon of social protest with the motive of destruction (as critique), is a powerful rhetorical act of violence that shapes public discourse about the protest. Arguably a type of "revolutionary argument" (Stewart, Smith, and Denton 197), arson depends upon dramatic rhetorical depictions: "the destruction of property is generally less important than the symbolic mileage gained from it" (197).

Historically, arson was an accessible medium of defiance for desperate peasants inflamed by landowner discrimination. During the sixteenth, seventeenth, and eighteenth centuries, European peasants burned the countryside to protest unjust governmental policies favoring landowners. Frederick Gamst finds that "such uprising of peasants often stem from increased rates of extraction of the fund of rent, or from attempts to alter the nature of their ties to the land" (48). Agrarian and peasant uses of fire have historically occurred during difficult times including harsh winters, failed harvests, and warfare. In the United States, arson has occurred most frequently in the South, while outside the United States and Europe, Kenya, India, Australia, and Argentina (among others) have a rich agrarian history incorporating arson (Kuhlken 345).

With the exception of Kevin DeLuca and Tamar Katriel, rhetorical studies of protest and social movements have not focused on the potential of arson as a vehicle of protest and resistance. DeLuca advocates that social movement scholarship focus on rhetoric, a point he reinforces by noting that social movement theory is "not rhetoric-centered" (28). DeLuca advocates critical attention both beyond the verbalized rhetoric of social movements as well as beyond the historical significance of a social movement. The nondiscursive rhetoric associated with violence, for example, is of critical importance to social movement theory. It is clear, then, that the history of arson used for political protest combined with a contemporary call for assessing anew the social movements that use such unorthodox rhetoric both warrant and provide an appropriate space for the examination of ELF arson.

ELF Arson: Depicting the Diatribe

Osborn's notion of rhetorical depiction and Windt's articulation of the diatribe are helpful constructs in understanding the rhetorical significance of ELF protest arson. Osborn notes that contemporary rhetoric is dominated by discursive and nondiscursive "visualizations" that exist in the collective memories of audiences. "Depiction," notes Osborn, "generates pictures for sharing that can be transmitted quickly and precisely by the mass media and possessed easily by mass audiences" (89). Symbolic acts that resonate with an audience's experiences are powerful rhetorical constructs because depictions present, intensify, identify, implement, and reaffirm the "contrast or juxtaposition of visual or sensual opposites, intended to represent moral opposition" (80). Windt points out that the diatribe, as incorporated by Diogenes and other Greek Cynics, "was intended to shock sensibilities, to scandalize by profaning societal customs" (6). Thus, any compromise with societal standards is a compromise of ethics, and because Diogenes and the Cynics opposed conventional morality, they proposed a counter-morality that embraced "the right of man to live his natural life without interference from society" (8). Accordingly, Windt notes that for Diogenes and the Cynics the diatribe provided a means for criticizing the self-interests of a society engrossed in luxuries and conveniences. "To live by men's conventions," notes Windt in his description of Diogenes and the Cynics, "is to embrace the death of person; to defy society is to embrace life" (4). Described by Windt as "an extemporaneous sermon," the diatribe criticizes and conveys how "man's conscience, his logic and emotions, his perspectives and attitudes have been corrupted by immoral institutions" (7). The diatribe certainly assaults the sensibilities of its audience, yet it is not a successful persuasive strategy. The diatribe, addressed herein, is a rhetorical strategy that identifies and reflects rhetorical motives without evoking social change. In sum, the diatribe is "successful" in shocking public perceptions, but it is not necessarily intended to change public perception.

The ELF promotes arson as an alternative to traditional public discourse and debate.[1] The ELF's identity is shaped by its use of arson. Since its inception in 1992 by Earth First! followers living in Brighton, England, the ELF has refused to abandon illegal criminal acts as a rhetorical tactic in defense of the Earth. The main goal behind these criminal tactics is to inflict economic and monetary damage on organizations that harm the Earth.

Unlike environmental organizations such as Greenpeace, The Sierra Club, and even Earth First! the ELF has no roster of members and no mailing list. ELF "members" operate in decentralized and anonymous "cells." As reported in *Newsweek,* ELF "members" may work alone or with a small collective of members, but they do not know one another nor do they know if other actions have been planned. Thus, if arrests happen, ELF "members" cannot implicate others or be forced to inform law enforcement of further actions (Murr, Morganthau, and Smalley 32). Consider this 1997 media release outlining the mission of the ELF:

> Welcome to the struggle of all species to be free. We are the burning rage of a dying planet. The war of greed ravages the earth and species die out every day. ELF works to speed up the collapse of industry, to scare the rich, and to undermine the foundations of the state. We embrace social and deep ecology as a practical resistance movement. We have to show the enemy that we are serious about defending what is sacred. Together we have teeth and claws to match our dreams. Our greatest weapons are imagination and the ability to strike when least expected. ("Our Inspiration")

As noted in their mission, the ELF considers itself the "burning rage" of an Earth at war with industry. The Earth is described as "sacred" and industry as the "enemy." The war over the sacred Earth will be fought with weapons of "imagination" and when "least expected." The allusions to fire and arson are obvious beyond the explicit description of "burning rage."

As a result of their fire protests from 1997–2001, the ELF has reportedly been responsible for causing nearly $37 million in damaged property in the United States and abroad ("Brutal" 28). The ELF claims that characterizing the use of arson as an "imaginative" weapon in confrontations to protect the "sacred" implies an inherently evil other, a self-serving judgment that works to reinforce the group's core beliefs, but does nothing to change social behavior.

RELIGIOUS TERROR AND THE FAILED DIATRIBE OF ARSON

ELF justification discourse for rhetorical arson is an interesting combination of anonymity, piety, and fiery baptism. The moral motive of the ELF is to scare the rich and humble industry. Its agent for promoting this moral change is arson (Glick 8). For the ELF, confronting the perceived immorality of industry requires religious notions of piety, mystery, and anonymity in charring the symbols of industrial vulgarity. Toward this end, "heating" up a moral confrontation with industry is as easy as rappeling down rugged mountain cliffs, snow-shoeing through moon-lit forests, secretly approaching a condominium construction project, striking a match and torching a construction project, and then fleeing the scene. The fuel for moral confrontation, according to the ELF, is provided by industries and scientists who invade natural habitats of spotted owls and mountain lynx, who splice poplar trees with pest resistant genes for urban renewal projects, or who haul logs from ancient redwood forests. An anonymous October 19, 1998, communiqué claiming credit for the arson fires atop Vail Mountain explains why cautionary arson is a necessary rhetorical response in attacking corporations:

> On behalf of the lynx, five buildings and four ski lifts at Vail were reduced to ashes on the night of Sunday, October 18th. Vail, Inc. is already the largest ski operation in North America and now wants to expand it even further. The 12 miles of roads and 885 acres of clearcuts will ruin the last, best lynx habitat in the state. Putting profits ahead of Colorado's wildlife will not be tolerated. This action is just a warning. We will be back if this greedy corporation continues to trespass into wild and unroaded areas.

For your safety and convenience, we strongly advise skiers to choose other destinations until Vail cancels its inexcusable plans for expansion. (Glick 3)

The ELF's response to corporatism is predominately incendiary reaction, a tactic former ELF spokesperson Craig Rosebraugh notes is an "act of love for the environment" (Cloud, Harrington, and Woodbury 77). Tactically, and rhetorically, arson is a religious response. Robert Scott and Donald Smith explain that radical moral confrontation reflects not only "a dramatic sense of division," but also an act of overcoming enemies (2). The protestors "picture themselves as radically divided for traditional society, questioning not simply the limitations of its benevolence but more fundamentally its purposes and modes of operation" (2). The ELF publication *Setting Fires with Electrical Timers: An Earth Liberation Front Guide* (available at no cost from the ELF Press Office Web site) outlines the ELF's contempt for traditional society. Here, the use of electrical timers is needed for "combating industry's relentless attack on the Earth" (2).

The use of arson facilitates a symbolic destruction of a manifestation of evil. The highly visual act of arson potentially works out the "rite of kill symbolically" (Scott and Smith 4). Through arson and rhetorical fire, the ELF destroys the cultural markers of industry (represented by housing developments, science and genetic research, and leisure) by causing economic damage to those projects sponsored by industry. ELF spokesperson Rosebraugh notes with pride the ELF's victory over industry in the 1998 Vail arson, stating: "Vail's insurance rates went up, and the international publicity was priceless" (Roosevelt 26). The ELF's identification of industry and science with evil is imperative to its rhetorical process of transcending the Earth to divine status.

In Burke's *The Rhetoric of Religion: Studies in Logology*, he points out that the "problem of evil" generally suggests the question "How to get evil out of the world?" In his analysis of Augustinian theology, Burke points out that for Augustine, the question is "How can evil get into the world?" for if God is good, His creation of the world is good and not capable of evil. For the ELF, the answer to Augustine's question of evil is evident: evil exists in the world because industry and science abuse the Earth for purposes of profit. The divinity of nature is attacked by evil manifestations of development that sacrifice the good and nurturing providences of nature. Evil-doers perceive the providences of nature as potential "riches" or "resources" for all while the ELF's response of arson acts symbolically as a vehicle of sacrifice: sacrifice for the sake of punishment, and sacrifice for the sake of salvation.

In the moral protest rhetoric of the ELF, the faithless require a baptism or conversion by arson as both a means of repentance and reform. ELF priests, similar to Thomas Lessl's priest-scientists, speak "from above as an epiphanic Word, filled with mystery and empowered with extra-human authority" (185). Distinctly, however, ELF priests use arson instead of words to enact their faith in the truisms of nature. In this enacted narrative, punishing the evil that threatens the Earth's authority, prominence, and goodness must sanctify the Earth's divinity.

Although moral confrontation ignites the rhetorical response of arson, this kind of fire retains its rhetorical potency via a visually depicted air of mystery. For the ELF, mystery is vital for its incendiary protests to successfully intensify its attack on industrial culture. Like the peasant arsonists of eighteenth century Europe, ELF followers secretly detonate fires. Here, the mystery of arson identifies human with nature: humans are part of the "larger plan" for attaining grace. Benjamin Farley notes that mystery and relatedness to nature are powerful religious themes, noting: "To live out the mystery of one's beingness with grace and humility, rigor and strength, is no small task. The theme is endemic to every religion, as humanity affirms the worthiness of life, in spite of finitude, anxiety, and the threat of non-being" (35). For the ELF, forces bent on destroying what is "wild, pure, and precious" (Glick 16) threaten the mysteries of nature and the attainment of nature's grace.

To glorify the mystery of nature, the ELF incorporates themes related to fantasy and folklore to justify its intimate courtship with nature. According to the ELF Web site, the ELF compares itself to the "mischievous elves of lore."

> We take inspiration from the Luddites, Levellers, Diggers, and Autonome squatter movement, ALF, the Zapatistas, and the little people—those mischievous elves of lore. Authorities can't see us because they don't believe in elves. We are practically invisible. We have no command structure, no spokespersons, no office, just many small groups working separately, seeking vulnerable targets and practicing our craft. ("Our Inspiration")

As a self-professed group of elves, the ELF takes on the personae of "little people" fighting the good fight against the evil corporation intent on destroying the Earth. Here, rhetorical fantasy justifies the idealism of the ELF perspective—a perspective that embraces both "naïve ecological romanticism and revolutionary idealism" (Prothero and Fitchett 46). The conditions for mystery are set by social distinctions, differences in social values, and beliefs.

In the Burkean sense, the moral confrontation between the self-professed virtues of the ELF and the vices of science and industry illustrates a rhetorical courtship. Burke notes in *A Rhetoric of Motives* that mystery is not only based on a perceived strangeness, but those parties involved must also be "thought of as in some way capable of communion" (115). Rhetorically, a mysterious courtship requires identification in a social and political debate. Burke notes, "there is the 'mystery' of courtship when 'different kinds of beings' communicate with each other" (115). The ELF rhetoric of confrontation and fiery protest thrives on mystery. For the ELF, conducting the mysterious and virtuous work of "saving the Earth" culminates in the sacramental duty of arson.

As Burke notes, mystery and courtship call "for a corresponding rhetoric, in form quite analogous to sexual expression; for the relations between classes are like the way of courtship, rape, seduction, jilting, prostitution, promiscuity, with variants of sadistic torture or masochistic invitation to mistreatment" (115). Both the ELF member and industrial-scientist—although made ideologically distinct in their beliefs about the Earth by the ELF—pursue an intimacy with the Earth. This courtship with the Earth is mysteriously depicted through ELF arson that identifies a critique of industrial culture and intensifies the ELF's shared commitment to its critique. For the ELF, mystery implies a love and intimacy with the Earth, perfected through the climatic release of purification through arson. Arson is a rhetorical strategy that depicts identification against industrial culture and intensification with the shared feelings associated with that identification.

Rhetorical power requires confrontation over a highly contentious social issue, a confrontation that spans a mysterious and highly rhetorical courtship. Heat and oxygen fuel the physical fire, while moral confrontation and mystery often fuel arson. In addition, arson requires a pious attitude that demonstrates a strong sense of loyalty and decorum to the cause. For the ELF, piety, decorum, and loyalty protect the Earth from those threatening its sanctity. Arson is the visible vehicle for waging not only protest, but also for sacrificing symbols of industry to the Earth for purification.

Although piety is generally associated with religion, Burke, in *Permanence and Change*, extends piety to secular rhetorical contexts. Burke notes that piety is *"the sense of what properly goes with what"* (74, emphasis in original). For Burke, piety is both an orientation and a process of organizing and categorizing, which according to Thomas Rosteck and Michael Leff, "function as stable frames of reference which direct human perception and determine our judgments about what is proper in a given circumstance" (329). A pious orientation requires a keen sense of "what goes with what," and "governs our sense of propriety" (329) and decorum. Because Burkean piety always rests upon principles of social order and challenges to it, social debates over "proper" and "improper" attitudes symbolically fuse into "standards of decorum defined in opposition to one another" (328). Burke, in *Permanence and Change*, ironically concludes that "vulgarity is pious" (77) since vulgarity competes rhetorically against cultural conceptions of refinement and because vulgarity "reveals the difference between standards of decorum defined in opposition to one another" (Rosteck and Leff 328). Ross Wolin notes that Burke suggests in *Permanence and Change* that criminality, the renouncement of piety, can actually be thought of as itself pious behavior (76). The "proper" attitude ELF members seek to evoke with arson is that industry's actions are vulgar in their promotion of the American dream.

In the pamphlet titled *Frequently Asked Questions about the Earth Liberation Front* published by the North American Earth Liberation Front Press Office, the actions of industry (particularly in the United States) are described as vulgar:

> Capitalism and the American Dream have long symbolized a form of economic opportunity and freedom. What wasn't and still isn't told to millions seeking the American Dream is that dream comes at a price,

always has and always will. That price consists of everything from taking advantage of slave labor, dumping toxic waste into our waterways, murdering those who take a stand for justice, destroying cultures, destroying environments and exploiting anyone or anything that poses to be a threat, nuisance, or a bump along the path to riches. The ELF realizes the profit motive, caused and reinforced by the capitalist society, is destroying all life on this planet. The only way, at this point in time, to stop the continued destruction of life is to by any means necessary take the profit motive out of killing. (7)

Pursuing riches, according to the ELF, involves vulgar action (including slavery, toxic waste dumping, and murder). The evils of capitalism, which "are destroying all life on this planet," initiate and perpetuate vulgar desires for purposes of profit. Of note is the desire to stop such actions "by any means necessary." Without the rhetorical construction of vulgarity by industry and perpetuated by the American dream, the ELF discourse of piety and justice seemingly justifies the vulgar act of arson. Interestingly, in ELF discourse, "vulgarity begets vulgarity." Incendiary protest, according to an ELF press release taking responsibility for causing $90,000 of damage to SUVs at an Erie, Pennsylvania, dealership, is justified as a direct and vulgar act against capitalism because "supporting this paradigm [capitalism] with our excessive lifestyles, and failing to offer direct resistance, we make ourselves accomplices in the greatest crime ever committed" ("ELF Torches"). Thus, arson demonstrates proper decorum for the Earth and for ELF members it is less of a crime than willingly supporting capitalism.

IMPLICATIONS

The ELF rejects the premises of the popular environmental movement as failing "miserably in its attempts to bring about the protection needed to stop the killing of life on this planet" (*Frequently* 5). ELF discourse not only deplores capitalism but also denounces the popular environmental movement. Conventional environmentalism works within the legal processes perpetuated by capitalism. According to the ELF, "state sanctioned means of social change rarely on their own have and will have any real effect in obtaining the desired results" (5). Seemingly the desired results of the ELF faithful require commitment not to societal law, but to enforcing the divinity of natural law. Natural law is defined by the ELF as "our dependence on the substances in the natural environment which enable all life to exist, primarily clean air, clean water, and clean soil" (6). Natural law provides and maintains life, while societal law, "particularly [since] the advent of the industrial revolution . . . has been in complete violation of natural law" (6).

In her analysis of Kant's notion of grace, Jacqueline Marina points out that Kant's views of divine justice and grace do not conflict with an authentically Christian understanding of these concepts (379). Neither does the ELF's theology of natural law. According to Marina, the Kantian notion of grace is based on "God's unmerited favor" with humans who turn away from evil and return to God's grace and accept it as universal moral law. For members of the ELF imbued with the insight of natural law, nature's grace is sanctified through sacramental duties facilitated by burning down symbols of capitalism. The evil and vulgarity inherent in capitalism, according to the ELF, reflects a "fall from nature's grace"; humans neglect their sacramental duty of embracing a universal natural law. Lacking nature's grace, capitalists and those not ordained in the divinity of natural law continue relying on "throw away conveniences, status symbols, and hoards of financial wealth [that] fuel brutality and oceans of bloodshed" ("ELF Torches"). Of note is the ELF assertion that their use of arson is not the work of terrorists. The ELF blames the mainstream media for biased coverage and ignorance of their actions, hence, the ELF uses parochial language in asserting that it is not a terrorist organization and again blames the unfaithful for rejecting sanctification.

> The ELF is not an ecoterrorist organization or any sort of terrorist organization but rather one that is working to protect all life on the planet. It is amazingly hypocritical for mainstream media and the federal government to label the ELF as a terrorist group yet at the same time ignoring the U.S. government and U.S. based corporations which every day exploit, torture, and murder people around the world. (*Frequently* 5)

ELF discourse rationalizes arson as an effective means of protest against evil by using language that is strikingly similar to religious discourse. The divinity and grace of natural law targets the evils of capitalism and ELF followers exhibit faith and fortitude. By torching the symbols of capitalism, ELF followers seemingly believe that they are baptizing and transforming evil with the grace of natural law. Hence, they are not terrorists bent only on causing economic damage, but rather are disciples blessed with nature's grace and are intent on sharing that grace in the redemption of industrialized evils. For the ELF, the true terrorists are those industrialists who ravage the Earth. Although arson is considered evil by the legal system, the ELF sees it as a "lesser evil" than those evils rejecting natural law. In *Attitudes Toward History,* Burke notes, "the problem of evil is met by transcendence—the process of secular prayer whereby a man sees an intermingling of good and evil factors, and 'votes' to select either the good ones or the evil ones as the 'essence' of the lot" (314). The ELF uses arson effectively to vote on the vulgarity of industry and the sanctity of the Earth.

The environmental movement is diverse in that many different political styles exist under the heading of "environmentalism." From home recycling to tree spiking, the movement has many different perspectives, all of which prescribe different means for "saving our Earth." Yet, the discourse of radical environmentalism has a spiritual component that potentially moralizes the use of arson as a symbolic depiction of faith and piety. Proponents of more "radical" protest methods exhibit a faith in nature and willingly battle through action and symbolism against those who disrespect nature. Their faith and fortitude comprise a stylistic and visual exhibition of sacramental duty. Environmental faith comes in a variety of forms. Faith in the popular environmental movement is the belief in the democracy of ideas and in civil opposition toward an established order that can bring about social and environmental change. This perspective is reminiscent of Freeman, Littlejohn, and Pearce's notion of "transcendent eloquence" that counters diatribes and violence, often associating moral confrontation with "levels of constructive dialogue, new contexts in which to understand differences, and new ways to compare and weight alternative choices" (319). Conversely, faith in nature is concerned with the courtly customs of revolution. To demonstrate faith in nature, "disciples" produce and stage confrontations with the aid of ignition switches and timers. The rhetorical power demonstrated in a highly visual and ritualized performance of sacramental faith illustrates a commitment to the Earth. Similarly, without the sacraments, religious icons, Eucharist, Koran, Star of David, and other stylistic rituals, mainstream faith is fleeting. For the ELF, nature provides a stylistic demonstration of faith and fortitude by providing an altar-like scene appropriate for sacrifice and valor. Faith, following this narrative, is compromised without sacramental duty and other demonstrations of faith upon the altar of nature and in the name of the Earth.

Returning to DeLuca's call to consider carefully the symbolic wares of environmental rhetors beyond the mere machinations of organization and leadership, it is clear that the thrust of ELF protest arson works to provide a new visual framework wherein so-called natural capitalist behavior is seen as anti-environmental. Through the visual diatribe, the incongruous perspective of evil capitalism is contrasted against the piousness of Earth protection. In parallel with Erving Goffman's assessment of media images as frameworks for viewing, ELF visual diatribes (including numerous images used by the media) provide new ways to frame traditional ideas of consumption as vulgar and evil. Toward this end, the ELF is similar to a religious sect given their direct action (burning with a purpose) and possesses a sense of realism (defense) as well as etiquette (symbolic conversion through reframing). As "disciples" of the Earth, ELF followers are not stewards of the Earth, but crusaders who incorporate arson as visual diatribes of faith and fortitude. Maintenance and defense of the Earth does not merely occur through the natural powers of life and death, but through the demonstration of faith and commitment. The duty of the faithful crusaders of the ELF is to take direct action against those who threaten the faith. Especially in the image-based medium of television and other visual media, faith in the Earth requires highly stylized rhetorical displays of decorum while providing a clear sense of realism. Arson is the ELF's rhetorical weapon of choice.

Note

[1] According to its Web site (http://www.eflpressoffice.org), from 1997–2001 the ELF predominately used arson as a protest strategy guided by three principles in its critique of industrial culture. First, the ELF pledged to inflict economic damage "to those who profit from the

destruction and exploitation of the natural environment." Moreover, the ELF hoped to edu-
cate the public on the "atrocities committed against the environment and all the species that
cohabitate in it," and, finally, the ELF was committed to "take all necessary precautions
against harming any animal, human, or non-human."

Works Cited

Arson Prevention Bureau. *Car Fires: The Growing Problem and How to Help Extinguish It.*
London: Arson Prevention Bureau P, 1998.

"Brutal Elves in the Woods." *Economist* 14 Apr. 2001: 28–30.

Burke, Kenneth. *Attitudes Toward History.* Berkeley: U of California P, 1984.

———. *Permanence and Change: An Anatomy of Purpose.* Berkeley: U of California P, 1984.

———. *A Rhetoric of Motives.* Berkeley: U of California P, 1969.

———. *The Rhetoric of Religion: Studies in Logology.* Berkeley: U of California P, 1970.

Cloud, John, Maureen Harrington, and Richard Woodbury. "Fire on the Mountain."
Time 2 Nov. 1998: 77.

Darsey, James. *The Prophetic Tradition and Radical Rhetoric in America.* New York: New
York UP, 1997.

DeLuca, Kevin M. *Image Politics: The New Rhetoric of Environmental Activism.* New
York: Guilford, 1999.

Earth Liberation Front. "ELF Torches SUVs in Erie, Pennsylvania." 2003. 4 Mar.
2004. <http://www.elfpressoffice.org>.

———. *Frequently Asked Questions about the Earth Liberation Front.* Portland, OR: North
American ELF Press Office, 2001. 19 Sept. 2003. <http://www.elfpressoffice.org>.

———. "Our Inspiration." 2001. 12 Oct. 2004. <http://www.elfpressoffice.org>.

———. *Setting Fires with Electrical Timers: An Earth Liberation Front Guide.* 2001. 14
Nov. 2003. <http://www.elfpressoffice.org>.

Farley, Benjamin W. *Son of the Morning Sky: Reflections on the Spirituality of the Earth.*
New York: UP of America, 1999.

Freeman, Sally A., Steven W. Littlejohn, and W. Barnett Pearce. "Communication
and Moral Conflict." *Western Journal of Communication* 56.4 (1992): 311–29.

Gamst, Frederick C. *Peasants in Complex Society.* New York: Holt, Rinehart, and Win-
ston, 1974.

Geller, Jeffery L. "Communicative Arson." *Hospital and Community Psychiatry* 43.1
(1992): 76–77.

Glick, Daniel. *Powder Burn: Arson, Money, and Mystery on Vail Mountain.* New York:
Public Affairs, 2001.

Goffman, Erving. *Frame Analysis.* Cambridge: Harvard UP, 1974.

Hardy-Short, Dale, and Brant Short. "Fire, Death, and Rebirth: A Metaphoric Analysis of the 1988 Yellowstone Fire Debate." *Western Journal of Communication* 59.2
(1995): 103–26.

Katriel, Tamar. "Rhetoric in Flames: Fire Inscriptions in Israeli Youth Movement
Ceremonials." *The Quarterly Journal of Speech* 73.4 (1987): 444–59.

Kuhlken, Robert. "Settin' the Woods on Fire: Rural Incendiarism as Protest." *The
Geographical Review* 89.3 (1999): 343–63.

Lange, Ehrig. "Arson as Symbolic Suicide." *Psychiatric, Neurological, and Medical Psychology* 41.5 (1989): 304–05.

Lessl, Thomas. "The Priestly Voice." *Quarterly Journal of Speech* 75.2 (1989): 183–97.

Lévi-Strauss, Claude. *The Raw and the Cooked.* New York: Harper, 1969.

Lowenstein, Lewis F. "Recent Research into Arson (1992–2000) Incidence, Causes, and Associated Features, Predictions, Comparative Studies, and Prevention and Treatment." *Police Journal* 74.2 (2001): 108–19.

Marina, Jacqueline. "Kant on Grace: A Reply to His Critics." *Religious Studies* 33.4 (1997): 379–401.

Murr, Andrew, Tom Morganthau, and Suzanne Smalley. "Burning Suburbia: An Elusive Group of Eco-terrorists Changes the Debate on Suburban Sprawl with a Dangerous Tactic—Arson." *Newsweek* 15 Jan. 2001: 32–33.

Osborn, Michael. "Rhetorical Depiction." *Form, Genre, and the Study of Political Discourse.* Ed. Herbert Simons and Aram Aghazarian. Columbia: U of South Carolina P, 1986.

Pettiway, Leon E. "Arson for Revenge: The Role of Environmental Situation, Age, Sex, and Race." *Journal of Quantitative Criminology* 3.2 (1987): 169–84.

Prothero, Andrea, and James Fitchett. "Greening Capitalism: Opportunities for a Green Commodity." *Journal of Macromarketing* 20.1 (2000): 46–55.

Pyne, Stephen J. "Consumed by Either Fire or Fire: A Prolegomenon to Athropogenic Fire." *Earth, Fire, and Water.* Ed. Jill Ker Conway, Kenneth Keniston, and Leo Marx. Amherst: U of Massachusetts P, 1999. 78–101.

———. *World Fire: The Culture of Fire on Earth.* New York: Henry Holt, 1995.

Roosevelt, Margot. "When Firebugs Bite." *Time* 16 July 2001: 26–28.

Rosteck, Thomas, and Michael Leff. "Piety, Propriety, and Perspective: An Interpretation and Application of Key Terms in Kenneth Burke's *Permanence and Change.*" *Western Journal of Speech Communication* 53.4 (1989): 327–41.

Sauer, Carl O. "Man's Dominance by Use of Fire." *Geoscience and Man* 10 (1975): 1–13.

Scott, Robert, and Donald Smith. "The Rhetoric of Confrontation." *Quarterly Journal of Speech* 55.1 (1969): 1–8.

Stewart, Charles J., Craig Allen Smith, and Robert E. Denton, Jr. *Persuasion and Social Movements.* 5th ed. Long Grove, IL: Waveland P, 2007.

White, Gilbert. "History of Fire in North America." *Fire in the Environment Symposium Proceedings.* Denver: U.S. Department of Agriculture, 1972.

Windt, Theodore O. "The Diatribe: Last Resort for Protest." *Quarterly Journal of Speech* 58.1 (1972): 1–14.

Wolin, Ross. *The Rhetorical Imagination of Kenneth Burke.* Columbia: U of South Carolina P, 2001.

"The Future Is Ours," or Is It?
The Rise and Fall of Totalitarian Rhetoric in Poland (and Elsewhere)

Cezar M. Ornatowski

In the once widely read and taught essay "Politics and the English Language," George Orwell proposed that the "present political chaos [Orwell writes this in 1946, just after the Second World War and on the brink of the cold war] is connected with the decay of language," adding, optimistically, "one can probably bring about some improvement by starting at the verbal end" (366). The essay used to be a staple in composition readers, but I note of late that many of the younger faculty members in my department have not heard of it. The decline in its popularity appears to have coincided roughly with the end of the cold war, which may be due to the essay's datedness, or perhaps to shifts in pedagogical trends. While Orwell's specific prescriptions for "political regeneration" through verbal self-discipline may indeed sound quaint today, his assumptions that (1) "if thought corrupts language, language can also corrupt thought" (364) and (2) that corrupted language produces a "reduced state of consciousness" (363) that has both political causes and consequences merit reconsideration in light of lessons learned since its publication and in the present chaos of the "war on terror."

The "war on terror" has led to some anxiety about the erosion of civil liberties and even possible creeping totalitarianism, or at least authoritarianism. Such anxieties may lurk behind the popularity of the 2006 film *V for Vendetta*,[1] in which a ruthless British politician exploits the threat of terrorism to become a dictator. Certainly, the "war on terror" has produced its share of verbal fog as the various agendas (which are less clearly defined than they were in Orwell's time, when the newly descended iron curtain provided a palpable symbol of ideological division) engage in the struggle for the hearts and minds of global opinion. One person's "terrorist" becomes another's "freedom fighter," and vice versa; I have heard the term "terrorist" applied by the various sides to Islamic extremists, Chechen separatists, Russian troops, Middle Eastern governments, Iran, Israel, Great Britain, and the United States.

In the midst of such verbal confusion, Orwell's call for semantic honesty, the use of concrete (as opposed to abstract), short (as opposed to long), and native English (as opposed to foreign) words, or active (as opposed to passive) voice may indeed seem as naïve as Professor Higgins's belief that correct pronunciation can overcome class distinctions.[2]

The complexities of the post-cold war and post-9/11 rhetorical situations, along with anxieties about and renewed interest in the future of a multicultural, global democratic society, invite a revisiting of the problem of politics and language—a project especially appropriate in the context of a volume exploring the "responsibilities of rhetoric." In this paper, this revisiting takes the form of a preliminary inquiry into the character of "totalitarian" rhetoric: What are the distinguishing features of "totalitarian" rhetoric? How would we know it if we saw it? Is "totalitarian" rhetoric fundamentally different, qua rhetoric, from "democratic" rhetoric, or is it the overall system of governance and jurisprudence that constitutes the difference? Can rhetoric be effectively separated from the latter? To begin to answer these questions, I examine selected features of the rhetoric of the "real socialist" regime in Poland during the periods of its ascendancy and decline, with comparative excursions into Nazi rhetoric, in an attempt to identify some features of "totalitarian" rhetorics as well as some rhetoric-regime relationships.

The idea that rhetoric has a reciprocal relationship to its political context, that is, the idea that political relations find rhetorical expression and, in turn, are to some extent shaped, or reshaped, through rhetoric, has been central to rhetorical theory. Aristotle's *Rhetoric* includes a consideration of regime types (monarchy, aristocracy, and polity—the "good" types of regimes—and tyranny, oligarchy, and democracy—the "corrupt" types), with the suggestion that each form of government evinces its own "character" or "tendency," and that this character is related to *ethos*—which Aristotle considers to be the primary factor in persuasion. In addition, in *Politics*, Aristotle discusses the adaptation of education, including rhetorical education, to the form of government and adds that "history shows that almost all tyrants have been demagogues" (V, 1410b, 13–14). The point is that, as Thomas Farrell has argued, political regimes are also rhetorical regimes in that they imply specific ways of speaking, arguing, writing, thinking, and being in the world that foreclose, limit, or proscribe other ways of speaking, arguing, writing, thinking, or being. Karlyn Kohrs Campbell and Kathleen Hall Jamieson have suggested that "public discourse reflects the philosophical presuppositions as well as the institutional structure of the state in which it is found" (6). And Gerard Hauser contends that "rhetoric is among the social practices by which society constitutes itself," since "we locate the possibilities for social action in and through our rhetoric" (114) and "our understanding of reality is a function of how we talk and write about it" (273).

The general assumption that political regimes are somehow embodied in their rhetoric and that the relationship is reciprocal and dialectical thus appears to be well established in general terms. What I am interested in here is identifying some general markers of "totalitarian" (or at least authoritarian and nondemocratic) rhetoric in order to perhaps better understand the relationship between rhetoric and democracy, as well as to help me make my way in the complex contemporary rhetorical situation.[3]

I am cognizant of the potential circularity implicit in trying to analyze "totalitarian" rhetoric by examining the discourse of a regime (or regimes) that I have already predesignated as "totalitarian." However, here one may apply the test of "by their fruit thou shalt know them." It is generally taken for granted that Nazism and Soviet communism constituted two principal "totalitarianisms" of the twentieth century, if you simply count the numbers of victims. Carl Friedrich and Zbigniew Brzezinski have defined the "ideal" totalitarian dictatorship as having the following characteristics: an elaborate ideology, consisting of an official body of doctrine covering all vital aspects of man's existence to which everyone living in the society is supposed to adhere; a single mass party, typically led by one man, and consisting of a relatively small percentage of the population (up to 10 percent); a system of terror, whether physical or psychological, effected through party and secret police control; a technologically conditioned, near-complete monopoly of control of all means of effective mass communication; a similarly technologically conditioned, near-complete monopoly on the effective use of all weapons; and a central control and direction of the economy through the bureaucratic coordination of corporate entities. Real-socialist Poland met all of these criteria.

The slogan "The Future Is Ours" in my title, taken from the purported British totalitarian regime represented in *V for Vendetta,* exhibits some features that one might consider "totalitarian": the future as already present ("the future is"—not "will be"—ours); wish fulfillment (the future "is" ours—not "might be" or "can be" ours); forced mass identification ("our" future includes "you," whether you want to participate or not); and monologism (no rejoinder, doubt, or debate is implicitly invited). By contrast, compare the also short and memorable "I Like Ike,"[4] with its dominance of the first-person singular ("I," thus an individual as opposed to mass) and its assertion of preference ("like"), and thus choice, as opposed to historical inevitability ("future is"). (A "totalitarian" version might run something like "All Americans Are for Ike," which loses in charm what it gains in coercive bent.)

While politicians everywhere may occasionally be guilty of having some "totalitarian" elements in their discourse (although, no matter what one's anxiety about the state of American democracy, it is still difficult to imagine a candidate of either party actually running for office under a slogan such as "The Future Is Ours"), one of the arguments of my paper is that while such features may be part of political rhetoric, it is their specific intensification, amplification, and persistence combined with cultural, historical, and institutional factors and regime-specific characteristics that make a particular rhetoric "totalitarian." On the other hand, it may happen that one's rhetoric may be at odds in this regard—at least to some extent—with ostensibly professed ideals, in which case I'd say: pay attention to the rhetoric as much as, or perhaps more than, the ideals.

WHAT *IS* TOTALITARIAN RHETORIC? REGIME RHETORIC IN POLAND, 1945–1989

In spite of many dramatic political changes in the country between 1945 and 1989, Polish real-socialist regime rhetoric remained relatively stable in its basic features, at least until 1988, just before the political transition. Specific expressions and terms went in and out of vogue, slogans changed, and there was a marked decrease in the stridency and aggressiveness of public discourse after 1956 as the country "normalized" after the excesses of Stalinism. However, the major rhetorical characteristics of regime discourse (which Polish scholar Michal Glowinski labeled "newspeak," following George Orwell's novel *1984*) remained substantially the same in kind, if not in substance.

Many of these features may be discerned in what may be regarded as one of the first official speeches by the leadership of the nascent regime: the opening speech delivered by Wladyslaw Gomulka, the first general secretary of the Polish Worker's Party—the newly installed ruling party—at its first congress in December 1945. In the speech, Gomulka declared:

> We are a young party because we have rejected everything that in the past has harmed the interests of the working class and working masses, we have rejected in our young party everything that did not allow the other old parties to lead the masses along the road to their social liberation, along the road of people's democracy. We are a young party because we have rejected the policies of all old parties, policies that led to fascism in Poland and as a consequence led our country to ruin. As a young party we were able to pose most correctly the problem of struggle for Democracy and Independence. Our youth, freed from the encrusted errors of old age of other parties allows us today to most consistently realize the building of Polish democracy and the building of the most enduring foundation of Poland's independence. (11)

This passage illustrates several features characteristic of real-socialist regime rhetoric.

Note, first, the categorical tone, amplified through modification: "rejected *everything*"; "*most* correctly," not just "correctly"; "*most* consistently," not just "consistently"; "*most* enduring foundation," not just "enduring." I have elsewhere referred to this feature, following the work of Michal Glowinski, as "pathetic amplification" (see Ornatowski, "Rhetorical"). Second, there is the theme of novelty and rebirth ("we lead the rebirth of the Polish Nation"; one of the sections of Gomulka's speech is called "We are Creating a New Life"), reinforced by the claim to radical difference ("we are a different party"), the claim to a specific, privileged relationship to historicity (we "surrender to the laws of history"), millenarianism (we represent the "fulfillment of history"), the claim to "correctness" (we represent the "correct stand in regard to all of the basic problems of the state"), and the claim to sole representation of collective interest ("our party has been built on the foundation of the entire Polish Nation, its aspirations and interests";

"nobody else can claim" to represent the people or national tradition). More-over, the "nation" and the "people" (the two are characteristically conflated) turn out to be limited to a specific segment of the population: only the "work-ing folk" "have the exclusive right to call themselves the nation," and it is this "nation" that the party represents (21). In fact, exactly such a delimited, class-based definition of the political nation was enshrined seven years later in the so-called "Stalinist" constitution of 1952, whose opening sentence read: "The Polish People's Republic is a republic of working folk" (Preamble, my translation). (By comparison, the Nazi *Volksgemeinschaft*, "folk commu-nity," was defined along a racial, rather than class, basis.) At this nascent stage of the regime, and in the context of the audience limited to party mem-bers, Gomulka is surprisingly candid about the consequences of such a redef-inition of the political community: the "reactionary class," which includes anyone of the "bourgeois" category, "has by the sentence of the people been condemned to annihilation." "Great social transformations cannot be affected without struggle and without victims," Gomulka declares: "new life is always born in pain and blood" (21).

Gomulka's rhetoric resembles Nazi rhetoric in its emphasis on rebirth and "new life," on struggle, on sacrifice and blood (Gomulka's explicit refer-ence to a "blood sacrifice" as constituting the "foundation" of the "New Poland" bears a striking similarity to Nazi phraseology and mythology); its claim to historicity and to exclusivity of political representation, along with an intolerance for alternatives or political competition; and its emphasis on unity, along with verbal stridency, amplification, and ruthlessness ("we want to and we will break down any obstacle that may stand in the way of [our] goal") (Burke, "The Rhetoric"; Klemperer). Gomulka also posits the "Enemy": "world fascism." The modifier "world" functions here similarly to the always modified Nazi figure of "*world* Jewry" or "*the* Jew," rather than simply "Jews." The modification identifies a single enemy (even if the enemy is in effect a mass noun, as in the case of "world Jewry"), yet makes the symbol capacious enough to include a range of potential actors and phenomena, as occasion may demand (cf. Burke, "The Rhetoric"; Klemperer). In Stalinist discourse, "world fascism" included American "imperialism," West German "revanchism," and domestic and émigré "reaction"; after the demise of Stalin-ism and through the 1970s, "world fascism" was replaced with "imperialism" and its foreign and domestic "agents"; while in the 1980s, following the rise of "Solidarity," the category was broadened to "enemies of socialism."

Communist discourse projected a sense of moving inexorably "forward" toward a final and inescapable "goal": the utopian state of "communism," the end of history. In the media, this forward energy was communicated through strident, emphatic narration (a delivery my mother used to refer to as "full steam ahead rhetoric"), similar to that in Nazi propaganda newsreels. This energy (combined with the idea of control, including control over nature itself) was embodied in iconography of harnessed energy: whirling machin-ery, billowing smokestacks, dams, locomotives, and the exertion of labor. The generally soporific delivery of communist officials may seem like an aberration in this context. However, unlike Nazism, communism was presumably based on a "scientific" analysis of society and (with the exception of Stalin's personality cult) thus was independent of any particular individual or leader and eschewed individualism as such (leaders were adulated while in power but were also dispensable and, once not in power, quickly erased from public memory). Unlike Hitler himself, in whose personalistic conception of history the leader embodied the collective spirit and actively "wooed" (the expression used in *Mein Kampf* and noted by Burke) the masses through oratory, the communist orator was merely a mouthpiece for the inexorable "logic of history." This "logic" also accounts for the formulaic, unchanging character of communist discourse, which, as possessed of the only "correct" vision, could not well adapt to changed circumstances. Certain things could be said only in certain ways and no other; no semantic or formal variety was tolerated. The slightest change in vocabulary, syntax, or arrangement signaled change in official policy; such changes were attended to carefully, which made attempts to understand a speech akin to trying to predict the future from tea leaves (such predicting was the occupation of highly specialized experts in the appropriate branches of the U.S. government).

Communist leaders avoided the singular personal pronoun "I" (while Hitler's speeches were redolent of it). Gomulka uses it only in the introductory part of his speech when he welcomes the delegates. Otherwise, he always uses the plural "we," which alternately designates the party, all good communists, and all Polish people: "At the foundation of the Independence of the Reborn Poland lie the blood and the bones of thousands of members of *our* party and soldiers who died in that struggle, who fought under *our national* banners" (14, emphasis added). This reified, shifting, and ambiguous "we," which at various moments in the same speech or even sentence includes members of the party, the political nation of workers and peasants, all "right-minded" Poles, or the entire nation, was a ubiquitous feature of communist rhetoric and constituted "forced identification"—a totalitarian "corruption" (to use Orwell's word) of one of the basic mechanisms of rhetoric (see also Ornatowski, "Rhetorical").

Other features of Polish regime discourse that are not shown in Gomulka's initiating speech include dominance of evaluation over description, hyperbole, magical wish fulfillment, verbal hypocrisy, and irony.

The dominance of evaluation over description was achieved through evaluative modification and the use of marked vocabulary: Gomulka speaks of "*real* freedom and Independence." The modifier "real" conveys positive evaluation (as opposed to presumably "unreal" freedom promoted by ideological opponents) without explaining what "freedom" means or implies in this context. Combining evaluative modification with hyperbole, Gomulka refers to the anticommunist underground as the "criminal fratricidal bullets of reactionary bandits" and the "venomous reactionary viper." Such phraseology made counterargument or questioning difficult; opposition amounted to

being against "freedom" (thus with "world fascism") or defending the indefensible (siding with "venomous vipers"). Questioning and discussion were
also forestalled through "magical wish-fulfillment" (the term is Glowinski's)
statements, such as Gomulka's claim that "the traditions of our struggle and
the struggle organized by us . . . have become the traditions of the entire Polish Nation" or "the Polish Workers' Party . . . has become not only the party
of one class but also the Party of the Polish Nation" (16–17). Statements of
what were in effect wishes as if they were already realities (another good
example is "the whole nation celebrates the May First holiday"—a typical
newspaper headline and staple of every May Day speech) also contained
implicit evaluation and coercion: if you don't celebrate May Day, you're not
part of the nation and therefore you single yourself out as its enemy, or at least
an outsider. Victor Klemperer notes similar mechanisms in Nazi rhetoric; he
observes "covert coercion," for instance, in the Nazi annual "winter charity"
(*Winterhilfe*), which one could not refuse on pain of admitting that one did not
consider oneself part of the "national community." (The expression "affirmative action," by the way, is "coercive"; everybody presumably knows what it
"means," but in itself it makes no specific sense besides conveying positive
evaluation: "affirming" as opposed to negating—and who wants to be seen as
negative—and promoting "action," presumably as opposed to inaction—and
who wants to be seen as obstructionist and thus, by implication, racist? Rhetorically, the expression represents absolute dominance of evaluation over
description—since in itself it describes nothing—along with covert coercion.
Thus, while its intent is noble, rhetorically the expression is authoritarian.)

Gomulka's speech does not contain any clear examples of verbal hypocrisy, but growing up in communist Poland I often had to participate in "voluntary service" for which one could not refuse to show up. State celebrations,
including May Day parades, were usually officially touted as "spontaneous,"
but nonparticipation might harm one's career, prevent one's children from getting into college, or result in other unpleasant consequences. (My own university, by the way, has recently been ordered to submit to a "Voluntary System
of Accountability"—an example of verbal hypocrisy—usually abbreviated as
"VSA," probably for "subtlety," so it does not sound quite as hypocritical.)

Still another feature of communist official rhetoric shared with Nazi rhetoric is what Klemperer calls an "ironic inverted comma": Western "democracy," the "civil rights" in the United States, the West's economic
"assistance" to Africa, and so on. The ironic inverted comma puts in doubt,
questions, gives the ostensible statement a lie, or implies ulterior motives
behind a seemingly benign word or statement. Through the use of ironic
inverted commas, opponents are never granted the good faith of their intentions, actions, or language, except when these actions are patently objectionable on the surface. Thus, in mentions of "American aggression" in Vietnam,
for instance, "aggression" was never put in quotes, presumably because it
simply described an objective fact, but if the United States provided "assistance" to South Vietnam, the word was usually "ironized," to signal that any

such assistance had to be in reality a cover for something else, something no doubt insidious. (Hitler's speeches were redolent of such ironizing, expressed by appropriate changes in tone, gestures, or facial expressions.)

While there are some variations (e.g., a different distribution of elements and accents for a very different final effect, and in service to a very different ideology), Polish communist rhetoric and Nazi rhetoric share the following features: insistent and tendentious modification; claims to sole correctness, representation, historicity, exclusivity, and radical difference or newness; forced identification through a shifting plural pronoun "we"; dominance of evaluation over description; wish-fulfilling and coercive statements; verbal hypocrisy; ironic inverted commas; along with the underlying assumption of ideological "unity." (These features are by no means exhaustive of the characteristics of communist, or Nazi, official discourse, but a detailed analysis and comparison is outside the scope of this paper.)

Discerning such similarities does not mean that communist and Nazi ideologies are similar; in fact, in most respects they are almost diametrically different. Nazi ideology (such as it was, since besides *Mein Kampf* there was not much explicit theorizing) was antirationalist (in contrast to communism, which claimed to be "scientific"), rejecting bourgeois rationalism as soulless and emphasizing action, spontaneous feeling, and the reintegration of individuals into the organic racial/ethnic/cultural community, which was led by a charismatic leader and based on the eternal values of the mythic Aryan culture. In this sense, as Hitler repeatedly emphasized in *Mein Kampf*, Nazism was primarily a "cultural" movement, as well as a political one; it was, paradoxically, also fundamentally romantic in its pervasive organicism, reliance on mythology, naturalization of the state, analogy between the state and the body, employment of the cult of heroism, genius, and collective "soul," and emphasis on the "natural" laws of struggle and survival. This antirationalist, "romantic" character was expressed in the aestheticization of politics and politicization of the aesthetic, as famously noted by Walter Benjamin (see also Schild). By contrast, communism in its Soviet (including Polish) variety was, or attempted to be, thoroughly rationalist, embracing the highest humanist ideals of the Enlightenment. Its "scientific" basis lay in volumes of economic and political theory and philosophy. In contrast to Nazi community building along racial, national, and cultural lines, Soviet communism emphasized class-based internationalism.

Any similarities between the rhetorics of the regimes are thus due less to similarities in ideology than their general character and forms of political practice (although this character and these practices were a function of ideology). Both Nazism and communism aimed at a total remaking of their respective cultures and people, in effect, producing a "new man" (and woman) in the image of their all-embracing ideologies. Both also aimed at a total integration of all aspects of life and culture with ideology and in service of ideology, at total politicization of every aspect of life (Arendt; Bytwerk; Clark; van der Will). This totalizing impulse was embodied in their characteristic political practices *and* rhetorics. In the latter, this impulse took the form of features that ranged from "totalizing" to "coercive."

The "totalizing" features include claims to sole correctness (only we are right), to sole representation of interests (only we represent the national or people's interests), to possessive historicity (history, and God, are on our side), to ideological exclusivity (nobody's ideas are similar to ours), and to radical newness (our ideas are completely new and have never been tried before; I often get this one from Marxist friends who tell me that Stalin had it all wrong and "real" communism has actually never been tried before, or that communism in Trotsky's version would have been different and better). These features make reasonable discussion, deliberation, or dissent impossible. Osama bin Laden's characterization of the current situation in the Middle East as a struggle between "two paths," "the divine, perfect belief, which has submitted to God's authority on all matters" and the "crudely secular way" (259–60) of "global unbelief" (250), represented and led by the United States, is "totalizing" in this sense (note the heavy modification and valuation: "divine" and "perfect"—not just "belief"; "all matters"—not just "submitted"; "crudely secular"—not just "secular"). One can hardly imagine how to begin to question such a vision without being classified (or in effect classifying oneself) as "crudely secular."

Expressions that smack of finality and absoluteness ("blood sacrifice," "inexorable logic of history") also belong to the "totalizing" category, as does "full steam ahead" delivery, and, perhaps, "forced identification" through the shifting plural pronoun "we" (which forcibly identifies the listener with the position and interests of the rhetor). Croatian dissident Slavenka Drakulić recalls "hating" the plural pronoun "we" as she grew up in communist Yugoslavia. "I grew up with 'we' and 'us': in the kindergarten, at school, in the pioneer and youth organizations, in the community, at work" (2). "Individuality, the first-person singular," she points out, was "exiled from public and political life and exercised in private" (4). On the other hand, by using the pronoun "I," "you stuck out; you risked being labeled an 'anarchic element' (not even a person), perhaps even a dissident" (3). Drakulić notes that the plural pronoun continued to hold sway when the nationalist myth replaced the communist one and led to the ethnic wars in the Balkans in the mid-1990s. Finally, absolutizing the "one enemy" ("world Jewry," "world fascism") may be considered "totalizing" by a mechanism similar to forced identification: any disagreement makes one a member of the "Jewish conspiracy" or a (probably) paid agent of imperialism, not to mention that it makes dealing effectively with perhaps separate and lesser enemies more difficult. (In this sense, President Bush's designation after 9/11 of the "enemy" as "world terrorism," or simply "terrorism," as if all who engage in political violence for very different reasons and in very different contexts were part of the same "conspiracy," was a rhetorical and strategic mistake.)

"Coercive" features of communist (and Nazi) discourse contain an explicit or implicit assumption of unity and one-mindedness and make reasonable dissent, deliberation, the search for alternatives, or compromise diffi cult. Such features include insistent and tendentious modification (how can one be against "real" freedom and for a "false" one?); dominance of evaluation over description (what exactly does "social justice" mean?); wish-fulfilling and coercive statements (which present wished-for states as a *fait accompli*, with no room to point to the gap between reality and rhetoric except at the cost of revealing one's "true colors"); verbal hypocrisy (a rhetorical analog of physical violence, which adds insult to injury); and ironic inverted commas (which enforce verbal conformity and prevent discussion by exclusionary appropriation of meanings).

It is significant that in the waning days of the Polish real-socialist regime, when, in the face of overwhelming popular opposition and economic collapse, the regime could no longer hope to maintain the monopoly of political (and rhetorical) power and began edging toward what was referred to as the "new social contract," regime rhetoric began to change, in fact precisely by abandoning its "totalizing" and "coercive" features. Two speeches delivered before parliament on September 27, 1988, by General Wojciech Jaruzelski (who throughout the 1980s was a virtual dictator of Poland) and Mieczyslaw Rakowski (the incoming prime minister backed by Jaruzelski) were especially significant in this regard.

Jaruzelski's speech in effect changed the entire representation of society that was implicit in the regime's discourse for over forty-five years. It was no longer the reified, unified, and passive "nation," "society," "the people," or "workers and peasants" that "enthusiastically" endorsed, hailed, and celebrated the regime's accomplishments while the monolithic authorities spoke in the name of everyone's best interest. Rather, society was represented as consisting of particular interests that may in fact be legitimately at odds, and where the government in power attempted to mediate and seek "accord," under the leadership of the party, which, far from being represented as the only possible and legitimate political force, stood for socialism as an ethical, rather than political, idea. In fact, "accord" emerged as Jaruzelski's new key word—a move impossible up to that time in regime discourse since its implicit antonym, "discord," was publicly unimaginable (under the assumption of, in the words of the ubiquitous 1970s slogan, "The Moral/Political Unity of the Nation"). Jaruzelski also, for the first time ever, mentioned "capitalism" by name in the same context as "socialism," thus bringing the former into legitimate existence, as it were, and even implying that there might be a choice between the two (gone were the "hooligans" and "dupes of Western imperialism" that populated official discourse through much of the 1980s). (For a detailed analysis of Jaruzelski's and Rakowski's speeches in the context of the 1980s regime rhetoric, see Ornatowski, "Rhetorical.")

Following the dramatic introduction by Jaruzelski, Rakowski, for the first time in a public speech by a communist leader, exclusively used the first person singular, even referring to the communist party as "my party" (not "our party," implicitly the only legitimately possible party, as would have been typical up to that time), thus also rhetorically legitimizing ideological differences and the potential existence of other political parties and individual political preferences. As a result, "partnership" emerged as one of the key terms of the Rakowski administration (whose slogan was "Respect the Partner"). Such rhetorical retreat from "totalizing" positions constituted a critical part of the process of compromise that led to the historic round table talks of February–April 1989 and to the "new social contract" that prepared the ground for the advent of political pluralism. More importantly perhaps, in terms of political realism (the regime did not surrender power out of the goodness of its heart), this retreat ensured the political survival of the Polish left; had the leadership insisted on the "total" course (and "totalizing" rhetoric) the left would have disappeared from the political spectrum, at least in the initial phase of the transition, perhaps even, as was widely feared, accompanied by violence.

POLITICS AND LANGUAGE REVISITED

Theodore Windt once suggested that "rhetoric is at the center of democratic politics. . . . A totalitarian society has no use for rhetoric, for persuasion, for debate. Compliance with laws and authorities is enforced through coercion either by the state police or through confinement" (xxxv). This statement is not only simply untrue, but also dangerous. Totalitarian regimes may have no use for debate (except in very narrow and isolated fora, like the Central Committee of the Communist Party), but rhetoric is central to both their character and power. Police and confinement may well constitute the sanctions that stand behind and thus bolster their rhetoric, but it is the rhetoric that does most of the work (in his diaries, Joseph Goebbels, Nazi chief of propaganda, expressed constant worry about the state of mind of the German people, which needed to be relentlessly and vigilantly tended through propaganda).

In this paper, I have tried to identify some of the features characteristic of totalitarian regime rhetorics. Specific "totalitarian rhetorics" combine these features in variable, localized ways with cultural, institutional, and historic factors and "regime specific" elements, including ideology, political practices, and the apparatus of constraint (police and confinement). For instance, while Polish communist leaders never used the first-person singular "I," only the collective "we," and so, in general, did rank-and-file Nazi speakers, Hitler himself reveled in the first-person singular "I." There are ideological reasons for this, namely the Nazi "Fuhrer principle," which contrasted with the collective leadership principle of communism. On the other hand, the singular first-person pronoun "I" was one of the most characteristic elements of Lech Walesa's speech, precisely in contrast to official rhetoric (for an analysis of Walesa's rhetoric in relation to regime rhetoric, see Ornatowski, "'I Leapt'"). It is instructive that when Walesa became president, his obsessive use of "I" (along with other characteristics of his speech that, under communism, contributed to his status as a popular opposition leader) became a liability; he lost the 1995 presidential election to the postcommunist Kwaśniewski, who, in turn, showed a preference for the collective plural (however, not in the old mode of forcibly identifying his party with the electorate and the nation, but rather as part of a rhetoric of reconciliation).

The specific effect of any particular rhetorical device is usually contextual, not only in the sense of the context of the "rhetorical situation," but in the broader context of ideology and regime-specific political practice and its attendant rhetorical practice. As Vaclav Havel has observed:

> The selfsame word can, at one moment, radiate great hopes, at another, it can emit lethal rays. The selfsame word can be true at one moment and false at next, at one moment, illuminating, at another, deceptive. On one occasion, it can open up glorious horizons; on another, it can lay down tracks to an entire archipelago of concentration camps. The selfsame words can, at one time be the cornerstone of peace, while at another, machine-gun fire resounds with every syllable. (12–13)

The speeches of "democratic" politicians may include "totalitarian" or "coercive" features, as may political or commercial advertising. It is the intensification, amplification, combination, and persistence of specific characteristics within an ideological and political framework that they support and that, in turn, backs them with other forms of sanction (psychological or physical) that make a rhetoric "totalitarian."

Hannah Arendt, for instance, notes that a "totalizing" rhetoric of "tribal consciousness" tends to come to the fore in times of collective crisis and danger; witness President Bush's speech in the wake of 9/11: "Tonight we are a country awakened to danger and called to defend freedom. Our grief has turned to anger, and anger to resolution." While Bush's speech was criticized as well as praised, it hardly augurs the ascent of totalitarianism in America (although, if some of its features became the norm in public discourse, I'd start getting worried). It is important, however, to be alert to such elements wherever they occur, no matter the avowed intention of the speaker. Even in a generally democratic context, the power of "totalizing" and "coercive" rhetoric may be considerable; I have sat through many a meeting feeling violated by an involuntary subscription to some "unity" (even if the cause itself was substantively good) that brooked no reasonable objection or response except explicit or silent support. Such rhetoric often becomes an invitation for people to jump on the bandwagon (people generally seem to enjoy being part of a like-minded group and the public approval that goes with it) and we're off toward some new, bright future.

In his reflections on politics and language, Orwell locates "corruption" (and, ultimately, the source of political dangers) in "insincerity": "when there is a gap between one's real and one's declared aims . . ." (363). Orwell's prescriptions for "political regeneration" are thus intended to ensure sincerity in discourse. Sincerity is a laudable goal, but it misses the essential rhetorical (and political) point: that language is not just a means of expression, representation, or "communication," but also, and perhaps primarily, at least in the context of "politics," a means of social action: action on, in relation to, and with, others. Definitions of "politics" typically emphasize its nature as both *social* and as *process*: it is "the process by which groups of people make decisions" and is observed in "all human group interactions." Politics "consists of social relations involving authority or power and applies to the methods and tactics used to formulate and apply policy" (Politics). Burke's celebrated definition of rhetoric may also effectively double as a definition of politics: "the use of words [or other symbols, even violence, as in the case of the attacks of 9/11] by human agents to form attitudes or to induce actions in other human agents . . ." (*Rhetoric of Motives* 41). Rhetoric emerges here as a critical function of ideology and a form of political practice: in effect the means of rendering one in terms of the other. The *politically* salient issue is not whether Gomulka, Hitler, Stalin, or anybody else is "sincere" in their beliefs or "clear" in their expressions (many mass murderers were no doubt quite sincere in their convictions), but what kind of political reality, including what forms of political practice and action, their rhetorics in effect help not only legitimate but also constitute and support.

Based on lessons from both the "hot" and "cold" wars, and in the midst of the "war on terror," I would thus revise Orwell's rhetorical prescriptions— not in the hope of anything as exalted as "political regeneration" but simply by way of learning from experience. I would replace injunctions such as "never use a long word where a short one will do" or "never use the passive where you can use the active" with injunctions such as "when you use 'we,' make certain that you are *describing* an actually existing group and not *subscribing* your audience to a community to which they may or may not want to belong or to beliefs they may or may not share" or "examine a modifier to see if evaluation dominates over description."

Ultimately, it is the combination of an ideology that aspires to an exhaustive and exclusive explanation of reality in the name of some ideal (even, or perhaps especially, if that ideal is in itself attractive, like "community" or "social justice") with "totalizing" rhetoric that is perhaps potentially most dangerous. Totalitarianisms usually arise, at least initially, with at least a measure of popular acquiescence and often out of fundamentally pluralistic contexts. Bits and pieces of "totalizing" and "coercive" rhetoric are all around us. It is when they come together, like filings around a magnet, around an idea that harnesses powerful feelings (like "Germany"), or harbors a powerful attraction (like "social justice"), or around compelling circumstances (like 9/11), that they become virulent. That does not mean one should not argue about or advocate, even passionately, for such ideals. It does mean that, especially in contexts such as the above, one should carefully attend to the workings of language, including one's own. Many well-meaning Poles, Russians, or Germans (many of them later dissidents) did not know what was in store for them when they followed, willingly or through rhetorical coercion, the beguiling visions of Gomulka, Stalin, or Hitler. It is only afterwards that one can say: "By their rhetoric thou should (have) know(n) them." That is a rhetorical lesson worth revisiting.

Notes

[1] Directed by James McTeigue and released in U.S. theaters in March 2006. The film was based on the graphic novel by Alan Moore and David Lloyd (parts of which appeared in Great Britain as early as 1982–1983 and in the United States in 1989–1990, the years of the world-shaking transformations in central/eastern Europe).

[2] In the 1964 Warner Brothers film *My Fair Lady*, directed by George Cukor and based on George Bernard Shaw's play *Pygmalion*, phonetics professor Henry Higgins promises to turn a London flower girl into a high society lady by teaching her correct speech.

[3] The reason to study communist rhetoric is, I submit, the same as the one offered by Kenneth Burke in his celebrated analysis of Hitler's *Mein Kampf*: "to discover what kind of 'medicine' this medicine-man has concocted, that we may know, with greater accuracy, exactly what to guard against, if we are to forestall the concocting of similar medicine in America" ("The Rhetoric" 191).

[4] The campaign slogan for Dwight David "Ike" Eisenhower during the 1952 presidential election in which Eisenhower defeated Adlai Stevenson to become the thirty-fourth president of the United States.

Works Cited

Arendt, Hannah. *The Origins of Totalitarianism*. New Edition. New York: Harcourt, Brace & World, 1966.

Aristotle. *Politics*. Trans. Benjamin Jowett. New York: Modern Library, 1943.

——. *The Rhetoric of Aristotle*. Trans. Lane Cooper. Englewood Cliffs, NJ: Prentice-Hall, 1960.

Benjamin, Walter. "The Work of Art in the Age of Mechanical Reproduction." *Illuminations: Essays and Reflections*. Ed. Hannah Arendt. New York: Schocken, 1985. 217–51.

bin Laden, Osama. "Depose the Tyrants." *Messages to the World: The Statements of Osama bin Laden*. Ed. Bruce Lawrence. Trans. John Howarth. London: Verso, 2005. 245–76.

Burke, Kenneth. "The Rhetoric of Hitler's 'Battle.'" *The Philosophy of Literary Form: Studies in Symbolic Action*. 3rd ed. Berkeley: U of California P, 1973. 191–220.

——. *A Rhetoric of Motives*. Berkeley: U of California P, 1969.

Bush, George W. *Address Before a Joint Session of the Congress of the United States: Response to the Terrorist Attacks of September 11*. The American Presidency Project. <http://www.presidency.ucsb.edu/ws/?pid=64731>.

Bytwerk, Randall L. *Bending Spines: The Propagandas of Nazi Germany and the German Democratic Republic*. Series ed. Martin J. Medhurst. East Lansing: Michigan State UP, 2004.

Campbell, Karlyn Kohrs, and Kathleen Hall Jamieson. *Deeds Done in Words: Presidential Rhetoric and the Genres of Governance*. Chicago: U of Chicago P, 1990.

Clark, Toby. *Art and Propaganda in the Twentieth Century*. New York: Abrams, 1997.

Drakulić, Slavenka. "Introduction: First-Person Singular." *Café Europa: Life After Communism*. New York: Norton, 1997. 1–5.

Farrell, Thomas B. *Norms of Rhetorical Culture*. New Haven: Yale UP, 1993.

Friedrich, Carl J., and Zbigniew K. Brzezinski. *Totalitarian Dictatorship and Autocracy*. Cambridge, MA: Harvard UP, 1975.

Glowinski, Michal. *Nowomowa po Polsku*. Warsaw, Poland: PEN, 1991.

Goebbels, Joseph. *The Goebbels Diaries 1942–43*. Trans. Louis P. Lochner. Garden City, NJ: Doubleday, 1948.

Gomulka, Wladyslaw. "Opening Speech of the General Secretary, December 6, 1945." *Ku Nowej Polsce: Sprawozdanie Polityczne i Przemowiania Wyglaszane na I Zjezdzie PPR*. Warszawa: Ksiazka, 1945.

Hauser, Gerard A. *Vernacular Voices: The Rhetoric of Publics and Public Spheres*. Columbia: U of South Carolina P, 1999.

Havel, Vaclav. "Words on Words." *Writing on the East: Selected Essays on Eastern Europe from the* New York Times *Review of Books*. New York: New York Review of Books, 1990. 7–21.

Klemperer, Victor. *The Language of the Third Reich: LTI—Lingua Tertii Imperii, A Philologist's Notebook*. Trans. Martin Brady. London: Continuum, 2006.

Ornatowski, Cezar M. "'I Leapt Over the Wall and They Made Me President': Historical Context, Rhetorical Agency, and the Amazing Career of Lech Walesa." *Advances in the History of Rhetoric* 8 (2005): 155–92.

———. "Rhetorical Regime in Crisis: The Rhetoric of Polish Leadership, 1980–1988." *Rhetoric of Transformation*. Ed. Jerzy Axer. Vol. 6. Warsaw, Poland: DIG, 2003. 91–106.

Orwell, George. "Politics and the English Language." *The Orwell Reader: Fiction, Essays, and Reportage*. New York: Harcourt Brace, 1950. 355–66.

Politics. Wikipedia. 28 Sept. 2008. <http://en.wikipedia.org/wiki/Politics>.

Preamble. Constitution of the Polish People's Republic of July 22, 1952. *Dziennik Ustaw* nr. 33.232. <http://www.trybunal.gov.pl/wszechnica/akty/konstytucja_prl.htm>.

Schild, Hans-Jochen. "Rhetorical Aesthetics and Power Politics: Problems of Research into Political Rhetoric." *Rhetoric of Transformation*. Ed. Jerzy Axer. Vol. 6. Warsaw, Poland: DIG, 2003. 9–15.

van der Will, Wilfried. "Culture and the Organization of National Socialist Ideology 1933 to 1945." *German Cultural Studies: An Introduction*. Ed. Rob Burns. New York: Oxford UP, 1995.

Windt, Theodore. "Presidential Rhetoric: Definition of a Discipline of Study." *Essays in Presidential Rhetoric*. 2nd ed. Ed. Theodore Windt and Beth Ingold. Dubuque, IA: Kendall/Hunt, 1987. xv–xliii.

Contributors

Ruth Amossy is Professor of French and coordinator of the ADARR research group (Discourse Analysis, Rhetoric and Argumentation) at Tel-Aviv University. Among her publications are *Stéréotypes et clichés* (1997), *Images de soi dans le discours. La construction de l'ethos* (ed.) (1999), *L'argumentation dans le discours* (2000, 2006), and "Doxa and Discourse; How Common Knowledge Works" (2002). She is the chief editor of the online journal *Argumentation et Analyse du discours*.

Maha Baddar is a PhD candidate in the Rhetoric, Composition, and the Teaching of English program at the University of Arizona. Her research interests include the work of medieval Arabic philosophers such as al-Kindi, al-Farabi, Ibn Sina, and Ibn Rushd; the history of the translation movements in Baghdad and Andalusia; postcolonial studies; and metaphor theory.

James J. Brown, Jr. is a PhD candidate in the University of Texas Department of English specializing in digital literacies and literatures. His work has been published in *Leisure Studies, Fast Capitalism,* and *The Computer Culture Reader,* and he is currently at work on a dissertation entitled "Hospitable Texts," which uses Wikipedia as a case study for shifting notions of rhetorical agency, community, and intellectual property.

Claudia Carlos is Assistant Professor of English and Rhetoric at Carnegie Mellon University. Her research interests include early modern French rhetoric, the art of "safe speaking" in rhetorical theory and practice, arguments by indirection, and the relationship between argumentation and style. Her most recent article, "Techniques of Bold Speaking, Safely, in Bossuet's 'Sermon sur la prédication évangélique' (1662)," will be forthcoming in the journal *Rhetorica*.

Jay P. Childers is Assistant Professor of Communication Studies at the University of Kansas. His work has appeared in a number of scholarly journals and collections including the *Quarterly Journal of Speech* and *Presidential Studies Quarterly.*

Gregory Clark is Professor of English and Associate Dean of the College of Humanities at Brigham Young University. He is author of *Rhetorical Landscapes in America* and coeditor with S. Michael Halloran of *Oratorical Culture in Nineteenth-Century America.* He is a former editor of *Rhetoric Society Quarterly* and is currently serving as Executive Director of the Rhetoric Society of America.

Kathleen Dixon, Professor of English at the University of North Dakota and recent Fulbright Scholar to Bulgaria, is the collaborative author of a forthcoming book on television talk shows titled *Revisiting the Global Village: Art, Politics, and Television Talk Shows* (Rowman, Littlefield). She is also the author of *Making Relationships: Gender in the Forming of Academic Community* (Peter Lang, 1997) and *Outbursts in Academe* (Heinemann, 1998).

Michael Bernard-Donals is the Nancy Hoefs Professor of English at the University of Wisconsin-Madison, where he is also an affiliate member of the Mosse-Weinstein Center for Jewish Studies. His books include *Mikhail Bakhtin: Between Phenomenology and Marxism, Rhetoric in an Antifoundational World* (coedited with Richard Glejzer) and, most recently, *Forgetful Memory: Remembrance and Representation in the Wake of the Holocaust*.

Kathryn E. Dobson is Assistant Professor of English at McDaniel College where she teaches rhetorical theory and literary nonfiction. Her research interests include rhetoric, affect, and historical representation.

William Duffy is completing a PhD in Rhetoric and Composition at the University of North Carolina at Greensboro. His dissertation considers how post-process composition theory can be used to understand collaboration as a form of rhetorical invention.

Richard C. Gebhardt is Professor of English and Director of the Rhetoric & Writing PhD Program at Bowling Green State University. His publications include *Academic Advancement in Composition Studies: Scholarship, Publication, Promotion, Tenure* and articles in *CCC, College English, Rhetoric Review, JAC,* and other journals. Rick is a former editor of *CCC* and a recipient of the Richard Braddock Award.

Cheryl Geisler is a joint Professor of Rhetoric and Composition and Information Technology at Rensselaer Polytechnic Institute where she serves as Head of Language, Literature, and Communication. She has received the Kneupper Award for Best Article in *Rhetoric Society Quarterly.* Her recent work, funded by the National Science Foundation, focuses on the advancement of women to the rank of full professor.

Curt Gilstrap is an Assistant Professor and Director of the Graduate Program in the Department of Communication at Drury University. His work includes environmental rhetoric and environmental entrepreneurship.

Richard Glejzer is Professor of English and Chair of the Department of English at North Central College. He is the coeditor of *Rhetoric in an Antifoundational World: Language, Culture, and Pedagogy* and *Witnessing the Disaster: Essays on Representation and the Holocaust*. He is also the coauthor of *Between Witness and Testimony: The Holocaust and the Limits of Representation*.

David C. Hoffman is an Associate Professor in the School of Public Affairs at Baruch College, City University of New York. He has served as President of the American Society for the History of Rhetoric and has published works in *Rhetorica, Rhetoric Society Quarterly, Rhetoric and Public Affairs, Advances in the History of Rhetoric,* and *Parabola*.

Charles Johnson, who holds the S. Wilson and Grace M. Pollock Professorship for Excellence in English at the University of Washington, is a renowned writer, artist, and public intellectual. He received the 1990 National Book Award for his novel *Middle Passage*, becoming the first African-American male to win this prize since Ralph Ellison. At the Seattle RSA conference, Johnson presented two short stories, including "The Cynic" (first published in *Boston Review* in 2007 and reprinted in this volume).

Lisa Jane Kabasin is an undergraduate English major at Niagara University. She has spent the last four years playing ice hockey and dedicating her time to the glorification of all things English. She aspires to break into journalism or become an English professor.

Todd Kelshaw is Assistant Professor of Communication Studies at Montclair State University. His writings pertaining to communication in democratic organizations, deliberative civic engagement, and service-learning pedagogies have appeared in journals such as the *International Journal of Public Participation* and *Communication Theory.* His forthcoming coedited book, *Partnerships for Service-learning: Impacts on Communities and Students*, will be published in 2009 by Jossey-Bass.

Krista Kennedy is a PhD candidate in the Department of Writing Studies at the University of Minnesota. Her research focuses on intellectual property in digital contexts, and she is completing a comparative study of authorship and agency in Chambers' *Cyclopaedia* (1728) and Wikipedia.

Joseph Little is Assistant Professor of English at Niagara University. His work on the role of analogy in science has been published in *Rhetoric Society Quarterly* and *Technical Communication Quarterly.*

Barbara Little Liu is an Associate Professor of English at Eastern Connecticut State University where she was also Coordinator of First-Year Writing from 1998 to 2009. She has presented at several RSA conferences, but this is her first publication of rhetorical criticism. Her other publications have been in the field of composition theory and pedagogy and include a chapter in *The Outcomes Book: Debate and Consensus after the WPA Outcomes Statement.*

Brian J. McNely is a doctoral candidate in Rhetoric and Writing Studies at the University of Texas at El Paso. His dissertation, "Un/Commonplaces: Redirecting Research and Curricula in Rhetoric and Writing Studies," seeks new approaches to writing research that respond to the complexities of contemporary knowledge work in ubiquitous and distributed computing environments.

Mark Meister is an Associate Professor in the Department of Communication at North Dakota State University. He is the coeditor of *Enviropop: Studies in Environmental Rhetoric and Popular Culture and of Communication Ethics, Media, and Popular Culture.*

Jane Munksgaard is currently a PhD student at the University of Georgia. She received her MA in Rhetoric and Public Advocacy from the University of Iowa in 2008. Her research interests include feminist theory, the politics of the body, and performance art.

Lester C. Olson is Professor of Communication at the University of Pittsburgh. His book publications include *Emblems of American Community* (1991), *Benjamin Franklin's Vision of American Community* (2004), and *Visual Rhetoric* (2008). He is a past recipient of the Rhetoric Society of America's book award and other recognitions from the National Communication Association, including the Karl Wallace Award, the Winans-Wichelns Award, and the Marie Hochmuch Nichols Award.

Cezar M. Ornatowski is Professor of Rhetoric and Writing Studies at San Diego State University. His publications include *Teaching Technical Communication* (coedited with Katherine Staples) and articles in journals and anthologies.

M. Karen Powers is Assistant Professor of English at Kent State University-Tuscara-was where she teaches composition, African-American literature, and the short story. Her research in rhetorical historiography most often considers intersections between political and educational discourses. Her work has appeared in *College Composition and Communication* and in *The Politics of Writing in the Two-Year College.*

Nathaniel A. Rivers is an Assistant Professor at Georgetown University. His publications include "Some Assembly Required: The Latourian Collective and the Banal Work of Technical and Professional Communication" and "First-Year Composition Takes the University's Agonism Online" (coauthored). He has also coedited a collection of Kenneth Burke's literary reviews entitled *Equipment for Living* (forthcoming), and has been named an emerging Kenneth Burke Scholar.

Julia M. Smith is a doctoral candidate in Writing Studies at the University of Illinois, Urbana-Champaign. She completed a Masters in Rhetoric and Composition at Florida State University. Her areas of special interest are the history of rhetoric, specifically the medieval era; recovering women in the history of rhetoric; rhetorical agency; new media studies; and activity theory.

Michelle Smith is a PhD candidate in Rhetoric and Composition in the English Department at Penn State University. Her dissertation examines the intersections of spatial and publics theory through a study of the rhetoric of nineteenth-century female members of intentional communities. Her work on the rhetoric of intentional communities won the Communal Studies Association's Starting Scholar Award and the University of Southern Indiana's Center for Communal Studies Prize and has been published in *Communal Societies.*

Kathleen A. Swift served as an English as a Foreign Language instructor in Asia and Mexico for over 11 years before becoming a candidate in the doctoral program of the Gevirtz Graduate School of Education at the University of California, Santa Barbara. Her research interests include the rhetoric of the U.S. eugenics movement and the sociology of knowledge. She is a member of the Kenneth Burke Society, the Modern Language Association, Rhetoricians for Peace, and the Rhetoric Society of America.

David Tell is Assistant Professor of Communication Studies at The University of Kansas.

Barbara Warnick is Professor and Chair in the Department of Communication at the University of Pittsburgh. Her areas of research are digital rhetoric and the history and theory of argumentation. She is a past editor of *Quarterly Journal of Speech.* Her most recent book, *Rhetoric Online: Persuasion and Politics on the World Wide Web*, was published by Peter Lang in 2007.

Eve Wiederhold is an Assistant Professor of English at George Mason University, where she teaches courses in rhetoric, critical theory, and the history of composition studies in the United States. Her current research explores representation and democratic politics in relation to rhetoric and public sphere theories.

Stephen R. Yarbrough is Professor of Rhetoric and Criticism at the University of North Carolina at Greensboro. His most recent book publications include *Inventive Intercourse: From Rhetorical Conflict to the Ethical Creation of Novel Truth*, *After Rhetoric: Studies in Discourse Beyond Language and Culture*, and *Delightful Conviction: Jonathan Edwards and the Rhetoric of Conversion.* He is a past recipient of the Everett Lee Hunt Scholarship Award.

David Zarefsky is the Owen L. Coon Professor of Communication Studies at Northwestern University, where he is a former dean of the School of Communication. His books include *President Johnson's War on Poverty: Rhetoric and History* and *Lincoln, Douglas, and Slavery: In the Crucible of Public Debate*. He is a past president of both the National Communication Association and the Rhetoric Society of America and has received NCA's Winans-Wichelns Award, Distinguished Scholar Award, Mentor Award, and Distinguished Service Award.

Name Index

Aalmuhammed, J., 306, 307
Abod, J., 82
Adams, P., 71, 72
Alcoff, L., 86
Al-Farabi, A-N., 230–241
Allen, D. S., 28, 29, 33, 34, 195
Althusser, L., 176
Amossy, R., 3, 4, 52, 56
Andelman, B., 312
Anderson, R., 122
Angenot, M., 54, 56, 60
Arendt, H., 25, 33, 34, 347, 351
Aristotle, 38, 39, 121, 125, 163, 220, 283, 284, 285, 286, 341
Arnett, R. C., 122
Asen, R., 72
Austin, J. L., 39, 86

Baddar, M., 8, 9, 230
Bakhtin, M. M., 97, 103
Barber, B., 25
Barilli, R., 159, 163
Bary, R., 45, 47, 48
Bates, B. R., 134, 135
Baumlin, J. S., 149n
Baxter, L. A., 117, 119,
Beerbohm, M., 121, 122, 125, 281, 282
Beikas, T., 196
Belova, O., 314
Benjamin, W., 224, 319, 347
Bercovitch, S., 134, 135
Berger, J., 318
Berkley, R. A., 271

Bernard-Donals, M., 8, 219, 228n
Bernstein, S., 228n
Berube, M., 163
Bethe, H., 294
Biesecker, B., 73
bin Laden, O., 348
Black, D., 235, 236, 237, 238, 239
Black, E., 186, 189, 214
Blair, C., 97
Bloch, R. H., 182
Blyth, D., 196
Boardman, K., 65
Bohman, J., 117
Bohr, N., 294
Bolter, J. D., 159, 162
Bormann, E., 176
Bostdorff, D. M., 134
Bourdaloue, L., 44, 48, 49
Bourdieu, P., 86, 144, 146
Bowden, J. J., 101
Boyer, E. L., 263, 265
Brandt, D., 155
Brooks, P., 160
Brown, J. J., Jr., 6, 151
Brown, P., 163
Brzezinski, Z., 342
Bunge, M., 290
Burke, K., 16, 156, 204, 211, 212, 217, 289, 317, 332, 333, 334, 336, 344, 352, 353n
Burkhardt, J., Jr., 266
Bush, G. W., 134, 187, 191, 192, 348, 351
Bushman, D., 41

Butler, J., 70, 71, 72, 77
Bytwerk, R. L., 347

Campbell, J. A., 290, 299
Campbell, K. K., 86, 166, 167, 174n, 304, 341
Carlos, C., 3, 44
Cartwright, L., 318
Catlin, G., 202
Caussin, N. S., 45, 46, 47, 48
Cavell, S., 319
Ceccarelli, L., 290
Chambers, T., 266
Channell, C. E., 283, 284
Charcot, J., 295
Charland, M., 175, 176, 177, 178, 181
Chase, B., 155, 156
Chasin, R., 122
Chasnoff, B., 155
Childers, J. P., 7, 186
Cho, Y.-C., 73
Cicero, 45
Cissna, K. N., 122
Clark, A., 283, 286, 287
Clark, G. F., 8, 201
Clark, R., 290
Clark, T., 347
Clement, C., 290
Clinton, H., 63, 64, 65, 67
Cloud, J., 332
Cohen, J., 123, 124
Colclough, D., 45, 46, 50
Colon, E., 317
Connolly, W., 31
Corder, J., 287
Cordova, N. I., 177

Crenson, M. A., 187
Crocker, L., 27
Cros, E., 76
Crowley, S., 37, 38, 39, 42, 43, 65, 73, 77
Crusius, T. W., 283, 284
Cukor, G., 353n
Cushman, E., 265

Darsey, J., 327
Dart, J., 130
Davidson, D., 144, 148
Davis, D., 156
De Boer, T. J., 232
De Certeau, M., 104, 106
de Man, P., 26
De Veaux, A., 80
Declercq, G., 56
Delaney, D., 102, 103, 104, 108
DeLuca, K. M., 327, 329, 337
Denton, R. E., Jr., 329
Derrida, J., 26, 27, 286
Diogenes, 245–247, 326, 330
Dixon, K., 6, 159
Dobson, K. E., 11, 310
Dow, B. J., 130
Drakulić, S., 348
Drechsler, D., 322
Duffy, W., 3, 37

Eemeren, F. H. van, 54, 60n
Eisenhower, D. D., 353n
Eisner, W., 312, 313, 315, 319, 320, 323
Enoch, J., 97

Fakhry, M., 232
Falwell, J., 142n
Farley, B., 327, 333
Farr, C. K., 159
Farrell, T., 341
Ferguson, R., 183
Fitchett, J., 333
Fleckenstein, K., 98, 102
Fleming, A. M., 320, 321
Flores, C., 108
Foix, M.-A. de la, 45
Foner, E., 178
Foucault, M., 33, 53, 102, 104, 109, 145
Foust, C., 73, 77
Frank, A., 221
Freeman, S. A., 326, 337

Freud, S., 295, 296, 297, 298, 300
Friedling, M., 75
Friedrich, C., 342
Fruchtman, J., Jr., 182

Gadamer, H-G., 118
Galton, F., 214
Gamow, G., 294, 295, 299, 300
Gamst, F., 329
Gardner, D. P., 250, 254, 260
Garsten, B., 25, 26, 27, 31, 32
Gastil, J., 117, 118, 122, 125
Gathercole, P. M., 168, 169, 172
Gay, P., 28
Gebhardt, R. C., 9, 10, 263
Geisler, C., 10, 269, 271, 304, 306
Geller, J., 329
Genette, G., 166
Gentner, D., 290, 299
Gergen, K., 144
Gibson, K., 290, 299
Giddens, A., 119
Gilstrap, C., 326
Ginsberg, B., 187
Glassick, C., 263, 265
Glejzer, R., 8, 219
Glick, D., 331, 332, 333
Glowinski, M., 343, 346
Goebbels, J., 350
Goetz, T., 154
Goffman, E., 337
Gomulka, W., 343, 344, 345, 346
Good, A., 206
Gosney, E. S., 215, 216
Graves, H. B., 299
Greimas, A.-J., 60n
Griffith, B., 318
Grignashi, M., 234
Gross, A. G., 86, 177, 289, 299
Gross, J., 221, 226, 227, 228n
Grusin, R., 159, 162
Guèret, G., 45
Gunn, J., 157n, 306
Guralnick, E., 249
Gutas, D., 231, 232, 239

Habermas, J., 125
Haddad, F. S., 232, 239

Hall, G. S., 296
Hamblin, C. L., 53
Hardy-Short, D., 328
Hargens, L. L., 274
Harrington, M., 332
Hart, R., 189
Hartley, J., 312
Hartman, S., 86
Hartmann, E. von, 296
Haskins, E. V., 177
Hauser, G. A., 97, 205, 341
Havel, V., 351
Hawhee, D., 283, 287
Hawke, D. F., 183
Heater, B., 317
Heilbron, J. L., 291
Helmholtz, H. von, 295
Hesford, W., 65
Hilberg, R., 221
Hill, A. S., 38
Hindman, S., 169, 170, 172
Hitler, A., 215, 216, 345, 347, 350, 352
Hoffman, D. C., 7, 175, 178
Holyoak, K., 290
Honig, B., 26, 32
Horowitz, D., 257, 258
Huber, M. T., 263, 265
Hutchinson, K. H., 311
Hyde, M. J., 313

Ibn-Khallikan, 233
Irigaray, L., 77

Jack, J., 97
Jackson, N., 97
Jacobson, S., 317
Jamieson, K. H., 86, 341
Janet, P., 295
Jarratt, S. C., 308
Jaruzelski, G. W., 349
Jay, K., 87
Jefferson, T., 190
Jendrysik, M. S., 142
Jeziorski, M., 290
Joas, H., 148
Johnson, C., 9, 243
Johnson, L. B., 17, 18
Jordan, J. W., 72
Jordan, R., 157n
Judson, H. F., 289

Kabasin, L. J., 11, 289
Kakalios, J., 312

Kaminski, D., 271
Kaner, S., 119
Kantorowicz, E. H., 252
Katriel, T., 328, 329
Kaveny, M., 117
Keane, J., 178
Kellogg, J. L., 173
Kelshaw, T., 5, 117, 118,
    122, 123, 124, 125
Kendler, H. H., 295, 296
Kennedy, G. A., 39, 285
Kennedy, J. F., 17
Kennedy, K., 11, 303
Kerbrat-Orecchioni, C., 52
Kezar, A., 266
King, M. L., Jr., 142
Kissinger, H., 217
Klemperer, V., 344, 346
Kokinov, B., 290
Kolodny, A., 259
Koren, R., 52
Kraft, M., 82
Kramnick, I., 178
Krips, H., 78
Kühl, S., 215
Kuhlken, R., 329

Lacan, J., 157n
Laidlaw, J., 165, 166
Lange, E., 329
Langhade, J., 234
Lattin, B. D., 131, 132, 141,
    142
Laughlin, H. H., 215
Law, H. G., 203
Le Bon, L., 76
Lee, S., 306, 307
LeFevre, K. B., 42
Lefevre, P., 318
Leff, M., 177, 304, 308, 334
Lemkin, R., 214
Lessl, T., 332
Lévi-Strauss, C., 328
Lewin, A., 221
Liell, S., 178
Lindberg, C., 306
Little, J., 11, 289, 290
Littlejohn, S. W., 117, 326,
    337
Liu, B. L., 5, 129
Lloyd, D., 353n
Loeb, J. W., 270
Long, J. S., 274
Longaker, M. G., 190

Lorde, A., 80, 94
Lovelace, C., 71
Lowenstein, L., 329
Lunsford, A., 304, 308

Macedo, S., 186
MacIntyre, A., 37, 182
Macri, L. C., 310n, 313, 315
Maeroff, G. I., 263, 265
Maingueneau, D., 54
Mallia, G., 311, 312
Marina, J., 335
Mathews, D., 118, 122, 124
Mathison, M., 89
McAffee, N., 124
McCain, J., 68n
McCloud, S., 318
McGee, M., 176, 177, 178,
    189
McHenry, R., 157n
McLuhan, M., 310, 318
McNely, B. J., 5, 96
McPhail, M., 89
McTeigue, J., 353n
Mead, G. H., 40, 41, 42, 43,
    144, 145, 146, 148
Mehler, B. A., 216
Meister, M., 12, 326
Mendelsohn, D., 219, 220,
    221, 222, 223, 224,
    227, 228
Merleau-Ponty, M., 313,
    314
Metz, L., 98, 100, 101
Milde, K., 303
Miller, C. R., 303, 305, 307,
    308
Mitchell, N. E., 142n
Mitchell, W. J. T., 106, 109
Montesquieu, C. de S., 182
Montgomery, B. M., 117,
    119, 121, 122, 125
Moore, A., 353n
Morganthau, T., 330
Morris, M. K., 86
Mouffe, C., 59
Mueller, J. E., 98, 99, 100
Munksgaard, J., 4, 70
Murr, A., 330

Nader, A., 233
Nagaoka, E. H., 289, 291,
    292, 293, 299, 300
Netton, I. R., 232, 233

O'Meara, K., 266
O'Reilly, B., 160
Obama, B., 63, 66, 68n
Olbermann, K., 62, 68n
Olbrechts-Tyteca, L., 14, 15,
    54, 59, 86, 205
Oléron, P., 56
Olmsted, F. L., 202, 206, 207
Olsen, E., 315
Olson, L. C., 4, 80, 81
Orlan, 70, 71, 72, 73, 74, 75,
    76, 77, 78
Orlowski, A., 153, 154, 155
Ornatowski, C. M., 12, 340,
    343, 350
Orwell, G., 340, 345, 351
Osborn, F., 216
Osborn, M., 327, 330
Ouy, G., 165

Paine, T., 176, 178, 179,
    180, 182, 183, 184
Pais, A., 294
Passavant, P., 74, 75
Pateman, C., 25, 26
Patterson, G., 296
Pauli, W., 295
Pearce, W. B., 117, 326, 337
Pekar, H., 315, 316
Perelman, C., 14, 15, 54, 55,
    59, 86, 205
Peters, R. J., 322
Pettiway, L., 329
Phelan, P., 73, 74
Phipps, K. S., 142n
Piskor, E., 315, 316
Pizan, C. de, 165–174
Plantin, C., 53, 55, 56
Pocock, J. G. A., 182
Popenoe, P. B., 215, 216
Poulet, G., 320
Powers, M. K., 9, 249
Prelli, L., 211
Prothero, A., 333
Przybylowicz, P., 71
Putnam, J. J., 296
Putnam, R., 186
Pyne, S. J., 328

Quilligan, M., 166
Quintilian, 46

Rahn, W., 186
Rakowski, M., 349, 350

Ramsey, D., 305
Reault, J., 76
Rehberg, V., 76
Reisman, D. C., 233, 239
Reno, C., 165
Rescher, N., 234
Rice, R. E., 263, 265, 266
Rich, F., 63, 64, 160, 161, 162
Richards, I. A., 38
Riker, W. H., 121
Ritchie, J., 65
Rivers, N. A., 10, 11, 281
Roberson, H., 315, 316
Roddy, K., 194
Romero, O., 138
Roosevelt, M., 332
Roosevelt, T., 203
Rorty, R., 29
Rosebraugh, C., 332
Ross, M. E., 250
Rosteck, T., 334
Rothman, M., 266
Rousseau, J-J., 25–34, 177
Royster, J. J., 101
Rutherford, E., 292

Sacco, J., 310, 322
Sack, R., 103, 104
Saito, R., 196
Satrapi, M., 310
Sauer, C., 327
Saussure, F. de, 144, 145
Sax, J., 202
Schier, S. E., 187
Schild, H-J., 347
Schott, G. A., 293
Schullery, P., 203
Schultz, R., 130
Schulz, C., 318
Scott, J. T., 30
Scott, J. W., 86, 87
Scott, R., 332
Segre, G., 294, 295
Seigenthaler, J., 151, 152,
    154, 155, 156
Sereno, M., 299
Shklar, J. N., 27
Short, B., 328
Shotter, J., 119
Sibley, D., 104
Sibley, R., 108
Simons, H. W., 117
Singer, B., 160
Sipiora, P., 149n

Skocpol, T., 187
Smalley, S., 330
Smith, C. A., 329
Smith, D., 332
Smith, J. M., 6, 165
Smith, L., 173
Smith, M., 12
Soarez, C., 45, 46, 47, 48
Sones, W. D., 311
Soulliere, L. E., 203
Spanos, W. V., 142
Spelman, E., 86
Spiegelman, A., 310, 317
Starobinski, J., 25, 26, 27
Stein, S. R., 177
Stepan, N., 289
Stevenson, A., 21
Stewart, C. J., 329
Stewart, D., 252, 253, 254,
    255
Stewart, G. R., 252, 255
Stone, G. R., 252, 256, 257,
    261
Strine, M., 89
Stuewer, R. H., 294
Sturken, M., 318
Sweet, E., 71
Swift, K. A., 8, 214

Taguieff, P-A., 59
Tanner, M., 320
Taylor, C., 28
Taylor, J. H. M., 173
Tell, D., 3, 25
Terdiman, D., 155
Thagard, P., 290
Thompson, J. E., 94n, 124
Tillerson, R., 193
Tonn, M. B., 130
Toulmin, S., 13, 14
Truc, G., 44
Truchet, J., 45
Truett, S., 102
Tweed, W., 203

Ulam, S., 300
Underhill, S., 131, 132, 141,
    142
Underwood, G. S., 207, 208
Utley, E. A., 177

Valone, D. A., 215, 217
Van de Ven, A. H., 265, 268
van der Will, W., 347

Ventura, J., 138
Versaci, R., 312
Vico, G., 227
Villa, R., 109
Votruba, J., 266

Wales, J., 151, 152
Walesa, L., 350
Wallis, J., 129–142
Walton, D., 53
Walzer, R., 237
Wander, P., 186, 189
Ward, K., 264, 267
Warner, M., 74
Warnick, B., 12
Washington, D., 306, 307
Wear, D., 86
Weaver, R., 17, 201
Wee, L., 290
Whatmore, S., 103
White, G., 328
White, H., 220, 221, 227
Whittlesey, L. H., 203
Wiederhold, E., 4, 62
Will, G. F., 68n
Willard, C. C., 166
Williams, L., 160, 163
Windt, T., 327, 330, 350
Winfrey, O., 159–163
Wolf, N., 251, 258, 259,
    260, 261
Wolin, R., 334
Wolin, S., 188
Wollstonecraft, M., 183
Woodbury, R., 332
Woodruff, P., 204, 205
Wright, E., 97
Wu, A., 307

Yagi, E., 291
Yarbrough, S. R., 6, 40, 41,
    42, 144, 145
Young, E., 102

Zaitlin, J., 207
Zarefsky, D., 1, 2, 13, 16, 18,
    19
Zimmermann, A., 74, 76
Zugazagoitia, J., 71

Subject Index

Aalmuhammed v. Lee,
306–307
Academia
erosion of civil liberties
in, 249–261
gender and advancement
within, 270–271
RSA and advancement
in, 271–274
Accomplishment/complica-
tion dialectic, 119–122
Ad hominem arguments,
53–54
Aesthetics, relationship with
ethos, 162
After Virtue (MacIntyre), 37
Agency
authorial, in bot-written
texts, 303–308
rhetorical, in Pizan's
"The City of
Ladies," 165–174
"Agency: Promiscuous and
Protean" (Campbell),
166–167
Aims of Argument, The (Crusius & Channell), 283
Al-Farabi, A.-N.
appeal of Aristotelian
concepts to an Arabic
readership, 239–240
Arabic translation of
Greek terms, 237–239
emanation, theory of,
233–234
on enthymeme, 238
grammar, theory of,
239–240

life and philosophy of,
233–234
on opinion and cer-
tainty, 236
on persuasion, 236
rhetoric of, 234–237
syllogism vs.
enthymeme, 238–239
*Al-Farabi: An Annotated Bibli-
ography* (Rescher), 234
American people
as more process than
phenomenon, 189
paternalistic rhetoric
and decline in civic
participation, 186,
197
transhistoric collective
sense of, in Paine's
Common Sense,
178–180
Analogy
in Freud's Clark lectures,
295–298
Gamow's liquid drop
theory as, 294–295
generativity and con-
straint in, 289–300
historiography of rhetor-
ical studies of, 299
Nagaoka's Saturnian
theory as, 291–293
rhetorical functions in
scientific discourse,
289–300
Anger, as empowering
resource, 83–85
Apolitical authenticity, 66

Arabic rhetoric, Al-Farabi's
logico-rhetorical the-
ory of, 230–241
Architecture, rhetorical/
nonverbal communica-
tive function of, 97,
201–212
Argumentation, polemical
discourse as, 52–60
Aristotle
al-Farabi's repurposing
of Aristotelian rheto-
ric, 234, 237
on *ethos,* 284–285, 287*n*
on forensic, occasional,
and deliberative
modes of rhetoric,
125
on *logos, pathos,* and
ethos, 121–122
on rhetoric vs. poetics,
163
on virtue, 38–39
Arson, rhetorical/cultural
significance of,
326–337
Art/artistry
capitalist co-optation/
commodification of,
76
counterhegemonic rhet-
oric in liminal areas,
108–111
in graphic novels,
310–323
medieval, rhetoric of
allegorical figures in,
165–174

performance, plastic surgery as, 70–78
shaping rhetorical agency through, 167–174
Association for Voluntary Sterilization (AVS), 216–217
Attitudes Toward History (Burke), 336
Audience, interpellation of, 176–184
Authorial agency
in automated/digital environments, 303–308
in *Malcolm X,* 306–307
Authorial image, in medieval manuscripts, 170–171
Authority/credibility, *ethos* defined as, 284, 287

Baghdad Peripatetics, 233, 237
Being There (Clark), 283
Black lesbian experiences, as resource for embodied invention, 80–94
Black, Edwin, implied auditor/second persona, 189
Bloodsaves, paternalistic rhetoric of, 194–195
Bodies That Matter (Butler), 71–72
Bodily Arts (Hawhee), 287
Body, the
as site for rhetorical invention, 80–94
as site of feminist voice and historical oppression, 70, 73–78
and symbolic deeds, 70–94
Book of Letters (Kitab al-Huruf) (al-Farabi), 240
Book on Logic: Rhetoric (Kitab fi al-Mantiq: Al-Khataba) (al-Farabi), 234, 236, 238–239
Bots, as textual curators, 305–306

Breast cancer, as resource for embodied invention, 80–94
Burke, Kenneth
dramatist pentad, scene/act ratio and eugenic rhetoric, 217
on the mystery of rhetorical courtship, 333–334
on piety in secular rhetorical contexts, 334
on the problem of evil, 332
on rhetoric of places, 212
on rhetoricality of lyric poetry, 204
Bush, G. W., paternalistic rhetoric of, 191–192
Butler, J., on performativity, 71–72

Cancer Journals, The (Lorde), 80–81, 83–84, 86–91
Chamizal National Memorial, 96–113
Christianity, political rhetoric of, 130
Cicero, on *licentia* and *parrhesia,* 45–46
"City of Ladies" (Pizan), agency and social responsibility in, 165–174
Civic virtue, Paine on, 182–183
Civil liberties
erosion of, in war on terror, 340
threat of loyalty oaths to, 249–261
Clinton, H., presidential campaign of, 63–64
Collective identity, 175–179, 181
Comics/comic books
embodied quality of speech in drawing, 317
ethos of, 313–317
harnessing the motivating capacity of, 313
multiple modes of "looking" in, 317–319

phenomenological approach to, 313
rhetorical qualities of, 311–312
as the un-photo, 319–322
visual redaction in, 318, 322–323
Communication
centripetal vs. centrifugal processes of, 118–119
Mead's interactionist approach to, 41–42
Communist rhetoric, 345–347, 353n
Communities
deliberative, 159–174
and publics, 117–197
Wikipedia as electronic means of building, 152–153
Composition, engaged scholarship in, 284–267
Conceptual vocabulary of rhetoric, 37
Constitutive rhetoric/discourse
in Paine's *Common Sense,* 175–184
paternalistic, 189–197
"Constitutive Rhetoric: The Case of the *Peuple Québécois*" (Charland), 175
Contract theory/contractual politics, 25–34
Corporate America, paternalistic rhetoric of, 192–194
Corporeal experiences, and embodied invention, 86–88
Counterhegemonic rhetoric, 108–111
Counterpublics, 72–74
Credibility/authority, *ethos* defined as, 284, 287
Cultural studies, renewed attention to aesthetics, 163
Cynicism and the rhetoric of diatribe, 326–327

Daddy's Girl (Drechsler), 322
De arte rhetorica libri tres
    (Soarez), 45
Debate, in republic democ-
    racy, 122
Dedicatory miniatures,
    168–172
Deliberation, dialogue vs.,
    122–124
Deliberative communities,
    159–174
Democracy, fascist shifts in,
    249
Democratic vs. republican
    mechanisms, func-
    tions of, 118
Demographic inertia,
    defined, 274
*Destruction of the European
    Jews, The* (Hilberg),
    221
Diachronism, and the
    nature of motion,
    144–145
Dialogue vs. deliberation, in
    republican democracy,
    122–124
Dialogues de Sourds
    (Angenot), 54, 56
Diatribe, 326–337
Didascalia in Rhetoricum (al-
    Farabi), 235–236
Discourse
    balanced, 117–126
    elite, in the U.S., 186
    feminist, of power, 65
    hegemonic, 190
    polemic, argumentation
        as, 52–60
    scientific, rhetorical
        functions in,
        289–300
    as temporal social
        action, 145
    visual/spatial, 96–113
Discursive interaction, ethi-
    cal shifting in,
    144–149
Displacement of representa-
    tion, in rhetorical nar-
    rative, 228
Display, rhetoric of, 211
Downsizing Democracy (Cren-
    son & Ginsberg), 187

Earth Liberation Front
    (ELF), 326–337
Elite discourse in the United
    States, 186
*Eloquentiae sacrae et humanae
    parallela* (Caussin), 45
Embodied invention, rheto-
    ric of, 80–94
End of America, The (Wolf),
    251
Engaged scholarship,
    263–267
*Engaged Scholarship: A Guide
    for Organizational and
    Social Research* (Van de
    Ven), 265
EngenderHealth, 215–217
*Entretiens sur l'éloquence de la
    chaire et du barreau*
    (Guèret), 45
*Enumeration of the Sciences
    (Ihsa' al-'Ulum)* (al-
    Farabi), 237, 240
Eroticism, as empowering
    resource, 83–85
*Establishing Universities as
    Citizens* (Rothman),
    266
Ethical shifting in discur-
    sive interaction,
    144–149
Ethics of rhetoric, establish-
    ing a shared set of val-
    ues, 38
Ethos
    aesthetics and, 162
    authority/credibility as
        defining characteris-
        tics of, 284, 287
    and character of one's
        government, 341
    graphic novels and,
        313–317
    interactionist under-
        standing of, 40
    masculine, of classical
        republicanism,
        182–183
    oppositional, liminal
        spaces reflecting, 96
    self-cultivating vs. self-
        stabilizing, 281–287
Ethos of Rhetoric, The (Hyde),
    313

Eugenics movement,
    214–218
Excess, rhetorical, tactical
    strategy/theoretical
    significance of, 77
Experience, distillation/
    metabolization of,
    82–83
Explicit Engaged Scholar-
    ship, 265–266
ExxonMobil Corporation,
    paternalistic rhetoric
    of, 192–194

Faces, photographed vs.
    drawn, 320–322
Faculty Priorities Reconsidered
    (O'Meara & Rice), 266
Feminism/feminist rhetoric
    embodied invention,
        80–94
    form as a feminist issue,
        62–68
    gendered nature of
        Paine's *Common
        Sense,* 183
    on misogyny, 165, 173
    resistance through perfor-
        mative bodily trans-
        formation, 70–78
    unmasking, concept of,
        71
Fire, as a cultural symbol,
    327–329
46 Pages (Liell), 178
Foucault, Michel
    on contractual politics,
        28–29, 33
    on polemics, 53
    on relationship of space
        and power, 102
FoxNews, exposure of polit-
    ical bias by, 62–68
Freud, Sigmund, in Clark
    lectures, 295–298

Gamow's liquid drop the-
    ory, 294–295
Gender Trouble (Butler), 70,
    77
Genetic determinism,
    215–216
Gestures, language as a con-
    versation of, 41

God's Politics: Why the Right Gets It Wrong and the Left Doesn't Get It (Wallis), 129–133, 139–141

Governing process, corporate interference in, 188

Grace, Kantian notion of, 335–336

Graffiti, spatio-discursive nature of, 106–111

Graphic novel, rhetoric of, 310–323. *See also* Comics/comic books

Greatest Story Ever Sold, The: The Decline and Fall of Truth from 9/11 to Katrina (Rich), 162

Greek rhetoric
al-Farabi's translation of, 237–239
on *parrhesia,* 45
on virtue, 38–39

Greek Thought, Arabic Culture (Gutas), 239

Griswold v. Connecticut, 20

Habitus, 146, 148

Happy Hypocrite, The: A Fairy Tale for Tired Men (Beerbohm), 281

Hegemonic discourse, constitutive identity articulated by, 190

Hereditarian eugenics, 218

Higher Education for the Public Good (Kezar et al.), 266

History
completeness (metonymy) and random chaos of (synecdoche), 225
displacement of representation in, 228
misrepresentation of Arabic rhetors in, 230–241
Orientalist view of medieval Arabic philosophy, 231–232
structural language of, 220
trope as the undercarriage of, 220

Holocaust, synecdoche as figure of, 219–228

Human Betterment Foundation (HBF), 215–218

Hypermediacy vs. immediacy, 162–163

Hypocrisy, verbal, 346, 349

Hysteria, analogy in Freud's lecture on, 295–297

Iconography of allegorical figures in medieval manuscripts, 171

"Iconography" (Hindman), 170

Iconology (Mitchell), 106

Identification
forced, in regime rhetoric, 345, 348
process of ("us" vs. "them"), 133, 156–157
rhetoric of display and, 211

Identity, transhistorical/collective, in constitutive rhetoric, 175–179, 181

Immediacy vs. hypermediacy, 162–163

"In Search of 'The People': A Rhetorical Alternative" (McGee), 176

Innocent rhetoric, appeal of, 66

Internet, digital rhetoric of, 151–157

Interpellation, 176–184

Inventive Intercourse: From Rhetorical Conflict to the Ethical Creation of Novel Truth (Yarbrough), 40

Inverted totalitarianism, 188

Ironic inverted comma, in regime rhetoric, 346–347

Isagogue (Porphyry), 233

Jastrow's duck-rabbit sketch, 147

Jeremiad, 131–132, 141–142
American, 134–142
for democrats, 138–140
for progressive Christians, 134–138

Judgment, Platonically inflected models of, 64

Kairos, 141, 149*n,* 239, 287

L'art de prêcher la parole de Dieu (Foix), 45

Landscape architecture, nonverbal rhetoric of, 201–212

Language, political regeneration through verbal self-discipline, 340–341, 351–352

Leaky self/soft self, rhetorical construction of, 286–287

Lesbian experiences, and embodied invention, 88–92

Letters and Notes on the Manners, Customs and Conditions of the North American Indians (Catlin), 202

Licentia, 44–50

Liminality of spatio-discursive locations, 96–113

Lincoln–Douglas debates, 15–16

Liquid drop theory, 294–295

Logic of Practice, The (Bourdieu), 144

Logocentrism, 283

Logos, 40, 121–122, 283–285, 290–292, 300

Lost, The: A Search for Six of the Six Million (Mendelsohn), 219

Loyalty oaths, and the erosion of civil liberties, 249–261

Macedonia (Pekar et al.), 315

Magical Life of Long Tack Sam, The (Fleming), 320–321

Mass mobilization vs. directed activation strategies, 187

Materiality of rhetoric, 97

Maus (Spiegelman), 310, 317

Media reporting, political bias in, 62–68

Mein Kampf (Hitler), 347
Melodrama theory,
    160–163
Metabolism/distillation of
    experience, Lorde on,
    82, 84–85
Metahistory (White), 220
Metaphor(s)
    bodily, 77, 84–85
    explanations of, 149*n*
    noticing new relation-
        ships through, 148
    of prosthesis, 89
Metonymy, 220–224, 318
Mimesis, Platonically
    inflected model of,
    64
Mimetic inversion/reversal,
    72
Misogyny, 165, 173
Murals, spatio-discursive
    nature of, 106–111

Nagaoka, H., Saturnian the-
    ory of, 291–293
Natural law, ELF's theory
    of, 335–336
Natural-Born Cyborgs (Clark),
    283
Nazi rhetoric, 341, 344,
    346–349
*Neighbors: The Destruction of
    the Jewish Community in
    Jedwabne, Poland*
    (Gross), 226
Neoplatonism, influence on
    al-Farabi's curricu-
    lum, 233–234
New Jersey Sterilization
    League, 216
New Rhetoric, The (Perelman
    & Olbrechts-Tyteca),
    14–15, 54, 59
Nicomachean Ethics (Aristo-
    tle), 39
9/11 Commission Report
    (Jacobson & Colon),
    317–319

Of Grammatology (Derrida),
    26
On Revolution (Arendt), 25
On Rhetoric (Aristotle), 231,
    240

*Opinions of the Inhabitants of
    the Virtuous City, The
    (Kitab Ara' Ahl)* (al-
    Farabi), 233–234, 236,
    239
Oprah Winfrey Show, The,
    159–163
Organon (Aristotle), 231,
    233–234, 236–237
Orientalist view of medi-
    eval Arabic philoso-
    phy, 231–241
Orthos logos, 290–292, 300
Overidentification, rhetori-
    cal strategy of, 78

Palestine (Sacco), 310, 322
Park Structures and Facilities
    (NPS handbook), 206
Parrhesia, 45–46
Paternalistic rhetoric
    in action, 190–195
    articulation of, 189–190
    of Bloodsaves, 194–195
    as constitutive dis-
        course, 189–190
    of ExxonMobil Corpo-
        ration, 192–194
    of George W. Bush,
        191–192
Pathos, 40, 55, 57, 121, 160,
    284, 327, 343
People
    as a transhistorical col-
        lective entity,
        178–179
    understanding the ideo-
        logical construction
        of, 189–190
Performativity, producing
    effective resistance by,
    70–78
Permanence and Change
    (Burke), 334
Persepolis (Satrapi), 310
Persuasion, 56, 236, 238,
    285
Phenomenology, rhetorical,
    313
"Philosophy of the Uncon-
    scious, The" (Hart-
    mann), 296
Picture Theory (Mitchell),
    109

Piety and vulgarity, rhetori-
    cal competition
    between, 334–335
Place, rhetorical construc-
    tion of, 96–113
Plato, 243–248
Plurality, 59–60
Poetic author, originality
    inherent in construct
    of, 303–304
Poetics (Aristotle), 233
Poetics vs. rhetoric, 163
Political foundation, sacri-
    fice of private judg-
    ment and liberty in, 27
Political rhetoric/discourse
    as a legitimate argumen-
        tative mode, 52–60
    of Oprah Winfrey, 161
    regime-based, 340–353
Politics (Aristotle), 341
Power
    feminist discourses of,
        65
    reconfiguring through
        counterpublics,
        72–73
Practices of Looking (Sturken
    & Cartwright), 318
Public advocacy, gaining
    through embodied
    invention, 93
Public debate/deliberation
    civic process of, 117–126
    developing a shared
        evaluation standard
        for, 37–43
    dialogic features of,
        123–124
    enactment of rhetorical
        balance in, 123–125
    Rousseau's model of,
        25–34
    telic features of, 124–125
    worldwide projects and
        programs on, 126
Public reason, promoting,
    25–113
Publicity, as integral resis-
    tance mechanism, 78

Racism, Lorde on, 84–85
Radical agents, rhetoric of
    protest through, 73

Raw and the Cooked, The
(Lévi-Strauss), 328
Reference texts, authorial
agency in, 304
Regime rhetoric, 340–353
characteristic features of,
345–346
forced identification in,
345
magical wish fulfillment
in, 346
verbal hypocrisy in, 346
Religious terror, and the
failed diatribe of arson,
328, 331–335
Repression, analogy in
Freud's lecture on,
297–298
Republic (Plato), 235
Republican democracy
oratory/public address
in, 121–122
rhetorical modes of,
120–123
rhetorical tensions of,
118–120
Republican vs. democratic
mechanisms, func-
tions of, 118
Research, engaged, 265–266
Reverence, attitude/rheto-
ric of, 204–205
Rhetoric
Al-Farabi's logico-rhetorical theory, 230–241
of arson, 326–337
constitutive, 175–184
counterhegemonic,
108–111
of diatribe, 326–337
digital, 151–157
of embodied invention,
80–94
of engaged scholarship,
263–267
eugenic, 214–218
feminist, 67, 70–94
hegemonic, 190
historical, agency and
social responsibility
in, 165, 174
jeremiad, 134–140
journalistic vs. populist,
160

licentia, 44, 50
materiality of, 97
nonverbal elements of,
201–212
paternalistic, 186, 197
politico/religious,
129–142
in public debate, 37–43
regime-based, 340–353
in republican democ-
racy, 120–123
of reverence, in national
parks, 205
in Rousseau's *The Social
Contract*, 29–32
of social contracts, 26–34
of space and place,
96–113
virtue ethical approach
to studying, 40–42
Rhetoric (Barilli), 159
Rhetoric of Motives, A
(Burke), 212, 333, 352
*Rhetoric of Religion, The:
Studies in Logology*
(Burke), 332
Rhetoric Society of Amer-
ica, gender equity in,
269–276
Rhetoric, The (Aristotle), 39,
233
Rhetorica Ad Herennium,
45–47
Rhetorical invention, bodily
experience in, 80–94
*Rhetorical Landscapes in
America* (Clark), 97
Rhetorical stratigraphies,
96–113
Rhetorics of Display (Prelli),
211
Rhétorique françoise, la
(Bary), 45, 47
Rousseau, Jean Jacques, on
role of rhetoric in the
state, 25–34
Rustic design, 201–213

Sanitized rhetoric/spatial
purification, 104–106,
108
Saturnian theory, 291–293
Scholarship Assessed (Glassick
et al.), 263

*Scholarship of Engagement,
The* (Boyer), 263
Scholarship Reconsidered
(Boyer), 263
Secularism, 131–134, 138,
140–142
Security questionnaires,
threat to democratic
civil liberties, 255–259
Self-cultivating vs. self-stabi-
lizing *ethos*, 281–287
Sermons, *licentia* practiced
in, 44–50
*Setting Fires with Electrical
Timers: An Earth Liber-
ation Front Guide*
(ELF), 332
Shaping Science with Rhetoric
(Ceccarelli), 290
Social contracts, Rous-
seau's theory of, 25–34
Social modernism, rhetori-
cal style of, 228
Social movement theory,
role of the diatribe in,
329
Social relationships, consen-
tient sets of, 146
Social responsibility in
Pizan's "The City of
Ladies," 165–174
Socio-scientific eugenics, 218
Soft self/leaky self, rhetori-
cal construction of,
286–287
Sojourners, rhetoric of,
129–142
Soul of Politics, The (Wallis),
131–132, 141
Spatialization
rhetorical perspective of,
97
U.S.–Mexico border,
96–113
Spatio-discursive locations,
liminality/territorial-
ity of, 96–113
"Speech in Defense of Q.
Ligarius" (Cicero), 46
Spirit of Laws (Montes-
quieu), 182
*Sterilization for Human Better-
ment* (Gosney & Pope-
noe), 215

Sterilization, compulsory, 215–216

Stratigraphies, rhetorical, 96–113

Structural architecture, non-verbal rhetoric of, 201–212

Structure mapping theory, 299

Synecdoche, 219–228

Television talk show, rhetoric of, 159–161

Telos, in public deliberation, 124–125

Territoriality of spatio-discursive locations, 96–113

Textual curation, 304–305, 308

Third persona, Wander's concept of, 189–190

Thresholds of Interpretation (Genette), 166

Time, diachronic perspective of, 144–145

Tom Paine and Revolutionary America (Foner), 178

Tom Paine: A Political Life (Keane), 178

Topoi, 82, 93, 218, 293, 299

Totalitarian rhetoric, 340–353

Totalitarianism, inverted, 188

Toward a Civic Discourse (Crowley), 37, 42

Transcendence, translating the meaning of, 67

Transhistoricism, in constitutive rhetoric, 177–179, 181

Tropics of Discourse (White), 220, 227

Truth, as relationship between judgment and reality, 41–42

U.S. National Park Service (NPS), 201–212

Uses of Argument, The (Toulmin), 13

Verbal hypocrisy, 346, 349

Vernacular Voices: The Rhetoric of Publics and Public Spheres (Hauser), 97

Vindication of the Rights of Woman (Wollstonecraft), 183

Virtue ethical critique of rhetoric, 39

Vulgarity and piety, competition between, 334–335

War on terror and erosion of civil liberties, 340

Ways of Seeing (Berger), 318

Wikipedia
    bot-written texts in, 303–308
    responsibilities for digital rhetoric on, 151–157

Winfrey, Oprah, 159–163

"With Ink and Mortar" (Hindman), 172–173

Women and the Book (Smith & Taylor), 172

Women
    changes in representation among doctoral degree holders, 272–274
    tracing patterns of professional advancement for, 269–276

World Viewed, The: Reflections on the Ontology of Film (Cavell), 319

Zion National Park, NPS Rustic aesthetic in, 207–211

Zippy the Pinhead (Griffith), 318